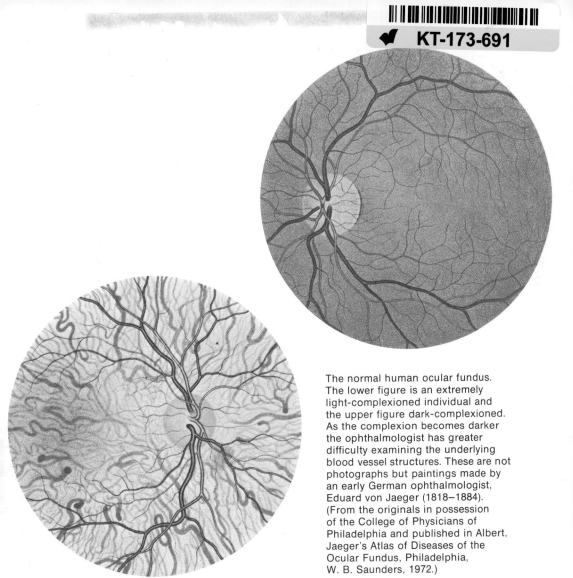

The normal human ocular fundus.
The lower figure is an extremely
light-complexioned individual and
the upper figure dark-complexioned.
As the complexion becomes darker
the ophthalmologist has greater
difficulty examining the underlying
blood vessel structures. These are not
photographs but paintings made by
an early German ophthalmologist,
Eduard von Jaeger (1818–1884).
(From the originals in possession
of the College of Physicians of
Philadelphia and published in Albert,
Jaeger's Atlas of Diseases of the
Ocular Fundus, Philadelphia,
W. B. Saunders, 1972.)

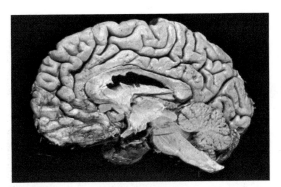

The medial surface of the human brain.
(From Curtis, Jacobson and Marcus,
An Introduction to the Neurosciences,
Philadelphia, W. B. Saunders, 1972.)

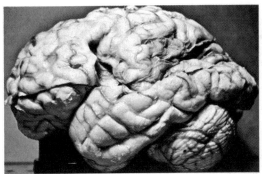

Left lateral view of the human brain.
Orange staining of the temporal parietal area
indicates hemorrhages. This individual had
focal seizures and paralysis of the right arm.
(Courtesy of Dr. John Hills, New England
Center Hospitals; and José Segarra, Boston
Veterans Administration Hospital.)

The pure scientist: knowledge for its own sake. (Cartoon by Charles Schultz.
© 1960 United Feature Syndicate, Inc.)

D. O. HEBB

Professor of Psychology, McGill University

Third Edition

textbook of psychology

W. B. SAUNDERS COMPANY

PHILADELPHIA · LONDON · TORONTO · 1972

W. B. Saunders Company: West Washington Square
Philadelphia, Pa. 19105

12 Dyott Street
London, WC1A 1DB

1835 Yonge Street
Toronto 7, Ontario

Listed here is the latest translated edition of this book together with the language
of the translation and the publisher.

Finnish (2nd edition) Tammi Publishing Company
Helsinki, Finland

German (1st edition) Julius Beltz Verlagsbuchverhandlung
Bergstrasse, Germany

Italian (2nd edition) La Nuova Italia
Florence, Italy

Japanese (2nd edition) Kinokuniya Shoten
Tokyo, Japan

Polish (2nd edition) Naukowe
Warsaw, Poland

Portuguese (2nd edition) Livraria Atheneu S.A.
Rio de Janeiro, Brazil

Spanish (2nd edition) Editorial Interamericana
Mexico

Swedish (2nd edition) C.W.K. Gleerup Forlag
Lund, Sweden

Textbook of Psychology   ISBN 0-7216-4622-0

Print No.:   9   8   7   6   5   4   3   2   1

To my wife Margaret

from the preface to the first edition

This book is meant both for the student who will go on to further courses in the subject, and for the one who takes only one, the "terminal," course. Both pedagogically and professionally, it seems to me that the terminal course should be no less scientific than the one which is an introduction to further work.

If psychology is a science, it should be presented as a science; it is at least as interesting, intellectually, as its applications, and I surely do not need to argue here that basic science is in the long run a very practical training. We would not think at the graduate level of turning out practitioners without a thorough basic training; we insist instead that a critical understanding is vital to the professional psychologist. Training in methods only, it is agreed, is a mistake. But if we give a first course which is primarily concerned with personal adjustment and the like, we are making precisely that mistake. The function of the course instead should be to develop critical understanding, to prepare the student to evaluate his later reading in the field of method, and prepare him also to understand the new methods that will be developed after he has left his "terminal" course. Valuable as the practical methods of psychology now are, I believe that those of the future will be more valuable still; if so, the theoretical and academic course is—as I have said—the most practical one in the long run.

D. O. HEBB

preface
to the third edition

The principal changes in this edition are as follows. Chapter 2 now deals only with phenomena of learning. The discussion of the Inference from Behavior is now put in Chapter 14, together with a discussion of how one is to know one's own mind—if at all. The material is intelligible to the student, but in Chapter 2 it came too early. The former Chapter 3 is broken into two, Chapters 3 and 4: the first deals mainly with anatomical relations, incorporating Sperry's remarkable human split-brain results; the second (Chapter 4) deals mainly with the functioning of the neuron and what it means for the questions of learning and the infant's early development. Here Inhibition is dealt with more adequately, with the incorporation of some recent experimental results. Chapter 6 now concludes with a more adequate introduction to study method (though it is no more than an introduction, and the student is urged to consult a study-method manual).

Bringing the text up to date requires some reference, in the section on language, to the Gardners (and Washoe's sign language) as well as to Chomsky. Though Chomsky's nativism may be overdone (as I think), his work is still of first importance, especially as a delineation of the problem. I have tried, here as elsewhere, to avoid a contentious tone in reference to such important developments. References to the literature have been listed somewhat more formally at the end of each chapter in this edition, though I have not abstained from a comment on a reference when I thought it might be of help.

I have constantly had in mind the beginning student; he is not talked down to here, but he does need help in threading his way through the jungle of the literature and I have tried to provide this help where I can. I have, for example, labored over the Index, with alternative entries, to make it as likely as possible that when the beginner looks for a page reference he will find it.

As I said in the Preface to the second edition, experience has shown that the approach represented here is practical: it does not assume a special group of superior students. It is intelligible at several levels, and the brighter student will get more from it than others, but the average or below-average student can still master it if he does a little work. He may also find it more interesting than the so-called eclectic texts.

In revising I have had help from Drs. Virginia Douglas, Ronald Melzack, Peter M. Milner, M. Sam Rabinovitch, Charles C. Torrey, and W. Gatewood Workman, and it is a pleasure to acknowledge my indebtedness to them. Figures 61 and 62 are from a test now out of print, privately published in 1941; the four drawings were done by Miss Elizabeth Peck, for whose volunteer work I was and still am most grateful. The new diagrams of this edition were prepared by Mrs. Jane Corcoran, my invaluable secretary; her help of course extended over a much wider area than just drawing diagrams, and I acknowledge it with pleasure. Finally, the staff of W. B. Saunders have been helpful, beyond the call of duty, besides being tolerant of an opinionated author.

Montreal   D. O. HEBB

contents

psychology and human behavior

The object of this book is to introduce the student to the serious scientific study of man's mind and behavior. A more accurate, and more complete, definition will be proposed later in this chapter, but that essentially is what psychology is about. Psychologists study animals too, and very fascinating they are, but the main reason for doing so is still to understand man, the highest animal. If we could once understand how the tiny brain of the rat or pigeon works, we would be a lot closer to understanding man's.

Our concern here is with scientific psychology and fundamental principles, for a very good reason. Until the student understands psychological theory, he cannot apply it intelligently. There are books that tell the student how to deal with adolescent depressions, for example, and what causes them. If these books make him feel better, they are good psychotherapy, and that is fine; but if they make him feel that he understands depression and can help other people who are depressed, they are dishonest and dangerous. Motivational disturbances and other hang-ups of human beings are complex matters, and the student will find that the more he learns about such things the less sure he is likely to be about the remedies.

The student who really wants to help human beings, and studies psychology for that reason, would not want to be one who gives bad advice. A half-baked psychologist is worse, much worse, than none at all. Unfortunately we already have a big supply of half-baked psychologists who have read a book. We also have those who have read *two* books, and now write newspaper columns and magazine articles. Sometimes they give sensible advice, but if so it is more or less by accident. Mostly what they write is nonsense pretending to be scientific.

A second reason for beginning with fundamental principles, instead of practice, is that each year more is known about human problems and the student should prepare himself to understand future methods and not just learn about the methods we have now. Present knowledge is often inadequate. Applied psychology has made great advances, but we can expect that it will have gone much further 10 years and 20 years from now. *This* should be prepared for too.

1

So the practical solution for the student, whether he is interested from a scientific *or* from a practical point of view — whether interested in advancing knowledge *or* in helping human beings — is to master the theory and principles of academic, ivory-tower, apparently irrelevant study of the mind. Even today, if he studies this book he will find more that is "relevant" than he may think at first. The problem of prejudice is one example: animal psychology — of all things — shows us that prejudice may be more deep-seated than most people have thought in the past. To deal with it effectively we must not regard it as superficial or simply a product of learning bad things about other people. Again, from animal psychology — of all places — it is possible to show what was never shown by those who worked with man alone: that human beings are by their nature kind and generous. We know only too well that they are mean and cruel and quarrelsome, too, but it is most important to see that there is another side to human nature. Knowing that it exists, we can look for ways of strengthening it.

STUDYING THE MIND

How are we to study the mind? It is not open to inspection and cannot be examined directly. In these circumstances we have to use theory as a means of finding out what mind is and how it works.

Not even one's own mind is open to inspection. It was once supposed that one could, somehow, look inward at any time and see what one was thinking, on any topic. Then Herbart, the German philosopher, realized about 1820 that there is much that goes on in one's mind that one knows nothing about, and about 1900 Freud made this a central part of his theory. Like Herbart, Freud assumed that it is unpleasant things, things one does not like or is ashamed of, that are suppressed and kept in the *unconscious.* He talked as if all other mental processes were available for examination (as indeed everyone else thought). But now it is clear, from the modern work of G. Humphrey and E. G. Boring, that this is not so. *Introspection,* "looking inward," does not exist. You are not conscious of your consciousness. What you are conscious of is your body and the world around you, not what is going on inside your mind.

Some of the things said here will not be fully clear till the student has studied the later parts of the book. After doing that he should come back to this first chapter and look at it again. The following paragraph is meant for when he studies this for the second time:

It was said above that one is not conscious of one's thoughts. But imagery is part of one's thought (Chapter 5), and you may feel that you are at least conscious of your imagery. But this isn't really so. Try a small experiment. Look for a few seconds at a bright object, long enough to have an afterimage. Now look away toward a plain wall. You see a dark patch, corresponding in shape to the bright object. Where does this dark patch seem to be? It is outside you, not inside. You know that there is not a real object there, because you can feel nothing if you put your hand out; and besides, the patch moves as your eyes move. So you conclude that there *is* nothing outside, it is just an image, caused by something going on in your visual system. This is a valid inference, but it is inference, not direct observation. What you are *conscious of* is something outside yourself, not the process of imagery that is going on inside.

So we must learn about the mind indirectly, from knowing how the human being is built and from what he says and does. There is complicated machinery inside. We can find out something about how it works by stimulating it in different ways and seeing what output follows a given input. But the mechanisms are indeed complex, and psychology, though it has learned a great deal, still has a long, long way to go before the problem will be solved — if it is ever completely solved. In principle, however, the method is straightforward: I must learn about others' mental processes from what they do, and even about my own, much of the time, in the same way. (The great American philosopher, C. S. Peirce, said that he might find out what he thought only when he heard himself speak or found himself acting in some other way on the conclusion his mind had come to.)

Clearly Freud was right in supposing that you can be thinking something and not know that you are thinking it, in ordinary everyday circumstances. It is common to hear someone say, "I don't know how I could have forgotten," or "I don't know what got into me" about something he did or did not do. Freud took his ideas further. He suggested that when I laugh at someone it shows I dislike him; that if I can't remember a name, or how to pronounce it, I may feel the same way even though I *think* I like the other person. These are examples of how one may use behavior to make inferences about thought. Inferences of this kind are not always true: before one could be sure, one would have to examine the person's behavior further. Laughter is not always malicious; plain forgetting does occur. But though we would not now generalize as much as Freud did when he proposed these ideas, we should see that in proposing them Freud was exploring the problem of how to think objectively in studying the mind. When he went so far as to study his own unconscious in this way — for example, when he himself forgot a name — he was clearly a pioneer in the development of objective psychological methods.

Now for the nature of mind itself, what it is or what it consists of:

We will take for granted, as a working assumption, that mind is a function of the brain and not something that can exist apart from the brain. We will assume that thought and consciousness arose in the course of evolution. They are not activities that man alone is capable of. Dogs and cats, monkeys and chimpanzees also think and have minds.

There are two theories of mind, speaking very generally. One in its clearest form is *animistic,* a theory of demonic possession: it assumes that the body is inhabited by an entity, a demon known as the mind or soul.* Less extreme (and less clear) forms of the same theory simply call themselves *dualistic,* and assert only that mind is not physical, not part of the workings of the body. The second theory is *physiological* or *mechanistic*: it assumes that mind is a bodily process, the activity of the brain or some part of that activity. This is *monistic* theory. Modern psychology works with monistic or mechanistic theory, and we will do the same in this book. It is a working assumption only, which may turn out to be wrong, and the student as neophyte scientist need not—should not—believe it. In his private capacity he may believe in either of the two theories; both are intellectually respectable, since there are men of the highest ability to be found on each side of the question (a great majority, probably, believing in the existence of the soul).

It is essential that the student understand this point. Logically, a scientific theory should never be believed. It is best regarded as a sophisticated statement of ignorance, a way of formulating *possible* ideas so that they can be tested, rather than an attempted statement of final truth. I may hold to the existence of an immortal soul as an agent in man's behavior; if so, how would I go about trying to demonstrate it? My best procedure would be to assume that it does not exist, try to explain everything in physiological terms, and expect to find—eventually, when such explanation is taken to its limit, a thousand years from now—that there is still something about man that is not accounted for. If such a result is obtained, it would then demonstrate the existence of the soul (or some nonphysiological controlling agent in behavior).

This is the *reductio ad absurdum* procedure of Euclid—to prove that two sides of some triangle are equal, assume that they are not, and show that this leads to absurdity: therefore, they *are* equal. In the case of psychology, whether you believe in the soul or whether you disbelieve, the working procedure—for the present—is to assume that it does not exist. The assumption does not imply anything whatsoever about your belief. There is no possible conflict here between religion and the scientific method. Scientific theory approaches truth by a series of approximations, and psychology is in no position to be dogmatic about the correctness of its notions about the nature of mind.

RESEARCH PROBLEMS: LEARNING

All the foregoing discussion is very general. It will have more meaning if we look now at some of the areas in which research is done. Psychologists do not spend all their time trying to settle outsize questions like what is the mind made of, or is there a soul. Their normal research deals with something easier to get at, such as learn-

---

*Demons are not necessarily evil. The Oxford English Dictionary quotes Shakespeare: "O Antony!... Thy Daemon,... thy spirit,... is Noble, Couragious, high unmatchable."

ing, motivation, perception, intelligence or memory—all of which must be understood if we are to understand the mind.

The first and main area of research is learning. More than anything else, the mark of a psychologist is an interest in learning and what it can or cannot explain about behavior. Now learning may seem very simple to the student, who has been doing it all his life. What need for research? Learning is just a matter of repetition. Practice makes perfect. The oftener you catch a ball the better you are at catching it, the more you drive a car the better driver you become, and so on. The way to learn the stuff in this *Textbook* is to read it over and over; the more you read, the more you will remember—

Or will you? That last statement may sound reasonable, but it is a trap. Things are not so simple. There are other ways in which you will learn more and remember more. Human learning is very peculiar in a number of respects. We will come back to it in later chapters, but here we can look at some points to give the student an idea of how much there is still to find out about learning and how interesting it can be (even study methods).

Let's take a moment to look at study methods (for a fuller account, see p. 108). It is possibly true that the more you read this *Textbook,* the more you will remember of its content (but not if you simply try to read and the book sends you to sleep). But it is not true that this would be a sensible way to learn. You will get more results, with less pain, from a different method. Less than half your time should be spent taking in information, more than half making notes on the material or trying to reorganize it, or to recall it. For example:

Stop reading at this point and look through the whole of this first chapter, to find out if possible why the parts are arranged as they are. Read the headings, *sample* the text, look at the Summary, and see if the organization of the chapter makes sense. If not, sample more of the text, and try again. How would *you* organize these points? Instead of just reading and trying to remember (and as like as not daydreaming while you try to read), see if you can find out what the pattern of ideas is. And the peculiar thing about this is, that you will remember more by not trying to remember but just to understand. And another peculiar thing is, that this method is easier as well as more efficient. It's also easier to talk yourself into study when you do it this way. This is how you should approach a new chapter or a new book. Look for the main picture and the details will look after themselves, mostly.

However, for any student there are times when straight memorization is necessary. When you are studying anatomy of the brain you must be able to name the twelve cranial nerves. In biology you must know the classificatory scheme of kingdom, phylum, and so on. Many generations ago students discovered something that psychologists still cannot explain to their own satisfaction: namely, that learning more is sometimes easier than learning less. Instead of pounding away at *olfactory, optic,* and the other ten names of the nerves till they can be repeated, the student adds something. He first learns a short ditty which goes as follows: "On old Olympus's tufted top, a fat-armed German viewed a hop.'' The first letter of each word is the first letter of the twelve cranial nerves: olfactory, optic, oculomotor, trochlear, trigeminal, abducens, facial, auditory, glossopharyngeal, vagus, accessory, hypoglossus. Similarly, ''King Peter came over from Germany seeking fortune'' will organize and help recall kingdom, phylum, class, order, family, genus, species, and form. It is probable that no English-speaking person has learned the number of days in each month without use of the familiar jingle, ''Thirty days hath September....'' Eventually one gets to the point of knowing that November, for example, has thirty days without having to go through that rhyme, but it is obviously easier to learn the rhyme too. In the case of the cranial nerves, it is quite clear that by adding something to the task, the task becomes easier. One must learn those anatomical terminological monstrosities, glossopharyngeal and the rest, in the end; yet it is easier to do so when the jingle is included. This surely is a surprising state of affairs.

One more example: the notorious case of learning which is your left hand, which your right. Everyone has difficulty mastering this problem, and many people all their lives will have to stop and think a moment before knowing what to do when someone says Take the next turn to the right. This should be simple: all one has to do is to associate the sound of the word ''right'' with a movement of the right hand, or moving the eyes to the right. Why is there trouble? Part of the trouble at least is the symmetry of the body: the similarity of left and right sides. Also, the child learns more than he has to, and in this case the ''more'' that he learns gives him trouble. He very early learns to associate the word left not with a particular hand or side of his body, but with laterality or sidedness: in other words, with one of the dimensions of his body in space. He also begins to learn which is the right and left of another person facing him, which of course is precisely opposite to his own left and right; and the result of all this is confusion.

It appears that the human brain, in its complexity, is unable to do simple things in a simple way. This makes things very interesting for students of behavior, but there are drawbacks in a practical world. If you meet anyone who thinks that learning is easily understood, ask him why it is so hard to learn which is left and which is right.

BEHAVIOR DISORDERS

Another way to show what is meant when we talk about the study of behavior is to look at some of the human problems in which behavior becomes disordered, or is not developing properly in the growing child. This will also help to show the student why he needs to spend time on academic psychology before starting to help other people. Motivation, learning, perception and so on are academic topics but they are not remote from human concerns.

A disturbance of motivation, for example, is always an important part of mental illness. Human motivations have a wide variety and can be disturbed in different ways, so this does not mean that all mental illness is the same. It does mean that we must know more about motivation if we are to learn how to do a better job of helping the patient who is depressed or anxious, or the one who has a phobia or ideas of persecution. The motivations we are concerned with range from the biologically primitive need of food and sleep to the very un-primitive motivations that we call ambition and the need of self-respect. Eating and sleeping are very often disturbed in mental illness, but this appears mostly to be an effect of the illness and not a cause. Human sexual motivation is more complex, and the disturbance that is often seen in mental illness may be either cause or effect — or both. (Some workers, following Freud's early views, have regarded sexual conflict as the main cause, even the only cause, of mental illness, but that view is too extreme; it seems probable that the disturbance is mostly an effect of some more deep-seated change.) But when we come to disturbances of the highest and most typically human forms of motivation, a disturbance whether cause or effect always means serious trouble. A loss of appetite or insomnia, or even frigidity or impotence, can exist without implying the presence of mental illness. Not so a spontaneous disappearance of self-respect.

A fundamental need of the human being is to *do,* to achieve, to make a career ("career" includes marriage and raising a family), to amount to something in one's own eyes and others'. It is essential to one's mental health and vigor to have some feeling of self-confidence, of competence in one's daily activities, and thus a moderate degree at least of self-respect. Such an attitude is part of mental stability. Any prolonged disturbance of it means serious trouble.

In one case for example a doctor began to have doubts about his diagnoses and the treatments he was prescribing. His colleagues could not persuade him to think differently. He began to avoid patients though this made him very unhappy, but no amount of reassurance could, by itself, restore his confidence in himself. Another case is that of a woman who had recurrent and long-lasting attacks of depression. She felt that she was worthless, and blamed herself for not living up to her religious beliefs, according to which if she had true faith she would not be unhappy. Telling her that she was far from worthless, that others admired her instead and thought highly of her professional work, only made her conclude that she was deceiving people.

These are cases of *neurosis.* The neurotic patient may suffer severely but he remains "in contact with reality." His disorder is different from a *psychosis,* in which the behavior is more seriously disturbed.

Note on Terminology: Today neurosis and psychosis are generally thought to be different in kind, not only in degree of severity, though some psychologists and psychiatrists do not agree. The behavior of the psychotic frequently gives evidence of a confusion of thought that is not shown by the neurotic. Psychosis usually implies insanity, but the student should note that insanity is a legal term, not medical or psychological. It means that the insane person is not fit to be in charge of his own life but must be cared for by others and if necessary locked up. But not all psychotics are insane. For example, there was a woman, a secretary in a department of physical science, who had a theory that solved all the important problems of physics and society. She soon found out that others laughed at her theory, so she concluded that the world was not quite ready for it yet and continued to work quietly at her job—waiting for the big day when she would be recognized. Obviously such persons need not be locked up: they are psychotic, but not insane. They come to no doctor's attention nor to that of the police; and there is a surprising number of them.

Schizophrenia is the most frequently occurring psychosis. It takes different forms: simple schizophrenia, mainly marked by the patient's lack of responsiveness to the world around him, carelessness about clothing and appearance, and failure of sexual motivation (but little or no hallucination or delusions); hebephrenic schizophrenia, with very disorganized behavior, some hallucinations, grandiose delusions and markedly infantile behavior; catatonic schizophrenia, principally marked by motor peculiarities such as prolonged immobility in odd postures alternating sometimes with sudden excitement, but again including delusions and hallucinations; and finally, paranoid schizophrenia, in which the patient shows less obvious external signs of disturbance but does have systematized delusions, often including the idea that others are spying on him and injuring him by mysterious means.

Manic-depressive psychosis is a second major category, now for some reason becoming less frequent, while schizophrenia becomes more frequent (or is detected more frequently). Manic-depressive psychosis is so named because it sometimes takes the form of periods of mania (hyperactivity, big notions, elation) alternating with depression, but it may occur as a depression only, or a series of depressions; or attacks of mania may alternate with periods of relatively normal behavior.

This psychosis could almost be defined as a disorder of motivation; and schizophrenia too, though the element of a confusion of thought seems greater in schizophrenia. What happens in either case is almost totally a mystery at present. Though we know a lot about pieces of the puzzle we can't yet put them together to make a true picture of the nature of mental illness. Anything that academic psychology can do to tell us more about motivation—about the higher motivations that are closely related to one's ideas about oneself and one's relation to others—might supply a missing piece or show us how to put together the ones we already have.

Learning and memory are relevant too, for the patient with depression may be disturbed by his memories of the past, and the paranoid builds into his delusions what he has learned about social processes and the current science. The paranoid with ideas of persecution may believe that he is being spied on by "them"; in the thirties it was radio that was being used mysteriously for this purpose; today it is television or radar. "They" may also be injuring him, perhaps destroying his sexual powers, by means of mysterious scientific rays—or maybe by lasers, if he knows about lasers.

But the special relevance of learning shows up when we ask what are the causes of mental illness and how childhood experiences contribute to it. This question is of the greatest importance, for if we knew what caused neurosis or schizophrenia we might know what to do to cure it and, even better, how to prevent it. However, there is no simple answer. There are psychoses in which learning has no important role; it may determine the content of delusions, but not whether the delusions will occur. These are the "organic" psychoses, as they are commonly known. They arise from some *constitutional* disturbance, not from the patient's past experience. The cause may be some brain damage or a syphilitic infection of the brain, or a glandular or dietary deficiency. On the other hand there are the so-called "functional" psychoses, which depend wholly or partly on experience. In the extreme case, it has been estimated (Swank and Marchand) that anyone will break down—develop a psychosis—in the stress of modern warfare if the stress and the conflict between fear and duty, and the affection for comrades who have been killed, is continued long enough.

Schizophrenia presents a more complex picture. The patient must have inherited a susceptible constitution, but heredity by itself does not determine that the illness will appear. We cannot say that schizophrenia is inherited; there must be an interaction with experience, and the person with the susceptibility may never develop the disease. Though there are still people who ask whether schizophrenia or manic-depressive psychosis is inherited or acquired, we know now that this is a bad question. The only answer is Both (or maybe Neither). We will return to this topic later (in Chapter 7), when we can see what the reasons are for saying that the question is bad. There are other things that depend like mental illness on a complex interaction of heredity, pre- and postnatal influences other than learning, and learning itself.

Here let us conclude by considering an example of mental disorder in a dog. Though this involves an animal lower than man, and cannot prove anything about human behavior, it does show that failure in a learning problem can produce a serious disorder in some animals and suggests, at least, the possibility that similar things may happen with human beings.

An experimenter in the laboratory of the great Russian physiologist, Pavlov, was trying to find out how small a difference the dog could detect between two objects, using the method of conditioned reflexes (p. 24). He taught the dog that food would be given following the sight of one object, and not following that of another. No punishment was given if the dog failed to discriminate between them. The objects were made more and more alike until, after several days of failing to discriminate, the dog's behavior changed, suddenly. Instead of coming eagerly to the experimental room the dog struggled to avoid it; instead of standing quietly in the apparatus, waiting for the next signal to appear, he bit and howled. Discrimination disappeared. The experimenter went back to easier forms of the problem which the dog had solved previously, but this had little effect on the changed behavior. The disturbance never completely disappeared; even after a long rest, the dog became excited again if he was put back into the experimental room.

The remarkable thing is that a simple perceptual conflict should have such drastic and long-lasting effects. No pain was involved, nor fear of pain. Can we conclude from this that a human neurotic disturbance might be produced in the same way, when something learned in childhood, say, conflicts with some adult experience? Is neurosis all a product of learning? Before leaping to that conclusion we must take one more fact into account: only a few dogs, perhaps one per cent, will develop a neurosis in that experimental situation. There must be a special susceptibility for the breakdown to occur, so it seems that here again we are dealing with an interaction between experience and a particular hereditary weakness. But the phenomenon does remind us that small things can have big effects when we are dealing with something as complex as a brain. Human beings are more vulnerable to emotional disturbance than the dog, as we will see later (Chapter 11), and so conceivably the human susceptibility to neurotic breakdown following minor stress may also be more widespread and not limited to such a small proportion of the population.

MENTAL RETARDATION

About three per cent of the population — three people out of every hundred, a high figure — make low enough scores on intelligence tests to be considered mentally deficient. IQ 70 is the dividing line. With a lower IQ, in the high sixties, the child may make some progress in school but with repeated failures. He may learn to read, but is unlikely ever to make enough use of reading to get through a book, and after leaving school he may regress to the point of being illiterate, retaining only enough to be able to sign his name and read a few words. (However, an IQ below 70 does not necessarily mean that the subject is incapable of managing his affairs; there are always a number of persons who have low IQs, perhaps because of limitation of experience in childhood, but who function better in practical matters than would be expected from their test scores. They are no geniuses, but they get along.) Children with lower IQs, below 60, may fail totally in the ordinary school, and at very low levels they may not even be able to dress themselves but must be cared for in all respects.

The causes vary widely. An important one is birth injury, so called. It includes any damage to the brain at or about the time of birth. Unfortunately, the neurons (nerve cells) of the brain do not regenerate, and they are very delicate. If the oxygen supply to the brain is cut off for more than a few seconds during birth, by pressure on the cord before the baby has emerged from the birth canal and can breathe for himself, brain cells will die and nothing can be done to replace them. How great the effect is will depend on what part of the brain is affected as well as the amount of destruction.

A different kind of cause is glandular or metabolic. An inherited deficiency of the thyroid gland results in *cretinism,* in which there is both stunted physical growth and mental retardation. If the condition is recognized in the first month or so of life and thyroid extract is given, normal development results. A rarer condition is *phenylketonuria,* which is an inability of the body to metabolize (to make use of, chemically) a substance called phenylalanine. If this condition also is recognized early and the baby is put on a diet that contains little phenylalanine, the baby's development is good; otherwise, he will be severely retarded.

A fascinating medical detective story concerns a related condition, though this is one that does not produce mental retardation. The victim was no less than George III of England, who it now appears was not insane at all in the usual sense of the word, but a sufferer from porphyria: a disease which is a hereditary disturbance of metabolism, like phenylketonuria, but which may show up only after the patient is full grown. For a while in this century the medical world was tempted to see all illness as *psychosomatic* — caused, that is, as much by mental as by physical factors — and two eminent psychiatrists some time ago proposed that the king's physical symptoms were of this kind or else merely invented by his doctors to cover up his insanity. Now however Macalpine and Hunter have shown that he had porphyria, and have traced the illness in the royal family from as far back as Mary Queen of Scots, and from there forward to include Frederick the Great of Germany, various other royal figures, and two anonymous descendants of George III now living, whose diagnoses provide confirmation that the hereditary constitutional defect was indeed present in the royal line.

A very different mental deficiency results not from any brain damage or hereditary defect, but from a lack of attention to the baby. Saddest of all cases, because there is no reason for it to happen, is that of children reared in an orphanage where babies receive complete physical care but little psychological care. A baby needs to be played with, talked to, and exposed to a normal human environment. A number of orphanages have been found in the past (we may hope that this does not happen any more, though the hope may be unfounded) in which the babies were fed well, kept clean in hygienic conditions, and otherwise left to lie in cots with sheets draped over the sides. They could stare at the ceiling, and hear other babies crying: and nothing else, except occasionally when a nurse showed up. Not a very stimulating environment. Such infants are severely retarded in motor development, some not having learned to walk by the age of three (R. Spitz; W. Dennis). W. Goldfarb showed that the mental retardation is severe also: three years spent in an orphanage, between the ages approximately of six months and three years six months, resulted in an average IQ of 72, whereas a similar group of orphans placed in foster homes (and thus in a more normal human environment) had an average IQ of 95. The tests were made at the age of 10 years or later, so this means that the effects of early psychological deprivation are permanent. Little change in the IQ occurs after the age of 12 to 15 years.

For the brain-damaged child, or the one with a hereditary defect, the environment is also a problem but in a different way. What suits the normal child does not suit him. His pace of mental growth is slower, he needs more time to master simple ideas, and he has more need of TLC (tender loving care). Parents and other children may simply conclude that he cannot learn; as a result he does not learn as much as in fact he could. There is a riddle here. In simple learning, such as the formation of a simple conditioned reflex, the retarded child is no slower, in general, than the normal—yet he is slower, or wholly incapable, at other learning which presents little difficulty for the normal child. The reason may be that the retarded child does not attend to the right things in the learning situation, or that he does not perceive in the situation what others perceive (which says the same thing in another way). It is clear that academic psychology still has much to learn about the normal course of learning in the development of perception in the normal child, the development of concepts, and so on. With a better understanding of normal growth we will be in a better situation to help the retarded child. Conversely, study of the retarded child's difficulties casts light on the nature of normal intelligence and draws our attention to things about the normal child that we may take too easily for granted.

HYPERACTIVITY

There are a number of disorders of child behavior that do not involve retardation and are even less well understood. *Autism* is one, a condition in which the apparently intelligent child seems almost schizophrenic in his unresponsiveness to the environment. Another is that of the child who seems normal in all respects except that he is unable to learn to read, or able to learn only with the greatest difficulty. Still another is the *hyperactivity* that can drive a teacher and parents to distraction and keeps the child himself from learning as he otherwise could. A case report follows.

Michael, 9 years of age, IQ 103, came from a middle-class home. His teacher reported that he could not sit still and constantly disturbed the class. His work was poor because of inattention and distractibility. He made just as much trouble at home, and his mother reported that he had been like this since he was a baby—quite unlike his brother and sister.

Some hyperactive children suffer from birth injury, but no evidence of such brain damage was found in Michael's case. His trouble seemed simply that he *had* to be active. He could not take time to think before answering, but he could also be distracted by anything that happened near him. It turned out that he was one of the hyperactive children who can be helped by a drug treatment. The drug reduced his activity somewhat—but greatly improved his ability to attend to what others were saying or to his work. This shows something very interesting: it was not his need of muscular activity, only, that was the problem. Michael himself was now much happier (not to mention his teacher and parents). The drug was not a depressant or tranquilizer but—surprisingly—a stimulant. This treatment does not work in all cases, and how it works is quite unknown, but the case is one example of the large number of behavior disorders for which psychologists, psychiatrists and neurologists are seeking explanations in joint research. Treatment at present is largely hit or miss, rule of thumb, and theoretical understanding is necessary before we can hope for any great improvement.

THE OBJECTIVE APPROACH TO BEHAVIOR

We have been looking at sample problem areas where the study of behavior takes on practical significance. There are others: racial and religious prejudice, the education of slum children deprived of a reasonable environment for stimulating mental growth, the effects of monotonous occupations on adults, programed learning in the schools, and so on. Modern psychology has not been handicapped, in its contribution to practical affairs, by having renounced subjective methods. Rather the opposite. Introspective psychology was almost totally out of touch with the real world about 1900 when, as we have seen, Freud was developing his essentially objective method. This was also the time at which the study of learning was getting under way (Hermann Ebbinghaus in Germany, Lloyd Morgan in England, Edward L. Thorndike in the United States), and the study of human intelligence was about to begin (Alfred Binet, in Paris): both objective in method, both bearing on the real problems of children.

A main reason for objectivity is the need to keep inferences separate from facts, to distinguish between theory and evidence. Theories may differ from one another, but it is no good arguing about theory if you can't agree on what the facts are. Psychology today is *behavioristic*, which means that it uses behavior as evidence: what people do, not what they think. What people do can be observed by others, and so agreement concerning the facts is possible at least in principle. The essence of a good observation for scientific purposes is that anyone can make the observation for himself, and so test its accuracy.

Psychology of course uses other objective evidence in constructing theory. It builds on the basic sciences of physics and chemistry, and on the anatomy and physiology of the sense organs, nervous system and muscles. An especially important item is the EEG (*electroencephalogram* or "brain waves," p. 175); less often used but also important are the EMG (*electromyogram,* recording changes of muscle tension) and the GSR (*galvanic skin response,* an electrical change in the skin accompanying emotion). The electrical activities that produce EEG, EMG and GSR are not classified as behavior but are still part of the objective total of human activity.

Most of the time we need not split hairs about what is subjective and what is objective. Pain itself is technically subjective, a "private" event that no one else can know about directly; but a *report* of pain by the person who feels it, saying Ouch!, screwing up the face and jerking the hand back from the sharp object that caused pain — all these are behavior. They are objective and permit a reliable *inference* that pain is occurring. Again, an afterimage is subjective and can only be observed by one person; but the report of afterimages in certain conditions is so consistent that we can be certain that in these conditions afterimages do occur. We can then take for granted that there is pain when a subject has burnt his hand, that there is an afterimage when he has stared at a bright object; and we need not be fussy in such cases about whether the evidence is subjective or objective. What the student should keep in mind is that when there is doubt or when one must choose between two hypotheses it is the objective evidence that carries weight.

So speech, including reports of subjective experience, is a most important form of behavior. Facial expression is also an important form of behavior in social communication. The muscles of the face can convey annoyance or pleasure or absentmindedness. Blushing (caused by changes of muscle tension in the blood vessels just under the skin) is behavior indicating embarrassment or anger (though we call it "flushing" when it is due to anger); breathing is behavior, and changes of breathing are part of the behavorial evidence used in the so-called lie-detector methods (which are really emotion-detecting). Behavior does not consist only of using the big muscles of arms and legs — to fight, to run away, to find food, to play games — nor of these plus the finer muscles of the fingers: it is the activity of *all* the muscles of the body, plus glandular secretions such as mouth-watering (secretion of saliva), tears and sweat.

It is important to observe that behavior tells us what is going on in the mind only when we take account of the circumstances in which it occurs. We must keep track of the *stimuli* or the *stimulus situation* as well as the *response* that is made to stimulation. We must keep track also of the *temporal pattern* of behavior: what follows what, the relation of what the subject does now to what he was doing before or to what he does next. The great American psychologist William James insisted that mental events are not discrete and separate from one another but form a flow, which he called "the stream of thought." The same is true of behavior. The flow of a stream may be smooth or tumultuous, it may meander gently in part of its course and elsewhere pour over the rocks with great violence, but it is a continuity.

So behavior has to be understood in terms of the circumstances in which it appears and its pattern over periods of time. Examples: not answering when spoken to means one thing when you are watching TV; it may mean something else when you are not busy, especially if your silence is followed by walking out and slamming the door. For a girl who is usually quiet at parties, not talking much means that she is her normal self; for another, usually one to keep the party going, exactly the same behavior means something else. She may be depressed or annoyed or trying to think how to get out of some difficulty. Her silence cannot show what the disturbance is, but it does show that she is in some way disturbed. This example shows two things: One is that feelings and emotions, when they are mild, are not recognized so much by one's present behavior as by its relation to the larger pattern of one's usual behavior; my good humor is apparent not because I act in a polite way but because I am more polite than usual. The second thing that is shown by the example of the silent girl is that *doing nothing*—silence, not moving, failing to respond—can be a most important feature of the behavioral pattern. By definition, it is not behavior, but it has meaning by contrast with past behavior.

This may sound more complex, more intimidating, than it really is. Everyone makes such judgments every day. From behavioral patterns, by long practice from infancy onward, we have learned in everyday life to infer what goes on in another person's mind: often wrongly, but very often correctly, especially when one can observe also what is happening to the other person at the time (what stimuli precede his responses). The inference from behavior is not a simple matter of seeing a smile and knowing that the smiler is happy (he may or may not be), but a complex judgment from all relevant data.

USE OF TERMS

We can now attempt some definitions, with commentary to avoid misunderstanding. The student should realize that the same word can mean different things to different people, and that "mind" for example may mean a ghostly, immaterial agent in one book, be dismissed as a meaningless term in another, and be defined as a brain process in a third. He must therefore learn how certain fundamental terms are used here.

Behavior, as a technical psychological term, may be defined as the publicly observable activity of muscle or glands of external secretion, as manifested for example in movements of parts of the body or the appearance of tears, sweat, saliva and so forth.

The student should note that this does not include glands of internal secretion (endocrine glands), whose activity is not directly observable. We know of the thyroid gland's activity, for example, only by inference: either as the result of elaborate chemical analyses, or by observing the changes that occur a week or so after the gland is injured; but we know of the tear gland's activity directly, because we can see it. Behavior is the factual basis of psychology and we do not include in the definition anything that is not at least potentially observable.

Psychology is then defined as the study of the more complex forms of integration or organization in behavior. It is implied that this includes also the study of processes such as learning, emotion or perception that are involved in organizing the behavior. "Integration" or "organization" refers to the pattern or combination of different segments of behavior in relation to each other and to external events impinging on the organism.

Note here that psychology is not defined simply as the study of behavior, as is often done. Such a definition would include too much. It is the physiologist, not the psychologist, who studies the units of behavior—for example, the mechanism of glandular secretion—and he is also the one who has obtained our knowledge of the integration of reflexes, an outstanding example being Sir Charles Sherrington's *Integrative Action of the Nervous System* in 1906 (a work which has had a profound effect on psychological thought). The fact is that we cannot really draw a sharp line between psychology and physiology. What we can say is that the physiologist is mostly concerned with the functioning of the different parts of the body and the segments of behavior that these parts exhibit; the psychologist with the functioning of the whole organism, and the way in which the segments of behavior are coordinated to form complex actions and sequences of action. The focal problem of psychology is found in the patterns of behavior shown by the whole animal of a higher species in adjusting to his environment over appreciable periods of time; to say the same thing in a different way, it is found in the mental processes of the higher animal.

If psychology cannot be sharply distinguished from physiology, it is even less easily distinguished from *ethology;* in fact, ethologists make the same kind of investigations of behavior that some animal psychologists do. What happened is that psychologists, though they claimed all behavior for their province, left large regions unexplored. They did little with species other than a few mammals (mostly rat, monkey and man) or with the problem of instinctive behavior (going so far about 1920, in fact, as to deny its existence). Meantime students of evolution were discovering that differences of behavior sometimes are the key to an evolutionary sequence and became aware, as psychologists were not, of the problem of the evolution of the striking and beautifully coordinated patterns of instinctive behavior in birds, fish and invertebrates. However, learning did not become a prime interest for them, nor did behavorial evolution in mammals. The ethologist, then, is a behavioral scientist with training in zoology, not always as informed about learning in mammals as he might be—or the animal psychologist is an ethologist who does not always know as much about the birds and the bees, and biological science in general, as he should. But there is more to know in this field than one man can master, and today there is an effective collaboration between the two sciences, each complementing the other's work.

Mind and *mental* are terms used in this book to refer to processes inside the head that determine the more complex levels of organization in behavior. (They are not exact terms but are still very useful; see p. 278.) It was said above that mental processes are the focal problem of psychology; but psychology also covers a wider field, having traditionally been concerned with the behavior of ant, earthworm, spider and wasp, which cannot be said to have minds or mental processes. Their learning, and their so-called instinctive behavior, has something to tell us about the mechanisms of learning and how it collaborates with the influence of heredity, but on our present evidence these animals lack thought and consciousness. Literally, "psychology" means the study of mind, but such a definition is inadequate today, since it does not include the whole field actually studied by psychologists.

SUMMARY

Psychology used to be called the study of mind; today it is usually called the study of behavior. If however mind is that which determines the complex behavior of higher animals, both definitions are approximately correct. In modern psychology mind is considered to be brain activity or some part of it—though this is held only as a working assumption—and is studied by objective methods. Mental events are known theoretically, being inferred from behavior. In such a framework the study of animals has a natural part, both for its own sake and for the light it casts on human behavior.

Use of objective methods is necessary because in science it is essential to be able to confirm the facts on which a theory is based. Private events are those that are peculiar to one person; they cannot be observed by anyone else and consequently they are unsatisfactory as scientific evidence. Also, it is known that introspection, direct observation of one's own mental processes, does not exist. But a verbal report of a private event is public or objective evidence, on which theory can be based, and certain private events like the afterimage are so uniformly reported that we know they exist. Using objective methods has not handicapped psychology but has made it more effective instead. Some samples of the problems dealt with in psychology—problems of learning, of mental disorder, of retardation, of hyperactivity—are considered briefly.

In reviewing, the student should note that this first chapter will not be fully intelligible, probably, until he has a fair understanding of the later chapters. What this means is that the text must be worked through several times, each time with a more complete understanding. It is suggested that the first step is to read through the whole book, skipping or skimming as necessary, well in advance of the lectures or assignments and without attempting detailed study. Then the student should plan to work seriously through the book twice, as suggested above.

Guide to Study

It may be a help, in mastering this chapter, to proceed as follows. Make sure you know, and can explain, how Freud made a contribution to objective method; why a sensation of pain is less satisfactory, as scientific evidence, than talking about it; what the two kinds of theory of mind are, how to distinguish animism and dualism from mechanism and monism, and which theory of mind is used in this book. How can one firmly believe in an immortal soul and still work with a mechanistic theory? What is a temporal pattern, and how can it make *doing nothing* an important feature of behavior? With respect to learning and the study method, how should you approach a new textbook? Do these questions that you are reading now fit in with the recommended method? Why is the old rhyme "Thirty days hath September ..." of psychological interest? It has been suggested by some people that any single act of a psychotic person might be done by a normal person: does this mean that it is only the *pattern* of acts, or the circumstances in which an act is done, that is abnormal? Does this agree with the idea that the essence of mental illness is motivation? What causes of mental retardation are there? What is puzzling about the retarded child's rate of learning? What is surprising about one treatment of hyperactivity? Finally, what is surprising about the cause of neurosis in Pavlov's dog?

NOTES AND REFERENCES

Alfred Binet, Hermann Ebbinghaus, Sigmund Freud, Lloyd Morgan, Ivan Petrovich Pavlov and Edward L. Thorndike are all great names in the history of psychology. The lives of these men and outlines of their work can be found in E. G. Boring, *History of Experimental Psychology,* Appleton-Century-Crofts, 1950. For Binet's work, see also Chapter 9. A good account of Freud's ideas is given in C. S. Hall, *A Primer of Freudian Psychology,* World, 1954. We will return in the following chapter to Pavlov's work, but he has given a very readable account of it himself in his *Lectures on Conditioned Reflexes* (trans. Gantt), 1928. The report of experimental neurosis is on page 342 of that book. (See also p. 290 of Pavlov's *Conditioned Reflexes:* Dover edition, 1960.)

OTHER REFERENCES IN THIS CHAPTER

Boring, E. G.: A history of introspection. *Psychological Bulletin,* 1953, 50, 169–189. Page 187: Consciousness is a construct, inferred, not observed.
Dennis, Wayne: For a review of the important work by Dennis and others on the intelligence of orphanage children, see J. McV. Hunt, *Intelligence and Experience,* Ronald, 1961.
Fox, M. W.: *Abnormal Behavior in Animals,* Saunders, 1968.
Herbart, Johann: German philosopher-psychologist, 1776–1841.
Humphrey, George: *Thinking,* Methuen, 1951.
Macalpine, Ida, and Hunter, Richard: *George III and the Mad Business.* Pantheon Books, 1970.
Peirce, Charles: Great American philosopher, 1839–1914.
Spitz, R. A.: See J. McV. Hunt, *Intelligence and Experience,* already referred to.
Swank, R. L., and Marchand, W. E.: Combat neuroses. *Archives of Neurology and Psychiatry,* 1946, 55, 236–247. Page 243: All infantrymen will break down if stress continues long enough—except when the soldier is psychotic to start with!

SPECIAL TOPICS
Ethology
Hinde, R. A.: *Animal Behavior* (2nd Ed.), McGraw-Hill, 1970. A systematic and good, but heavy, synthesis of ethology and comparative psychology.
Lorenz, K.: *King Solomon's Ring.* Very readable, by the founder of modern ethology, but not at all a systematic account.

Mental Illness and Hyperactivity
Millon, T.: *Modern Psychopathology,* Saunders, 1969.
Rosen, E., Fox, R., and Gregory, I.: *Abnormal Psychology,* 2nd ed., Saunders, 1972.
White, R. W.: *The Abnormal Personality* (3rd Ed.), Ronald Press, 1964.

Retardation
Estes, W. K.: *Learning Theory and Mental Development,* Academic Press, 1970.
Goldfarb, W.: The effects of early institutional care on adolescent personality. *Child Development,* 1943, 14, 213–223.
Robinson, H. B., and Robinson, N. M.: *The Mentally Retarded Child.* McGraw-Hill, 1965.

GENERAL REFERENCES

The following three books are useful for reference purposes on most of the topics in this textbook. All three are somewhat out of date now, but they provide authoritative background information.

Osgood, C. E.: *Method and Theory in Experimental Psychology*. Oxford University Press, 1953. Emphasis—the theory of learning.

Stevens, S. S. (Ed.): *Handbook of Experimental Psychology*. The 36 chapters by different authors range from neuroanatomy to the higher processes of human thought.

Woodworth, R. S., and Schlosberg, H.: *Experimental Psychology,* Holt, 1954. An excellent integration of classical topics such as imagery and imageless thought, with a modern approach to theory. The 1971 revision cited below has become very "sensory" and has lost the special values of the earlier edition:

Kling, J. W., and Riggs, L. A. (Eds.): *Woodworth and Schlosberg's Experimental Psychology,* Holt, Rinehart & Winston, 1971.

2

conditioning and learning

We must begin with the phenomena of learning in our systematic examination of behavior and behavior theory. ("Learning" includes conditioning, which must have been the earliest form of learning to appear in evolution and is still fundamental.) We will not be able in this chapter to deal with the topic completely, since learning involves all aspects of psychology, but must return to it repeatedly in the following chapters.

The two chief variables that determine behavior are learning and heredity. They interact closely, and in Chapter 7 we will see what some of the details of the interaction are; for the present, the student should keep both variables in mind. Apart from unconditioned reflexes (a term that will be explained shortly), all the behavior of human beings and of other mammals is influenced by learning; but *all* behavior, reflex or not, is fundamentally influenced by heredity. In a normal environment, heredity determines what sort of brain, sense organs and motor equipment the subject will have; and on them depends absolutely what he can learn. Because of differences of heredity a man can learn what an elephant or a weasel cannot; dogs and cats and monkeys learn different things from the same situation; and so on. Learning is always a fundamental influence in the behavior of higher animals; but so is heredity, and this is sometimes forgotten. If the student will just remember that what he learns in any situation is as much determined by how he is made as by that particular experience, he will be better able to keep both things in mind.

DEVELOPING IDEAS ABOUT LEARNING

In the past most progress has been made when learning has been studied in its simpler forms. This applies especially to the study of conditioning in animal subjects. However, the study of learning did not begin with animals or with conditioning. We have already seen (p. 6) that human learning may be surprisingly complex, but Ebbinghaus in 1885 found a way of avoiding some of the complexities and it was he who opened up the topic for study.

Till 1885 it seems to have been thought that learning could never be handled experimentally. Of course it was known to occur, even young children can learn, and notions about "the association of ideas" (another form of learning) and how it takes place had been discussed since the time of Aristotle; but the process seemed too elusive and subtle to be attacked in the laboratory. All this was changed at one blow by Ebbinghaus. He simplified the problem by inventing a new kind of material to be learned by human beings and showed how readily learning could be experimented with. Lloyd Morgan then made the first steps toward the study of learning in animals. Thorndike followed Morgan with a systematic study just at the end of the 19th century, and in doing so determined the main questions that psychologists would be asking for the next half-century. It was four years later, in 1902, that the equally crucial work of Pavlov began in Russia. Pavlov, a physiologist, apparently had no knowledge of any of this psychological work till much later; and on the other hand psychologists had no effective knowledge of Pavlov's work till about 1918. From then on, however, the two lines of research interacted closely and now can be regarded as a single body of experimentation.

Ebbinghaus's invention was the nonsense syllable, a short combination of letters such as *dak, wom, cib, nug*. He made up lists of such syllables to memorize. Using such lists it is possible to study the rate of learning, by finding out how many times a list has to be read over before it can be repeated correctly; and also the rate of forgetting, which is what Ebbinghaus was mainly interested in. Figure 1 for example shows the rate of forgetting: very fast at first, then becoming very slow. The shape of this curve of course depends on the kind of material and the conditions in which it is learned; the rate of forgetting, or whether forgetting occurs at all, is influenced by many things.

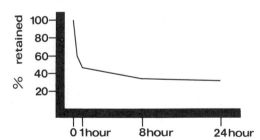

Figure 1. Ebbinghaus's curve of retention (memory) using 13-syllable lists of nonsense syllables. Separate lists were used for the 20-min. interval, the one-hr. interval, and so on; on the curve is an average obtained from a number of lists. Ebbinghaus first learned a list, counting the number of times it had to be read before it was completely learned. Then he relearned it, again counting the number of trials. The curve shows that at 20 min. relearning took 60% fewer trials than original learning; at one hr. 45% fewer trials; and so on. So at 20 min. he had retained 60% of the original learning, at one hr. only 45%. (These are approximate values: see Woodworth and Schlosberg [p. 726] under Notes and References, p. 19.)

Thorndike's early work was done with animals, but there are few experiments that have had more influence on our ideas about man. What he did, very simply, was to put hungry cats into problem boxes with food outside. In one box the cat had to press a lever to escape; in another he had to pull a loop of string; and so on. Rate of learning was measured by the time it took to escape in successive trials in the same box, as the cat got quicker and quicker with practice. Figure 2 shows how this can be represented in learning curves. (Learning can also be measured by counting "errors"—false moves made on each trial—as well as by the number of trials needed to achieve an errorless performance.)

No one really cares much about how long it takes a tomcat to pull a string to open a door to get to food. But these experiments of Thorndike's led him to look in a new way at learning and thinking—*any* learning and thinking, not only the cat's—and this raised fundamental questions that have since had a dominant influence in psychology. Not that Thorndike's views were generally accepted: on the contrary, they gave rise to violent argument. On one side were psychologists who more or less agreed with his ideas but were apt to make them more extreme. On the other side were the majority, who strongly disagreed. Today we have mostly recovered from these extremes and can see better what Thorndike's contribution to knowledge was.

The first question he raised was whether cats have minds and mental processes. Do they think about the situation and then decide what to do, or is there some simpler way in which animals may learn? Watching his cats, Thorndike thought the learning was very mechanical and showed little sign of intelligence or thought. It looked to him as if the cat's brain somehow made a connection between *stimulus* and *response,* so that when the cat saw a loop of string and learned to pull it, or a wooden button and learned to turn it, a message could go straight from the cat's eye to his paw and no thinking would occur. The two possibilities are diagramed in Figure 3. Lloyd Morgan had thought that learning was possible only if an animal was conscious: he thought the animal would have to remember the pleasure that followed a correct response and the lack of pleasure or the pain following an incorrect one. Thorndike made psychologists realize the

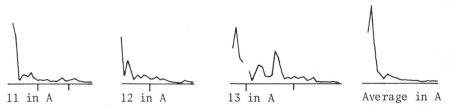

11 in A   12 in A   13 in A   Average in A

Figure 2. *Learning curves from Thorndike's experiments of 1897–98: the time scores for cats 11, 12 and 13 in problem box A, and the average scores on 24 trials for 13 cats in the same problem box. (Adapted from E. L. Thorndike,* Animal Intelligence, *1911.)*

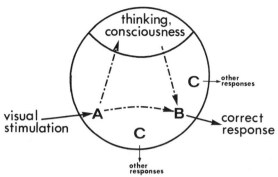

Figure 3. *Thorndike's question about learning and the mind. Suppose that the large circle represents the cat's brain. When the cat sees a loop of string in a puzzle box, the brain has received excitation from the eye. How does this produce the correct response? Two different possibilities: (1) the excitation goes to a part of the brain where there is thinking and consciousness, and this mental activity then excites the motor path leading to the response; (2) a much simpler possibility is that A gets connected directly with B, a stimulus-response connection with no thinking involved — the stimulus excites the response directly. Learning then has nothing to do with the mind but consists of making S-R connections.*

importance of another possibility: the sort of stimulus-response (S-R) connection that is represented by the line *A-B* in Figure 3.

We will see in Chapter 5 that this is the S-R formula, a fundamental idea in psychology. We may also note that cats can and do think, since they are capable of delayed response, which as we will see in Chapter 5 is evidence of thinking. But Thorndike was right to raise the question, since at that time there was no proof at all that any animal except man could think. One result of his work was to stimulate others to find the proof.

Thorndike's second main question was, Why does an animal learn some responses and not others? When will a connection like *A-B* in Figure 3 be formed? When an animal or human being is learning to make some response, he makes many wrong moves. Yet they are not remembered and repeated. The oftener the wrong response is made the *less* likely it is to be made again, so mere repetition is not enough. Thorndike proposed that there is another factor operating, a special effect of reward or punishment. He said that when a connection like *A-B* operates and the cat gets to food, *the effect of this reward is to strengthen* A-B. When the cat looks at the loop of string and then pulls it, food follows, so that the next time the cat sees the loop he is more likely to pull it, or pulls it sooner. On the other hand if a connection *A-C* should operate, there is no reward and the connection is not strengthened. So, as trials go on, *A-B* becomes stronger and stronger. Thorndike's *law of effect* said that an S-R connection is strengthened if it is active and a pleasant state of affairs follows, but weakened if an unpleasant state of affairs follows. In modern psychology Thorndike's "effect" is referred to as *reinforcement,* a conception that we will return to.

CONDITIONED REFLEXES: PAVLOV

Shortly after Thorndike began experimenting, Pavlov turned to the study of conditioned reflexes. He was already famous for his studies of digestion; now, in a second career beginning in 1902, he began the work on the brain that made him even more famous.

Pavlov's experimental situation is illustrated in Figure 4. For almost all his work he used the secretion of saliva by a dog as the response to be studied. The stimulus to be conditioned was most often auditory—a bell, a buzzer, a metronome ticking at a particular rate—but he also used visual and tactual stimuli. The dog in Figure 4 is shown with attachments for mechanically stimulating (scratching) his shoulder and thigh, but these would not be the only stimuli used. To collect saliva, Pavlov made a minor operation to let one of the salivary glands secrete outward, into a small cup cemented to the dog's cheek.

Pavlov then proceeded as follows. Some more or less neutral stimulus such as the sound of the buzzer was presented repeatedly, each time followed by food. (A buzzer or metronome is "neutral," since it does not excite the dog to make any strong response and by itself would soon be disregarded.) The buzzer was sounded for 15 sec., then food was moved into the dog's reach (while the buzzer continued for another 15 sec.). This sequence, buzzer followed by

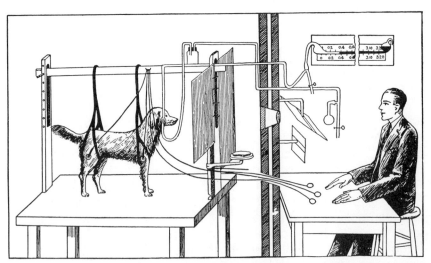

Figure 4. *Pavlov's procedure for conditioning salivary responses. Dog and experimenter are in separate rooms; before the experimenter's hands are the controls for stimulating the dog's skin (note the attachments on shoulder and thigh) and feeding (the food dish swings round into the dog's reach). Attached to the dog's cheek by cement is a tube that leads to the manometer at upper right, by which the amount of salivary secretion can be measured. (From I. P. Pavlov.* Lectures on Conditioned Reflexes, *International Publishers.)*

food, was repeated about 10 times, at irregular intervals, in a one-hour session. Perhaps by the fifteenth or twentieth trial, in the second session, the dog would begin to secrete some saliva on hearing the buzzer, before the food appeared; by the fortieth trial he would do so copiously and reliably. Now a *conditioned reflex* was established.

In this procedure the neutral stimulus is referred to as the *conditioned stimulus* or *CS;* food in the mouth is the *unconditioned stimulus* or *UCS;* the secretion of saliva as a response to the neutral stimulus (before the food appears) is the *conditioned response* or *CR;* and the secretion of saliva when food is in the mouth is the *unconditioned response* or *UCR.* In other work, the UCS might be electric shock applied to a dog's paw, the UCR lifting the paw. Or, with a human subject, the UCS might be a puff of air hitting the cheek near the eye, and the UCR would then be an eye-blink.

The UCS-UCR sequence is the operation of an *unconditioned reflex,* which simply means that the response is not learned; the stimulus evokes the response because of "inherited" connections in the nervous system—ones that are determined by the subject's heredity and normal growth processes. Examples are the constriction of the pupil when the eye is exposed to bright light, coughing when the throat is irritated, sweating in warm air and shivering in cold air, and pulling back the hand from a painful contact. The salivary reflex does not seem a likely prospect for the study of learning, but Pavlov showed in fact that it is a very good one.

The learning that Pavlov studied was quite different from what Thorndike was studying in the United States about the same time. No doubt this was due partly to the fact that one man studied cats, the other dogs, but the main cause was a difference of method. Pavlov worked with glandular responses and limited all other activity by his subject; Thorndike worked with muscular responses, which are more closely controlled by higher brain centers (that is, they are voluntary rather than involuntary: p. 91), and his subjects could move around more freely. Also, Pavlov's procedure is what is now known as *Type-S conditioning,* Thorndike's *Type-R conditioning.*

In Type-S conditioning the experimenter uses a UCS to control the response that is to be conditioned. In Type-R conditioning there is no UCS; the experimenter waits till the response occurs, more or less by chance, and then rewards it. In Type-S conditioning the response is *elicited* by stimulation, when the experimenter wants it to occur; in Type-R conditioning the response is *emitted* by the subject and is not the result of any particular stimulation. Pavlov wanted to make an association between the sound of a bell (for example) and the secretion of saliva: he rang the bell and then *made* the dog salivate (by giving him food). To make an association between seeing a loop of string and pulling it, Thorndike had to wait till the cat happened to pull it—and then reward the cat with food. In the first or Type-S case, food is both a stimulus and a reward; in the second or Type-R case, a reward only. Type-S conditioning attaches old responses to new stimuli; Type-R develops new response patterns, sometimes in familiar situations, sometimes in unfamiliar ones.

One of Pavlov's important discoveries is the way in which animals show *generalization.* Let us suppose that a dog's first CR has been established, the CS being a tone of 500 *cps* (cycles per second). Now a new stimulus is presented, a tone of 600 cps. The dog secretes saliva. Why—since he hears this now for the first time? The answer is that dogs, like people, generalize: having learned to make a response in one situation they will make the same response in other more or less similar situations. The dog does not confuse 600 cps with 500 cps, but can distinguish such tones perfectly well, as Pavlov also showed. By continuing to feed the dog following 500 cps, but never feeding following 600 cps, 400 cps, and so on, he could readily get a dog to a stage at which the CR was always elicited by the 500-cps tone and not by any others.

Another important item is Pavlov's demonstration of *inhibition.* In the preceding example, when the 600-cps tone is presented and the dog does not respond, one might think that the response has gradually weakened and disappeared. Pavlov showed that the connection between stimulus and response is still there, but inhibited. A sudden unexpected noise can break up the inhibition temporarily (this is known as disinhibition), and now the 600-cps tone will elicit salivation again. The inhibition is extensive when it is present: it not only prevents response to the 600-cps tone, but also prevents other responses. For example, if the 500-cps tone is presented immediately after the 600-cps tone it will not elicit salivation. A negative CS—one that is not followed by the UCS—sets up an inhibitory state in the dog's brain which takes several minutes to disappear.

Inhibition also appears in the *extinction* of a CR with massed trials (Pavlovian extinction, cf. p. 105). After a CR has been well established it can be extinguished by presenting the CS by itself (without the UCS) for about eight times, at three- or four-minute intervals. Now there is no salivation to the CS, and other CRs are affected also. But the CR is not wiped out but subject to a temporary inhibition, for when the animal is brought back to the experimental room next day the CR reappears.

TYPE-R CONDITIONING AND REINFORCEMENT

Type-R conditioning is so named because of the emphasis it puts on the selection of a particular *response* from several possible ones (whereas the *S* of "Type-S" points to the importance of CS and UCS in this other method). But another strong reason for the name might have been the large part that *reinforcement* plays in Type-R conditioning. Before we go into this, let us define some terms.

Reinforcement in its general sense is an event immediately following a response which increases the probability that the response will be repeated when the subject finds himself in the same situation again. The increased probability means that the response is being learned.

Primary reinforcement is the satisfaction of some biologically primitive need: food when hungry, escape from painful stimulation, and sexual satisfaction are examples.

Secondary reinforcement is sensory stimulation that is associated with primary reinforcement; having occurred at the same time or just before primary reinforcement, it has acquired some of the same power to promote learning. Examples: the smell of food or sound of the dinner bell, seeing a chair when one is tired standing, the first touch of a cool breeze on a hot day (before it has time to do any cooling: the actual cooling, when one is too hot, is primary reinforcement).

The modern development of Type-R conditioning is chiefly the work of B. F. Skinner. It is in following his procedures that the nature of reinforcement, and its effectiveness, becomes clearest.

Type-R Procedure

Put a pigeon in a box with a button on the wall and a delivery chute for grain or put a rat in a similar box with a bar or lever sticking out of the wall and a mechanism for dropping food pellets into the box (consider Fig. 5; as for the pigeon, see Fig. 102). The food can be supplied by hand, or automatically. Then we wait. The hungry subject moves about the box, more or less at random (we can speak so, though the behavior always shows a considerable amount of organization and is not really random), pecking at the walls and floor or sniffing in corners and investigating anything investigable. Sooner or later the bird pecks the button, or the rat puts his forefeet on the bar and depresses it. Immediately food appears. The subject eats and then resumes the investigation. The same sequence of events is repeated as soon as the subject again makes contact with button or bar, and before long the subject begins making the response systematically as soon as he is put in the apparatus.

The subject is conditioned. There is not one CS but many (cf. Fig. 38, p. 83)—visual, olfactory, tactual—simply from the subject's being

Figure 5. *Rats in a Skinner box, one about to press. The original caption in the Columbia* Jester *read, "Boy, have I got this guy conditioned! Every time I press the bar he drops in a piece of food." (Reproduced from* Cumulative Record *by B. F. Skinner. Copyright © 1959, 1961 by Appleton-Century-Crofts, Inc. Reproduced by permission of Appleton-Century-Crofts.)*

exposed to the experimental chamber itself. And the CR does not need to have any natural connection with the reinforcement that is used (whereas a salivary CR is related to eating, or withdrawal related to pain). So this method easily allows us to condition any behavior in the animal's repertoire. Also, it is possible to reinforce only every second or third or tenth response, thus producing more responses per minute than if the animal got a piece of food every time and stopped to eat it. With this procedure, which is called *partial reinforcement,* very high rates of responding can be obtained.

What we have been talking about here, of course, is primary reinforcement (food for a hungry animal). The role of secondary reinforcement is next seen in a procedure which uses Type-R conditioning to *shape up* new forms of behavior: behavior that is not in the animal's original repertoire, though each individual action of the complex is.

The first step is to make a secondary reinforcer of some easily produced noise. The noise is made and then food is given, repeatedly, until the animal looks for food as soon as he hears the noise. Now when the animal makes any movement toward where you want him to go, or performs the first of the sequence of actions you want him to perform, you make the noise instantly and follow it with the food. After a few repetitions the first part of the movement you want is being made reliably. Now wait till the animal moves a little farther toward the desired goal, then give the secondary reinforcement (make the noise) again, and feed; and so on.

Here the practical importance of secondary reinforcement is that it can be given *at once,* as soon as the right movement is made. Primary reinforcement takes longer to give, and the secret of shaping up is to reinforce, without delay, the first slight movement in the right direction, then, when this is established, the slight further movement that takes the animal a step closer; and so on. To do this efficiently requires skill, and the skilled operator can manipulate an animal's behavior—establishing a new pattern of behavior in a matter of minutes, or *extinguishing* one and substituting another with equal speed—in an almost miraculous manner; but the beginner will find that even he, with care, can produce surprising results by consciously using secondary reinforcement. He must separate it in his thinking from the primary reinforcement, which is also necessary (otherwise the secondary reinforcement loses its effect), but which is more difficult to present rapidly.

LATENT LEARNING

The learning we have considered so far is by no means representative of the whole range of learning that is characteristic of human beings in their ordinary affairs. For the purposes of the laboratory—especially in the earlier exploratory stages when the field was new and no one knew what complications might turn up—it was desirable to study the mastery of well-defined tasks, with definite responses to be made, in definite stimulus situations. It was also a great advantage to study rote learning in which a number of trials is necessary, since then the course of acquisition can be followed from trial to trial, whereas in other "insightful" or "intelligent" learning this may be impossible. ("Rote" learning means learning by heart, or simple memorization, as distinct from learning in which it is ideas that matter and not the exact words.) But important as memorization may be (in mastery of the multiplication table, for example, or learning the names of people met at a business meeting) and fundamental as conditioning is in man's adaptation to the environment, there are other forms of learning.

Having a human brain predisposes one to certain kinds of learning that are remarkable in one particular respect: they involve no apparent response at the time the learning occurs. When it is another person that is concerned, one can find out that learning did occur only because of something the person does later. This is known as *latent learning.*

A first simple example will help to make it clear. A girl watching an exciting TV program makes no move when the phone rings, and someone else answers. Did she hear? Two minutes later, during a commercial, she asks who called: so she did hear, a stimulus had its effect on brain activity, and the brain activity caused a response *later.* Learning had occurred, but there was no evidence of it at the time. As we will see, latent learning can be found in some infrahuman animals and may presumably occur frequently, but it is occurring constantly in the waking hours of human beings. It is of fundamental importance in man's behavior.

There are several forms of latent learning to be considered here, the first being perceptual learning.

Perceptual Learning

Perceptual learning can be defined as a lasting change in the perception of an object or event resulting from earlier perceptions of the same thing or related things. Primarily, the change is in the direction of a clearer or more distinctive perception, but in some cases the clearer perception of one aspect of the object means that other aspects are seen less clearly.

An example of an increased distinctiveness with practice comes from study of the *two-point limen,* a measure of ability to discriminate points on the skin. Procedure: with the subject blindfolded, his skin is touched sometimes with one, sometimes with two points (points such as those of a pair of dividers). Each time the subject is asked to report whether he feels one or two. The most sensitive areas are the tip of the tongue, the tip of the forefinger, and the lips; here the subject can tell that he is touched on two separate spots even when there is only one millimeter or so between them (I mm. for tongue, 2 mm. for fingertip), whereas on the upper arm or back they must be 40 to 70 mm. apart. For our present purposes, however, the important thing is that prolonged testing in any area will decrease the two-point limen to a half or less of its original value. Repeated sensory input has changed the functioning of the central processes involved in the perception. By definition, this is perceptual learning.

Another example of an increased distinctiveness of perception with repetition comes from everyday experience. Those Occidentals who have seen few Orientals (and vice versa) complain that all Orientals (or Occidentals) look alike. With continued frequent exposure to Oriental/Occidental faces the Occidental/Oriental begins to see differences and these become so clear that he wonders how the faces could have looked alike to him at first. His perceptions have changed as a result of perceiving. We will return to the question of reinforcement, but here it may be remarked that in this form of the learning, at least, no reinforcement appears to be necessary: simple repeated exposure is enough to produce changes of perception. Note also that no specific response appears to be learned. At this stage it appears that the subject is simply learning to see more clearly, and only when he does so—only when he can differentiate individuals of the other group—can he begin to make discriminative responses (by applying their proper names, for example).

An experiment by R. W. Leeper provides a final example: this one of learning which, in making the perception of one aspect of an object more distinct, makes others less so. Figure 6 shows at the left an old woman, at the right a young woman, and in the center a sort of combination or composite of the two. The center one is an *ambiguous figure,* since it may be seen either as an old woman or as a young woman, but not both at the same time (for another example of an ambiguous figure, see p. 235 and Figure 89). The subjects of the experiment were college students. One group was shown only the center (ambiguous) figure for 15 sec.; one was first shown the old woman (left) for 30 sec., and then the center figure (15 sec.); and one was shown the young woman (right) for 30 sec., and then the center figure (15 sec.). Thirty-five per cent of those who saw only the center

Old Women   Composite (—from Boring)   Young Women

Figure 6. *The center panel is the ambiguous figure, redrawn from a cartoon in Puck, 1915, by W. E. Hill (title, "My wife and my mother-in-law"), rescued for psychology by E. G. Boring (Amer. J. Psychol., 1930), and used by Leeper in his perceptual learning experiment. The side panels each accentuate one of the two ways of seeing the center panel. (From R. W. Leeper, J. Genet. Psychol., 1935.)*

figure saw it as an old woman, 65 per cent as a young woman; but of those who were shown the left figure first, 97 per cent saw an old woman in the center figure and of those who saw the right figure first, 100 per cent saw a young woman in the center figure. Clearly the perceptions of the center picture were affected by previous experience; and it is also clear that perceiving one of the two aspects of the picture better than before meant that the second aspect was less well perceived (this is not always so: in a second experiment with a different ambiguous figure Leeper found that some of his subjects saw both aspects of the figure, so improving one does not always worsen the other). Thus perceptual learning may make a given perception more difficult, or may interfere with one by strengthening another.

An interesting example in ordinary life is the tendency, in reading, to see whole words and phrases and not see the individual letters as such, or not see all of them. It is this that makes proofreading difficult: you perceive the word that *should* be there, and fail to perceive that one of the letters is wrong; or perceive the phrase that naturally follows in the sentence, and fail to realize that one of the words is missing.

S-S Learning: The Association of Ideas

"Association of ideas" is an unfashionable term—much used in the 19th century, it has almost disappeared in this one—but the time may have come to put it back to work again. The reason for its disappearance was the doubt, earlier, whether ideas and thought exist at all. We have seen that Thorndike raised this question about cats; John B. Watson took it further, and suggested that human thinking is only a series of tiny muscular contractions, each contraction providing a stimulus to the next one, so that in thinking one is really talking to oneself under one's breath. In that case ideas would not exist, and because of this doubt the term *idea* practically disappeared from psychology. We now know however that ideas do exist as special processes in the brain, and we know also that connections can be set up between them. The classical term "association of ideas" thus becomes useful again. *S-S learning* or stimulus-stimulus association has much the same significance. Its value lies in its clear distinction of S-S from S-R learning, and its direct reference to laboratory procedures. It is clearly shown in the fundamentally important demonstration of *sensory preconditioning* by W. J. Brogden, with both dogs and human beings as subjects, in several experiments.

With the dog as subject, the first step is to have him make an association between two sensory events, such as a light and a sound. The light and a buzzer are presented together some six to ten times for this purpose. This is represented in the first diagram of Figure 7. Next, the light is made the CS for an avoidance CR, lifting the paw to avoid electric shock (second diagram). Then comes the crucial test. The buzzer is presented, and the dog lifts his paw. Why, since the

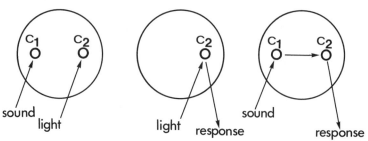

Figure 7. *The large circles represent the brain at three different stages in the experiment (sensory preconditioning). The first diagram represents the simultaneous presentation of auditory and visual stimuli; C_1 and C_2 are the "central processes" aroused together by the two stimuli. In the second stage, the light is made the CS for a conditioned avoidance response; the sound is not presented, so it is not a CS. But in the third stage, the sound is presented without the light and evokes the CR. The explanation must be that there is a connection between C_1 and C_2 (shown by an arrow in the third diagram), owing to the earlier presentation of sound and light together, in stage 1.*

buzzer is not the CS? The only answer seems to be what is represented in the third diagram of Figure 7: the central process or brain activity excited by the buzzer has become connected with the central process excited by the light. The latter is part of the conditioned-reflex pathway, so the sound of the buzzer is able to evoke the response. A number of *control* procedures (cf. Chapter 8) have been employed to show that this is what it seems—for example, for one half of the subjects the light is made the CS, for the other half the buzzer; or control groups are exposed to light and buzzer, but without pairing these stimuli—and it now appears clearly that sensory preconditioning is a genuine phenomenon. It also seems that the explanation of it is the sort of connection between brain processes that is diagramed in Figure 7.

In this experiment we have the perfect example of latent learning. After the two stimuli, light and sound, have been presented together several times, the learning has taken place, but there is still no sign at all that it has done so. Only the later test makes it evident that the subjects (which in Brogden's first work were dogs) had made the association between the two sensory events.

Such associations are a common phenomenon with human beings. The relation of thunder and lightning, of knife and fork (or the smell of food and eating), of the presence of mosquitoes and an itching skin, or of dark clouds and rain, is in each case so obvious that we are apt to forget that such relations are examples of a kind of learning that human beings are extremely good at and one that is of essential importance in their behavior.

KNOWLEDGE: A PREPARATION FOR RESPONSE

The third and last form of latent learning to be discussed here is one for which no special technical term has been developed in psychology, though its existence is an important feature of higher behavior, and of man's behavior particularly. It is, in short, the acquisition of *knowledge.*

In dealing with a familiar object or event, which in the past has been encountered in different situations and responded to in different ways, the higher animal has learned not one but a number of ways of reacting to it. When he perceives such an object and remembers its position or its size or its color, further learning has occurred.

But what kind of learning? Not learning to *do* something, for in most such cases (and this is something that is happening to the normal human being all the time) one never does anything more and before long forgets the event completely. Yet in another sense, one has acquired a great many *potential* responses to other stimuli, depending on what may happen to one later. You learn that "msec." means milliseconds, or "amp." amperes, and (if you don't move your lips when you read) you make no response at the time. But in later situations, such as a physics exam or in using printed instructions on a new piece of equipment, your behavior is different from what it would have been without this knowledge.

Another example, perhaps clearer: Looking for glue in a friend's workshop I perceive a screwdriver lying under a pile of shavings. Having no use for the tool I do no more than let my eye rest on it for a moment, and go on with my search. But if my friend *X* should say, "Is the screwdriver on the bench?" I would at once say "Yes," instead of having to look first. If *X* should say, "The screwdriver must have been left outside," I would answer, "No, it's here." If I should find the glue but could not get the lid off, I would reach directly for the screwdriver instead of looking for it first or getting out the pocket knife I might otherwise have used. And so forth. Perceiving the screwdriver, or knowing that it is on the bench, has changed the response that I would make to each of a large class of potential stimulations; it would not be possible to list them all. Also, there is no single definitive way of reacting to a screwdriver (which may be used to drive screws or remove them, to pry cans open or to pierce them, to prop open windows, to close electrical circuits or to throw at cats). So the learning is not learning to do any particular thing — it is not an incomplete S-R connection. What it really amounts to is changing some of the connections in the brain: resetting the switchboard, so that now any of a number of later stimuli will produce a different response from what it would have otherwise.

THE DISTINCTION BETWEEN LEARNING AND PERFORMANCE

Implicit in the preceding discussion is a distinction that should be made explicit: the distinction between learning and performance, or between learning and learned behavior.

Actually, the distinction applies to all learning, not latent learning alone. Learning is not something we see or observe directly. Instead, it is something inferred from behavior: a presumed change in the nervous system that produces changes in performance. Psychologists sometimes try to define learning as the behavioral change itself, but this is unsatisfactory. For example, a rat is trained to press a bar for food; then we satiate him and put him back in the apparatus, and we find that the behavioral change (bar-pressing) has disappeared. If learning is a change of behavior, then we must say that the learning has ceased to exist—but this is wrong, for when we make the rat hungry again he presses at once, without having slowly to acquire the habit all over again. The learning is a neural change which continues to exist when the animal is not hungry, but it makes itself evident only under the proper conditions.

This logical distinction becomes essential in the learning we have been discussing. In sensory preconditioning, the learning takes place without giving any evidence that it is happening, until the later test is made; in fact, in the procedure as described it sometimes does not take place, and one can only be sure by making the special test. In the acquisition of knowledge, again, there is a similar situation. You see another car driver get stuck on an icy hill: did learning take place, or what learning took place? And is it retained? At that time I cannot tell; but when later I observe you putting on chains for driving in icy weather, or telling someone else about chains, or taking care to be moving fast as you approach an icy hill, I obtain the behavioral evidence.

In sensory preconditioning and the acquisition of knowledge the difference between learning and performance is inescapable, but it is important in S-R learning also. The distinction must be made if the student is to think clearly about learning as it has already been discussed and, in a later chapter, about memory and forgetting.

SUMMARY

This chapter begins by reminding the student that learning and heredity cooperate closely. An interest in learning need not decrease one's interest in heredity. The chapter then outlines the beginning of research on learning by giving a brief account of the work of three men: Ebbinghaus, human learning (memorization), 1885; Thorndike, cats in problem boxes, 1898; and Pavlov, conditioned salivation in dogs, 1902. All three lines of research have continued, and form a large part of modern experimental psychology. It was Pavlov who produced the most interesting data (Pavlovian inhibition, for example), Thorndike who asked the most interesting questions (have cats got minds? why does one connection form in the brain, and not another?). Pavlov's method is Type-S conditioning; Thorndike's "trial-and-error learning" can be regarded as Type-R conditioning, and Skinner showed how this latter method can be used to shape new forms of behavior by an efficient use of primary and secondary reinforcement.

Less experimental work has been done on latent learning, though this is much the commonest form in ordinary life, outside the classroom and the laboratory. Three forms are described: perceptual learning (things look or sound or taste or feel differently due to past experience), S-S learning or the association of ideas, and the acquisition of knowledge. In each of these there is no necessary response at the time, and the occurrence of learning is shown only by a modification of response made at some later time. In such latent learning, it is obvious that learning and performance are different, since there is no response at the time of learning. The same distinction is important in other learning. Learning itself is a change of connections in the brain; performance is the response or responses that the changed connections determine.

Guide to Study

For his review, the student should first see that he can explain or define: CS, UCS, CR, UCR; Type-S and Type-R conditioning; primary and secondary reinforcement, and reinforcement in its general sense; latent learning, perceptual learning, S-S and S-R learning, and sensory preconditioning. How does the acquisition of knowledge differ from the acquisition of a particular habit? The student should also remember the names of Ebbinghaus, Lloyd Morgan, Thorndike and Skinner, as principal architects of the modern theory of learning.

NOTES AND REFERENCES

The work of Ebbinghaus and of Thorndike is discussed in a large number of texts, but a good account of each can be found in Woodworth, R. S., and Schlosberg, H.: *Experimental Psychology*, Holt, Rinehart & Winston, 1954. A brief account is given there of C. Lloyd Morgan's work, with reference to his book. *An Introduction to Comparative Psychology*, 1894.

SPECIAL TOPICS

Conditioning

Pavlov, I. P.: *Conditioned Reflexes*, 1927. Dover edition, 1960.
Skinner, B. F.: *Cumulative Record*, Appleton-Century-Crofts, 1961. This is a collection of papers that vary in technical difficulty. The student's attention is drawn particularly to "A case history in the scientific method," and "How to teach animals," but the whole book is valuable.

Sensory Preconditioning

Brogden, W. J.: Sensory preconditioning. *Journal of Experimental Psychology*, 1939, 25, 323–332. The original report.
Seidel, R. J.: A review of sensory preconditioning. *Psychological Bulletin*, 1959, 56, 58–73. The interpretation of Brogden's results as a form of S-S conditioning raised doubts, but this review (with the following paper by Tyler) dispels them.
Tyler, V. O.: Sensory integration with and without reinforcement. *Journal of Experimental Psychology*, 1962, 63, 381–386.

Perceptual Learning

Leeper, R. W.: A study of a neglected portion of the field of learning—the development of sensory organization. *Journal of Genetic Psychology*, 1935, 46, 41–75. An important paper, without apparent effect for a rather long time, probably because S-R learning was all that psychologists were interested in.
Gibson, J. J., and Gibson, E. J.: Perceptual learning: differentiation or enrichment? *Psychological Review*, 1955, 62, 32–41. This paper was an important influence in reviving the question raised by Leeper.

3

pathways in learning and perception

In Chapter 2 references were made to the nervous system, and it is time now to look at it more closely.

In principle the nervous system consists of a collection of *neurons,** which are elongated cells specialized for conducting tiny excitations from one point to another. The primary function is to connect *receptors* with *effectors,* directly or indirectly, so sensory stimulation can guide behavior. Receptors are sensory cells, specialized for sensitivity to environmental stimulation; effectors are the cells of muscle and gland whose activity is behavior. Some neurons lead from receptors into the *central nervous system* or *CNS* (the brain and the spinal cord); some of them lead out of the CNS to the effectors; and great numbers of them connect different points within the CNS itself.

The neurons are microscopic in cross section, but vary in length from a fraction of a millimeter to a meter or more. In higher animals their number is enormous: some ten billion (10^{10}) in the human nervous system, for example. They are packed together by thousands to form the macroscopic (easily seen) structures of nerves,** spinal cord and brain. The general plan of the nervous system is the same for all vertebrates; differences from one species to another are due to different sizes of the parts, not to the way in which the parts are connected. In mammals especially, the design is the same. Man's brain, weighing on the average about 1350 gm., is some 600 times the size of the laboratory rat's. The two look very different in shape (Fig. 15), but this is because some parts of man's brain have developed more

---

*It also contains blood vessels and supporting membranes, as well as glial cells, or glia—of which there are many more than there are neurons. The glia may have a supporting function, helping to hold the jelly-like neurons in place, but are believed also to have something to do with the nutrition or the maintenance of the neurons.

**It is important for the student to notice the difference between "neuron" and "nerve." A neuron is a single cell; a nerve is a bundle of many of the long fibers that grow out of the cell-bodies of neurons—that is, a bundle of axons or dendrites or both (p. 57). Inside the CNS such bundles of connecting fibers form the "white matter," while "gray matter" consists of closely packed cell-bodies. White matter then is like the cable or cables that connect different parts in an electrical system.

than others; the outer layer in particular has increased tremendously, and become wrinkled in doing so. The same parts are present in both rat and man, with the same internal relations. Accordingly, we will be concerned with the structure of the mammalian brain in general, referring to man in particular only when some question arises concerning one of his special abilities, such as speech, which is thought to be due to a greater development of one part of his brain (the *speech areas* of the cortex: p. 53).

Figure 8 shows man's nervous system: the large mass of the *cerebrum* on top, with its convoluted outer surface, the *cortex* or "bark"; the *cerebellum* below and at the back of the head; and the long narrow spinal cord running down inside the bones of the spinal column. The plan of its construction, however, and relations of its parts, can be better understood by looking at Figures 9 to 11. The basic plan is that of a hollow tube with some swellings at the front end (the brain) and tiny branches growing out of it (the nerves, which

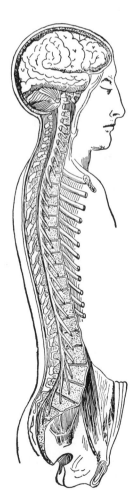

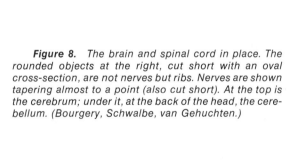

Figure 8. The brain and spinal cord in place. The rounded objects at the right, cut short with an oval cross-section, are not nerves but ribs. Nerves are shown tapering almost to a point (also cut short). At the top is the cerebrum; under it, at the back of the head, the cerebellum. (Bourgery, Schwalbe, van Gehuchten.)

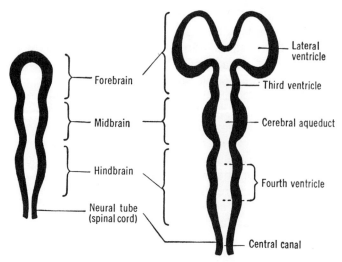

Figure 9. *Two early stages in the development of the brain. Left, the tubular form is still evident. Right, at a later stage, the two swellings are the beginning of the cerebral hemispheres; the spinal cord, of which only the end is shown, remains tubular. (From E. Gardner,* Fundamentals of Neurology, *Saunders.)*

are not shown except in Figure 8). It starts out, in the embryo, as a simple tube running the length of the organism (parallel to another great tube running from mouth to anus, the alimentary canal). The only complication at first is that the forward end is larger than the after end (Fig. 9). With growth, the connections inside the walls of the tube become complex, but it remains a hollow structure whose walls are thicker in some places than in others, with bulges here and constrictions there. The hollow of the tube in the spinal cord is so small it can hardly be seen; but in the brain it is enlarged in four places (the "ventricles"), which are filled with the "cerebrospinal fluid" which

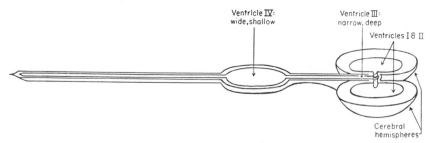

Figure 10. *Schematic representation of the adult brain, right, and spinal cord, left, with top half cut away to show the ventricles. Inside the skull the hollow of the tube widens out to form ventricle IV (beneath the cerebellum, not shown), narrows again to form the "aqueduct" and then deepens in the narrow ventricle III at the forward end of the tube. Ventricles I and II open off from III. This is the shape the brain might have if it had plenty of room to grow in, but with limited space in the skull the parts are crowded together, as shown in the following figures.*

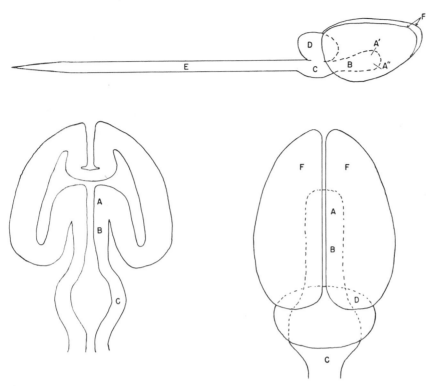

Figure 11. *Main divisions of the CNS, slightly less schematic, in an animal such as the rat. Above, side view; below, left, horizontal section; below, right, view from above. Instead of ballooning out, as in Figure 10, the hemispheres are crowded together around the front end of the tube, up over the top, and back so that they hide the central tube completely except from below, and hide much of the cerebellum. A, diencephalon, of which the upper half (A') is the thalamus, lower half (A") is the hypothalamus; B, midbrain; C, medulla and pons; D, cerebellum; E, cord; F, cerebral hemispheres. A, B and C together form the brain stem.*

The human CNS differs in two main respects: because man is built to walk erect, the brain stem is bent downwards at B; and the cortex is deeply wrinkled (as shown in Figures 12 and 14).

also surrounds the brain and cushions it within the bony box of the skull (Figs. 10 and 11).

The brain consists of the *brain stem,* the front end of the original tube (inside the skull), and three main outgrowths, the *cerebellum* and the two *cerebral hemispheres.* The cerebellum is concerned with the coordination of muscular movement, but we have no adequate knowledge of its function (such a large mass must play a bigger part in behavior than our present knowledge suggests) and we will not be concerned with it further in this book. The cerebral hemispheres are another matter. They are essential to mental processes; their development makes the difference between lower and higher animals, and when they are removed nothing remains that can be called thought or consciousness. (However, thinking does not occur in these hemispheres alone, or in the cerebral cortex alone: they are necessary to it, but they function as a unit with the anterior [forward] end of the brain stem, so this is necessary for thinking also.)

As the student will see from Figure 9 and the schematic diagrams of Figures 10 and 11, the hemispheres are attached to a very small part of the brain stem. Each is really a sort of ballooning out of the wall, like a soft spot in an automobile tire, but flattened to fit into the skull. This is seen clearly in the cross-sectional diagram of the rat brain (Fig. 11, lower left). The "balloon" spreads forward and back, and up over the top of the brain stem it is attached to, hiding the place of attachment. In higher mammals, and especially man, the great growth of its outer layer, the cortex, also results in a folding and wrinkling (Figs. 12 and 14) so that much of the cortex itself is hidden from sight in the *fissures* (wrinkles or clefts; the protruding part, between clefts, is a *gyrus).*

The forward end of the brain stem is the *diencephalon,* of which the upper half is the *thalamus,* the lower half the *hypothalamus* (Figs. 11 and 12). This is where the cerebral hemispheres are attached to the stem, and all their complex connections with the rest of the brain and the spinal cord funnel through this region. The thalamus is a way-station for incoming paths; all sensory input to the cortex (with the single exception of olfactory excitations) is relayed here. The hypothalamus has motor functions rather than sensory ones. It is closely connected to the hemispheres, but may be considered as the highest level of reflex organization in the brain stem; in the hypothalamus for example are control centers for the water balance of the body, temperature regulation and appetite. The unconditioned reflex is subject to some control from thought processes, so this does not mean that the hypothalamus is uninfluenced by the cortex—quite the contrary—but for much of its activity the cortex does not appear to be necessary.

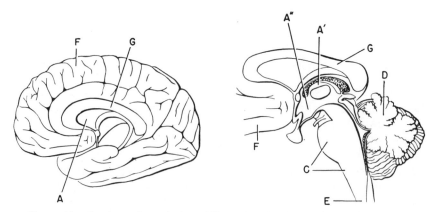

Figure 12. Sections through the midline of the human brain (the frontal lobe is to the left). In the left-hand diagram the lower part of the brain stem has been cut off; at the right, it is shown in full, with the cerebellum attached. Labels as in Figure 11; G, corpus callosum.

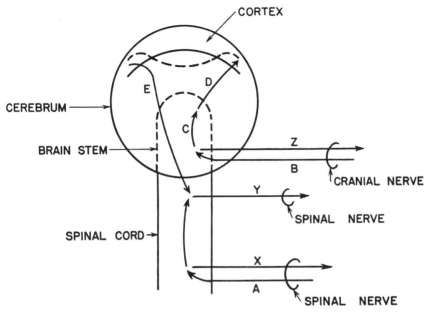

Figure 13. *The "long-circuiting" of learned paths through the cerebrum, as distinct from the more direct but less modifiable reflex paths. A and B, afferents; X, Y and Z, efferents. The broken-line connection, top, between D and E would not likely be a straight-through connection, but would involve some of the loops discussed in Chapter 4.*

The brain stem with its subdivisions has a complex structure but it is not necessary to go into this for our purposes. If the student will think of it in principle as simply being the forward end of the spinal cord, where it projects into the skull *(A, B* and *C* in Fig. 11), he will see the situation more clearly. The cord and stem are thought of as having reflex functions only, and the cerebral hemispheres as the seat of higher processes and learning. This probably oversimplifies things; some learning may occur in the cord and stem, though whether to any important extent is doubtful, and parts of the hemispheres may well be the loci of some (unconditioned) reflex activities. However, on the basis of our present knowledge we can regard the brain stem (and cerebellum) as the highest level of reflex function, and the cerebral hemispheres as the still higher level at which learning occurs. The cord and stem represent the built-in or reflex connections, the rigid part of the switchboard; the hemispheres a collection of unallocated lines which are available to form new connections and to make possible the *central processes* of thought (p. 69).

Figure 13 shows this diagrammatically. *A–X* and *A–Y* are two built-in connections in the cord, ones provided for by growth processes, apparently without any need of learning to make them work. They are the basis, consequently, of unconditioned reflexes (see also Figure 18). *B–Z* is another such pathway; though *A, X* and *Y* lie in spinal nerves (*A* and *X* in one, *Y* in another) and *B* and *Z* in a cranial nerve, their operations are in the same class. But that of the pathway

B–C–D ... *E–Y* is not. *B–C–D* is provided for innately, and so is *E–Y;* but the connection between *D* and *E* is established only by some form of conditioning or learning. This "long-circuiting" through the cortex illustrates the special role of the hemispheres. Heredity and growth processes lay down the "short" reflex circuits, providing an automatic and unchanging form of adaptation to the immediate environment; when modification of this behavior is called for, it is not effected by changing connections in the reflex circuits themselves, but by changes at the level of the cortex.

Paths in the nervous system are classified as *afferent, efferent,* and *internuncial.* Afferent paths conduct from receptors to the CNS, and within the CNS from lower to higher centers; efferent paths conduct from higher to lower centers, and from CNS to effectors. Internuncial paths are ones that connect different points inside the CNS at about the same level.

The terms *neuron* and *synapse* will be considered in more detail in Chapter 4; for the present, a neuron is a single nerve cell, and a synapse is the place where one neuron makes connection with another; it is the switching point, the place where it is determined what direction a neural "message" will take. The student may think of the synapse as a sort of barrier that an excitation must get past. Some barriers are hard to pass, others easy, and there is often a choice: which of two or more paths will be followed at this point? The difficulty of getting through any one synapse is supposed to change with learning. If neuron *A* has synapses with *B* and *C,* the difficulty of passing them determines whether an excitation, the neural message, traveling along *A* will follow *B* or *C*—or both, or neither. Learning means a change in the direction of messages in the CNS. Because of the all-or-none principle (p. 58), which means that an excitation once started in an axon must sweep across all its branches, switching is not possible halfway along a neural fiber. Therefore it must occur at the synapse, though how it occurs we do not yet know for certain.

In Figure 13 saying that *A–X* and *A–Y* are "built-in" paths means that the synapses between *A* and *X,* and *A* and *Y,* are effective from the first. The barriers are easy to pass. But the synapses in the path between *D* and *E,* the "long-circuit" that represents some learned habit, are ones that function effectively only as a result of certain experiences. If the experiences had been different, messages arriving over the afferent path *D* would not be delivered to *E* at all, but to some other efferent path—via other synapses.

Some of the changes of learning consist in the suppression of responses—learning *not* to do something—or suppression of a component of the response, changing its pattern. Part of this is done by *inhibitory neurons,* which are found throughout the CNS; their effect is to block transmission. Inhibition makes the neuron temporarily hard to excite. (The other way suppression occurs is by strengthening a competing muscular response: e.g., learning to turn left, which prevents turning right.)

INTO AND OUT OF THE CORTEX

Now let us see how excitations get from the sense organ to the cortex, where we assume that the changes take place in the learning of mammals, and out of the cortex to the motor organ. (Lower animals have little cortex or none, so the changes must occur in other structures, but the present text will concern itself with the mammalian brain.)

Except for smell, each sensory surface (skin, retina, etc.) on one side of the body is directly connected with a *cortical sensory area,* specialized for that sense, on the opposite side of the brain. As we will see, there are also connections with the same side, but in general the paths are so laid out that a stimulus event on one side of the body has its main effect on the opposite side of the brain. There are also two *motor areas,* one on each side of the brain, and these too have crossed-over connections so that the right side of the cortex controls the left side of the body, and vice versa. The remainder of the cortex, all that is not included in the specialized sensory and motor areas, is known as the *association cortex.*

To see where these areas lie, consider first Figure 14. It shows the division of the cerebrum into *frontal, parietal, temporal* and *occipital lobes.* The division, made by the old anatomists, centuries before much was known about how the brain functions, is more or less arbitrary. Some of the dividing lines do not mean much, psychologically or physiologically. However, two of them are important landmarks: the *sylvian fissure* and the *central fissure.* The sylvian fissure is the deep cleft that partly separates the temporal lobe from the rest of the brain, and in Figure 15 it can be seen, for example, that the *auditory area* lies on the lower lip of the fissure. Also, man's *speech area* can be described roughly as the cortical region surrounding the sylvian fissure on one side of the brain—usually the left side. The central fissure is less easy to see, but equally important. It is the dividing line

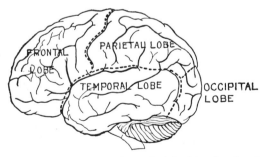

Figure 14. *The human brain seen from the left side, showing the four lobes. The central fissure is the one separating the frontal from the parietal lobe; the sylvian fissure is the one that first runs upward, then horizontally to the right, separating frontal from temporal lobe, and partly separating temporal from parietal lobe. (From C. J. Herrick,* An Introduction to Neurology, *Saunders.)*

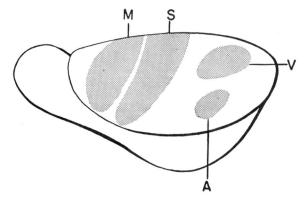

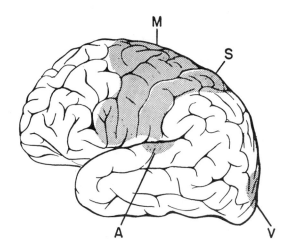

Figure 15. Approximate loci of sensory and motor areas in rat and man. Man's visual area is pushed round into the cleft between the two hemispheres, so it can hardly be seen. The auditory area proper is buried in the sylvian fissure. M, *motor;* S, *somesthetic;* A, *auditory;* V, *visual.*

between the frontal and parietal lobes, and it also separates the motor area, in front, from the somesthetic area, behind (Fig. 15).

The *somesthetic* or *somatosensory area* on one side receives sensory messages from all parts of the body on the opposite side (plus some from the same side, but these are fewer and less important). *Somesthesis* means "body sensitivity," including sensations of touch, warmth, cold and itch from the skin; sensations of deep pressure and muscle tension and joint pressure, inside the skin; and sensations from the visceral organs. It also includes pain, from any of these regions.

Figure 15 shows the locus of these specialized areas for a lower mammal, the rat, and for man. One can see here the kind of structural change that has occurred with the growth and infolding of the cortex in the higher animal. The rat is a smooth-brained animal and there is no basis for dividing his brain into lobes. His specialized sensory areas are in plain sight; in man, with an enlarged and wrinkled cortex, the visual area has practically disappeared into the posterior cleft between the two hemispheres, and the auditory area into the sylvian fissure. Thus it is worth looking at the two diagrams side by side, for the simpler rat's brain shows more clearly than man's how these specialized areas relate to one another.

It has been said already that there is no cortical area specialized for smell. Taste is localized at the foot of the somesthetic area, but as far as we know at present has not the same degree of internal organization as somesthesis, and for the purposes of this text smell and taste will both be regarded as more primitive senses. The cortical areas for the other three senses, vision, audition and somesthesis, are the highly organized end-stations of the afferent paths from the corresponding sense organs. These paths are specialized for rapid conduction to the cortex and for keeping distinct the excitations produced by stimulation of even slightly different points in the sensory surface.

As we have seen, these more highly developed senses are "lateralized," so that the left side of the body is chiefly represented in the right somesthetic area; the right ear though it conducts to both auditory areas does so more quickly and strongly to the left; and though both eyes are connected to both visual areas, the connections are such that the left visual *field*—not the left retina—is represented only in the right visual cortex.

The *retina* is the light-sensitive sensory surface at the back of the eye. In lower vertebrates the retina of the left eye appears to be connected solely with the right hemisphere of the brain, and vice versa; but in mammals there is a peculiar departure from this scheme, which reaches its highest development in man (Fig. 16). The outer (tem-

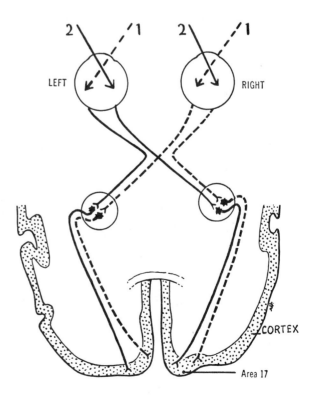

Figure 16. The visual pathways. Above, light rays from an object (1) in the right visual field and (2) in the left visual field enter the two eyeballs, crossing as they pass through the lens. The left parts of both retinas then connect with the left visual cortex at the back of the brain ("area 17"), and the right retinas with the right visual cortex. Thus an object in the right visual field excites the left visual cortical area only. (After E. Gardner, Fundamentals of Neurology, Saunders.)

poral) side of each retina is connected with the occipital lobe on the same side (ipsilateral connection), the inner (nasal) side with the occipital lobe on the opposite side (contralateral connection). In lower mammals, most of the connections are still contralateral, but in man all of the retina to one side of the *fovea* (the central fixation point and the region of clearest vision) is connected to the occipital lobe on the same side, so that nearly half of the connections are ipsilateral. Light rays from the left and right visual fields cross as they pass through the lens. All optical events to the left of where the subject is looking, therefore, stimulate the right halves of both retinas and are conducted to the right occipital lobe. Thus the right side of the brain deals with the left visual field, just as it predominantly deals with the left-sided auditory and somesthetic events, and also controls motor activity on the left side via the crossed-over paths from the motor cortex.

Damage to one side of the brain, then, causes both sensory and motor defects on the other side of the body. Left-sided wounds in the frontal region produce a right-sided paralysis. If the injury is extensive, it is likely to involve also the somesthetic area just behind the motor area (i.e., behind the central fissure: Figure 15) and then the patient will have a "hemianesthesia," or loss of sensation on the same side of the body as the paralysis; and since a large injury on the left side of the brain is also likely to involve the speech areas surrounding the sylvian fissure, there may also be *aphasia*—a general disturbance of speech—to a more or less serious degree.

In the auditory system, the connections of one ear with both sides of the brain are good enough so that no deafness may be noticed after brain damage to one of the auditory areas, but the patient will actually have some loss of ability to localize sounds, as well as some other defects that are harder to detect except with special tests. For vision, however, the "lateralization" seems to be complete. Damage to one occipital lobe can produce a "hemianopia," or half-loss of vision, in which state the patient can see nothing to one side of the place he is directly looking at. If the wound is on the left side of the head, the patient cannot see things in his right field, and vice versa.

Another important matter is the internal arrangement of the somesthetic, visual and auditory systems. There is a "point-to-point projection" of the sensory surface on the cortex. Each sensory point connects with a particular cortical point,* and two adjacent points in the skin, or in the retina, or in the *basilar membrane* of the *cochlea* (the sensory surface that is excited in hearing, buried deep in the skull behind the ear), connect with adjacent points on the cortex. This is *parallel conduction* (p. 71) and very efficient, since the excitation carried by one neuron is reinforced by that carried by another when several neurons, side by side, are excited together.

The arrangement means that any pattern of sensory excitation is

---

*Since there is overlap and spread of connections at each synaptic junction on the way to the cortex (inset, Fig. 35), a sensory point actually connects with a fairly wide cortical region but its principal connection is with the center of the region.

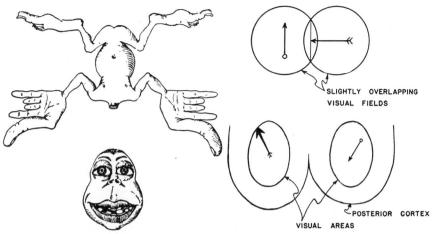

Figure 17. *The organization of the somesthetic and visual cortex. A, showing the way in which the different parts of the body are represented in the cortex (legs at the top, head at the bottom) and the relative amount of cortex devoted to the different parts (mouth area and thumb well represented, top of the head and trunk with small representation). (From W. Penfield and E. Boldrey,* Brain, *1957.) B, showing how a horizontal and a vertical arrow in the visual field of a rat (above) are projected on the cortex (below). (After K. S. Lashley,* J. Comp. Neurol., *1934.)*

reproduced in the cortex (Fig. 17). The pattern does not keep the same orientation, and there are distortions of size. In the somesthetic cortex, the legs are at the top, the head at the bottom; "up" in the visual field becomes "down" in the visual cortex. The face and hand areas in the somesthetic cortex are enlarged—which agrees with the fact that skin of face and hand is more sensitive, more discriminative, than that of upper arms, legs or trunk—and the fovea and the central area of the retina also have an enlarged representation. But, as above, points that are side by side in the periphery are side by side in the cortex, and the patterns are recognizable despite the distortions.

The motor area, similarly, has a point-to-point correspondence with the periphery, and the connections are also in parallel: that is, two fibers from the cortex that lead toward a leg muscle lie close together, and so can reinforce one another's excitations and produce contraction of the muscle more reliably (p. 71). The motor cortex is organized in the same way as the somesthetic cortex, with leg movement represented at the top, hand and arm movement below, and face movement (and voice production) at the bottom of the motor strip that lies in front of the central fissure (cf. Fig. 17).

The principal path from the motor cortex to the lower centers is a large bundle of fibers known as the *pyramidal tract.* Not all of the motor connections from the cortex are in this tract, and the tract also includes some other connections from the brain stem to the spinal cord, but the main point is that there are direct connections between the cortex and motor centers of the cord. When the brain of a patient is being operated on under local anesthetic only (so that cutting open the skull does not cause pain, and the patient can remain fully conscious), stimulation of the hand area of the motor cortex produces a movement of the patient's hand that he cannot prevent. The conduction is highly reliable, and the same effect can be produced time after time. This appears to be because the connections of the pyramidal tract are in parallel, as noted above, and because some neurons reach all the way from the cortex to where the motor nerve leaves the spinal cord, with no synapse till they near the motor neurons. Some neurons for example run all the way from the leg area at the top of the motor strip down nearly to the end of the cord.

These out-going or efferent connections are made in the *ventral* half of the cord (next to the belly), while incoming or afferent connections are made in the *dorsal* half (next to the back), conforming to a general rule that motor functions in the spinal cord and brain stem are ventral and sensory functions dorsal. The student will recall that the predominantly motor hypothalamus is in the ventral part of the diencephalon, the predominantly sensory thalamus more dorsal. Figure 18 shows a cross section of the spinal cord: A, diagrammatically, showing how the spinal nerve (right) divides near the cord to allow all the afferent fibers to enter the "dorsal root" (top of the diagram) and the efferent fibers to leave by the "ventral root." The afferent fibers branch inside the cord, making connections with the efferent fibers at this level but also sending branches upward in the cord to connect with higher centers (as shown in Figure 13).

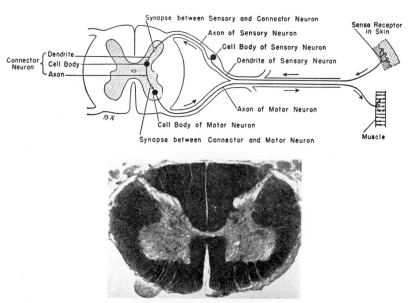

Figure 18. *Cross sections of the spinal cord. A, diagram of the pathway of an unconditioned reflex; a "connector neuron" is internuncial. (From C. A. Villee,* Biology, Saunders.) *B, photomicrograph of human cord; the white matter of the cord is stained black so it can be seen under the microscope, the gray matter remains gray, forming the dorsal horns (toward the top) and the ventral horns (bottom). (From E. Gardner,* Fundamentals of Neurology, Saunders.)

LATERAL CONNECTIONS; THE SPLIT-BRAIN EXPERIMENT

We have now seen how afferent excitations get to the sensory projection areas of the cortex, and how efferent excitations get from the motor cortex to the muscles. Our next question concerns the coordination of the two halves of the cortex. For example, we have separate visual areas, one on each side of the brain: how is it that we do not see the world in two halves but as a single unified visual field?

The CNS like the rest of the body is constructed in two symmetrical parts, with cortical sensory areas and motor areas duplicated, one on each side, and at first glance it might seem that the result must be a split personality, a left-hand mind and a right-hand mind, the left hand not knowing what the right hand doeth and so forth. But at all levels of the CNS there are internuncial paths connecting corresponding areas on the two sides. Such connections are known as *commissures.* The biggest of them is the *corpus callosum* (Figs. 12, 19, and 20), which provides a great bridge between the two halves of the cortex, connecting visual area with visual area, auditory with auditory, and so on — in each case, also, connecting their corresponding parts, so that in the somesthetic cortex the thumb area on one side is connected with the thumb area on the other. Thus the left hand *does* know what the right is doing, and the normal subject has one visual world, not two.

This bridge, together with smaller ones at all levels of the brain stem, makes it possible for the organism to have one mind — one set of reaction tendencies, with coordinated perceptions and thought processes — instead of two. Experimentally, however, it is possible to cut the monkey's corpus callosum and enough of the commissures below it so that much of the coordination is lost. This is shown in Figures 19 and 20. As Figure 19 shows, a longitudinal cut is also made in the *optic chiasm* (this is the place where the two optic nerves are intertangled, as half the fibers from each eye cross over to the other side). Now the left eye is connected with the left cortex only, and so with the right eye and the right cortex. This is the *split-brain preparation* of R. W. Sperry, and the two halves of the brain can be taught different things without apparent conflict. With the right eye covered, the monkey is trained to choose a square and reject a circle to get food; with the left eye covered, to avoid the square and choose the circle. The second task is learned as easily as if the first — opposite — task had not been learned, and both are remembered just as if two different animals had been taught these two things.

It is not too much now to say that the monkey has two separate minds. They are very similar minds, since they were connected during growth and must have learned the same things and be used to reacting in the same way. But it is possible by a brain operation on one side to make one of the minds quite different from the other (J. L. Downer). Removing the temporal lobe from one hemisphere makes for calmness and a lack of hostility at the approach of the caretaker;

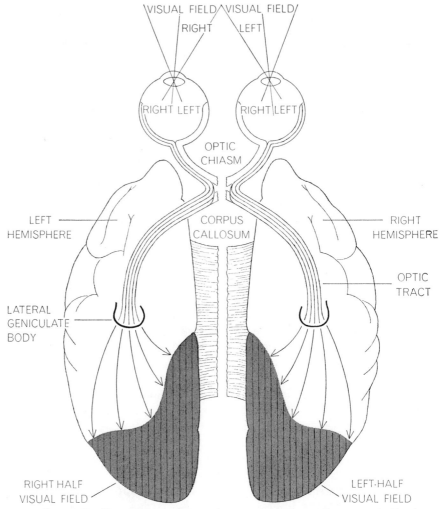

Figure 19. *The split-brain preparation seen from above, diagrammatically, show-ing how the visual system is separated into two, as well as the cutting of the corpus callosum. (From "The Great Cerebral Commissure" by R. W. Sperry. Copyright © 1964 by Scientific American, Inc. All rights reserved.)*

when the eye is open that is connected only with that hemisphere, and the other eye closed, the monkey appears to be tame; but when the eye connected with the normal hemisphere is open the macaque becomes his normal, unlovely, mean-spirited self (unlovely and mean-spirited toward human jailers, at least). The two monkey minds now are different personalities.

These results are dramatic enough, but even more dramatic ones have been obtained by Sperry in the case of certain human patients in whom the corpus callosum was cut (only the callosum, not all the other structures cut in the experimental work with monkeys) for the relief of epilepsy. As we will see in the next section, the right and left halves of the human brain have different functions; and the result of the operation is not only two minds, but two minds that are different.

One can talk, for example, and the other cannot, though it has some comprehension of speech. When Sperry talked to the patient, therefore, he was giving information to both minds. He could however give information to one only by means of vision or touch. An object shown briefly in the left visual field while the patient looks straight ahead can be seen and recognized by the right hemisphere only (Figs. 16 and 21). Or if the object is put in the left hand, out of sight, it is only the right hemisphere that gets the information. Now the experimenter can set out a number of objects and ask the patient to pick out the object (Fig. 22). The right hand, under the control of the (ignorant) left hemisphere, starts to make a wrong choice, more or less at random—and the left hand pulls the right hand away and makes the correct choice.

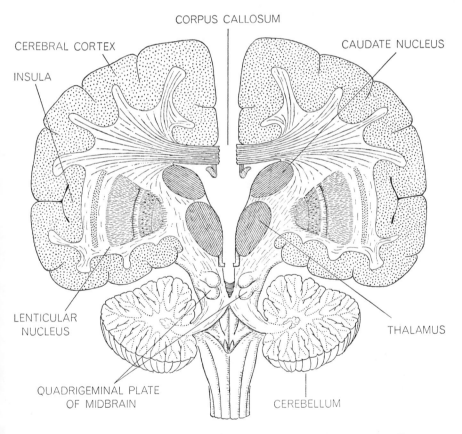

CORPUS CALLOSUM

CEREBRAL CORTEX

CAUDATE NUCLEUS

INSULA

LENTICULAR NUCLEUS

THALAMUS

QUADRIGEMINAL PLATE OF MIDBRAIN

CEREBELLUM

Figure 20. *Showing the deeper cut made in the split-brain preparation. The upper part of the figure represents a cross section of the monkey brain, the lower part shows schematically how the cerebellum and lower end of the brain stem might look if the brain were removed from the skull: the figure, that is, combines cross-sectional with three-dimensional drawing. (From "The Great Cerebral Commissure" by R. W. Sperry. Copyright © 1964 by Scientific American, Inc. All rights reserved.)*

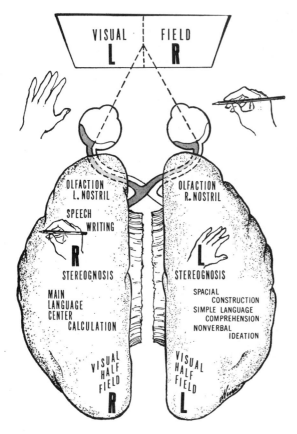

Figure 21. Schematic representation of the functions of the two hemispheres in Sperry's study of patients with section of the corpus callosum. If the eyes are focused on the middle of the screen labeled "Visual field," the L will be seen only by the right hemisphere, the R only by the left hemisphere; writing (shown by the hand with the pen) is controlled from the left hemisphere; and so on. "Stereognosis" is the perception of shape by means of touch. (From R. W. Sperry, "Hemisphere disconnection and unity in conscious awareness." American Psychologist, *Vol. 23, 1968, pp. 723–733.*)

Figure 22. One of the test situations used by Sperry. When the patient is looking directly at the middle of the screen, the experimenter flashes a picture of an object on the back of the translucent screen, so that it falls in either the right visual field or the left visual field of the patient. He is then asked to use a hand to find, by touch, the object he was shown. The objects are hidden from sight by the screen. (From R. W. Sperry, "Hemisphere disconnection and unity in conscious awareness." American Psychologist, *Vol. 23, 1968, pp. 723–733.*)

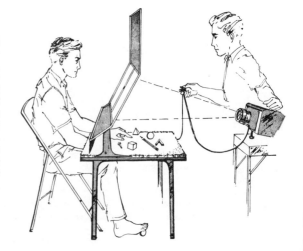

Or the experimenter gets the subject to look at the midpoint of a screen, then flashes briefly two diagrams on the screen, a dollar sign on the left and a question mark on the right. He asks the patient to draw what he saw, with the left hand but out of sight. The left hand draws a dollar sign. Now the patient is asked what was drawn, and answers that it was a question mark—the left hemisphere does not know what was drawn but thinks it does, while the right hemisphere, which does know, is unable to talk.

Two halves of the brain, with different thoughts, different knowledge, different intentions: two minds in one head.

LATERALIZATION AND DOMINANCE

The human brain has in the course of evolution developed a feature that is not known in any other animal: the two halves of the brain are specialized in some of their activities. In most persons the left half of the brain is dominant, controlling speech and the activity of a more skilled right hand. The right half of the brain, however, is specialized for form perception and perception of spatial relations. These differences are not absolute: the right hemisphere has some speech comprehension (Sperry's split-brain patients showed this), and the left hemisphere does not completely lack space and form perception. But large injury to the left temporal lobe in most persons produces a severe aphasia, with disturbance of comprehension as well as of the production of speech, and injury to the right temporal lobe disturbs visual pattern perception and other nonverbal abilities.

Handedness—having one hand that is more easily used for skilled movements, and preferred when a choice is possible—is the most familiar sign of the lateralization of brain function. It is not known in any animal but man. Any monkey or chimpanzee, or cat or dog, may have a preferred hand or paw, but this appears to be a matter of learning instead of heredity (whereas handedness in man is familial: i.e., it runs in families), and if the monkey's preferred hand is blocked the animal can readily shift to the other. And this reminds us that the lateralization is not the same in all persons. Some five to seven per cent of human beings are left-handed, and 15 to 20 per cent more or less ambidextrous. It is uncertain how many people have speech centers on the right: it is perhaps five to ten per cent; or how many have a mixture of left and right localization (like ambidexterity in handedness). But it is definite that speech and handedness do not always go together: a left-handed man may be found, when his brain is being operated on, to have speech localization on the other side—that is, the preferred hand is controlled from the right side, but his speech is still controlled from the left.

When speech is on the right, it may be so due to heredity—just as handedness is hereditary—but it may more often be due to brain injury on the left side, at or about the time of birth. In that case the right half of the brain may take over part or all of the control of speech.

SUMMARY

The nervous system is made up of a very large number of neurons, cells that are tiny in cross section but vary in length from a millimeter or so to a meter or more in large animals. A nerve is a bundle of hundreds or thousands of neurons. These connect directly with the spinal cord and brain stem, forming the basis of unconditioned reflexes; conditioned reflexes involve higher brain centers (especially the cortex, in mammals). The structure of the brain is a development from a hollow tube, and the large hollows that remain are the ventricles. The highest centers are in the two cerebral hemispheres, one on each side of the original tube, with first and second ventricles inside and the cortex like the bark of a tree on the outside.

In man, unlike any other known animal, there is a specialization of function in the two hemispheres: one, usually the left, containing centers for speech production and control of the preferred hand (on the opposite side); the other specialized for form and space perception and control of the less preferred hand. The two hemispheres are normally coordinated by the corpus callosum, a great bridge consisting of fibers that connect corresponding points on the two sides; it is possible, however, to cut this bridge, and then the functioning of the two sides of the brain may be so independent of one another that there are, in effect, two minds in one head.

Guide to Study

Subdividing the brain into different parts is mostly artificial, since they work so closely together, but doing so and naming them is useful in communication. The student in reviewing should be able to name and locate four lobes of the cerebrum in a sketch, with central and sylvian fissures and sensory and motor areas marked; he should be able to show the anatomical relations of thalamus and hypothalamus, and of cerebrum, diencephalon, brain stem, cerebellum and cord. He should know how the two halves of the two retinas connect with the cortex, and how parts of the body are represented in the somesthetic and motor areas. He should be sure he understands the split-brain study with monkeys, and the kind of evidence in the case of human patients with cut corpus callosum that led Sperry to speak of the patient as having two minds.

NOTES AND REFERENCES

SPECIAL TOPICS

Anatomical References

Gardner, E.: *Fundamentals of Neurology,* Saunders, 1968. A very good briefer guide to human neural anatomy.

Zeman, W., and Innes, J. R. M.: *Craigie's Neuroanatomy of the Rat,* Academic Press, 1963.

Speech and Handedness

Penfield, W., and Roberts, L.: *Speech and Brain Mechanisms.* Princeton University Press, 1959.

Milner, B., Branch, C., and Rasmussen, T.: Observations on cerebral dominance. In A. V. S. de Reuck, and M. O'Connor (Eds.); *Ciba Foundation Symposium on Disorders of Language*, London: Churchill, 1964.

Milner, P.: *Physiological Psychology*. Holt, Rinehart & Winston, 1970.

Split-Brain Preparations

Sperry, R. W.: The great cerebral commissure. *Psychobiology*, pp. 240–250. (Originally in *Scientific American*, January, 1964). A report of the original experiments with monkeys.

Sperry, R. W.: Hemisphere deconnection and unity in conscious awareness. *American Psychologist*, 1968, 23, 723–733. The dramatic description of work with human patients.

Downer, J. L. deC.: Changes in visual gnostic functions and emotional behavior following unilateral temporal lobe damage in the "split-brain" monkey. *Nature*, 1961, 191, 50–51.

4

mechanisms of learning and development

In Chapter 2 we saw that learning takes a number of forms. Some learning seems simple and easily explained by direct S-R connections, but other kinds are more puzzling. However, it turns out that even the simpler learned responses in mammals – a CR, for example, in which a dog lifts a paw to avoid shock – is unlikely to be explained by direct connections. Even farther removed from such a simple explanation is perceptual learning, and what was called, in Chapter 2, the acquisition of knowledge. It is possible that direct S-R connections may be the explanation of learning in certain lower forms, but it seems that the ordinary learning of mammals must be more complex.

Also, learning is not the same at all stages in development, but changes with experience. The infant is not at all capable of learning in the same way as an adult. The remarkable learning capacities of the adult, so familiar to us that we do not see how remarkable they are, result from learning that went on in infancy and childhood. We have to learn in order to learn: just as a capitalist must have money before he can make money, so the student who has already learned a lot in his normal experiences before entering school is in the best position to learn more. Early latent learning is the prerequisite for much that follows. Learning people's names, for example, requires having first learned to see faces as distinctive entities, learning to use words demands having learned to hear the distinctive sounds of the language. Much learning during childhood is, obviously, motor learning, and lays the basis of motor skills later on; but much of it is the latent learning that is a foundation for intellectual development.

Here then we will proceed by first taking a look at neuron and synapse, since a change of neural connections (the basic phenomenon of learning) must involve the interaction of single neurons at the synapse. We will also look at certain anatomical peculiarities of the nervous system, to see how these may help us to understand such things as latent learning, selective attention and the difficulty of concentration when one is studying.

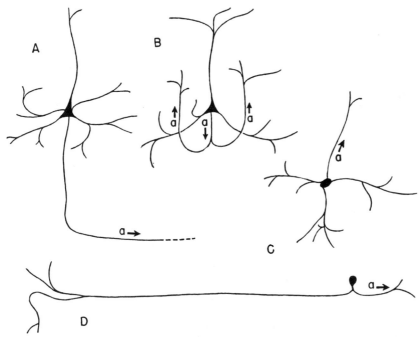

Figure 23. *Different forms taken by neurons; a, axon. In neuron A, only part of the axon is shown; in B, C and D the whole cell is shown. B and C are short-axon cells from the CNS (note how the axon in B comes back toward the dendrites of the same cell, as if to form a closed loop). D is an afferent neuron, from a spinal-cord nerve.*

NEURON AND SYNAPSE

Examples of some of the different forms taken by neurons are provided in Figure 23 (see also Figs. 32 and 34). What these have in common is that they are all one-way streets, each with a receiving and a sending end. The *dendrites* are fibrils at the receiving end; the neuron may have more than one of these. There is only one *axon,* the fibril that conducts away from the cell-body and toward the next cell, but it usually has a number of branches or collaterals.* Though the dendrites have the function of receiving excitation from other cells, the cell-body itself also receives excitation directly, by-passing the dendrites (Fig. 24). Conduction by the dendrite may be slow and inefficient; it has been suggested that this is the primitive arrangement, and that direct excitation of the cell-body is an evolutionary development which permits more efficient conduction.

The *synapse* is the point at which an axon makes contact with the dendrite or cell-body of another neuron (Fig. 24). The enlargement of the axon fibril at the point of contact is known as a *synaptic knob.* When synaptic transmission is improved in learning, one possible

---

*This is the traditional view. However, T. H. Bullock *(Science,* 1959, 129, 997–1002) has reported that there are neurons which have two axons, and can deliver at the same time two differently "coded" messages (see p. 227).

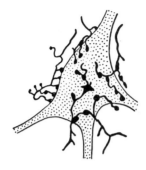

Figure 24. Synapses: synaptic knobs (black) making contact with a cell-body (stippled). Only a few knobs are shown; the cell-body and its dendrites may be completely covered by them. (From E. Gardner, Fundamentals of Neurology, *Saunders.)*

basis for the improvement is an enlargement of the knob, or a closer contact of knob with cell-body or dendrite. This explanation is not a necessary one, for the change may be in the chemical functioning of the knob rather than its size. Or, of course, both explanations may be correct.

Both dendrite and axon are conductors, but it appears that a large part of the dendrite has different properties from those of the axon. The axon (like the cell-body itself) works on the *all-or-none principle* (except possibly at its very end). The dendrite over much of its extent does not.* The all-or-none principle means that the axon, when it fires, expends all its accumulated energy ("firing" means that the cell is excited and begins to conduct, not that it goes off like a firecracker). It is like a shotgun that either fires or does not fire, with no half-way measures; pulling the trigger gently does not produce a gentler explosion. The dendrite is more like a bow-and-arrow system, in which a weak pull produces a weak effect, a strong pull a strong effect.

The axon conducts "without decrement": since it burns all of whatever fuel is available at each point, the electrochemical disturbance does not decrease with distance as it travels along the fiber. In this respect the axon is like a train of gunpowder; a large part of the dendrite is like a damp match in which the flame gets smaller and smaller as it moves along, so that it may go out before the end of the match is reached. The dendrite conducts "decrementally." Often, therefore, a dendrite may be excited at some distance from the cell-body and not excite the latter; the greater the disturbance in the dendrite, the greater the probability that the disturbance will reach the cell-body and fire it. The cell-body and the axon tend to act as a unit, both all-or-none in action; so that, if the cell-body is excited, the excitation sweeps over it and on over the axon, including all its branches.

This event, the *nerve impulse,* is the fundamental process of neural transmission. The important facts for our present purposes are summarized as follows. (1) The impulse is a change, both electrical and chemical, that moves across the neuron at a fast but limited

---

*W. Hild and I. Tasaki (*J. Neurophysiol.,* 1962, 25, 277–304) report all-or-none conduction in cell-cultured dendrites, in the region adjoining the cell-body.

speed,* the rate varying with the diameter of the fiber (up to 120 meters per second in large fibers, less than 1 m./sec. in the smallest); (2) this disturbance can set off a similar one in a second neuron, across the synapse, or when it reaches a gland or muscle cell can cause it to secrete or contract; (3) the neuron needs a definite time to "recharge" itself after firing in this way; (4) immediately after firing nothing can fire the neuron again, but a little later, before recharging is complete, the neuron can be fired by a strong stimulation; and (5) when the neuron fires, its cell-body and axon fire completely — the all-or-none principle.

The *absolute refractory period* is the first stage of recharging, about a millisecond in duration (0.5–2.0 msec.), when the cell is incapable of firing no matter how strong the stimulation. The *relative refractory period* follows, in which a strong stimulation can fire the cell; this is about a tenth of a second (100 msec.) or longer. The term *limen* or *threshold* refers to the strength of stimulation necessary to produce a reaction, so we can say that in the absolute refractory period the limen (or threshold) is infinitely high, and that it is higher in the relative refractory phase than when the cell is resting. For large cells the refractory period is shorter and the resting limen is lower — that is, large cells can be re-excited sooner, and are more easily excited, than small ones.

Next we can look at some of the elementary consequences of these facts. Any nerve or bundle of neurons is made up of fibers varying in size, and hence in speed of conduction. If, therefore, a strong stimulus fires all the neurons in a given bundle, the "volley" of impulses starts out at the same time but is dispersed, in time of arrival, at the other end. A short sharp stimulation of the foot, for example, does not produce an equally brief excitation at the level of the cord, but a scattering of impulses extending over an appreciable part of a second. (The dispersion in time is still greater at the level of the cerebrum.) Next, the refractory period means that the fastest frequency of firing in a single fiber is of the order of 1000 per second, since it takes about a thousandth of a second (1 msec.) for the fiber to recover each time.

The logical consequences of the all-or-none principle are quite clear, though students usually have some trouble with them. A strong stimulation does not produce bigger impulses in a fiber. It can, however, fire the cell more frequently, by catching it earlier in the relative refractory period. Thus intensity of stimulation is translated into frequency in the CNS. Furthermore, since different afferent cells have different limens, a stronger stimulation excites more cells,

---

*Students are sometimes confused about the speed of an "electrical" nerve impulse, and think that it must travel at the same rate as electrical current. Instead, the impulse is an electrical (and chemical) *disturbance* which travels much more slowly. It may be thought of as like a thunderstorm which moves across the countryside; electrical currents, in the form of lightning flashes, may travel at the speed of light, but the storm itself moves, perhaps, at a rate of only 10 to 15 miles per hour, just as a hurricane does, though it consists of 100-mile-per-hour winds. The current flow in and around the nerve impulse may be at the speed of light but the locus of disturbance, the impulse, moves in a relatively slow way along the nerve fiber.

which again means an increased frequency of firing. Thus the all-or-none principle applies to a single impulse in a single fiber, but not to the repetitive firing of the fiber nor to a bundle of fibers.

At this point in discussions such as this it is customary to introduce a simple diagram like Figure 25A, hallowed by long use, to explain the nerve impulse. Let us introduce it by all means. In the resting state the cell has more positive ions on the outside and more negative ions inside, separated by a membrane which is semipermeable (i.e., it allows some ions to pass through, but not others). This is an unstable equilibrium; a very slight disturbance in the neighborhood of the membrane can upset the balance and allow the positive ions on the outside to pass through the membrane. When this happens the outer surface of that part of the neuron becomes negative, an electrical effect referred to as the "action potential." The polarization (i.e., the separation of positive and negative ions by the membrane) has disappeared; the depolarization then spreads by disturbing the equilibrium of the region next to it, so that it travels along the axon. No sooner is the equilibrium upset, however, than the cell begins to restore it by moving the positive ions outward, a process that takes altogether about 1 msec.; the nerve impulse, that is, lasts about 1 msec. at any one point in the cell (0.5 msec. in large fibers, 2.0 in small) (Fig. 25B).

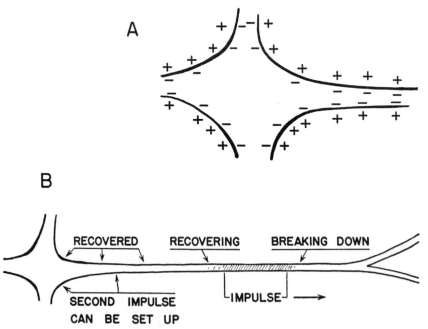

Figure 25. A, *polarization of resting neuron. B, passage of one impulse (shaded region) along the axon: showing that two or more impulses can occur at the same time in the neuron, since a second one can be started in the "recovered" region as soon as the first has moved along the fiber and the cell-body has recharged itself. The process is known to be far more complex than diagram A would suggest.*

The whole process is known to be more complex than this; the positive ions moving inward are sodium ions, but positive potassium ions are moving outward while this is going on (just to confuse the picture), and no one knows how the sodium ions are moved out in the process of recovery. Something must do it, and this something is known as the sodium pump, an entity that has some relation to unicorn or phoenix, or the celestial spheres that move the stars in their courses. Psychologists frequently have to give names to things they have not seen and do not understand; it is reassuring to observe that others must do so too.

The all-or-none action of the axon makes possible a rapid conduction to distant points. A further contribution to this end is made by the myelin sheath, a fatty covering surrounding many nerve fibers (this is what makes the white matter white). At intervals of a millimeter or so there are gaps in the sheath (at the "nodes"); the electrical potential at one gap produces an excitation in the next, starting what is really a second nerve impulse at that point. The myelin sheath over the intervening part of the fiber appears also to prevent the impulse from occurring in the internodal region. Thus the impulse does not travel continuously along the fiber, but jumps from node to node at a faster rate perhaps than continuous travel would permit. (It may also demand less energy expenditure.)

WHEN ARE NEURONS ACTIVE?

The neuron is a living cell and, being alive, must be active. If it is not excited from outside it tends nonetheless to fire *spontaneously*: that is, the cell stores up energy received from the blood stream until a point is reached at which the membrane polarization breaks down—so the cell fires. Some neurons, it seems, will eventually die if not excited from outside (p. 120), but they may be the exception. It is true, however, that in normal circumstances the cells of the brain are always active, as shown by the EEG or by recording electrodes inserted in the brain. The activity continues even in sleep, although the pattern of activity is changed (p. 177).

Facilitation and Summation

Facilitation is the delivery of an excitatory impulse by one neuron to another—whether the excitation is strong enough to make the second neuron fire or not. ("Facilitation" has the same meaning as "stimulation" except that it is customary to distinguish (1) excitatory events from outside the nervous system, which are *stimuli*, from (2) the excitation of neurons by other neurons, inside the nervous system: *facilitation*.)

It is important for the student to realize that one impulse at the synapse is usually not enough to fire the postsynaptic neuron. It is always possible that the neuron has been building up toward spontaneous firing, and then, when the neuron is almost ready to fire anyway, one impulse is enough to do the trick; but for reliable trans-

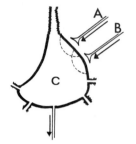

Figure 26. Summation at the synapse. A and B, axons; C, cell-body. A alone may not be able to fire C; A and B together produce a greater area of breakdown and a higher probability that C will fire.

mission across the synapse it may be necessary to have two or more neurons *sum* their effects.

Summation is the reinforcement of the action of one stimulus, or one facilitation, by that of another. If one touch on the skin or one slight sound or one glimmer of light is not enough to affect behavior, two together may sum their effects and be able to do so. This is part of the reason why a strong stimulus is more likely to be effective than a weak one: as we have seen, the strong stimulus cannot produce bigger nerve impulses, but it can excite more impulses which sum and are more likely to reach the limen of behavioral response.

At the synapse, summation must normally be essential. A single axon, delivering an impulse to another neuron, produces a slight depolarization that is not usually extensive enough to result in firing. Two such axons side by side, however, will produce a greater area of depolarization (Fig. 26) which is more likely to be effective. Especially with continued rapid firing, the postsynaptic neuron must be relatively refractory and the summation of impulses from a number of presynaptic axons will be necessary if the firing is to be maintained. Since the impulses must arrive close together in time in order to sum, perhaps within a millisecond or so, timing becomes very important in neural functioning.

Fatigue and Inhibition

Fatigue in the neuron is, first, the refractory period. The absolute refractory period lasts only for the duration of the impulse at one point, about 1 msec. During the relative refractory period the cell can be fired again, but full recovery takes from 80 msec. (in large fibers) to a second or so (in small ones). Secondly, a cell that fires at a rapid rate begins to have a kind of supply problem. For example, the sodium ions that move inward when the cell fires are not excreted completely by the sodium pump for some time, and so accumulate when the cell is continuously active. Full recovery may take an hour or more.

Inhibition occurs in two ways. In one the postsynaptic neuron is made harder to fire; in the other, the presynaptic impulse is made less effective. The two mechanisms are diagrammed in Figure 27.

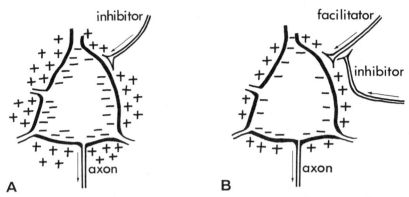

Figure 27. *Two mechanisms of inhibition: A, the "normal" postsynaptic mechanism, where the inhibitor acts directly to prevent depolarization in the postsynaptic neuron; B, presynaptic inhibition, where the inhibitor acts on the excitatory axon and decreases its capacity to deliver excitatory impulses. In A, the postsynaptic cell is hyperpolarized; in B, the postsynaptic cell is not directly affected.*

In the first mechanism an inhibitory neuron produces *hyperpolarization* — the opposite of the depolarization that takes place in firing — in the postsynaptic neuron, which makes it harder to fire. In the second, it is not an inhibitory but an excitatory neuron that has the inhibitory effect, by delivering an apparently weak excitation to the presynaptic axonal ending. This makes a partial depolarization of the ending, so that when a normal impulse arrives its effect is diminished and the postsynaptic neuron does not fire.

It is known that some neurons in the spinal cord (Renshaw cells) are specialized for inhibition, and it is believed that many of the short-axon cells found in the brain have the same function, with the sort of interaction between neurons that is diagramed in Figure 28. They are of the highest importance in learning, for learning is the elimination of wrong or irrelevant activity as well as the establishment of the right activity. Learning must be both the formation of new associations and the elimination or suppression of previously existing ones that interfere. As we saw above, however, not all inhibition is produced by inhibitory neurons, and H. Wachtel and E. R. Kandel

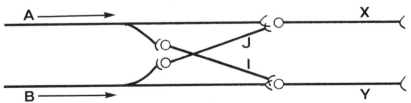

Figure 28. *The mechanism of inhibition. Neuron A excites X in the usual manner; a collateral also excites I, which is specialized for inhibition. I then acts to hyperpolarize Y and prevent it from firing at the same time as X. Similarly, B excites Y, but (via J) inhibits X. (This is known as reciprocal innervation.)*

describe neurons that are both excitatory and inhibitory. The same neuron may excite one postsynaptic neuron and inhibit another; or may excite a second neuron when firing at a low rate but inhibit the same neuron when firing at a high rate.

SYNAPTIC CHANGES IN LEARNING

Now we come to the crucial question: what happens at the synapse when something is learned? And the answer is that after three-quarters of a century of research on the problem, we still do not know for certain. This is an area in which we deal mostly in theory, not fact, and it is important for the student to remember that this is so. We know much about the end results of learning and the conditions in which it is likely to happen, but fine details of the process? No. What we must do is see if we can arrive at theoretical ideas about neuron and synapse that would account for the phenomena we know.

There is a long-standing idea that when two brain processes are active at the same time they tend to make connection with each other. This explains the association of ideas and sensory-motor associations, and there is good reason to think that something of the kind does happen. How might it work? Figure 29 shows what is implied concerning individual neurons at the synapse. Two brain activities *A* and *B* are excited at the same time. This might be in the sensory preconditioning experiment (p. 31), *A* perhaps being the perception of the light, *B* perception of the sound. A neuron *a*, in activity *A*, happens to be one whose axon ends near *b*, a neuron that is part of activity *B*. The impulses in *a* then arrive near *b* while *b* is being fired (by *c* and *d*), so the impulses from *a* help to fire *b*. Theory says when this happens a connection is formed between *a* and *b*, or if there is one already it will be strengthened. We can put the theoretical idea in general terms:

When an axon of a neuron x *is near enough to help fire a neuron*

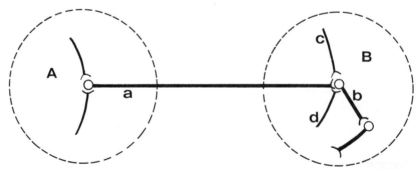

Figure 29. *A mechanism of establishing synaptic connections. A, a group of active neurons, of which only one (a) is shown completely; B, a second group of neurons active at the same time, of which only two are shown completely. Since a and b are active together and an axon of a is close to b, a will become connected with (better able to facilitate) b.*

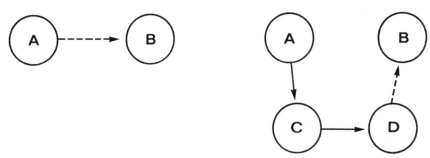

Figure 30. Direct and indirect associations. Left: some axons from neurons in group A end close enough to neurons in group B so that a direct A-B connection can be established when the two are active together. Right: no axons from A approach B, but among A's many connections (associations from common experience) is one with C, which is connected with D, whose axons do reach B and thus make a connection A-C-D-B possible.

y and does so, some change takes place such that x becomes more effective at exciting y.

What is this change, or how does it work? This is the question to which we have no final answer. Transmission at the synapse is chemical, the axon tip or synaptic knob secreting a small quantity of an exciting substance (in the cortex, probably acetylcholine). When transmission at the synapse becomes more effective, in learning, it may be because there is more transmitter substance accumulated in the presynaptic axon (x), or possibly because there is a closer or more extensive contact between the synaptic knob and the cell wall: or both.

Now the mechanism of association diagramed in Figure 29 requires that the axon a must be close to b, so it can help to fire it, before the learning begins. How often would this be so? Not often, surely. And when we talk about an association between two perceptions (e.g., sound and light in the sensory preconditioning experiment), we must suppose that a *number* of single-neuron contacts are required — a single neuron a could not reliably excite all the neurons making up the group B. It is not likely that any brain activity has such contacts with any other brain activity, to make direct association possible. But if A in Figure 29 does not have such potential connections with B, it will have many other connections already formed (the associations of common experience), including one with some process C or D which *can* connect with B. When a direct A–B connection is impossible, an A–C–B or A–C–D–B connection may be formed instead (Fig. 30). A can excite B, but indirectly.

The scientific literature tells us nothing about how inhibitory synaptic changes are made. For excitation we have a theoretical idea, at least: if x excites y and y then fires, x becomes more capable of exciting y. No such rule has been suggested for inhibition, but we might consider one. This is the converse of the excitatory rule:

When a neuron x delivers an impulse to a neuron y and y does *not* fire, further impulses from x make y *less* likely to fire.

In other words, *x* now inhibits *y*. It is Pavlov's work that has given us the most direct and detailed information about learned inhibition, and this theoretical rule seems consistent with his data, though working it out exactly would involve us in too much detail. The student must keep in mind that all this is theory and there are limits to the extent to which such theory should be elaborated in the absence of physiological data.

Finally, to complete this account of what happens at the synapse in the course of learning, some mention of *reinforcement* and *consolidation* is necessary. We will come back to this topic in discussing memory (Chapter 6). Here it is enough to say that the synaptic changes of learning are temporary until they have had a chance to become consolidated. Consolidation takes some period of time up to an hour or so, and the effect of reinforcement may be to promote consolidation.

THE INFANT'S FIRST LEARNING

Some of the things that were said in the preceding section give us some clue to the nature of mental growth, and suggest why the growth depends on stimulation from the baby's environment. The stimulation must have two effects, according to the theoretical ideas we have been discussing. One is perceptual learning, which enables the baby to perceive better and develops a capacity for images and ideas. The other is to establish many associations, which provides a basis for making new associations by means of indirect connections, when direct connections are not available (Fig. 30).

First the perceptual learning: common events in the baby's experience—sight of a face or a hand or the milk bottle, the sound of mother's footsteps, the taste of milk, the touch of a finger on cloth—repeatedly excite groups of neurons in the cortex. The neurons that are excited when one of these things happens are not the same every time, but there is a common core of ones that are excited every time. The core neurons therefore tend to become connected with one another in a single system that we will call a *cell-assembly.* Many of these neurons are in closed self-re-exciting circuits (Figs. 31, 32, and 33) and so, as we will see shortly, the system can continue to be active after outside stimulation has ceased. Also, the system may be excited by another system, instead of by the sensory event that developed it originally. While it is being excited by its own proper sensory stimulation, *the activity of the cell-assembly is perception,* theoretically; if it is active after the sensory stimulation has ceased, or if it is excited by another cell-assembly and not sensorily, *the activity is imagery* or *ideation* or a *mediating process* (for the meaning of this term, see p. 84). The increase of organization of the cell-assembly, with experience, is perceptual learning, which theoretically (none of the babies have told us about this) means increased clarity and distinctiveness of perception; but since it is also laying a basis for ideation, we can think of this as *conceptual* learning too.

A word should be said about the increase in the distinctiveness of perception. At an early stage in the learning many of the cortical neurons that are excited by seeing a face (e.g.) must be different from one time to another, so it would make little difference to the baby's behavior if he sees the same face a second time, or a different face. But the common core of neurons excited by one face are different from those excited by the second face, and if both faces are seen often the two core groups will be organized in two assemblies, becoming more distinct as organization goes on. For behavior, the existence of two distinctive cortical processes — two different assemblies — means that two different responses become possible. Inhibition presumably will play a part in this process, tending to suppress firing by neurons that are not part of the assembly and thus making the perception more clear-cut and distinctive.

Secondly, establishing the network of associations: cell-assemblies that are active at the same time become interconnected. Common events in the child's environment establish assemblies, and then when these events occur together the assemblies become connected (because they are active together). When the baby hears footsteps, let us say, an assembly is excited; while this is still active he sees a face and feels hands picking him up, which excites other assemblies — so the "footsteps assembly" becomes connected with the "face assembly" and the "being-picked-up assembly." After this has happened, when the baby hears footsteps only, *all three* assemblies are excited; the baby then has something like a perception of the mother's face and the contact of her hands before she has come in sight — but since the sensory stimulations have not yet taken place, this is ideation or imagery, not perception. According to the work of the great Swiss psychologist Jean Piaget, ideation can be detected about the age of four to five months.* At this point the baby is ready for the development of a wide network of associations — he is no longer limited, in his brain activities, to ones that are excited by here-and-now sensory stimulations — which (again theoretically) must help in the formation of new associations.

The variety of CRs that can be established in a baby's first weeks of life is limited, and in part the reason may be the absence of that network to provide for indirect associations (Fig. 30). (We know that indirect association is important at least for adult learning, in everyday life as in the laboratory. In the laboratory, for example, a subject with the task of associating "rock" and "run," in a long list of paired associates, tied this particular pair together in memory by thinking,

---

*Piaget's simple but very significant observation is this. The baby is shown some bright attractive object such as a watch, and reaches for it while it is in sight; but if it is put under a cushion or covered by a piece of cloth, the baby stops reaching and acts as if there was no attractive object even though it was in sight only a moment before. When the baby is a month or two older, however, he keeps on looking for the watch. Earlier his behavior was influenced only by actual sensory events; now something is happening in his head that makes him act as if the watch was still in sight: a "representative process," which is the general name for an image or an idea (or a hallucination).

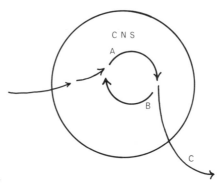

Figure 31. *Diagrammatic representation of a re-entrant, closed or reverberatory pathway: when incoming excitation excites A, A excites B which again excites A, and so on. The continuing excitation may then be transmitted to motor organs via C.*

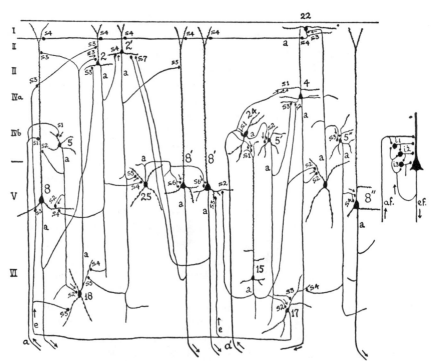

Figure 32. *Diagram of closed path in the human cortex. This is more realistic than Figure 31 but still diagrammatic since it shows only about one one-thousandth of the connections that would actually be found in a block of cortex. The small diagram at the right is a simplification of the larger one. Arrows show the direction of transmission in different cells. (From Lorente de Nó, in J. F. Fulton,* Physiology of the Nervous System, *Oxford University Press.)*

"Throw rocks at a dog and he runs.") The characteristics of learning change greatly as a child grows — there is, for example, no immediate one-trial learning in early infancy — and this must be partly due to the fact that the brain is not yet fully developed, but part of the reason also seems to be that learning takes place increasingly against a broad background of common associations.

CELL-ASSEMBLIES: THE BASIS OF THOUGHT

Another way of putting what has just been said is that the development of *thought processes* is what changes infant-style learning to adult-style. Though we do not know exactly how cell-assemblies are constituted, with respect to the details of their function, there is a good deal of empirical evidence to indicate that they exist and are the basis of thought.

Much of the CNS, but especially association cortex and certain closely connected subcortical structures, is filled with paths that lead back into themselves as well as leading on to other paths. The simplest case is shown diagrammatically in Figure 31. A and B form a loop circuit or re-entrant pathway; if A is excited it excites B, which can then re-excite A, and so on — the excitation chasing its tail round and round the loop, or "reverberating." Such a reverberatory mechanism can hold an excitation, at the same time sending out impulses to other central processes or to a motor path, via pathway C.

Figure 31 shows this in schematic form. Figure 32 is a drawing by R. Lorente de Nó, the distinguished neuroanatomist and physiologist to whom we owe most of our knowledge of these matters (following the great neuroanatomist of an earlier generation, S. Ramón y Cajal). Figure 33 is a schematization of another such drawing, allowing the closed loops to be seen more clearly. Figure 34 then shows the kind of photomicrograph from which such drawings were made, to give some idea of the actual complexity of the structures we are discussing. The student, when he looks at the schematic diagrams which in this text represent closed circuits in the brain, should remember that Figure 31 stands for something much more complex.

For convenience, these paths will be discussed as if they were *in* the association cortex. Actually, some of them are in the cortex, but many of the closed loops are "corticothalamic," running from cortex to thalamus and back to cortex; and some of them must similarly involve other subcortical structures, such as the *hippocampus,* which in man lies inside the tip of the temporal lobe and, as we will see (p. 100), appears to have an important part to play in memory.

We assume that a cell-assembly consists of a number of these reentrant paths that have become connected with each other by the processes of perceptual learning discussed above. Thus the assembly is a system that is organized in the first place by a particular sen-

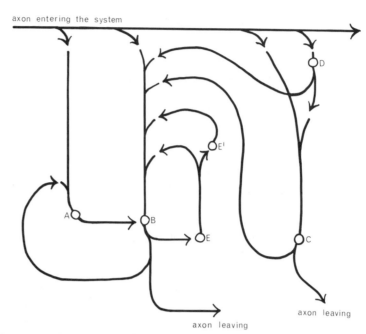

Figure 33. Diagram of relations between neurons actually observed by Lorente de Nó. The entering axon excites the dendrites of four neurons, A, B, C and D. Of these B and C send impulses out of the system to excite other systems, but impulses from A and D are delivered only within the system itself. A–B, B–E, and B–E–E′ form closed circuits which can hold excitations and cause B to continue delivering impulses outside the system. (After F. A. Beach, et al. (Eds.), The Neuropsychology of Lashley, McGraw-Hill; cf. p. 467.)

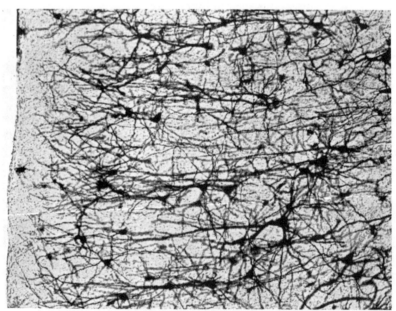

Figure 34. Photomicrograph of a section of cat cortex, giving a better idea of the complexity of connections — but still only about one neuron in 60 is shown here, stained by the Golgi-Cox method which for some unknown reason is selective. If all were stained, no detail could be observed, only a solid mass of stained tissue. The outer layer of the cortex is at left. (From D. A. Sholl, Organization of the Cerebral Cortex, Methuen.)

sory event but is capable of continuing its activity after that stimulation has ceased. Not only is it made up of self–re-exciting closed loops, neuron *A* exciting *B* and *B* exciting *A,* but two loops or sets of loops may also have that self–re-exciting relation to each other. The whole system therefore is such as to maintain an internal activity for short periods of time.*

Further, the system may be excited by other similar systems, in the total absence of the sensory event that originally organized it. It thus meets the requirements of an ideational process. The very essence of an "idea" is that a brain activity is occurring in the absence of the environmental event it corresponds to. You need not have an elephant present to think about elephants, the discomfort of being caught in the rain can be thought about long after your clothing has dried.

Note finally that latent learning now becomes intelligible. It is a change of connection between cell-assemblies at a time when the assemblies are not exciting other assemblies that have direct motor connections. The need of summation must mean that one assembly may be able to fire another only with support from other assemblies, so these systems may be active, in certain combinations, without producing a behavioral effect. Other combinations result in behavior. In the first case, when there is no motor outflow, interaction between assemblies makes changes at the synapse, which affects the relations between them. For example, it may be proposed now that the two "central activities" in Figure 7 (p. 32) are cell-assemblies. Also, the development of an assembly, as a form of perceptual learning, is itself latent learning. Latent learning has been regarded as mysterious in the past, but it need not be.

Let us see next why the sort of direct S-R connection that Pavlov and Thorndike talked about is unlikely to exist. The nervous system does contain straight-through pathways, especially from sense organ to cortex, and from motor cortex to spinal cord, but this seems not to apply to the cortex — and it is in the cortex that learning takes place.

DIVERGENT VS. PARALLEL CONDUCTION: ATTENTION

When dendrites and cell-bodies lie close together, they tend to be excited together; and if their axons also lie side by side, ending at about the same place, impulses reaching the ends of the axons at the same time can sum their effects on the dendrites or cell-bodies of neurons at the next level, past the synapse. This arrangement of fibers is found all the way from the skin, for example, to the cortex,

---

*It is believed that a very mild fatigue, which builds up quickly, is enough to put an end to activity in an assembly after some short period of time such as half a second. However, recovery from fatigue may be rapid also, and when several assemblies are facilitating each other the activity may go on for much longer periods of time: one assembly excites a second and then stops firing, but the second excites a third, which by this time can re-excite the first, and so on.

and the result is that skin stimulation produces an excitation in the corresponding region of the somesthetic cortex with high reliability. But when we look at the way in which the excitation is carried from the sensory to the association cortex, we find *divergent conduction* instead. The neurons lead in different directions, and transmission must be less reliable. Is this a defect? No, we will find that there is good reason for it. It allows central processes to do things they could not do otherwise. The "unreliability" of divergent conduction allows central processes to receive, and to be affected by, relevant sensory messages only. If transmission in the association cortex was always effective, these processes would be bombarded by too many messages at the same time. In effect, divergent conduction screens sensory input and allows the higher animal to respond selectively to events around him: the fundamental mechanism of attention.

Figure 35 represents the change from parallel to divergent conduction as a sensory excitation is transmitted first to the sensory area of cortex and then on to the association cortex. In parallel conduction, branching at the axonal ends of the neurons (inset, Figure 35) allows each neuron at the next level to receive excitation from several axons, so summation can occur. But where divergent conduction begins, at the right of the figure, summation is not provided for except when by chance two neurons starting in different places happen to converge. In Figure 35, the stimulation *S* which fires a group of cells *A* will have a high probability of firing group *B,* and also the single cells *C, D* and *E,* but the excitation is likely to peter out at the level of *F, G* and *H unless other neurons* (not shown in the figure) *provide supporting excitation.* There is a low probability, for example,

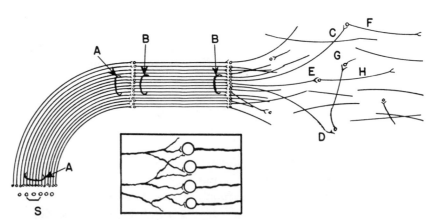

Figure 35. *Neural conduction: parallel on the left, divergent on the right. S, stimulation of part of a receptor surface, excites a group of neurons A which converge at the next synaptic level and provide summation in a postsynaptic group B, which therefore fires reliably. At the next synapse there is divergence; B produces summation in C, D and E, and so fires them reliably, but there is no summation for F, G and H (some of these diverging paths may meet by chance, when a very large number is involved). Inset: the convergence in greater detail, showing the overlap of branching fibers that produces summation.*

that *E* will fire *H,* unless something else in this region is sending impulses to *H* at the same time. So the region of divergent conduction will act like a screen, allowing through only the "messages" that can obtain some support from other activities that are already going on.*

These are the reasons why it seems most unlikely that there are direct S-R connections formed in the cortex during learning. This conclusion was long ago reached by K. S. Lashley, who showed by means of brain operations that there is no clear-cut loss of single habits when parts of the cortex—even fairly large amounts, as much as 15 to 20 per cent of the total cortex—are removed. Direct connections should be interrupted by such removals. Also, there is plenty of other evidence to support the idea that the mammal's cortex is constantly screening out sensory messages and not allowing them to be responded to behaviorally. The cortex is always exposed to messages from the sense organs: from the pressures on all parts of the body that are touched by clothing and the change in these pressures with every movement, from joints and muscle reporting to the brain the position of the limbs, the constant information being received from all parts of the visual field as long as the eyes are open, the constant low-level background noise received by the ears. Not 1 per cent of this information is responded to, or enters awareness (that is, it does not affect the ongoing thought process).

We may think instead of transmission via cell-assemblies, which may be relatively direct and reliable, if the assemblies are strongly connected, or very indirect and unreliable. Figure 36 shows, schematically and theoretically, how selective transmission from sensory cortex would occur. In the figure, *X, Y* and *Z* are excitations coming from sensory cortex into association cortex, in a region where a cell-assembly *A* is already active. Facilitation from both *A* and *X* sum to make *B* fire, and now *B* can sum with *Y* to fire *C. B* and *C* in turn fire *D,* which sends excitation back to help keep *B* active. The effect is to produce a temporal series of central activities, *A–B–C–D* firing in that order.

On the other hand, the assembly *F* is not active, so there is nothing to sum with the sensory input *Z,* so this will have no central effect. If *F* was active and *A* not active, *X* and *Y* would have no effect, but *Z* would excite *E*; a different cortical activity—and therefore a different behavioral response—would be excited by the same total sen-

---

*As we will see in Chapter 10, p. 173, it is also necessary to have support from the arousal system for *any* message to get through. It appears from our present knowledge that activity in the sub-cortical arousal system produces a more or less indiscriminate bombardment of cortical synapses, thus providing summation for any cortical transmission. The summation is not selective. If arousal is high, this support will be great enough to allow messages to get through that are not related to what the subject is now thinking about, as well as the ones that are (a sudden loud noise or a sharp pain, for example, produces high arousal and thus can break into the train of thought). But with moderate levels of arousal it seems that summation is required from *both* the arousal system and the cortical activity already going on. Thus the latter can still have its selective effect, and the topic of arousal need not be gone into at this stage in the discussion. It is mentioned here to keep the record straight for the student when he comes to review, after reading Chapter 10.

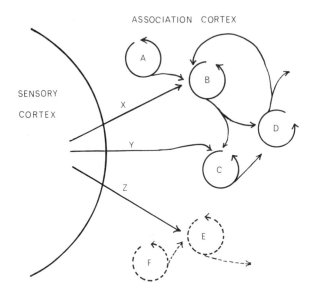

ASSOCIATION CORTEX

SENSORY

CORTEX

Figure 36. Selective transmission from the sensory cortex. X, Y and Z, sensory transmissions; A, B, C and D, closed systems (cell-assemblies), A being active before the sensory input occurs, B, C and D becoming active thereafter; E and F, inactive systems. In these circumstances excitation X would have its effect, and then Y, but Z would not have an effect.

sory excitation *(XYZ)*. The response that is made to a given stimulation depends on what activity is already going on in the brain.

This is the selective action made possible by divergent conduction in association cortex, and transmission via cell-assemblies instead of straight-through pathways with neurons organized in parallel.

ATTENTION AND CONCENTRATION

The selectivity of brain response is, from a psychological point of view, *attention* or *set,* to which we will return in the following chapter. Before we conclude the present account of the development of perception and thought, there is one further point which is suggested by what we know of the anatomy and physiology of the brain.

The large size of the human brain is needed to allow human beings to learn so many different things, but it also means that there are many more neurons in the brain than are needed for learning any one thing. As we have already seen, neurons fire spontaneously if they are not being kept active. The many neurons that are not necessary for a learning task may, when the task is prolonged, become active anyway, producing other thoughts besides the ones that concern the present task. This is the student's problem of attention and "concentration": to respond to, and think about, only the subject-matter before him. How is it possible?

For one thing, the cell-assemblies that are active tend presumably to inhibit random activity by other neurons, and this inhibitory action may become more and more effective as mental growth goes on and assemblies become better and better organized. Young children have a notoriously short "span of attention," but this span increases as they grow older. Secondly, the span of attention is longer for the more intelligent subjects at any particular age, provided the topics they attend to have many facets for one to think about. We may suppose that the more intelligent person has developed more cell-assemblies, which would provide more inhibition to control the random extra activity in the brain. What the full story is here we do not know, but it seems that the "interesting" task — the one that is easy to concentrate on — involves both complexity and some level of *arousal* (Chapter 10). The complexity makes it possible to find different ways of thinking about the material, making more assemblies active. Another way to add somewhat to the interest of a dull learning task, as we will see in the discussion of study method in Chapter 6 (p. 108), is to make the learning active, though it is not clear theoretically why this should contribute to the inhibition of that random extra activity of the brain cells that are for the moment unused.

SUMMARY

This chapter provides a short account of what is known about the functioning of the single neuron, and a more theoretical account of the changes that occur at the synapse in learning. Inhibition is an important part of the process, eliminating irrelevant or conflicting response. It is proposed that in mammals, especially man, an essential part of learning is the development of cell-assemblies — closed systems capable of briefly maintaining their own activity — and a background of interconnections between assemblies corresponding to familiar events. It is also proposed that this development is what happens as the baby's style of learning changes to a more adult style. The structure of the cortex appears to rule out direct S-R connections in mammalian learning. Cortical transmission thus appears relatively inefficient, from one point of view, but from another it has the advantage that much irrelevant excitation from the sense organs is screened out and not allowed to disturb behavior. Finally, the chapter points to a disadvantage arising from the large size of the human brain, related to the student's problem of concentration.

Guide to Study

The student should be clear about the meaning of all the italicized terms in this chapter, but especially the following: axon, dendrite, synapse, all-or-none principle, nerve impulse, relative and absolute refractory periods, facilitation (vs. stimulation) and summation. He should be able to state a theoretical rule for the strengthening of connection at the synapse, and a converse rule for inhibition. He should be able to explain why it is possible that a wide background of associations may make further associations easier to form. How is a cell-assembly formed, and how can it maintain its own excitation? Why is parallel conduction more "efficient" than divergent conduction? If divergent conduction screens out some messages, what messages will it let through, and why? And why may a large brain be a handicap to the learner—in some ways?

NOTES AND REFERENCES

NEURON AND SYNAPSE

Doty, R. W.: The brain. In *Britannica Yearbook of Science and the Future,* 1970. Includes a brief but interesting and intelligible account of neuron and synapse, and transmission at the synapse.

Eccles, J. C.: *The Neurophysiological Basis of Mind,* Oxford University Press, 1953. This book is now somewhat out of date, but still valuable. Eccles is the discoverer (or co-discoverer, with Brock and Coombs) of direct experimental evidence of inhibition.

Milner, P. M.: *Physiological Psychology,* Holt, Rinehart and Winston, 1970. A psychologically oriented account of neural function, in considerable detail but intelligible.

Ruch, T. C., and Fulton, J. F. (Eds.): *Medical Physiology and Biophysics,* Saunders, 1960. Contains a multi-authored, complete and authoritative (as of 1960), account of the nervous system.

Wachtel, H., and Kandel, E. R.: Conversion of synaptic excitation to inhibition at a dual chemical synapse. *Journal of Neurophysiology,* 1971, 34, 56–68.

LEARNING PROBLEMS

Early Learning

Elkind, D., and Sameroff, A.: Developmental psychology. *Annual Reviews of Psychology,* 1970, 21, 149–238. A review of current research.

Kessen, W., Haith, M. M., and Salapatek, P.: Human infancy: a bibliography and guide. In P. M. Mussen (Ed.): *Carmichael's Manual of Child Psychology,* Wiley, 1970. Cf. p. 322, "The infant as learner."

Marquis, D. P.: Can conditioned responses be established in the newborn infant? *Journal of Genetic Psychology,* 1931, 39, 479–492. The early study: how much has been done since will be seen by comparison of this paper with the two reviews above.

Neural Mechanisms in Learning

Hebb, D. O.: *Organization of Behavior,* Wiley, 1949. Proposing the theory of cell-assemblies in learning.

Hebb, D. O.: Distinctive features of learning in the higher animal. In J. F. Delafresnaye (Ed.): *Brain Mechanisms and Learning,* Blackwell, 1961.

Lashley, K. S.: In search of the engram. In F. A. Beach, D. O. Hebb, C. T. Morgan and H. W. Nissen (Eds.): *The Neuropsychology of Lashley,* McGraw-Hill, 1960. This is probably the most frequently cited of Lashley's papers.

the control of behavior: cognitive and noncognitive

At several points in the preceding chapters the discussion has referred to higher behavior, or has implied a difference between behavior that involves thought and other behavior. Ultimately all behavior is a reaction to environmental stimulation, but the relation between stimulus and response varies from direct to extremely indirect. At one extreme is the unconditioned reflex, where the stimulus has its effect at once; the neural connections between receptor and effector are straight-through. At the other extreme, the stimulus has the effect of exciting complex cortical circuits and the behavioral effect may be long delayed (when latent learning occurs, for example).

Knowing something about the way the nervous system works will now help us to find order in these behavioral phenomena. Some psychologists have talked as if all behavior was *cognitive:* meaning that it involves thought. Others have talked as if all behavior fitted the *S-R formula:* meaning that thought does not enter into it, that all behavior is fully controlled by the stimulation from the environment. In the light of what has been said about the nervous system, the student will see that both kinds of behavior do occur and that the real question is the directness of the connections between stimulus and response. There is no opposition between two kinds of behavior but a gradation from one to the other, though at the extremes they seem quite different.

What is the difference between the behavior of a spider building a web and that of a man ploughing a field to plant potatoes? Both will obtain food as a result of what they are now doing, but one is consciously planning, one is not; what is the meaning of this difference? A girl at a dance is cold; she shivers reflexively, but then goes to get a scarf to put over her shoulders. On what principles do we distinguish between her two kinds of response to the environment?

In general, the answer to these questions is that some behavior shows a close temporal relation between stimulus and response, and depends on direct, or relatively direct, connections in the CNS; other behavior does not show this close relation, and we must assume that the connections are more indirect. The first kind is *reflexive* or *sense-dominated;* the second kind is cognitive behavior, dependent on *mediating processes* (ideas, thinking), which in this text are assumed to consist of the activity of cell-assemblies (p. 69). The presence of cell-assemblies permits a delay betwen stimulus and response but also, when two or more stimuli are involved, may introduce other kinds of complications: for example, the phenomenon of *set.*

But having mediating processes, and so being less directly controlled by sensory events, does not mean that the higher animal has less need of sensory information or is less influenced by it. All behavior is affected by sensation all the time. Behavior is fundamentally an adaptation to the environment under sensory guidance. It takes the organism away from harmful events and toward favorable ones, or introduces changes in the immediate environment that make survival more likely. Not all behavior is adaptive in such a narrow sense; sex and maternal behavior are not necessary to the behaver's survival, nor is play. But with these forms of behavior also (for example, in finding the mate, avoiding obstacles in moving to and from the nest, or maintaining bodily orientation in play), sensory guidance is always an essential factor. No organized behavior is possible without it.

A simple one-celled organism such as ameba does not have the specialization of parts, sensory and motor, found in higher animals. In obtaining nourishment, for example, the same tissue must act to detect the presence of food, move toward it, ingest and absorb it, and excrete wastes: a single cell must be nose, mouth, legs and alimentary canal. As a result, the ameba has very limited ability to capture food and avoid destruction. Only events in its immediate vicinity, at the present moment, affect its behavior. In a higher animal, specialization of parts permits an extraordinary sensitivity of some cells (the receptors) to environmental events, so that food or danger is detected at a distance, and an equally extraordinary speed and precision of movement in others (the muscles). But specialization means that the receptors and effectors are spatially separated, and there must be some means of communication from one to the other. This is the first function of the nervous system: a *spatial integration* or coordination of parts. The specialization of effectors also means that they must be active in a definite sequence or at just the proper time in order to have their effect; this *temporal integration* is also achieved by the nervous system.

For example: when a mosquito alights on the forehead and begins operations, the skin of the forehead has no adequate means of self-defense. Nerve fibers in the skin transmit the excitation, originating in the skin, to the central nervous system, whence it is relayed to effectors at a distance, the muscles of a hand and arm. The mosquito is swatted. For successful defense, cells at a distance must be called upon, and they must be called upon in the proper order; the muscular contractions involved in a swift, accurate movement must have very precise timing or the hand will reach the wrong place. Another example: the nose of a hungry animal smells food but, though it needs nutrition as much as the rest of the body, it cannot obtain the food directly; what it must do is initiate a complex series of activities in other parts of the body, in definite order. The end effect is that food gets into the stomach and the blood stream delivers to the olfactory cells of the nose (and of course to other parts) the proteins, salts, sugar and so forth that they need in order to keep on serving their function.

The role of sensation is clear, not only in initiating the activity but in continuing to guide it throughout. In swatting a mosquito the muscular contractions to be made depend on the initial position of the hand, so they are determined by the sensory processes which, coming from muscle and joint (p. 90), "tell" us where our limbs are at any moment. Similarly, the predatory animal seeking food must change the course of his movements as the prey changes position. Sensory control is involved in any form of adaptation to the environment, simple or complex, and we must recognize it as a first principle of behavior.

The directness of control, however, and its complexity, vary. Think of the nervous system as a communications network, and of the brain and spinal cord as the switchboard where messages coming in get passed on to the proper destination. The primary function of the switchboard is to connect the sender (sensory) directly with the receiver (motor): a simple routing function. This is all the nervous system does in animals at the lower end of the evolutionary scale. But in higher animals the switchboard has developed, one may say, a mind of its own and is no longer fully controlled by its input.

What can such a statement mean? Figuratively, the phrase "a mind of one's own" means that one does not merely follow instructions, but may go counter to, or act without, instruction. In the present discussion the phrase is applicable both figuratively and literally, and seeing why this is so should help the student to think psychologically. The figurative meaning applies, for the complex network in higher animals does not merely transmit signals from receptor to effector; sometimes the signal is held and not transmitted at all, sometimes it is transmitted only after being changed, and sometimes signals originate in the switchboard itself, arising from the continuing activity that goes on within. The brain does not merely "do what it is told" by sense organs.

The literal meaning also applies, when mind is defined as the higher activities of brain; for the complex communications network of the higher animal has developed so that messages run to and fro within it, as well as into and out of it. Such internal activity, infinitely more complex than these words can suggest, *is* mind; and possession of this internal complexity is what distinguishes higher from lower animal, making the behavior of the higher animal less directly under the control of sensory input.

For example: a barefoot boy steps on a sharp stone and pulls back his foot. We may think of this as simple in-out (reflex) transmission: in from the skin of the foot to spinal cord, out to leg-muscles. But something else may happen also. The boy stops, stands for a moment, then goes back for his sandals. He has "thought" about it, and "decided" that the beach is too rough for barefoot walking. Something has gone on in the closed loops of the switchboard, a complicating factor in the relation of sensory events to the concomitant behavior.

Thus we have two main classes of behavior, roughly speaking, though one shades into the other. One of them is reflexive, one involves a thought process to some degree. In both, sensory guidance is essential; but in the first the guidance is a full control — sensory events by themselves take charge and elicit the complete pattern of response as long as no other event interferes. The second class involves a much more complex process at the level of the association cortex in the cerebrum.

CLASSIFYING BEHAVIOR BY MEANS OF THE S-R FORMULA

We can distinguish the two classes of behavior by means of the *stimulus-response* or *S-R formula*. The formula describes the fundamental pattern of behavior: each movement of the animal is a response to an immediately preceding stimulation, and is predictable from that stimulation. Behavior that fits this formula is reflexive behavior, explained by the operation of through routes from sense to motor organ. This is the first class of behavior. Behavior that does not fit the S-R formula belongs to the second class.

As far as we know at present all the behavior of lower organisms, such as ant, bee, housefly, jellyfish, cockroach and spider, is comprised by the S-R formula and does not justify any reference to mental processes: there is no mind, consciousness, emotion, purpose or perception. Also, in higher animals — even man — there is a great deal of reflexive behavior which is likewise comprised by the formula. To understand the problem of mind it is essential that we first separate lower from higher behavior and not make the mistake of seeing mental processes everywhere. It is possible that mental processes occur in the spider but we have no evidence that this is so (and much evidence that it is not). It is quite possible, even probable, that conditioned reflexes in man involve mental processes: but there is no clear evidence that this is so, and until such evidence is obtained we will be on firmer ground by working with the assumption that the ordinary CR is the operation of a relatively simple through route, even though part of the route goes through the cortex (cf. route *B–C–D–E–Y* in Figure 13).

So we assume that some (lower) behavior is fully controlled by direct S-R connections, and that other (higher) behavior is not. Since neural conduction is rapid, the direct connection means that a response should occur promptly, unless some other process interferes with it, and obviously the response cannot occur when the stimulus is not present. When analyzing some new piece of behavior we apply the S-R formula—that is, we ask whether it meets the above conditions—and if it agrees with the formula we conclude that it can be explained by the more direct S-R pathways, with no need to assume any self-maintained activity within the switchboard. If the behavior does not meet these conditions, even if it still seems simple, the more complex switchboard activity (mediating processes, ideation) is involved and we are dealing with cognitive behavior. Given the same sensory input, cognitive behavior varies from one time to another; what the response will be is not determined by the stimulus alone. This point will be clearer below, where set is discussed.

These are broad classes of behavior, and one merges into the other with no clear dividing line. And to this it should be added that the fundamental principles of neural action are the same at both ends of the continuum, just as the fundamental principles of chemical union are the same in inorganic and organic chemistry. Organic chemistry deals with far more complex molecules than inorganic chemistry, and hence with superficially different phenomena, but the atoms are the same in both cases and obey the same laws. In psychology, we know more about the relatively simpler behavior corresponding to the S-R formula, and what we must find out is how to apply this knowledge to "higher" (i.e., more complex) mechanisms.

First, then, reflexive behavior, more closely controlled by the present sensory input.

SENSE-DOMINATED BEHAVIOR: UCR AND CR

In psychology as in other fields of scientific thought one prefers the simpler explanation rather than the more complex one, as long as the facts permit it. We must prefer the S-R connection to ideation, as involving fewer steps of inference and thus being more nearly factual. But in doing this, we must ask what properties of behavior are implied by S-R connections if the explanation is to be satisfactory. For example, it was suggested in the preceding section that the conditioned reflex fits the S-R formula. When we apply our criteria, however, we find that while some CR's fit, others are doubtful cases.

The essential idea is that behavior is produced by sensory stimulation. This means that the response coincides in time with the stimulus, within a second or so; and that the same response follows the stimulus each time, provided there is no interference from background stimulation and that learning has not changed the S-R connection in the meantime (if, for example, pain followed the response on the preceding occasion, the response might not be repeated: but this would mean that learning had occurred). Neural conduction is fast (ranging from about a meter per second in small fibers to 120 m./sec. in large ones). With a direct S-R connection consequently there can be little delay of response following stimulation, barring interference. We saw in Chapter 4 that connections through the cortex, where mammalian learning occurs, can hardly be direct; but they may be relatively direct. Cell-assemblies, though they make a delay of transmission possible, might also be connected so as to permit prompt and reliable transmission. The essential question concerns the behavioral evidence: is the response predictable from knowing (a) the physiological state of the animal (whether he is hungry or not, for example) and (b) what the environmental stimulation is?

The UCR meets the requirements of the S-R formula completely. It begins and ends with stimulation and it is highly predictable. If stimulation for two incompatible reflexes is given simultaneously, of course, only one of the two can occur. A pinprick in the foot of a new-born infant produces a flexion (withdrawal) response of the leg, mild pressure on the sole of the foot produces an extensor thrust; if both stimuli occur at the same time, only one response can be made: it is usually the flexion. Also, especially in older subjects, the higher centers of the brain are capable of interfering with reflex processes. The reflex response to a pain stimulus in the fingers, for example, is to pull back the hand; but if one is holding a valuable teacup which becomes too hot, the pain reflex is usually inhibited long enough for one to set the cup down before letting go of it. Similarly, one can often inhibit a cough.

Otherwise, however, the UCR is highly constant and predictable. There is a long list of separate reflexes: the pupillary response to increased light in the eye, producing contraction of the pupil; salivary reflexes produced by stimulation of the mouth; sucking reflexes in the baby, produced by stimulation of the lips; sneezing, coughing, eye-watering, produced by irritations of nose, throat or eyeball; reflexes of heart and arteries, regulating the flow of blood to different parts of the body; reflexes of the stomach and gut, controlling digestion and the movement of food through the alimentary canal; a large number of postural reflexes, producing maintenance of orientation of the body in space; and so on. All these UCR's are highly consistent in their action; there is no doubt that the responses are controlled sensorily, and depend on straight-through S-R connections.

Now let us see how these considerations apply to the learned reflex-like responses, the CR's or acquired S-R connections.

In our first example, the CS is a buzzer; the UCS is an electric shock to the foot, delivered two seconds after the buzzer begins. After a few trials, the animal raises his foot off the grid immediately when the buzzer sounds, and continues to do so on almost every trial. We may then think of a fairly direct pathway from certain cells in the ear to the muscles of the leg (Fig. 37).

If the connection does not work every time, we need not reject this conclusion; any path through the nervous system must thread its way through a tangle of other paths, and is exposed to possible interference from other processes, especially inhibition. What we can ask is whether a given stimulus combination *tends* to arouse always the

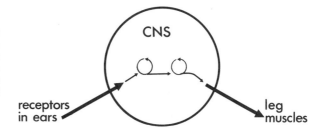

Figure 37. Schematic diagram of an S–R connection via the mammalian cortex: not a straight-through connection, as Thorndike would perhaps have suggested, because the cortex does not seem to work that way, but still relatively direct.

same response (any deviations from this response being referable to interference or fatigue); or whether, on the other hand, the same total pattern of stimulation produces systematically different responses on different occasions.

Thinking not of single stimuli but of the total pattern of stimulation, as in the preceding paragraph, helps us deal with another possible difficulty. Having established a CR to the buzzer, we take the animal out of the apparatus and sound the buzzer again. The CR does not appear. This does not necessarily mean that the response is not controlled by S-R pathways, but shows that a pathway from ear to leg muscles is not enough, by itself, to account for the response. But we can assume that the path is supported by others (Fig. 38) from eye, nose and skin—that is, by sight, smell and touch of the apparatus. The S-R formula may have seemed overly simple to the student at first glance, but when we begin to deal with actual behavior it involves us in complexity enough. But the principle still remains clear. In the apparatus, at least, the experimenter can elicit the CR whenever he wishes by manipulating the animal's environment: thus the behavior is controlled by sensory stimulation.

Another problem is this. In Pavlov's procedure the CS is presented for 15 seconds before the UCS. Early in conditioning the animal secretes saliva as soon as the CS is presented; but then the CR is delayed and eventually is made only in the last two or three seconds before food appears. The same thing happens in conditioned-avoidance experiments. A buzzer is presented for 10 seconds, followed by shock if the rat does not move off the grid that delivers the shock. Early in conditioning the rat jumps as soon as he hears the buzzer; but eventually a time comes when he does not move till 7, 8 or 9 seconds later. Are these delays compatible with the S-R formula,

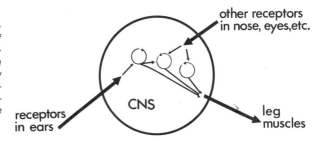

Figure 38. If the primary pathway of Figure 37 is not capable of evoking a response outside the apparatus, this may mean only that in the apparatus it is supported by other pathways, from different receptors. The mechanism is somewhat more complex, but can still be comprised by the S-R formula.

which says that response should be prompt? They are, perhaps, if the response is being inhibited—as Pavlov's results indicate—and if the inhibition itself is under sensory control. (Sense dominance may be inhibitory as well as excitatory.) A more likely hypothesis, however, is that the inhibition is controlled by a mediating process—a combination of cell-assemblies—with limited duration. With these data, no final decision is possible.

A clearer case, however: we change the experimental conditions further, and get a different kind of conditioning. Instead of presenting the CS for the whole delay period of 10 seconds, we present it for 1 second, and give the UCS 9 seconds later. Once again we obtain a 7- or 8-second delay in response. What produces the CR, when it does occur—8 seconds after cessation of the CS? In some manner the brain holds the activity aroused by the CS, instead of transmitting it at once to the effectors. Such behavior is not comprised by the S-R formula, but involves the question of the mediating process, to which we now turn.

THE MEDIATING PROCESS

The typical problem of higher behavior arises when there is a delay between stimulus and response. What bridges the S-R gap? In everyday language, "thinking" does it; the stimulus gives rise to thoughts or ideas that continue during the delay period, and then cause the response. And in fact, we are now talking about the thought process. But the words "thought" and "idea" have been around for a long time and have acquired a number of meanings, so it is hard to use them precisely though they are still useful in a general sense.

Mediating process has a more exact and more limited meaning. It may be defined as an activity of the brain which can hold the excitation delivered by a sensory event after this event has ceased, and thus permit a stimulus to have its effect at some later time. To "mediate" means to form a connecting link, and the simplest function of the mediating process is to connect S with R. Theoretically, however, a mediating process can also be excited by other mediating processes as well as its own sensory event, and when a number of mediating processes interact in this way—being excited by each other as well as by sensory events—the result is thinking; so, theoretically, a mediating process might also be defined as the unit or elementary component of thought, replacing the term "idea."*

---

*The careful reader may observe that the discussion deals with mediating *processes* only, not with mediating *responses*. A distinction is maintained in this text between responses, as observable behavior, and unobserved processes in the CNS, on the ground that we must not use a terminology that confuses facts with hypotheses (p. 13). Some other writers are not as persnickety, but when they say "mediating response" they are apt to mean an actual muscular contraction—one that bridges a gap in time between a stimulus and a response. Instead of a closed path in the brain itself, the closed path here is from brain to muscle (causing contraction), back from muscle to brain (sensations of muscle contraction), and so on. This kind of mediating or bridging certainly occurs and is important in behavior (cf. "feedback," p. 90), but "mediating response" is avoided in the present text because of the inevitable risk of confusion with "mediating process" as a purely intracranial (i.e., ideational) mechanism.

We do not know, certainly, what a mediating process is, as a physiological mechanism. By definition, however, it can hold an excitation for some short period of time, and the only way in which this can happen according to present knowledge is by means of the closed loops or reverberatory circuits discussed in Chapter 4 (Figs. 31, 32, 33). One of these circuits consisting of two or three neurons could not hold an excitation long enough to correspond to an idea, because with steady firing fatigue would build up in 10 or 20 msec., but a number of them combined in a cell-assembly (p. 69) might do so. Still longer holding could occur with several cell-assemblies, assembly A exciting assembly B, which excites C, which excites A again. In this text therefore it will be assumed that a mediating process consists of one or more cell-assemblies. The student must remember that the *cell-assembly idea is a hypothesis* of how a mediating process works. We know from behavior that mediating processes exist; that they consist of cell-assemblies is theory, which may turn out to be wrong, or only partly right (that is, there may be some other mechanism of holding in addition to cell-assemblies). Consequently, we can speak of mediating processes without committing ourselves to any definite idea of how they may work; when we speak of cell-assemblies we are talking about a specific theoretical construct.

Now let us look at the behavioral evidence. Figure 39 might represent the situation in which a schoolboy has been told to add some numbers, but before he has been told *what* numbers, so he cannot make the response yet. Five seconds later the teacher says, "Four, seven." The pupil at once says, "Eleven." It is a simple task, but how did he do it? He could not make the response to the first stimulation ("Please add") alone, nor to the second ("Four, seven") alone; the response can only be made to both, so the effect of the first must have been *held* for five seconds until it could be combined with the second, and Figure 39 shows how a reverberatory path could hold it (though the path would have to be complex—probably two or more cell-assemblies—to hold for as long as five seconds). This kind of

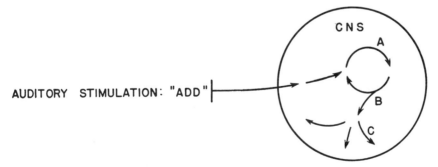

Figure 39. *Diagrammatic representation of a reverberatory pathway: incoming stimulation excites* A, *which excites* B, *which re-excites* A *and so on. It is suggested that this is the mechanism of holding or trace activity, in principle.* C *represents other paths which may be excited by collateral fibers (branches) from* B, *and which might be excited each time the excitation travels round the closed pathway.*

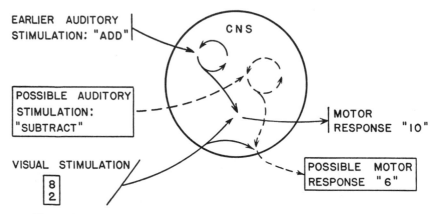

Figure 40. *Diagram of a possible mechanism of a set to add. The excitation from the prior stimulus, "add," is held in a reverberatory loop. The second stimulus (8, 2) is connected with two motor paths, and can evoke "ten" or "six"; but the reverberatory activity supports only one of these, and the response is "ten." If the prior stimulation had been "subtract," a different reverberatory circuit would have been active and would have determined the response "six." Needless to say, this diagram is entirely schematic (any resemblance to neural tissue is entirely coincidental).*

behavior, thoroughly familiar to everyone, is the simplest and clearest evidence of the existence of mediating processes. The behavior takes us beyond what is comprised by the S-R formula. *The capacity for holding an excitation in the central nervous system is the primary mark of the higher animal.*

The student is reminded that the simple closed paths of Figure 39 and the figures that follow in the present chapter are conventional representations, deliberately schematized so they will not be taken for reality (cf. Figs. 32 and 33). The closed-loop diagram of one or two arrows is a symbol to represent a self-re-exciting system, just as the chemist has his conventional symbols for the improbable atomic structures he talks about, and the physicist has his to represent battery, condenser or ground in electrical circuits. In other words the loops of Figures 39 and 40 are not pictures, but a kind of pictorial shorthand.

SET AND DELAYED RESPONSE

Let us take as an experimental subject an intelligent student for whom simple arithmetical operations are automatic. We seat him before a screen, tell him that pairs of numbers will be flashed on it, and instruct him to give their sums as quickly as possible. We present then a series which is made up of combinations such as $\frac{8}{2}$. To each we obtain a correct and rapid response. A given stimulus pattern always produces the same response, and the reaction time is short, of the order of a second. This is a highly practiced form of behavior; no thought appears to be involved, and we might conclude that the behavior meets the criteria of the S-R formula: promptness and reliability.

But the response depends on the subject's being *set* to add. The 8, 2 combination produces the response "ten" every time—until we say to the subject, "Now subtract" (or divide, or multiply); whereupon the same stimulus pattern produces, with equal speed and reliability, the response "six" (or "four" or "sixteen"). It is therefore clear that the response is not determined by the present stimulus pattern (8, 2) alone, so the behavior does not fit the S-R formula. *The response is determined by two stimulations, one of which has to be held and has its effect only after an interval.* The highly schematic diagram of Figure 40 illustrates how this might occur, developing further the idea presented in Figure 39. (It shows also, in the broken lines, what would have happened if the earlier stimulation had been different and had produced a set to subtract.)

The paradigm (the clear representative example) of set is as follows: Stimulus *A* is applied to the organism, and then a different stimulus *B; B* elicits promptly a response *C,* but only if *A* was presented first. *A* sets the switchboard, or prepares it, so *B* can have its effect.

The *delayed-response* procedure provides us with another example of set, in the behavior of the monkey. (The preceding discussion has referred several times to a delay in responding, but the term "delayed response" refers technically to W. S. Hunter's method, about to be described.) The monkey is allowed to see food put in one of two containers out of reach. A screen is then put between him and the containers, so that he cannot later find the food simply by keeping his eyes fixed on the correct container. After a delay of five seconds, ten seconds, or more, the screen is removed, the two containers are brought within reach, and the monkey is permitted to choose between them.

The monkey is quite capable of success with this task, in a way that provides some evidence of the presence of mediating processes. In one experiment, particularly, the evidence was decisive (O. L. Tinklepaugh). In it the experimenter sometimes used lettuce, which the monkeys liked, as the food reward, and sometimes banana, which they liked better. When the monkey saw lettuce put into one of the containers, chose the right one, and found lettuce in it, he took it and ate it. But when he saw banana put in, and then found lettuce—the experimenter having deceitfully made a change during the delay period—the monkey did not take the lettuce, but showed surprise and searched in and around the container (apparently looking for the missing piece of banana). On occasion the animal simply had a temper tantrum instead.

Here is our holding process again. Seeing banana put into the food container had some lasting effect, as shown by the conflict that appeared when lettuce was found instead. We know that when the monkey found lettuce without having an expectancy of banana he reached for it and ate it. This is consistent with a direct sensory control of response. But the temper tantrum, and failure to take the lettuce, is not: this behavior must be *jointly* determined by a mediating process resulting from the earlier stimulation and the effects of the present stimulation.

The problem of holding does not always arise when there appears to be a delay of response. A lower animal may succeed in delayed-response tests by making a postural adjustment immediately and maintaining it. For example, when the animal sees food put into the right-hand container he may move over to that side of the cage and wait there until the screen is raised; then he simply chooses the near container. Monkeys and chimpanzees do not solve the problem in this way; they usually move around during the delay period. It would be possible, if we did not have any other data, to suppose that the monkey might tense the muscles of the hand nearest the food and keep them tensed while moving around; when the screen is raised and he turns back to face the containers, he could then choose the correct one by using the hand whose muscles were contracted.

However, there is usually no sign at all of the monkey's "remembering" the location of the food in this way; and the lettuce-versus-banana experiment has special importance in ruling out such an explanation as far as the higher animal is concerned.

SELECTIVITY IN BEHAVIOR: ATTENTION RELATED TO SET

It was said above that the distinguishing mark of the higher animal is the capacity to hold an excitation for some time before it has its effect on behavior. The mediating process that does the holding is apt to introduce selectivity into the behavior, in either or both of two ways, in the form of *attention* and *set.* Accordingly, these also are marks of higher behavior. Attention is selectivity in what is responded to, or sensory selectivity; set is a selectivity of response, motor rather than sensory. Very often, however, attention and set go together.

Notice that the selectivity is constant at any one time, but is easily changed from one time to another. This has already been illustrated by the set to add. Presented with a visual stimulation of a pair of numbers, the subject *consistently* produces one response to each pair as long as that set lasts; when the set is changed to subtraction, a different response to each pair is made—again consistently. It is characteristic of such sets that they change readily, so with the same stimulation the response varies systematically from one time to another. With the visual stimulus of 6, 3 we do not get a random variation of "nine" and "three," but a response that is highly predictable, provided we know what the subject's set is. Thus the mark of higher behavior is not mere selectivity of response: the lower animal is also selective, but he is always selective in the same way, because he is built to behave in that way only. The higher animal is capable of responding in many different ways, and does so at different times, but at any one time he tends to respond in one of those ways only: a *changeable selectivity* of response.

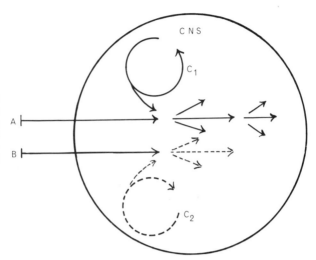

Figure 41. Schematic diagram of a mechanism of attention in which a central process, C_1, supports one sensory input (from A), C_2 supports another (B). Event A will be responded to if C_1 is active, event B if C_2 is active.

Attention is closely related to set. In Figure 40 is suggested a way in which a mediating process would support one response and not another. Figure 41 shows how the mediating process would support the effects of one *sensory* input and not another. A and B are two stimulus events whose effects are transmitted to the higher levels of the CNS. C_1 is a mediating process which supports the input from A—that is, it excites the same central paths that A does—so that the excitation from A is transmitted farther. A is, as we say, "noticed" by the subject, and is likely to affect behavior. C_2 is a mediating process that would similarly support B, but it is not active, and so it is much less likely that B will have any effect. It is not noticed. This would be true especially if C_1 tends to inhibit C_2 and vice versa: A or B will be attended to, but not both. *Attention* may then be defined as an activity of mediating processes (C_1 or C_2) which supports the central effects of a sensory event, usually with the implication that other sensory events are shut out.

If the student will now compare Figures 40 and 41 he will see that we are talking about a process very similar to that of set. The two terms really have almost identical meanings, but "set" is usually applied when the process is thought of as a selection of one response rather than another, and also when one can point to a specific preceding experience which excites the mediating process that does the selecting, or "sets" the animal. The similarity of the two is such that we sometimes speak of a "perceptual set," a set to perceive one way rather than another, and this obviously is a form of attention as defined above.

TEMPORAL INTEGRATION IN BEHAVIOR

Next we can see how the selectivity (of set and attention) appears when there is an extended series of responses, rather than the single responses we have talked about so far. This is the question of how the links are connected in a chain of responses, or how one step in behavior leads to the next—in general, the question of how it is that man or animal in responding to his environment appears to be doing one thing in a coordinated series of movements, rather than responding randomly, now to this stimulation, now to that, in a disorganized way.

For the lower animal, as we have seen, the whole process is sensorily controlled, and the organization or integration of individual movements into a unified, directed whole is determined by the animal's environment, for any given physiological state of the animal. (A hungry animal, or a sexually active one, will respond differently from the way he would at other times, but this is because the low level of nutrient chemical substances in the blood stream, or the presence of sex hormones, changes the way in which certain synapses in the CNS function. The S-R paths are changed, but they are still S-R connections and the animal is still under sensory control.) Each leg movement of the animal, for example, produces a further stimulation, which leads to the next movement. This may be by feedback from the muscles of the leg (sensation of movement); by changing the animal's position in space, which changes visual or tactual input; by sensation from the foot as it meets the ground; and so on. Each of these new stimulations can give rise to a new response, and the continuity of the behavior derives from the situation in which the animal finds himself.

Feedback stimulation is equally important for the higher animal, though here mediating processes take part in producing the directedness and unity of behavior, sharing the control with sensory input moment by moment. Figure 42 shows how one may think of the shared control. C_1, C_2 and C_3 represent the combined central processes of the brain at three successive moments in time. X and Y represent the central processes that might have occurred, but did not. S is sensory input. S_1, occurring at the same time as C_1, tends to excite

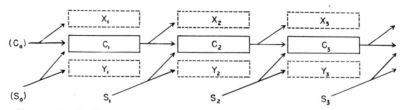

Figure 42. *To illustrate the selective process in thinking. C, central processes (simultaneously active assemblies) at three successive moments in time; S, corresponding sensory inputs; X and Y, subliminally excited assemblies. X receives excitation from one source (central) only, Y from one source (sensory) only, so these have lower probabilities of being active. C consists of the assemblies which receive excitations from both sources and which consequently are active. Thus C_1 selectively determines which of the assemblies will be active, from among those that S_1 tends to excite; and contrariwise. This selective central influence is* attention, *represented by the horizontal arrows of the diagram.*

the cell-assemblies of the C_2 group and also the Y_2 group (that is, it delivers facilitation to both). C_1 tends to excite C_2 and X_2. The one that is excited, therefore, is C_2, which receives the summed facilitations of two sources, C and S; X_2 and Y_2 are not excited, each receiving facilitation from one source only, without summation.

There will be motor outflow — facilitation delivered to some part of the motor system — from these central activities, though it is not shown in Figure 42. Thus behavior is determined by C_1, C_2 and C_3, and since each of these groups of activities is controlled by (a) sensory input and (b) facilitation from the preceding central activity, the behavior is under the joint control of sensory and central processes. Both the environment in which the animal or human subject is, and the continuity of central processes — that is, thought processes — make for continuity and direction in what the subject does.

This describes a single unified train of thought, which we may perhaps think of as the normal state of affairs. However, it is possible that the facilitation from C_1 on X_2 may sometimes be strong enough so that X_2 is activated. It is also possible that when this happens there may be enough summation among the cell-assemblies making up X that it can excite another group, and this one still another — and so on. That is, there might be a separate X series of activities that starts and continues at the same time as the C series, in parallel with it, provided that the cell-assemblies in question did not cause interference with one another. This means that there would be two trains of thought at the same time, one of them in control of behavior. Something of the sort seems actually to occur in man. Sometimes when one is reading aloud, from a not-too-interesting book and for an extended period of time, one finds that though one has kept on reading intelligibly (since the audience has not complained) one's thoughts have wandered. Reading requires mediating processes, and so does a daydream, so there must have been two separate series at the same time. Again, lecturers commonly have the experience while speaking one sentence of thinking about the next one, or wondering whether an illustration is clear, or sometimes even thinking that the lecture is rather dull. Speech is not interrupted while all this is going on, and it seems definite that two independent thought processes must be running in parallel.

Speech is the most interesting example of temporal integration in behavior, and we will return to it in Chapter 13.

SENSORY DOMINANCE AND VOLUNTARY BEHAVIOR

"Volition" represents an old and troublesome philosophic problem, chiefly because the nature of the underlying *psychological* issue was not clearly formulated. The problem does not arise with the behavior of lower organisms such as the ant, in which there is no clear departure from direct sensory control; nor does it arise when the behavior of higher organisms remains under such control. It does arise at other times, and it is, in short, the problem of understanding how mediating processes are involved in a response.

In an earlier day the nervous system was thought of as simply a sensory-motor system. As we have seen, this would imply a direct sensory control; so whenever the control was absent, the behavior became a mysterious business. "Volition" or "will" was a power of some separate agency, which somehow could be exerted on the brain or on the motor system to make it behave in a way in which it would not otherwise behave. "Will power" thus was something that one might have a lot of, or little. "Free will" also might seem to mean that voluntary behavior was not subject to scientific law, not determined by cause and effect.

But all this, in a much earlier day, was related to a very crude idea of how the bodily machinery operates, and especially the machinery of the brain. If the higher animal responds in two different ways to the same total pattern of stimulation, it is because the activity of the central switchboard is not the same on the two occasions, but "set" differently; as a result the sensory input is routed to different muscles. It is evident that we are as yet far from understanding these problems in detail, and must not be dogmatic about their eventual explanation in terms of brain processes; but at the same time there is no fundamental philosophic problem about voluntary behavior as such.

Consequently, in modern psychology the terms "volition" and "will" or "will power" have disappeared. "Voluntary behavior" still has a certain usefulness, as a rough classification; it is, in short, behavior that cannot be predicted from a knowledge of the present environmental stimulation alone because a systematic variability is introduced by mediating processes.

SUMMARY

All behavior is under sensory guidance, through the switchboard of the central nervous system. Reflexive or sense-dominated behavior is controlled by direct connections; higher behavior involves mediating processes (roughly, ideas or images). The mediating process is an activity of the switchboard itself, not a straight-through transmission. It can hold a sensory input for an appreciable time before transmitting it; it may also be excited by other central activities (i.e., other mediating processes), instead of by sensory input.

Set is like closing one switch and opening others before current is applied to the line. It prepares the switchboard for a particular kind of output. Attention is closely related: it prepares the switchboard for receiving a particular class of input. Both involve mediating processes, and a holding of the prior stimulation that prepares the switchboard.

The chief problem is to understand how mediating processes can hold an excitation. An available theory (which may or may not be right) proposes that this is done mainly by complex closed circuits (cell-assemblies: Chapter 4) in which excitation can travel round and round without dying out immediately. "Volition" appears to refer to the selective effect of mediating processes on behavior.

Guide to Study

For review, the student might see whether he can produce schematic diagrams representing what happens in holding, set, and attention. He might find, for example, that the delayed-response procedure, involving holding followed by a later stimulation (when the screen is raised so the animal can make his choice between the two containers), calls for the same diagram as that of set—and consequently he would be able to say why the delayed response is a special case of set, or set another form of delayed response. He should understand how the holding process frees the subject from immediate sensory dominance, and how "free will" essentially means the absence of such dominance. He should see what problem is raised by the CR which occurs only after the CS has lasted for 5 seconds, as distinct from a CR that appears at once, and how a delayed CR (5 sec. after the CS has stopped) raises the problem of holding or mediating process. He should be clear about the meaning of feedback and be able to give examples of his own, and he should be able to explain how feedback contributes to organized sequences of behavior.

NOTES AND REFERENCES

The hope in this chapter is to get the student to think of the S-R formula as a means of classifying behavior, and of S-R connections and thought as allies—not opposed to each other, but complementary—in the control of behavior. This becomes apparent as soon as one tries to "physiologize" about higher animals' behavior, and ask how the CNS does its job. But psychologists have been reluctant to speculate about the mechanisms of thought and there is not much of a literature on the topic. Most of the current discussion takes the the point of view of a *computer simulation* of thought (see, e.g., Miller, Galanter and Pribram, and Reitman, below).

SET AND DELAYED RESPONSE

Gibson, J. J.: A critical review of the concept of set in contemporary experimental psychology. *Psychological Bulletin,* 1941, 38, 781–817. A good review of the phenomenon, but treats it as a mystery (which it was in 1940): no explanation attempted.
Hunter, W. S.: The delayed reaction in animals and children. *Behavior Monographs,* 1913, 2, No. 6. Report of the original experiments.
Hunter, W. S.: The delayed reaction in a child. *Psychological* Review, 1917, 24, 75–87. Report of an improved procedure, still in use.
Leeper, R. W.: Cognitive processes. In S. S. Stevens (Ed.): *Handbook of Experimental Psychology,* Wiley, 1951. Still a valuable review despite its date. Includes a report of Hunter's and Tinklepaugh's experiments.
Tinklepaugh, O. L.: An experimental study of representative factors in monkeys. *Journal of Comparative Psychology,* 1928, 8, 197–236.

MECHANICS OF THOUGHT

Hebb, D. O.: The American Revolution. *American Psychologist,* 1960, 15, 735–745.
Hebb, D. O.: The semiautonomous process, its nature and nurture. *American Psychologist,* 1963, 18, 16–27.
Meehl, P. E., and MacCorquodale, K.: Some methodological comments concerning expectancy theory. *Psychological Review,* 1951, 58, 230–233.
Miller, G. A., Galanter, E., and Pribram, K. H.: *Plans and the Structure of Behavior,* Holt, 1960. A

readable, interesting and stimulating account of thought in terms of the functioning of a computer.

Osgood, C. E.: *Method and Theory in Experimental Psychology,* Oxford University Press, 1953. This book, like the papers by Meehl and MacCorquodale and Hebb (1960), argues that S-R theory and cognitive theory are complementary.

Reitman, W. R.: *Cognition and Thought,* Wiley, 1965. Also concerned with computer simulation of thought, like Miller, Galanter and Pribram (above), but somewhat more technical. It is concerned with simulation but is still primarily directed at the psychological problem.

6

learning, memory and forgetting

Any student knows that learning a formula or a definition is only part of the job—he must also remember it, correctly, till he has passed the examination. In the present chapter we will consider memory and forgetting: what it is that makes the results of learning persist or not persist, and how error may be introduced into memories.

Some learning is used at once and not again. You ask, "What time is it?" and need remember the answer only long enough to set your watch. This is known as *short-term memory.* If instead you are a character in a detective story and need to fix an alibi, you will have to remember the answer until after you have been cross-examined in court and set free: this we call *long-term memory.* In these two situations the *acquisition* of the learning is about the same—a momentary stimulation and one-trial learning—but the *retention* differs. A question to be discussed, then, is what determines retention.

"Memory" is a slippery term. Primarily, it means the retention of the effects of learning of any kind (which is what it means in the heading of this chapter), and this is the way it is generally used in psychological discussions. But it has a popular meaning too, which causes trouble. The popular meaning includes only what the human subject can recall and tell you about, or have a "memory image" of (p. 242). The two meanings are very different. Two years ago, let us say, you took a course on Patagonia and learned the names of all the principal villages, but today you cannot recall one; have you forgotten completely? It would be easy to show that forgetting is not complete—that memory is not at a zero level. There might be perhaps 50 per cent retention, as you would see if, when you relearned the names, you needed only half as many trials to learn as you needed the first time (the *savings method* of measuring retention). Or, in another example, ask an experienced typist what finger she uses to type the letter *s.* There is a fairly good chance that she cannot tell you, especially if you make her keep her fingers still; does this mean that she has no "memory" of where *s* is on the keyboard? Of course not. If you sit her down at the typewriter and ask her to type "Mississippi" without looking, she does so at once, without a mistake. It is easy to deal with this sort of thing in terms of "acquisition" and "retention"; in the first or Patagonian case, we can speak of 50 per cent retention; in the second (Mississippi) we say that the typist's early training established two modes of response, verbal and manual, that there is some loss of the verbal response, but that the retention of the manual response is perfect.

MEMORY: A CHEMICAL MOLECULE?

Recent work on a chemical factor in learning and retention has led some psychologists, neurologists and biochemists to talk as if memory might be a chemical substance that could be given by mouth or by injection. The experimental work on which this idea is based is valuable, but this interpretation must not be taken seriously.

The chemical factor is RNA (ribonucleic acid) or some closely related substance. RNA is a macromolecule—a big organic molecule—found inside the neuron and elsewhere. It is thought that when learning takes place the RNA inside a neuron is modified to correspond to its changed pattern of activity. The modified RNA is what maintains that pattern. As long as it is present, therefore, the learning is retained: so the changed RNA is called *memory.* Not only that: this "memory" may be extracted from one animal and fed to another, or injected, and then the second animal will have the first animal's memory and be able to do what the trained animal learned to do, but without having done the learning.

This sounds fine till we ask how the RNA (or other related chemical) sets up the neural pathway that determines response. To have an animal make a particular reaction to a stimulus means that the sensory excitation must be conducted to particular muscles, in a particular order. To set up such a pathway, the RNA that is given to the second animal must be carried by the blood stream to the particular neurons making up the pathway and affect them only. No one has explained how this might happen. It is not inconceivable, for neurons in different parts of the nervous system may be chemically distinct and the RNA that originated in a particular structure in one animal might be absorbed only by the corresponding structure in a second animal of the same species: possible, but unlikely.

It is more likely, on our present knowledge, that the effect of RNA on the second animal is more general. Instead of acting only on specific neurons and synapses it may have the effect of speeding up learning: *any* learning.

This is consistent with the results reported by J. V. McConnell with planarians (flatworms), the best-known and best-established results in this field. A planarian is conditioned with light as CS and electric shock as UCS, the CR being a twisting movement by the planarian. When one animal is thus conditioned it is minced up and fed to another. The second animal is then conditioned in the same way, and the conditioning takes fewer trials than conditioning the first animal did. This is the result that has led some investigators to think of memory as a chemical that can be taken from one animal and given to another. But there is no evidence here that a specific reaction has been transferred. (The evidence is consistent with the simpler — but still very significant — conclusion, that a chemical substance to be found in a trained animal may accelerate the training of another animal.)

Fundamentally, learning is a modification of transmission routes in the nervous system, and memory is the retention of that modification. Conceivably, injection of RNA into the system might set up the equivalent of a memory (though this seems most unlikely), but even so it would be unjustified to speak of the macromolecule itself as a memory that can be taken from one animal and given to another.

SHORT-TERM AND LONG-TERM MEMORY

Much of man's learning is transient and unstable. Human beings are continuously engaged in perceiving, during waking hours, and the result is a continuous acquisition of knowledge; but most of this turns out to have no significance and is rapidly forgotten. Some of it, however, does last. What makes the difference between short-term and long-term memory?

On our present knowledge it seems that short-term memory may be a reverberation in the closed loops of the cell-assembly and between cell-assemblies while long-term memory is more structural, a lasting change of synaptic connections. Synaptic change would take time, presumably, and might be possible only if the reverberation of short-term memory lasted long enough to give it a good start. All this is theory, but it suggests that the two kinds of memory work together. The longer the reverberation of short-term memory lasts, the more likely it is that a long-term memory will be established. Thus exciting events, causing the arousal that is discussed in Chapter 10, would be remembered because arousal would make for longer-lasting reverberation.

A simple experiment will illustrate the two kinds of memory. College students were asked to repeat series of nine digits (the same nine digits each time, but in different orders, read aloud one digit per second). An example is 951437826. Nine digits is too many to be reliably repeated after hearing them once, so only a few subjects succeeded with the first series. But the experiment had a special feature. Unknown to the subjects, every third series was the same. The question was, would this series be learned because of being repeated? Would hearing it on the third trial leave behind some effect that would be added to when the same series was repeated on the sixth trial, and so on, or would the intervening series prevent this? The results are shown in Figure 43. There was steady improvement with the repeated series, not with the others.

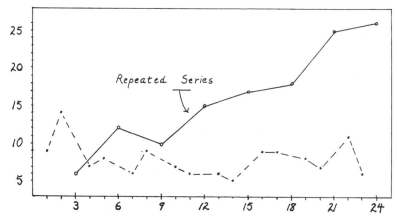

Figure 43. *Number of subjects (out of 40) successfully repeating nine digits on each of 24 trials. Points on the broken line, number of successes with nonrepeated series; points on the solid line, number of successes with the repeated series. (From J. F. Delafresnaye,* Brain Mechanisms and Learning, *Oxford.)*

The short-term memory for nine digits is very brief. There is no hope of succeeding with the task unless one listens carefully to the series as it is read and then repeats it *at once.* What this experiment shows is that listening to a set of digits does more than set up a short-term memory. There is also some trace of another kind, some beginning of a long-term structural change that is left behind. The memory of one series seems completely wiped out by hearing the following one and there is no interference from one on the next (that is, there seems to be no tendency to repeat some of the digits in the order given in the preceding series); but it is only the short-term memory that is wiped out completely. It leaves behind it a trace that is added to on every third trial and forms the basis of a long-term memory. The two mechanisms seem different in kind, but they collaborate closely with each other.

SYNAPTIC CHANGE AND CONSOLIDATION IN LONG-TERM MEMORY

In long-term memory there is another factor. Once begun, presumably by the short-term mechanism just described, the long-term memory trace needs to be left relatively undisturbed for some time if it is to become firmly established. The necessary synaptic changes must be allowed to mature, as it were, much as raw whiskey must be left to sit awhile in its oaken barrels if it is to become fit to drink. Whiskey takes a year or more; learning needs something between 15 minutes and an hour or thereabouts. The maturing process is known as *consolidation,* and its duration is the *consolidation period.*

The existence of the consolidation period (or the need of consolidation) is shown by failure of retention when brain function is disrupted soon after learning is—apparently—complete. *Retrograde amnesia* is the failure of retention that follows concussion, when a blow on the head has caused partial or complete loss of consciousness. Suppose a car driver on his own side of the highway is hit by a car from the other direction—one that has gone out of control and has crossed into his lane. He is knocked out briefly, then gradually comes back to full consciousness. It is not surprising that his memory is impaired for events following the accident, his brain being more or less addled for the time being, but it is very significant that he cannot remember what happened just *before* the accident, when his brain was functioning normally. If he had not been hit on the head—if at the last instant the other car had managed to avoid him—he certainly would have remembered seeing the car headed straight for him: the learning would have been retained. So the concussion wiped out learning that we know must have occurred. But it does not wipe out all learning, only recent learning; old, well-established memories are unimpaired, and the longer the interval between acquisition and concussion, the less the impairment. In that interval, therefore, something is happening to make memory less vulnerable to disruption. The something is what is known as consolidation.

Electroconvulsive shock (or electroconvulsive therapy: ECS or ECT in abbreviation) has the same effect on consolidation, and can be used experimentally, with man or animal. The human experiments are possible because the shock—a current passed through the head causing a brief convulsion—is frequently used for the psychiatric treatment of depression. It is very effective and in general appears to have no lasting bad effects. If a patient is scheduled to have the treatment at 11:00 A.M., he can be asked to learn something just before it—for example, at 10:30 he can be given ten nonsense syllables to memorize. Next day at 10:30 A.M., when he has fully recovered from the immediate state of confusion following the shock, he is tested to see how many of the syllables he can repeat. If the shock was given right after the learning, we can expect to find that he cannot repeat any of them. Even the savings method shows no retention in such experiments, the patient usually taking as many trials to learn the list of syllables the second time as the first.

To make sure that the forgetting is not due merely to the passage of time, we can make a control test (p. 147) on some other day when he is not having shock, using another list of ten syllables of about the same difficulty. Now we might find the patient able to repeat three, four, or five syllables after 24 hours, and a considerable saving on relearning the list. The loss following shock, therefore, is more than normal forgetting can account for.

This is the means by which consolidation has been studied formally, and it shows that the longer the shock is delayed, following learning, the less the disruptive effect on retention. But informally the effect of electroshock on retention is even clearer; for the patient not only forgets nonsense syllables, he also forgets entering the treatment room, having the electrodes placed on his temples, and receiving the shock itself (fortunately, for it is usually necessary to give the patient a series of shocks once or twice a week).

There is a small number of unfortunate patients who have one more thing to tell us about consolidation. Inside the tip of the temporal lobe is a small structure called the *hippocampus*. For the treatment of severe cases of epilepsy it has sometimes been necessary to remove the hippocampus on both sides, together with some of the overlying cortex. The patient then loses the power of consolidating learning (B. Milner). Things learned before the operation are not forgotten, and short-term or immediate memory, lasting one or two minutes but not much longer, is not impaired; but there is a practically complete loss of new long-term memories. It therefore seems that the hippocampus, by itself or with neighboring cortex, plays a large part in the consolidation process. It probably does not control the whole process by itself; if it did, we would expect to find a comparable failure of retention in lower mammals with injury to the hippocampus, and this is not observed although there are some defects.

What consolidation is we do not know, nor how the hippocampus affects it. The results with lower animals, however, suggest a relation to reinforcement. The animal experiments used primary reinforcement, whereas the human (clinical) observations concerned cognitive learning with no primary reward. One possibility therefore is that the hippocampus is needed for unreinforced cognitive learning, to supply some sort of substitute for primary reinforcement.

Both consolidation and reinforcement act *after* the response being learned has been made. May reinforcement have its effect by promoting consolidation? There has been great argument in the past about reinforcement and how it has its effects. One view, called *reinforcement theory,* is that reinforcement is needed for all learning, and that it has its effect by somehow strengthening S-R connections. This was Thorndike's early proposal. Pavlov on the other hand thought that the food he gave his dog served only to make CS and UCR occur at the same time, in temporal contiguity. Occurring together was enough to form the association. This is *contiguity theory.* But both views may contain some truth. We have seen how readily latent learning takes place, and this without apparent reinforcement. Reinforcement in Thorndike's sense, at least, is not necessary. On the other hand there is learning that is hard to understand except in terms of reinforcement and a strengthening of connections. Skinner's shaping up (p. 28) is an example. How could the strengthening result? A possibility is that some gland such as the adrenal cortex may, on the termination of hunger or pain, release a hormone into the blood stream that is picked up only by synapses that have just been active—thus strengthening the response that has just been made, the one that was followed by reward. The adrenal cortex is active in stressful conditions and may reasonably be suspected of such a role. Cognitive learning, without stress or primary reinforcement, may need help from the hippocampus to make the gland secrete the same hormone. When a mediating process causes a response whose feedback corresponds to that mediating process—when expectation is confirmed, when the intention to make a skilled movement is, *mirabile dictu,* followed by just that movement—it may be the hippocampus that throws the adrenal cortex into action to cement the synapses that did it. However (since we are now using Latin tags), *caveat emptor*: let the student beware, this is all gross speculation, except that the parallel between reinforcement and consolidation seems important and should be noted.

FORGETTING: INTERFERENCE AND DISUSE

"Forgetting" here refers to normal forgetting, by a subject whose hippocampus is intact and whose brain is otherwise in a presumably normal state. Also, it means that no special training has been given to cause a failure of response. When special training is used we speak of the *extinction* of response, which is dealt with later (p. 104).

Spontaneous forgetting, then, or failure of retention in the ordinary course of living, is what we are now concerned with. It may be due to *interference* from other learning or to *disuse*—or to both. Interference may be *proactive* or *retroactive*. Proactive interference (also called *proactive inhibition)* is an impairment of retention of one thing, *B,* because of having learned something else, *A,* beforehand. Retroactive interference (also, and classically, known as *retroactive inhibition)* is an impairment of retention of *A* because of learning *B* subsequently. Figure 44 shows how the two are demonstrated experimentally. The impairment is greatest when *A* and *B* contain similar but not identical material.

Disuse refers to the possibility that the synaptic changes of learning, even though consolidation has occurred, tend to regress and become less effective as time passes if the synaptic connections are not activated. Disuse is the common-sense popular notion of forgetting: if you don't practice your basketball shots or your French verbs you will forget them, just from lack of practice. There is some truth in this notion, but there is also much forgetting in which disuse plays little part and which must be attributed to retroactive interference instead.

It seems likely that proactive interference and retroactive interference must have their effects in different ways. What proactive interference seems to do is make later learning intrinsically less sta-

GROUPS	PROCEDURES		
	Proactive interference with learning		
Experimental	Learn A	Learn B	Tested with B
Control	-------	Learn B	Tested with B
	Retroactive interference with learning		
Experimental	Learn A	Learn B	Tested with A
Control	Learn A	-------	Tested with A

Figure 44. The order of procedures in demonstrating proactive and retroactive interference. In each case the experimental group when tested shows an impairment of retention compared to the control group.

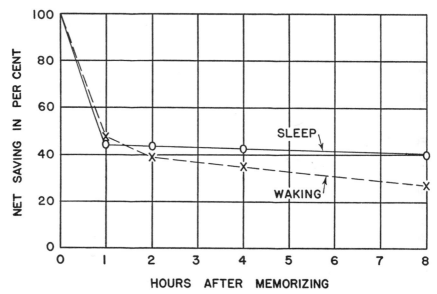

Figure 45. *Retroactive inhibition is shown in the difference between retention when the interval between learning and a later test is spent in sleep, and that when it is spent awake. (After van Ormer, adapted from R. S. Woodworth and H. Schlosberg,* Experimental Psychology, *Holt.)*

ble, while retroactive interference exerts a positive suppression.* Also, retroactive interference may be an impairment of consolidation, for the second learning has the greatest effect on the prior learning when it occurs immediately afterward.

Retroactive interference appears also to be the most powerful of the three mechanisms discussed here (i.e., more powerful than proactive interference or disuse). Its existence has been thoroughly established in subjects as different as cockroach and man. The evidence indicates that *any* activity, between learning and testing, must cause some learning and hence some interference with the retention of the prior learning. Now it is impossible for a normal waking subject to do nothing — to perceive and remember nothing of what is happening around him — just because he is told to do so. Therefore the control group we need would also have some retroactive interference from such incidental learning. To try to get a control group that learns *nothing* during the waiting interval, experiments have been done in which the subject sleeps during the interval. With the same subject, the retention of nonsense syllables can be measured when the syllables were learned just before going to bed, and when they were learned before a normal day's activity. The results of one such experiment are shown in Figure 45. In the first hour the subject lost as much

---

*The difference is a little like the difference between the fighter who gives his opponent a sedative before the fight, and one who knocks his opponent out; or between greasing the steps before the debt-collector calls so he falls down stairs all by himself, and hitting him over the head after he arrives.

in the sleeping condition as in the normal-activity condition, but of course one cannot go to sleep instantly, so there would be retroactive interference at first; after the first hour in the sleeping condition, when the subject actually was asleep, there was practically no forgetting.

The existence of retroactive interference is firmly established. However, there is some evidence to show that disuse must have its effect also. For example, goldfish that were active during the period between learning a simple maze and being retested, retained more of the original learning than goldfish that were less active (J.W. French); if the forgetting was due to retroactive interference the result should have been the other way round.

Again, Figure 46 shows forgetting that seems to require both retroactive interference and disuse for its explanation. Cockroaches were trained to avoid the dark end of an alley. Each of the control animals was then allowed to enter a small hole, where the animal immediately became inactive, in a possibly sleep-like state; each experimental animal was kept in a small cage, and was moderately active for the same length of time. All were then tested. From the figure it can be seen that the active animals lost more (i.e., took more trials on relearning: the savings method) than the inactive ones, which clearly indicates retroactive interference. But the inactive ones

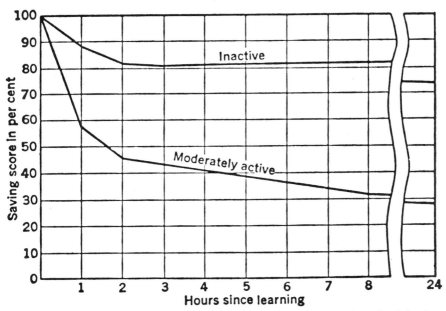

Figure 46. *Retroactive interference demonstrated in the cockroach. Animals that were inactive between learning and testing make better retention scores in the test than animals that were active in the interval and thus presumably learning other things. Note however the loss by the inactive group during the first two hours, which suggests an effect of disuse. (Data of H. Minami and K. M. Dallenbach, from R. S. Woodworth and H. Schlosberg,* Experimental Psychology, Holt.*)*

also lost a good deal in the first two hours, and this cannot be explained away by supposing that it takes a cockroach two hours to go to sleep in these conditions. The results are best understood by supposing that the loss by the inactive animals is mostly due to disuse, and the greater loss by the active animals due both to disuse and to retroactive interference.

There is clinical evidence to support the conclusion that some forgetting is due to disuse. The human child who has normal vision for the first two years of life and then becomes blind will have lost, by the time he has grown up, all his visual learning and will be indistinguishable from one who has been blind from birth.* It might be suggested that this also is due to retroactive interference, the effect of all the other learning the blind child must do. But if he does not become blind until the age of five he does not lose all the effects of visual learning, although retroactive interference should have its effect here as well as with the child who becomes blind earlier. Retroactive interference undoubtedly has some effect, but it does not explain the whole loss in the child who becomes blind at the younger age.

These clinical observations are confirmed experimentally by the results of putting a young chimpanzee in a dark room, thus depriving him of any visual activity, from eight months of age to 24 months (A. H. Riesen, K. L. Chow). At eight months (corresponding to an age of about 12 months in the human baby) he had been making extensive use of vision; when brought out of the dark room at 24 months he had lost all signs of visual learning, and behaved just like other chimpanzees who had been reared from birth in the dark room. As we will see later, there is some loss of neurons in the visual system of an infant reared in darkness. This loss accounts for some of the apparent blindness of the experimental subject, but it cannot account for the whole loss of learning since the infant who had spent only part of his life in darkness was able to learn again, and therefore still had enough neurons left to make visual responses possible (p. 121).

The loss of visual responses—and indeed, the loss of neural cells itself—is therefore due to disuse.

EXTINCTION AND THE ELIMINATION OF ERROR

The clinical data just referred to show us that there is some memory that is permanent, and indeed common experience tells us the same thing though psychology is hard put, in some cases, to explain

---

*There are definite defects in space perception in the congenitally blind. Compared to those who became blind later in life, the congenitally blind make amorphous clay models, are poorer at estimating size or identifying shapes (thus doing badly in form-board tests in which blocks are fitted into receptacles which they fit exactly), and make worse scores than blindfolded normal subjects in maze learning.

why one thing is retained and another is not. Frequency of repetition is one factor that makes for longer retention. Another is the degree of emotional excitement aroused in the learning situation. Some learning persists, however, that may have been based on a single exposure to a not-very-exciting situation; and sometimes the persistence of a habit or of a cognitive memory may be undesirable.

Extinction is the process of abolishing a learned response by withholding reinforcement. Obviously, it applies only in the situation in which there is a known reinforcer, but we will consider it first. There are two forms of extinction, temporary and lasting.

The phenomenon of temporary extinction was discovered by Pavlov. When a salivary CR has been established, the repeated presentation of the CS without the UCS in one training session (lasting about an hour) makes the CR first diminish and then disappear. When the dog is brought back next day, however, the CS again elicits the CR. Pavlov showed that the temporary disappearance of the CR is due to some sort of inhibitory process which is generalized and affects all other CR's while it is present. This is extinction with *massed trials.*

With *spaced trials,* one or two a day for a number of days, or with massed trials repeated day after day (still without reinforcement), the result is a lasting disappearance of the CR (though it can be reestablished with training, and shows savings in the number of trials necessary). Just what happens — the nature of the basic mechanism — is not clear. The response that is extinguished may be a well-established one, for which consolidation has long been complete, so the process is not a reversal of the synaptic changes of learning. It seems therefore that the extinction trials must add some further learning that modifies or inhibits the earlier learning.

The elimination of error — that is, the extinction of a wrong response — in the acquisition period is somewhat easier to understand. Figure 47 represents a simple T-maze for the study of learning in the rat. The animal is started at *A,* and food is put at *D.* Suppose he turns left when he reaches the choice point, *B,* then goes to *C,* then turns back and reaches the food at *D;* and suppose that, because of some accident of past learning, he does this repeatedly. At first glance one might think that the oftener the left-turning response follows the stimuli of the choice point, the stronger the S-R connections would be, and the more likely the rat would be to turn left; but we know, of course, that this does not happen — the oftener he turns left, the less likely he is to do so the next time — and we can understand this from the principles of reinforcement. The response of going toward *C* is not reinforced*, whereas a turn toward *D* is positively reinforced whenever it occurs.

Once the right-turning response at *B* is well established, elimin-

---

*Besides being unreinforced, entry into the blind alley may cause frustration, an emotional disturbance that, if it is strong, is disruptive of the behavior it accompanies. (cf. p. 194.)

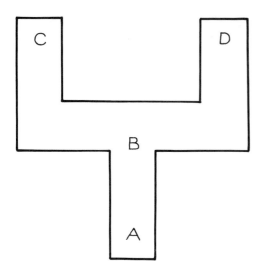

Figure 47. *Plan of a simple T-maze. A, starting-point; B, choice point. The goal box, where food is put, may be either C or D.*

ating it may be more difficult. We place the food at *C* instead of *D,* but it may take considerably more trials to extinguish the right-turning response than it took to establish it. What is happening, however, is easily understood as the addition of further learning that interferes with the earlier learning. Turning left at *B* prevents turning right.

We can regard this as the normal mechanism of eliminating error: the establishment of a correct response which prevents the occurrence of a wrong one, by rewarding the correct response and not rewarding the other. But there are certain situations in which this method of dealing with error encounters difficulties, and this is especially characteristic of some human learning situations.

For example: every amateur typist knows that typewriters spell badly, much worse than a good pencil, and that the errors in question may be extraordinarily persistent. Each person has his own particular difficulties (the writer of this text produces "experiemnt" for "experiment," with annoying frequency), but a common example is "hte" for "the." How should one eliminate these repetitive errors? One logical procedure is to practice the troublesome word, typing it correctly by itself for hundreds of times. But another way is to type the error, also for hundreds of times. In one experiment (K. Dunlap) in which these two methods were compared, practicing the wrong response was more effective than practicing the right one; in a later test of this result, no difference was found—but even this second result seems remarkable: to perfect a response *A,* it is just as effective to practice a different one, *B,* as it is to practice *A* itself. But if the rat in the T-maze is recalled, we see that the cases are quite parallel, for the oftener the rat "practiced" entering the blind alley, the less likely that response was to be made. So perhaps we can regard the effects of typing the wrong response as a form of extinction, though here, as in other forms of extinction, exactly what happens is not too clear.

DISTORTIONS OF MEMORY: TESTIMONY

It is obvious that distortions of memory for complex events may occur because essential parts of the story are lost, and what remains may be meaningless or misleading. We need not spend more time on this mode of distortion, since it is comprised by the previous discussion of the need for consolidation; it is understandable, with an exciting situation particularly, that some of the learning is not consolidated and drops out.

Two other ways in which distortion occurs, however, need consideration. In these there need be no "forgetting," in the sense of a failure of consolidation: all the synaptic changes of learning may be retained, but the addition of further changes—the occurrence of further learning—alters recall, so that the subject's testimony becomes unreliable even though he is honest in his attempts to describe what happened. One of the two ways involves a simple change in the order in which the items are reported, the other an addition of things that did not happen.

1. Changed Order of Report. It is evident that in some situations the order of events is crucial. An elementary example: Susie hits Willie with a stone, Willie hits Susie in return, and Susie runs to mother crying. If Susie reports that Willie threw the first stone, Willie is in trouble; yet just such a change of memory can occur, and Susie need not be lying. An idea sequence A–B–C in Susie's head can become A–C–B simply by strengthening the A–C connections: as Susie thinks about the event while hunting for mother, she is activating the cell-assemblies concerned, and in the course of this activity further synaptic changes can occur. Children's "lying" is well known, not only in connection with quarrels; and though of course some of it is intentional deceit, much of it occurs simply because in thinking about events the child has added synaptic connections that change the whole story.

As for adults, there is a classic experiment that has been reported many times. About 1902 Professor von Liszt, criminologist at the University of Berlin, was lecturing about a book when a student suddenly shouted, "I wanted to throw light on the matter from the standpoint of Christianity!" but another shouted, "I cannot stand that!" The first jumped up shouting "You have insulted me!" The second replied, the first drew a revolver, the second ran at him and as Professor Liszt stepped between them the revolver went off. After he had got control of the situation, Liszt asked the other students to write reports of the incident. He of course had planned the incident and could now compare the eyewitnesses' accounts with what had actually gone on. In the accounts were alterations as well as omissions and additions: clear evidence that even intelligent witnesses, with nothing to gain from false reports, can make gross errors in testimony concerning a relatively simple incident. The relevance for the law court (as well as for the theory of memory) is obvious.

2. Additions as Well as Alterations. If what a subject recalls does not make sense to him, he is likely to think and think about it, and add in thought further incidents that make sense out of it. In this process he is likely to be influenced by other memories of earlier events, and to combine some of them with his memory of the incident in question. Having worked out a different and more coherent account (of "what must have happened") he is likely to recall this account rather than the original puzzling memory.

The behavior of human beings in disaster situations or in battle differs very much from what one would expect. Ten to 25 per cent of those told that the apartment house is on fire, or that a flash flood is about to descend on them and they must get out at once, may behave with complete futility; about the same proportion of soldiers in the presence of the enemy may be incapable of firing their rifles even in the direction of the enemy, let alone aiming with care (p. 199). When the survivors are questioned immediately after emerging from either situation, they can give an accurate account of what happened (accuracy is shown by agreement between different survivors), even though they are still dazed. But once a survivor has recovered, and has had time to recall and to think about his behavior and that of his fellows, his report is changed—not necessarily to make himself and others look more heroic, but to make their behavior more understandable, to make it conform to stereotypes of human behavior, whether cowardly or brave. The memory of complex events is to a great extent a reconstruction, made up in part of the actual retention of what was perceived at the time, but also made up in part of the thoughts that the subject had about the event later.

STUDY METHOD

The theory of learning and memory as discussed so far has been very academic, without much practical application. Psychologists, it seems, spend their time on the learning of animals or, with human subjects, giving thought to a memory for nonsense syllables instead of something useful like calculus or biochemistry or the Cardinals' batting averages. The reason of course is that theory will eventually pay off with practical values; and in the meantime, psychologists have *also* done work on the practical aspects of human learning. A prime example concerns study method.

At the first of this chapter it was observed that the student's problem is not merely to learn but to learn *and remember,* long enough to pass examinations. He may even want to remember longer than that. It is easy to read a paragraph in a textbook and—for the moment—know what's in it; but then comes retroactive interference, due to learning the next paragraph and the one after that. The net result is that having read through a whole chapter you may find you can recall the last page or so only. How is this to be avoided—how is the learning to be retained?

Good study method provides an answer. What is more, it provides an answer for the student's other main problem: how to get himself to do the studying, at least to the extent that it makes study less unpleasant—even enjoyable at times.*

Almost any student can benefit from a book on study methods. The sad thing is that the one who needs it least will benefit most; for others, with bad habits, find it hard to change. A typical example: the student gets the book and means to use it, but using a book effectively is just what he does not know how to do and he complains that he has not time to devote to this one now—though if he did he would save the time ten times over. Nonetheless, this must be said: *If you have trouble with getting down to study, find it hard to concentrate or cannot recall what you have read, get a book on study methods and use it.* Study it; it will repay the time invested. The following brief survey, all that can be offered here, is made with the hope that it will induce the student to go further.

A good study method makes study easier and more tolerable as well as more efficient. Bad study method is inefficient and makes the task unpleasant and hard to face. Many students, including some very intelligent ones, do not realize that there is more than one way of attacking a chapter of history (for example). They sit down to read the chapter through, trying to retain detail at the same time—almost to memorize. No technical book is meant to be read that way, still less to be memorized. Retroactive interference has full opportunity to take effect and the concentration on detail keeps the student from attending to the large picture, the tenor of the chapter as a whole. His attention wanders, he realizes that he is not concentrating as he meant to, he knits his brow, stares harder at the page, resolves to stop thinking about other things, and tries again to read and remember. It is an impossible task with technical material of more than a few paragraphs. Attempting it is unpleasant as well as inefficient.

No good student goes at the task in such a way. One who knows how to study does *not* begin by reading the chapter, but sets out to see first what it is about: by reading the summary if there is one, looking at the headings, sampling and skimming and relating what he finds in this way to what he thinks the author's views are—all with the intention of knowing what the chapter says and what its general meaning is before ever reading it. This allows a minimal opportunity for retroactive interference. Instead of learning series of details, meaningless in themselves until related to the main theme, the details when eventually the student gets to them are fitted into and become part of a single larger picture. No interference is involved. The larger picture is what is remembered, not the details, though in fact it also has the effect of making detail easy to recall. Also, no heavy effort at concentrating is called for, either in the preliminary scanning of the chapter or in the later mastery in detail.

---

*A strong statement.

A further step toward the avoidance of that strain of concentration made necessary by bad study habits comes with the extensive use of note-taking. Merely making a note on a difficult passage is an effective mechanism of attending to it; and if there is something that you particularly want to fix in memory, make a note—write it out on a separate piece of paper, even if you throw the paper away afterward. *Do not underline* as a means of recall; write it out. The student's aim should be that of a lazy man, at getting the most for the least work: but a lazy man with intelligence, and the underlining method is not intelligent. Take the trouble to make notes. It more than repays the extra time and effort.

Your notes should not merely summarize. You should be asking questions, commenting and criticizing, looking for evidence to support ideas of your own, and in general taking an active attitude toward your task instead of passive retention of what you read. It is not true that we learn only by doing—as we have seen, latent learning is an outstanding characteristic of the human species—but even latent learning is supported and maintained by a critical and active mental attitude.

For the student with good study habits, study is not the nightmare it sometimes is for others but may almost be fun. If it is a nightmare for you, or if you have difficulty in persuading yourself to get down to work, or if you have trouble recalling what you have studied or trouble getting it down on paper in the examination, consider: it may not be your intelligence but your study method that is at fault. Get hold of a good book and use it. What has been said here is only a beginning.

SUMMARY

Before he goes farther, the student might use this chapter as material for *a practical exercise in study method.* It is suggested that he first look through the chapter and make a list of the headings; under each heading, make a list of the technical terms found in that section of the book (mainly the italicized terms, but he should look also for technical terms he is already familiar with); and then make a list of the principal problems that are discussed. Then he might prepare a summary, and a brief study guide as he would make it for another student, along the lines of the suggestions for review in the previous Chapter Summaries of the present text. When he has got through doing this, organizing the chapter for someone else to study, he may be surprised to find that he does not need much more study himself—all that remains, for mastery of the material, may be to fill in the chinks.

Now for a summary, which the student may compare with his own: If learning is to last, a period of consolidation is necessary. We do not know what happens in this period, but this may be where primary reinforcement has its effect. The need of consolidation is shown by the disturbing effects of shock following learning. The hippocampus appears to be essential for consolidation of human learning, less necessary with lower mammals (but this may be because the human learning studied was cognitive, without primary reinforcement, whereas the animal experiments used primary reinforcement).

Normal forgetting seems mainly due to retroactive interference, a disturbing effect of later learning on the retention of earlier learning, but there is proactive interference as well and some evidence of an effect also of disuse. We speak of "forgetting" when no active steps are taken to change the response. When one deliberately sets out to suppress a habit, this is called "extinction," and takes two forms: a temporary extinction with massed trials, due to inhibition, and a lasting extinction with spaced trials (probably a form of new learning that prevents the old learning from having its behavorial effect).

Distortions of memory are of great practical importance, as for example in legal testimony. They may occur because some items in a complex memory have dropped out, but also thought processes (recalling and thinking about the events in question) may have the effect of rearranging and adding to the retained items ("it must have happened that way").

The theory of learning does not add much to the practical advice one can give the student, but empirically we know a good deal. Any student, whether he is doing well or badly, should make himself really familiar with a good book on how to study.

NOTES AND REFERENCES

SPECIAL TOPICS

Chemical Factors in Learning
Byrne, W. L., Samuel, D., et al.: Memory transfer. Science, 1966, 153, 658–659. Twenty-three authors in all: they report failure to confirm earlier reports of transfer of specific memories from trained to untrained rats.
McConnell, J. V.: Memory transfer through cannibalism in planarians. Journal of Neuropsychiatry, 1962, 3, 542–548.

Short- and Long-Term Memory
Hebb, D. O.: Distinctive features of learning in the higher animal. In J. F. Delafresnaye (Ed.): Brain mechanisms and Learning, Blackwell, 1961. Reporting the repetition of digits experiment; on this topic, see also—
Melton, A. W.: Implications of short-term memory for a general theory of memory. Journal of Verbal Learning and Verbal Behavior, 1963, 2, 1–21.
Milner, B.: Memory and the medial temporal regions of the brain. In K. H. Pribram and D. E. Broadbent (Eds.): Biology of Memory, Academic Press, 1970.

Study Methods
Morgan, C. T., and Deese, J.: How to Study, McGraw-Hill, 1969.
Smith, D. E. P. (Ed.): Learning to Learn, Harcourt, Brace and World, 1970.
Voeks, V.: On Becoming an Educated Person, Saunders, 1970.

OTHER REFERENCES
Carr, H. A.: The influence of visual guidance on maze learning. Journal of Experimental Psychology, 1921, 4, 399–417. Maze learning by the congenitally blind is reported on.
Dunlap, K.: The technique of negative practice. American Journal of Psychology, 1942, 55, 270–273. For a summary account of related experiments, see also—
Hovland, C. I.: Human learning and retention. Chapter 17 in S. S. Stevens (Ed.): Handbook of Experimental Psychology, Wiley, 1951.

Minami, H., and Dallenbach, K. M.: The effect of activity upon learning and retention in the cockroach. *American Journal of Psychology*, 1946, 59, 1–58.

Riesen, A. H.: Stimulation as a requirement for growth and function in behavioral development. In D. W. Fiske and S. R. Maddi (Eds.): *Functions of Varied Experience*, Dorsey Press, 1961. Includes a review of the work of Riesen and Chow and co-workers on young chimpanzees reared in darkness.

Sylvester, R. H.: The mental imagery of the blind. *Psychological Bulletin*, 1913, 10, 210–211. The congenitally blind are deficient in various aspects of tactual form perception.

7

heredity, maturation, early learning

The preceding chapters at several points have raised the question of the relation between heredity and environment and the effect of early experience in the development of behavior. We must now look more closely at these issues and a related one: the age-old but still confused question of instinct.

The student has already been warned to avoid opposing heredity to environment as is commonly done. It is common to talk as if a perception, for example, might be entirely inherited *or* entirely learned; as if maternal behavior must be inherited *or* learned; and so on. Such opposition is confused, the confusion due in the first place to thinking of two variables only—there are more—and in the second place to forgetting the role of early experience. In 1955 F. A. Beach showed what the confusion is and how to avoid it. It is time that behavioral scientists learned to do so.

A central issue in all aspects of psychological analysis is the nature of learning, and the part it plays in the development of adult characteristics. But equally central—the same problem in reverse, the other side of the coin—is the role of *physical maturation,* or growth, in determining the structures in which the learning must occur. In our thinking, theoretically, we can distinguish between these different kinds of influence, but in practice they are inseparable: there is no behavior that is independent of the animal's heredity, or of the supporting environment; and no higher behavior that is uninfluenced by learning.

INSTINCTIVE BEHAVIOR AND MATURATION

"Instinct" is a term of doubtful scientific value, for reasons that we will come to later, but "instinctive" is more useful as a rough term for designating certain kinds of behavior. *Instinctive behavior* may be defined as complex species-predictable behavior: at a higher level than reflex behavior, not requiring special conditions of learning for its appearance, but predictable simply from knowing that we are dealing with a particular species in its ordinary habitat.

The distinction between instinctive behavior and reflex behavior (which of course is also species-predictable) is clear in principle, though in practice the two classes shade into one another and a sharp dichotomy is probably impossible. *A reflex response occurs in a specific group of effectors,* and is evoked by *stimulation of a specific sensory surface.* Light falling on the retina results in pupillary contraction; acid in the mouth results in salivary secretion; stimulation of the palm of the newborn infant's hand produces clasping by that hand, and stimulation of the lips produces sucking movements. The pupillary reflex is not possible without the retina, the clasp reflex is not possible without the receptors of the palm, and so on. Instinctive behavior, on the other hand, is usually not dependent upon any specific receptors, and it characteristically involves a large proportion of the effectors of the whole body, rather than being limited to one gland or muscle group. Also, it commonly includes elements of learning.

All instinctive behavior involves reflex elements,* so part of the pattern can be eliminated by loss of a sense organ or muscle group, but the overall pattern may still remain fully identifiable. The instinctive maternal behavior of the female rat is only slightly affected by the loss of any one of the senses of vision, smell, or the tactual sensitivity in the snout. Loss of two of these senses does affect the behavior significantly, showing that they are all involved in the behavior, but no one is essential (Beach).

Instinctive sexual behavior by the male rat shows the same picture. Even if the genitalia are removed the pattern of mating behavior can be obtained, complete up to the point of intromission and ejaculation; thus an essential reflex element of the total pattern is missing, but the pattern is recognizable and complete as far as it is mechanically possible. Reflex behavior is primarily a local process; instinctive behavior primarily involves the whole animal (Fig. 48).

The special attribute of instinctive behavior is that it does not have to be taught or acquired by practice. A female rat may be brought up in isolation and never have an opportunity to observe another female caring for her young. At maturity the female is mated, and put in a cage in which strips of paper are available. A day or so before giving birth she begins gathering paper together to form a primitive kind of nest. When the young are born she promptly cleans

---

*As any complex behavior does. In the first place, any response must affect the animal's posture, which is reflexively controlled though higher centers can impose changes on these reflexes and thus produce what we classify as a nonreflexive action. Thus if a male animal has a leg amputated there will be a recognizable change in his approach to the female, but the overall picture of male sex behavior will also be recognizable. In the second place, instinctive behavior in general includes two phases, *preparatory* and *consummatory,* and the consummatory phase is essentially reflexive. In food-getting behavior, the search for food and seizing it are preparatory, whereas mastication, salivation and swallowing are consummatory. Damage to throat muscles would prevent completion of the consummatory activity, but the instinctive pattern would still be identifiable.

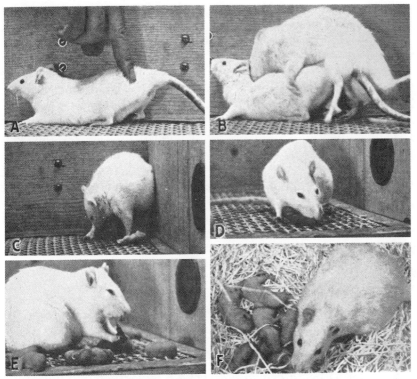

Figure 48. *Instinctive behavior in the female rat. A, tactual stimulation elicits the receptive posture reflexively. B, mounting by the male. C, delivery of the young. D, cleaning a pup and removing the amniotic membrane. E, eating the placenta (the mother seldom pays attention to the young until the placenta has been eaten). F, the litter has been gathered together in the nest; in a cold environment the nesting material would be pulled up over mother and young so that they could hardly be seen. (Photographs taken in The Wistar Institute by Dr. Edmond J. Farris and William Sykes. From E. J. Farris and J. Q. Griffith,* The Rat in Laboratory Investigation, *Lippincott.)*

them and collects them into the nest, and crouches over them in a way that makes suckling possible. With no opportunity for practice, in short, she performs a complex task quite adequately. Many such examples could be given: the web-building of spiders, each making a web characteristic of its particular species; the complex courting and mating behavior of birds; or the migration of some fish for great distances to spawn in a particular stream, and the nest-building and fighting patterns of others.

The farther down the animal scale we look, the more rigid and unvarying the predictable pattern of behavior is, but it is quite evident that there is much that is "species-predictable" about the behavior of the higher mammals, including man. Is this instinctive too? For man, at least, the usual answer is no, because some learning is involved and instinct is supposed to be incompatible with learning. We will see, however, that the question is more complex than this. An act may be unlearned, in the sense that one does not have to practice it or be shown or told how to do it, and yet be fully dependent on the prior occurrence of other learning. "Instinctive behavior" is regarded here as being only a rough designation because, in its long history, it has picked up connotations that prevent its being used precisely. Because of these connotations it is not possible to give a clear yes or no to the question as to whether man has instincts. Instinct is thought of as a substitute for learning, or for intelligence; man shows some very marked forms of species-predictable behavior at a complex level, which (according to the definition above) means that it is instinctive, yet it is evident also that learning and intelligence are involved in the behavior, which (according to the connotations referred to) means that it is not instinctive. Such contradictions make it desirable to use other terms in discussing human behavior (as well as when we wish to be precise in any context) but it should be clear that the essential problem exists with man as much as with the rat or the spider.

TWO KINDS OF BEHAVIOR, LEARNED AND INHERITED?

Much of our difficulty with these questions comes from thinking of behavior as being of two different kinds: learned and unlearned, with the idea that the learned is more or less independent of heredity and the unlearned determined by heredity alone. But now consider this case. Neither a human nor a chimpanzee baby needs to learn how to have a temper tantrum. The behavior is complex but quite characteristic in form, so that no experienced observer has any difficulty in identifying it. The baby does not have to practice it (nor to see how others do it) in order to produce, on the first try, a first-class sample. It is therefore "unlearned." But it is not independent of learning, for the baby must have learned to want something outside his reach and to see that it is being withheld from him. That is, the tantrum itself is not learned, but it *is* dependent on the existence of other learning (W. Dennis).

Another example is the fear of strangers, which occurs only when the child has first learned to recognize familiar persons, but does not require that he must have any previous exposure to strangers, or any unpleasant event associated with strangers. Another example is Pavlov's experimental neurosis (p. 9): the dog's breakdown in behavior was not learned, but it could not have occurred until after the conditioning process had established the discriminative behavior with the test objects (an oval and a circle).

There are other situations in which similar relations hold. Shall we then conclude that there are three kinds of behavior: (1) learned, (2) unlearned but dependent on learning, and (3) unlearned, determined by heredity alone? Instead, we might ask whether this kind of classification is justified at all. Let us now consider two other sets of relevant facts, one concerning maturation, the second the effects of early experience; we will then be in a position to make a different approach to the whole heredity-environment question.

MATURATION

It is obvious that some of the changes of behavior following birth are due to physical growth, especially the increase of the infant's muscular strength. It is not so obvious that growth is also going on in the nervous system, and that learning is not the whole explanation of other changes that are observed. The human brain at birth has all the neurons it will ever have, but many connecting fibers are still incomplete.* Learning processes cannot strengthen synaptic connections between two neurons until axon and dendrite, or axon and cellbody, are in close proximity. Learning, that is, cannot occur until physical maturation has reached the proper stage.

Thus we think of the infant as learning to walk, once his muscles are strong enough to hold him. But throughout this period, apparently one of practice, what is going on is at least partly the completion of a certain level of growth in the nervous system. When this stage has been reached, a comparatively short practice period is enough to achieve walking.

Another example is the feeding behavior of young chicks. Shortly after hatching, as the chick begins to peck at things about it, it will succeed in hitting kernels of grain, holding them in the beak and swallowing them. But errors (failing to hit the kernel, but more often failing to hold it until it can be swallowed) are frequent. The accuracy improves rapidly in the first 5 to 10 days, as the chick practices, and this looks like learning. Figure 49 gives the results of an experiment by W. W. Cruze which shows instead that much of the change is due to maturation. Some chicks began their pecking one day after hatching; others were kept in darkness and fed by hand for one to five days before they began to practice pecking. The figure shows two things: the older the chick, the more accurate it is without any practice (e.g., the curve for the three-day group begins at a lower level of errors than that for the two-day group); but the practice has its effect also, for the three-day group does not begin at the level which the one-day or two-day group has reached by the third day.

This example is particularly instructive. For one thing, it shows clearly how physical growth and learning processes can collaborate in the development of behavior. They are not opposed but work

---

*Many of the axons also lack the myelin sheath (p. 61), the growth of which continues long after birth. The brain at birth weighs about 425 gm. (250–600 gm.); at maturity, about 1350 gm. (1000–2000 gm.). The great increase is partly due to outgrowth of axon and dendrite, but must be due more to the addition of myelin and the proliferation of capillaries and larger blood vessels. There may also be an increase in the number of glia.

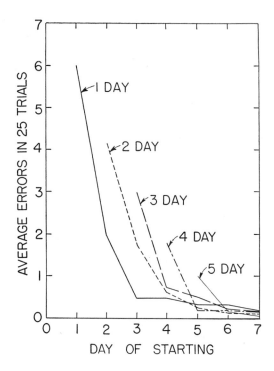

Figure 49. *Maturation of pecking skill in chicks: the number of misses ("errors") made by chicks allowed to begin practice at different intervals after hatching. (After W. W. Cruze, J. Comp. Psychol., 1935.)*

together, and only by ingenious experimentation can they be distinguished for theoretical purposes. Another important point is that the learning must occur at the right time; if the chick is kept in darkness very long, grossly abnormal feeding behavior is the eventual result. We must note also that learning is not essential for all aspects of the behavior: the tendency to peck at small objects is present in the newly hatched chick, and it has been reported that no prior experience is needed to make the chick peck at rounded objects rather than sharp-cornered ones.

This innately established pecking may be classed as reflexive. Unconditioned reflex paths are in general laid down by heredity and growth processes; no learning is involved. Some of them are functional at birth, as in the chick's pecking tendency or the sucking reflex of the newborn mammal, but others apparently have to wait until the neural fibers involved have made connection with each other. When the sole of the foot is scratched in the newborn infant the toes curl upward and outward ("Babinski reflex"), but in the older child or adult they curl downward (a Babinski reflex in the adult means that motor paths in the spinal cord have been injured).

Another classic demonstration of reflex maturation is one in which larval salamanders are placed in an anesthetic solution before any swimming movements have begun. The anesthesia prevents any movement during the period in which others from the same hatch seem to be learning to swim. They are then taken out of the anesthetic and placed in ordinary water, and as soon as the anesthesia has worn off they show swimming movements identical with those of their normally reared fellows. The development of reflexive swimming in the normal animals is therefore a product of physical maturation, with no important effect from practice (L. Carmichael).

Maturation is an important phenomenon in primate behavior. An obvious example is sexual development, which depends on the growth of the gonads. Another example is the baby's fear of strangers, which characteristically does not appear until the age of four months or so in the chimpanzee (Fig. 53), six months in man. Still another is the fear of imaginary creatures or events associated with darkness, which in the human child is rare before the age of three years, common thereafter. In these examples we are not dealing with maturation in the narrower sense of physical growth alone (a distinction is made later between *physical* and *psychological maturation:* p. 129), but it seems highly probable that the physical development of the nervous system is an essential factor in determining the delayed appearance of such phenomena.

THE EFFECTS OF EARLY EXPERIENCE

In the phenomena of maturation the probability that learning is going on strikes the eye, and the experimental problem is to find a way of showing that the development of behavior is not due to learning alone. Now we turn to another complication: to examples in which the problem, on the contrary, is to show that any learning is occurring. The very young infant seems to be doing nothing much but eating, defecating and growing; vegetating in the intervals between feedings, with some random movement of the limbs and eyes, and some random noise-making, but not being affected by what is going on around him. But this is a period of latent learning that lays the basis for all future mental development.

Even before birth, the mammal is exposed to complex tactual stimulation, in the various pressures exerted by the uterine wall and by contacts of one part of the fetal body with another. From birth onward, the complexity of this stimulation is enormously increased. The human baby lying in his crib is exposed to a continuously changing pattern of stimulation*; even if he is in a quiet room in which nothing else is happening, his own movement of eyes and limbs varies the visual and tactual input, and there is auditory stimulation from his own breathing and any vocalization he happens to make. The baby seems mostly unaffected by the stimulation, and it used to be thought that this was a period of physical growth during which the environment was unimportant, except for a supply of food and maintenance of an adequate temperature.

---

*Normally, that is; not if the baby was one of those in certain orphanages (p. 11).

We now know that the situation is quite different. The sensory stimulations of the early environment are necessary for the maintenance of some neural structures, which would otherwise degenerate, and for the occurrence of learning which is essential for normal adult behavior.

Maintenance of Neural Structures.   When chimpanzees are reared in darkness to the age of 16 months, the lack of visual stimulation results in a loss of many of the "ganglion cells" in the retina (the neurons whose axons form the optic nerve, connecting the retina with the rest of the nervous system: p. 220). If the animal is reared normally, in light, to the age of eight months, and then placed in darkness for 16 months, there is again a loss of ganglion cells. A normal sensory environment, therefore, is necessary for the continued existence of these neurons. When the animal is reared with exposure to diffuse light—when the head is surrounded by a translucent shield that admits light but does not allow the animal to see pattern or form—no loss of cells can be found, and the visual system seems unimpaired (K. L. Chow, A. H. Riesen, F. W. Newell). But there may still be defects in the system, for cats reared in darkness show no loss of ganglion cells and yet the following experiment shows that rearing either in darkness or in diffuse light produces serious damage somewhere in the visual system.

Certain individual neurons in the visual cortex are so connected with cells in the retina that they are specialized for response to lines or edges of a particular slope in the visual field. Thus a line with slope ╱ excites one set of neurons in the cortex; a line with slope ╲ or — excites a different set of neurons, even though it falls in the same retinal area (cf. p. 221). In the normal animal the connections are present at birth as well as at maturity, but if one of the newborn kitten's eyes is kept closed for two months (or covered with a translucent shield) the retina of that eye will no longer be capable of exciting the specialized cells. *Innate* connections—ones present at birth—are lost by disuse (D. H. Hubel, T. N. Wiesel).

Early Learning.   The sensory events of infancy also determine adult patterns of behavior in invertebrates, fish, birds and mammals. Examples follow: Ants discriminate members of their own colony by odor, and attack others, even members of the same colony that have been given the wrong odor; but early experience determines the behavior, for normally antagonistic species will live amicably together if the two are mixed within 12 hours of hatching, and the effect is apparently permanent. The sexual behavior of certain fish at maturity is changed by rearing in isolation, the males attempting to mate with both males and females. Many species of birds show *imprinting,* a lasting social attachment to members of the species to which they are first exposed—normally, of course, their own species, as the parent cares for them. Infrahuman mammals, abnormally reared, show striking effects of deprivation of normal early experience. These are changes of social behavior, of somesthetic perception (including pain reactions — see p. 124), and of intelligence and learning capacity. As for man, several references have already been made to the effects of different environments on mental development, and the effect of early environment on intelligence, both animal and human, will be discussed in Chapter 9 (p. 161).

In an earlier edition of this textbook it was assumed that the importance of early learning is also shown by the effects of rearing animals in darkness or diffuse light, and by deficiencies of perception in human beings who are born blind and given vision by a surgical operation at an age when they can talk and report what they see (M. v. Senden). This evidence is now suspect, because of the more recent evidence concerning the maintenance of neural connections in kittens reared in diffuse light, referred to above. In the case of congenital blindness there may be a greater loss of connections than seemed possible earlier, which would account for much of the difficulty the patient has in learning to perceive visually.

However, it does not seem that structural loss can account for this difficulty completely, especially for the slow development of pattern perception after the subject has shown that he is able to see the elements of the pattern (i.e., lines or edges, and corners). Neurons do not regenerate in the brain, and the fact that the human patient ultimately is able to perceive patterns shows that the necessary neurons were present immediately after the operation. Similarly, the dark-reared chimpanzee learns to see, though his vision remains defective. It is hard to understand how structural defects can account fully for these phenomena: the absence of visual perception but the presence of visual reflexes, which are well developed when the animal first comes out of the dark room; the similarity of dark-reared and diffuse-light-reared animals in this respect; and the subsequent course of development of pattern perception. It seems clear that early experience results in learning as well as in the maintenance of neural structures, and that this learning is essential for normal visual perception.

IMPRINTING IN BIRDS

When a bird emerges from the egg the first moving object it sees is normally one of the parent birds. In the first 24 hours or thereabouts of the chick's life this exposure has a lasting effect, very important in many species as a determinant of the bird's behavior at maturity. This is true at least of "precocial" species, in which the newly hatched chick can walk and follow an adult bird. An early learning occurs which, in part, produces the proper species-predictable behavior. For if instead of an adult of the same species, it is some other species to which the chick is exposed, the bird responds later to that other species as it normally would to its own. The degree of this effect varies from one kind of bird to another, but greylag geese, for example, hatched in an incubator and exposed only to a human being (who feeds and cares for them) will at maturity consort with people, and the ganders will tend to make their sexual advances to people and not to females of their own species. The birds are then said to be *imprinted* on man (K. Lorenz). In the ordinary course of events such learning would be directed toward the parent bird, and would produce normal social behavior at maturity.

Imprinting has been extensively studied in the laboratory. One form of experiment is shown in Figure 50. A duckling is exposed to a wooden model that moves in a circular track; the duckling follows, and in doing so becomes imprinted (E. H. Hess). Such experiments show that there is a critical period after which imprinting will not occur, the period being usually the first 12 to 24 hours of life, depending on the species. They also show that this is a very special kind of learning in other respects. The learning does not require primary reinforcement (a wooden model, as in Figure 50, provides neither food nor warmth), but appears to depend on the amount of effort expended in following. Mere visual exposure is not enough, though the visual stimulation is obviously important when the bird discriminates visually between the imprinted-on object and others; and imprinting has also been obtained in chicks of a domestic breed of hen merely by allowing them to approach a motionless object close to a flickering light at one end of a long runway (H. James).

EARLY LEARNING IN MAMMALS

In its clearest and most dramatic form, imprinting is a phenomenon that is characteristic of birds (though there are great differences

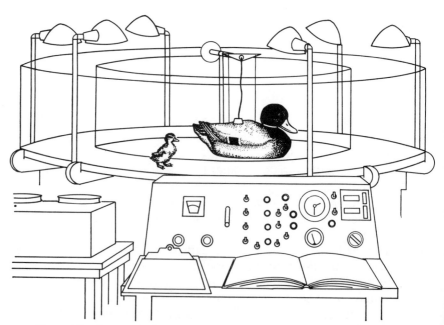

Figure 50. *The apparatus used for the study of imprinting. The large decoy moves on a circular track under the experimenter's control; the duckling follows and is thereby imprinted. (From E. H. Hess,* Science, *1959.)*

from one species to another). However, the same kind of effect may appear in mammals, though the learning period needed may be much longer. It is reported that guinea pigs, sheep, goats, and deer brought up by man tend to act like pets only, and not to respond normally to their own kind. The sheep that has been reared by hand and kept away from other sheep during growth does not join the flock when turned out in the field, and will approach the human caretaker instead if given a choice. Pet dogs are perhaps showing the same thing when they attempt to mount (make a sexual approach to) the foot and leg of a human being. Female chimpanzees reared in a nursery by human caretakers and ones reared normally by their mothers differ markedly in their preference for human company at maturity; and some of the nursery-reared females are less sexually responsive to male chimpanzees than the others. These observations in general seem to show that some kind of lasting social identification results from the early experience of mammals, though it is less dramatic than the imprinting of birds.

The *experimental* study of early learning in mammals, as distinct from the incidental or naturalistic observations of the preceding paragraph, includes the work on chimpanzees reared in darkness (referred to above, p. 120), and a number of investigations of the development of learning and problem solving that will be discussed under the heading of the growth of intelligence (Chapter 9, p. 162). Here we will consider some of the drastic changes in the behavior of the dog when reared in isolation: changes in social behavior and in the reaction to pain stimuli, and more generally, changes that can only be summed up as changes of *personality*.

Scottish terriers were reared in partial isolation, from early weaning onward (R. Melzack, W. R. Thompson). They could hear and smell other dogs and the human caretakers in the same room, but otherwise were cut off from all social contacts, in small cages just large enough to allow them to stand and turn round comfortably. They grew well and stayed in excellent health until they were removed for testing at ages between 9 and 12 months (Fig. 51). There was no sign that they were unhappy; a dog that is reared normally and then put in isolation is obviously miserable, but these dogs had known no other existence. They were "happy as larks" and physically "as strong as bulls," in the words of the Scottie expert who supervised their rearing and who won a number of first class ribbons with them at dog shows. Such prizes are awarded only for physical form and posture; in obedience tests the isolation-reared dogs would have got nowhere, for they turned out to be almost untrainable. The whole picture of their social behavior was aberrant in a way that is hard to describe; they were dominated by normal dogs, would permit another dog to eat simultaneously from the same food dish (the normal Scottie reared outside the laboratory will not permit this) and reacted to familiar or unfamiliar people with a strange combination of approach and avoidance—a sort of diffuse or disorganized emotional behavior—that was never seen in normally reared dogs. The peculiarities

Figure 51. *Littermate Scotties, one reared normally, one in restriction. Visitors were sometimes invited to tell which was which when the two groups were put in a pen together, and usually made the wrong choice. The normal dog is at the left, rather bored with the photographic process; the restricted dog "didn't have brains enough to be bored," in the perceptive comment of the handler—i.e., boredom is a function of intellectual capacity. Cf. Chapter 11.*

diminished with time but did not disappear, and the personalities remained grossly abnormal.

The response to noxious stimuli (ones that cause pain in normal animals) was at least as unusual. At such a stimulus the restricted dog pulled back reflexively as a normal dog would, but made no attempt to avoid a repetition of the stimulus and appeared not to be upset by it; thus one dog, when a lighted cigar fell on the floor, smelt it, burned his nose and pulled back, but then thrust his nose into the live coal twice more. When an experimenter stuck a dissecting needle into the dog's skin repeatedly, the dog squirmed each time but made no attempt to escape or to pull out the needle although its wooden handle was sticking out from his flank. He gave no sign of feeling pain.

These results with pain are paralleled by ones obtained by rearing a chimpanzee in a lesser degree of restriction (Fig. 52)—with

Figure 52. *Rob at 30 months of age, as reared in conditions of somesthetic restriction. The cylinders permitted fairly free joint movement but radically limited his tactual experience. Note the abnormal sitting posture (cf. Fig. 53.) (Courtesy of H. W. Nissen, from Nissen, Chow and Semmes,* Amer. J. Psychol., *1951.)*

large cardboard "cuffs" over forearms and lower legs, loose enough to allow joint movements but still preventing the ordinary tactual exploration of the young animal's own body and his surroundings (H. W. Nissen, K. L. Chow, J. Semmes). One point of interest is the unusual posture, different from that of a normally reared chimpanzee of about the same age (Fig. 53); the most important difference, however, is in the experimental animal's response to somesthetic stimulation in tests made when the cuffs were removed at the age of 30 months (corresponding roughly to an age of three to four years in man). When the normally reared animal was pinched at some point on his body (vision being prevented), he would reach directly and accurately to the spot, to stop the pinching. The experimental animal made inaccurate movements, with apparent need for exploration before reaching the right spot. A most interesting further observation was this: to make sure the animal was doing his best to find the spot as quickly as possible, pin prick was used. A normal control animal objected vociferously, and wasted no movements in removing the painful object. The experimental animal, on the other hand, showed no sign that the pin prick was disturbing, even acting as if it was pleasant as much as unpleasant.

A situation was also set up to test simple somesthetic learning. The subject was placed with a shelf under his chin so that he could

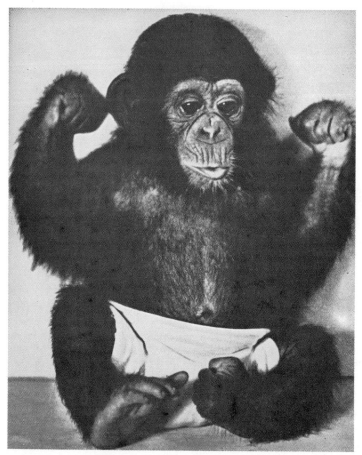

Figure 53. *Jed, a nursery-reared chimpanzee infant at four months, the age at which fear of strangers appears. The leg posture is the normal one for the sitting animal; an abnormal posture appears in Figure 52. (Courtesy of H. W. Nissen and R. K. Helmle, the Yerkes Laboratories of Primate Biology.)*

not see his hands; the food reward (milk in a nursing bottle) was presented sometimes from the right, sometimes from the left, and the hand on the same side was touched first. The normal control animal learned reliably in 200 trials to turn his head to the left when his left hand was touched, and to the right when the right hand was touched; but the experimental animal had not fully learned in 2000 trials.

It is clear that the higher behavior of the adult, in mammals as in birds, is fundamentally dependent on the experience of infancy. There are a number of pieces of evidence indicating that this need not be true, or is true to a minimal extent only, of reflex behavior; but normal motivation, perception, and intelligence require a normal early experience.

At first, this may sound like a denial of the importance of heredity, but nothing could be more erroneous. It is as true of higher behavior as of the innate reflex that it is fundamentally a function of heredity. Higher behavior depends on early experience; but it *also* depends on heredity and the growth processes that give us eyes and ears and skin receptors and a nervous system in which learning can occur. Instead of asking whether a given action is hereditary or learned—opposing these two influences to one another—we need to ask how the two have collaborated in producing it.

The student should note that heredity, by itself, can produce no behavior whatever; the fertilized ovum must have a nutritive, supporting environment for its growth, before behavior is possible. Similarly, learning can produce no behavior by itself, without the heredity and the prenatal environment that produce the structures in which learning can occur. The two collaborate. Further, it seems highly probable that heredity makes some kinds of learning easy or inevitable, others hard, and thus guides learning. Some things that are considered to be unlearned, for example in the insects, may in fact be the result of a very rapid learning which the sensory and neural structure of the insect makes inevitable.

In the higher animal too some learning is inevitable, in ordinary circumstances, but now there is a larger mass of neural tissue involved, and if we assume, as in Chapter 4, that cell-assemblies must be developed before effective transmission can occur at higher levels, this implies that the first course of learning may be slow. Theoretically, therefore, we may consider that the function of early experience in the mammal is to build up the mediating processes which, once they are established, make possible the very rapid learning of which the mature animal is capable.

CODIFYING THE FACTORS IN DEVELOPMENT

In all matters touching on the heredity-environment or maturation-learning question, long experience shows that it is extremely difficult to think or speak with logical consistency, or without omitting some obviously important factor from discussion. A codification of the factors in development is presented in Table 1, which may oversimplify the question, but which will help to avoid the worse oversimplifications that abound in the literature: not only the literature of psychology, but also that of medicine, zoology, genetics—in short, the whole field of biological investigation, as far as it touches on the determinants of physical or behavioral growth.

The purpose of Table 1 is to provide a working classification only, one that will at least keep us reminded that there are more than two kinds of factors in development, and allow us to talk about them less ambiguously. The scheme is really a sort of mnemonic device, not an exhaustive analysis; if it is carried too far shortcomings will appear. Factor I is classed as genetic, for example, as if the ovum consisted of genetic structures alone. Many ova consist of genetic structures *plus* nutritive matter (as birds' eggs clearly do), which means that they

TABLE 1. CLASSES OF FACTORS IN BEHAVIORAL DEVELOPMENT

No.	Class	Source, Mode of Action, etc.
I	genetic	physiological properties of the fertilized ovum
II	chemical, prenatal	nutritive or toxic influence in the uterine environment
III	chemical, postnatal	nutritive or toxic influence: food, water, oxygen, drugs, etc.
IV	sensory, constant	pre- and postnatal experience normally inevitable for all members of the species
V	sensory, variable	experience that varies from one member of the species to another
VI	traumatic	physical events tending to destroy cells: an "abnormal" class of events to which an animal might conceivably never be exposed, unlike Factors I to V

comprise both Factor I as defined and part of Factor II, the nutritive environment of the developing embryo. This applies in some degree to mammalian ova as well. Factor II should include also temperature, which is physical rather than chemical, and so on.

But if we regard the table as a working approximation, it will help us to avoid certain common fallacies. Much of the discussion of instinct is based implicitly on this kind of argument: such-and-such behavior needs no special experience—that is, it does not require practice, or observation of others' performance—hence it must depend on heredity alone. Table 1 permits us to restate this: Factor V is not involved, therefore Factor I alone is the cause. But this omits Factors II, III and IV (assuming that VI is not involved). In other words, the roles of the nutritive and constant-sensory environments, as causal factors in behavior, have been overlooked—and there is plenty of evidence to show that they must not be overlooked.

The schematizing of Table 1 will help one to remember that no behavior whatever can be caused by one of these factors alone. No "learned behavior" is possible without Factors I to III, which together make possible the existence of the sense organs, nervous system and so forth. No "innate behavior" can be produced by Factor I alone; the nutritive environment must act on the fertilized ovum to produce something that can manifest behavior at all.

Factor I, evidently, is the hereditary variable in behavior. Factors II to VI are the environmental variables. Factors II and III are the same in principle, but in practice II is apt to be forgotten: for example, a deficient diet for the mother may impair the infant's brain, and this impairment may be mistaken for a genetically determined lack of intelligence in the case of slum children.* It is not genetic, it is environ-

---

*See M. T. Kennedy, Science, 1967, 157, 1210.

mental. Also, II is harder to control experimentally, III easier, so it is worth while (especially for mnemonic purposes) to separate them. Similarly, Factors IV and V are the same in principle — though IV is predominantly a cause of early learning, and V of later learning, and in higher species these have rather different properties. But Factor IV, again, is hard to control experimentally and is very often overlooked, so these two may also be kept separate in our codification.

Factors I to III and Factor VI, together, comprise the *constitutional* variables in behavior; Factors IV and V the *experiential* variables. In speaking of maturation, we may mean either of two things: the influence of Factors I to III, which we may refer to as *physical maturation* (the effects of heredity plus growth, only); or the influence of Factors I to IV, referred to as *psychological maturation* (heredity, growth *and* early experience). The student will find that these two things are confused in the literature. For example, in the case of children learning to walk, let us say between the twelfth and the fifteenth months, we arrange it so that none of the children in one group are allowed to practice — that is, to get into a vertical position with feet on the floor — until they are 12 months old. We see how long it then takes for walking to occur. Ten per cent, let us say, are walking after three days' practice; in another group, not allowed to practice until the age of 15 months, we find that perhaps 75 per cent can walk after three days' practice. We say then that the difference between the two groups must be due to the "maturation" that occurs between the twelfth and the fifteenth month. But is this physical maturation, the operation of Factors I to III alone? During this time we have not controlled all the aspects of somesthetic experience that come under the heading of Factor IV, and their effects cannot be excluded. We have seen that some sort of somesthetic learning, or development of perception of tactual locus and of the position of the limbs with respect to the body, is going on in this period. We cannot doubt that physical maturation is also going on, but such experiments as this do not show that physical maturation alone produces the increased walking readiness of the child at 15 months of age as compared with 12 months. On the other hand, the change is not due to practice in the specific skill of walking, so we can regard it as psychological maturation: the operation of Factors I to IV, apart from the ad hoc learning of Factor V.

FURTHER ON FACTOR IV AND INSTINCT

The general conclusion to which all this leads us is that, apart from the unconditioned reflex, all behavior depends on the generalized learning resulting from Factor IV stimulation. This does not say that all higher behavior is "learned," in the usual sense of that word: *much of it is unlearned, but dependent on previous learning.* The first temper tantrum; the spontaneous avoidance of strangers that appears at about six months of age in man, four months in the chimpanzee; the first new sentence constructed by the child, or the first imaginative response: none of these can be called learned behavior but all require other learning that has resulted from exposure to the normal environment of the species.

Instinctive behavior also requires prior learning, and all our evidence indicates that it is wrong to think of instinctive behavior as a separate class, wholly distinct from another class of learned behavior. Instead, the two classes shade into one another, with no clear line of demarcation. As for the term "instinct," it must be, by definition, that process within the nervous system that produces instinctive behavior, and we can see now why it is a misleading term. It implies that instinctive behavior is produced by a *special* activity or part of the brain, separate from the brain processes that control learned behavior, and separate from those that make up what we call intelligence. But this is not so.

In addition to the facts already discussed, Beach has provided another kind of evidence to show that instinct is not separate from learning or intelligence. He has shown that learning ability in the male rat, as measured by maze performance, is correlated with the level of sexual activity. The better learner copulates more efficiently and frequently. Sex behavior in the female at this phyletic level is largely reflexive, and does not correlate with learning ability; but maternal behavior does. The female that is best at maze learning is the best mother. Similarly, cortical removals which affect intelligence and learning ability in the rat produce a lowered rate of copulation in the male and a deterioration of maternal behavior in the female.

There is no ground, therefore, for thinking of instinctive behavior as having a special kind of neural control, immune to the effects of learning and distinct from the operations of intelligence. Instinct by definition is that which determines instinctive behavior—that is to say, it is the presence in the individual animal of certain neural paths which are characteristic of the species. How are these paths determined? Also by definition, instinctive behavior does not depend on practice (or imitation), and thus is not learned in the usual sense of the term; yet, as we have seen, the learning induced by Factor IV may play a significant part in it. What we conclude is that instinct is the neural organization, over and above reflex paths, which is common to a whole species: determined by a common heredity *and* the common features of the environment. The learning that is part of it is learning that inevitably occurs in the whole species (except when an individual animal's environment differs significantly from the usual environment of the species, and produces aberrant behavior). Growth processes and early experience between them determine the presence of neural paths which mean, when the animal is faced for the first time with a particular class of situation, that he will tend to respond in a particular way. These processes are incredibly complex, and we have hardly begun to unravel them, but in principle there is nothing any more mysterious about instinct than about other aspects of behavior.

The student should be clear, for example, that instinctive behavior does not imply advance knowledge of its end effects, inherited from the animal's ancestors. It is done for its own sake, not for what it will achieve in the future. The pregnant rat builds a nest before her first litter is born because she wants to build a nest, not because she knows why her belly is swollen and that the pups will need shelter. The primary reason that human beings engage in sex behavior is not to produce another generation of troublemakers in this troubled world but because human beings like sex behavior.

Human Instinct?

It has already been said that it makes for confusion to apply the term "instinctive" to man's behavior, because of the word's persistent connotations. It is almost an article of faith for many psychologists that man has no instinctive behavior, no matter how the term might be defined. The student, however, should recognize how species-predictable human behavior is, in many of its aspects.

If instinct is a poor theoretical conception we must abandon it for technical purposes, but we must not forget the problems of behavior to which in the past it has been applied. Man everywhere has a fondness for the sound of his own voice, singing and listening to songs, telling elaborate tales for their own sake (some of them being true), or talking when there is no need of communication. Man everywhere uses tools, organizes social groups, avoids darkness in strange places. All cultures are said to have developed string games, related to the childhood game of cat's cradle. The taboos of incest or of food use, the belief in spirits good or evil, the tendency to ornament the body in particular ways and to impose strong sanctions against ornamenting it in other ways—all these are things which, in their details, are subject to the influence of special learning, but which in one form or another spring up in every society of which we have knowledge. In detail, therefore, they are not species-predictable; but in a larger sense they are very much so. The fact that the specific way in which the hair may be worn varies from culture to culture, or from one time to another in the same culture, does not change the fact that all cultures at all times have such rules, and that they play an important part in the behavior of man in the presence of his fellows. We cannot predict the content of folk tales in a culture encountered for the first time; but we can safely predict that there will be folk tales, learned and passed on from generation to generation. A false opposition of the "instinctive" to the "learned" has tended in the past to prevent us from seeing these common features of human behavior and from recognizing that they must result, much as the instinctive behavior of rodent and carnivore does, from (a) the way we are made, and (b) the universal features of the human environment.

HEREDITY AND MENTAL ILLNESS

The confusion characteristic of discussions of heredity and environment is very marked when it comes to mental illness. The issues here are so serious that one can understand a lack of judicial calm in thinking about them, but their seriousness also makes it important to be clear about them as far as we can.

Implicitly or explicitly the question has been approached as the old dichotomy: Is mental illness caused by an abnormal heredity, some weakness of the germ plasm of the patient's parents, *or* by bad experiences and the special learning produced by such experiences? This is a false dichotomy, an "either-or" approach that nearly always leads one astray. Translate the question into the terms of Table 1, and it becomes, Is Factor I the cause of mental illness, or Factor V? In the first place, this leaves out Factors II, III, and IV; and in the second place, it rules out the important possibility of an interaction between factors. A certain heredity may predispose to mental illness in one set of environmental conditions, but may produce a highly stable, well-adjusted man in another; or a given set of environmental conditions may bring out the best in persons of one heredity and cause breakdown in others.

Present attitudes toward these questions are greatly affected by the work of F. J. Kallman in a study of the incidence of *schizophrenia* among close relatives of schizophrenics. The study shows that the closer the genetic relationship, the more likely it is that the relative will be schizophrenic. Thirteen per cent of the brothers and sisters of schizophrenics (excluding twins) are also schizophrenic. Twelve to 13 per cent of ordinary (fraternal) twins also have the disease, but 91 to 92 per cent have it if they are identical twins of schizophrenics. Identical twins, of course, have identical genetic constitutions since they grow from a single fertilized ovum; fraternal twins result from the chance fertilization of two ova at about the same time, and are no more closely related, genetically, than other brothers and sisters.

These results have sometimes been taken to mean that heredity is the whole cause of mental illness, or nearly the whole cause. The easiest way to show that this is not so is provided by M. Roth, using further data from Kallman (Table 2). Tuberculosis shows a similar pic-

TABLE 2. INCIDENCE OF TUBERCULOSIS AND OF SCHIZOPHRENIA AMONG RELATIVES OF PATIENTS HAVING THOSE DISEASES (in Per Cent)*

Degree of Relation	Frequency of TB in the Relatives	Frequency of Schizophrenia in the Relatives
Half-brothers or sisters	11.9	7.3
Brothers or sisters	25.5	12.9
Ordinary twins	25.6	12.5
Identical twins	87.3	91.5

*After Roth, from Kallman.

ture, and in tuberculosis we know that the environment plays the decisive part. An environmental action — exposure to infection by the tubercle bacillus — is essential, and we cannot possibly conclude that heredity is the whole cause of tuberculosis. The similar figures for schizophrenia, therefore, mean that one may inherit *susceptibility* to the disease, but do not make heredity the whole cause.

Table 2 has the same kind of significance as Figure 49, which showed that improvement in pecking by the newly hatched chick is a joint product of physical maturation and experience or learning. The table shows that heredity and environment can interact similarly in disease. It makes clear that the heredity of the person exposed to tuberculosis has a large part in determining his susceptibility to the infection. Otherwise we cannot understand the difference between 26 per cent for fraternal twins and 87 per cent for identical twins. Of course, twins are usually brought up in the same environment and if one is exposed the other is very likely to be exposed also. But as far as tuberculosis is concerned, this is just about as true of fraternal twins as of identical twins, so the great difference in the incidence of the disease can only be explained by the fact that the identical twins have the same hereditary susceptibilities.

Now if we look at the figures for schizophrenia we can see better what they show. The difference between 13 per cent for fraternal twins and 92 per cent for identical twins can only be understood by concluding that there is a hereditary susceptibility to schizophrenia. But this does not make stresses from the environment unimportant; just as tuberculosis occurs only by an environmental action on a susceptible constitution, so schizophrenia may occur only with some social stress.

There are in fact cases that show this. One of a pair of identical twin girls, very strictly brought up, had an unhappy affair and developed schizophrenia (but recovered later). Her twin stayed on an even keel, psychiatrically speaking, throughout the episode. However, the stresses that are involved in schizophrenia are not usually so well defined, and are probably the more long-continued and general stresses of home and social environments. Such influences would affect both of a pair of twins equally, and this helps to account for the very high frequency with which both have the disease when one has it.

SUMMARY

The development of behavior, and the characteristics of behavior at maturity, depend on a number of influences which are classified here as Factors I to VI. Heredity by itself (Factor I) cannot produce any behavior whatsoever; nor can learning by itself, without heredity and the nutritive environment necessary to produce an organism in which learning can occur. The unconditioned reflex does not require learning for its development; but all other behavior, including instinctive behavior in mammals and much instinctive behavior in other animals, involves learning determined by the experience of infancy (Factor IV). An essential point is that there is much behavior that is not learned but still is dependent on the existence of other, prior, learning.

Guide to Study

In reviewing, the student should make sure that he understands and can define, describe or explain: instinctive behavior as distinguished from instinct, and also from reflexes; physical vs. psychological maturation; the phrase "maintenance of neural structures by experience," and the term "experience" itself; imprinting; and the six "factors" or classes of influences on behavior. He should also be able to say what the behavioral evidence is that shows that salamanders do not have to learn to swim; how it is shown that learning and growth interact in chickens' pecking, and that early experience affects important aspects of behavior in species as different as ants, geese, dogs and apes; how it is shown that instinct is closely related to learning and intelligence in the rat; and what evidence, comparing schizophrenia and tuberculosis, shows that mental illness is determined by both heredity and environment. A useful exercise also is to see what other predictable aspects of human behavior can be listed, in addition to those mentioned in the text.

NOTES AND REFERENCES

The general point of view of this chapter derives from Frank Beach's paper of 1955, a culmination of a series of studies of instinctive behavior in mammals. One important early study appeared in 1939:

Beach, F. A.: The neural basis of innate behavior: III. Comparison of learning ability and instinctive behavior in the rat. *Journal of Comparative Psychology*, 1939, 28, 225–262.

Beach, F. A.: The descent of instinct. *Psychological Review*, 1955, 62, 401–410. The first real clarification of the heredity-environment problem with respect to behavior.

SPECIAL TOPICS

Emphasis on the Innate

Carmichael, L.: A further study of the development of behavior in vertebrates experimentally removed from the influence of external stimulation. *Psychological Review*, 1927, 34, 34–47. The maturation of reflexive responses.

Cruze, W. W.: Maturation and learning in chicks. *Journal of Comparative Psychology*, 1935, 19, 371–409.

Dennis, W.: Infant reaction to restraint: an evaluation of Watson's theory. *Transactions of the New York Academy of Science,* 1940, Series 2, 2, 202–218.

Roth, M.: Interaction of genetic and environmental factors in the causation of schizophrenia. In D. Richter (Ed.): *Schizophrenia: Somatic Aspects.* Macmillan, 1957.

Tinbergen, N.: *The Study of Instinct.* Oxford University Press, 1951.

Effects of Early Experience

Chow, K. L., Riesen, A. H., and Newell, F. W.: Degeneration of retinal ganglion cells in infant chimpanzees reared in darkness. *Journal of Comparative Neurology*, 1957, 107, 27–42.

Hess, E. H.: Imprinting. *Science,* 1959, 130, 133–141.

Hubel, D. H., and Wiesel, T. N.: Effects of visual deprivation on morphology and physiology of cells in the cat's lateral geniculate body. *Journal of Neurophysiology*, 1963, 26, 978–993.

James, H.: Imprinting with visual flicker. *Canadian Journal of Psychology*, 1960, 14, 13–20.

Lorenz, K.: *King Solomon's Ring.* Cited earlier (Chap. 1) but very relevant here also.

Melzack, R., and Thompson, W. R.: Effects of early experience on social behavior. *Canadian Journal of Psychology, 1956,* 10, 82–90.

Nissen, H. W., Chow, K. L., and Semmes, J.: Effects of restricted tactual . . . experience on the behavior of a chimpanzee. *American Journal of Psychology*, 1951, 64, 485–507.

Riesen, A. H.: Arrested vision. In S. Coopersmith (Ed.): *Frontiers of Psychological Research,* Freeman, 1964. (Originally in *Scientific American,* July, 1950.)

Senden, M. v.: *Space and Sight.* Methuen, 1960. Translation of the original German monograph (1932).

statistics and the control group

At some point in his introduction to psychology the student must be told something about statistics. It is not necessary for him to learn how to calculate *standard deviations* and *correlation coefficients* until he does research of his own, but he must know what such things are and how they are used if he is to understand the research of others. A large part of psychology must otherwise be taken on faith, which is no way to become a scientist. We have already had occasion to refer to control groups, whose use is statistical, and the following chapter on the study of intelligence will make further demands of this sort. Accordingly, it seems time now for a sort of interlude on the nature of statistical thought.

All scientific measurement is subject to error, and it is important to be able to estimate the probable extent of such error. Also, when predicting a specific event on the basis of preceding observations, or when drawing conclusions about a general class of phenomena from experience with a limited number of them, one is dealing not in certainties but in probabilities. To evaluate such probabilities we use statistics, which makes statistics an essential part of the scientific method.

The difference between biological and physical science is not that one is inexact, the other exact. Instead, the difference is in degree of exactness, this being related to the number of variables which must be dealt with simultaneously and the extent to which they can be controlled. In general, the biological sciences must deal with larger errors than the physical sciences; but this is not uniformly true, as the student will see if he considers the accuracy of meteorological prediction or if he comprehends the meaning of the fact that the structural engineer very often considers it necessary to use a safety factor of two or three hundred per cent. The statistical principles used in dealing with error in measurement, or in prediction and generalization, are the same whether the errors are large or small. Statistics is not a substitute for obtaining clear answers but a means of checking and controlling hasty conclusions, by providing an estimate of the error to which a conclusion is subject.

Statistical method has been highly developed mathematically, and is usually presented to the student in mathematical terms. Essentially, however, it is a way of thinking, which very often involves no computations and no use of formulas. It has two functions: describing empirical data, permitting one to see a mass of facts as a whole; and, secondly, providing the rules for inference and generalization from a limited set of observations to a larger universe of which one has observed only a part. It is sometimes said that science is not interested in the unique event. This is certainly not true. If the sun turned a mottled green for 30 seconds, just once, then returned to its usual sunny disposition and remained so with no sign of further upset, we can imagine what a commotion would be stirred up in astronomical circles. But it is true that the scientist is inveterately concerned with general classes of events, with regularities in repeated observations, and the unique event may be considered of interest because it implies the existence of a *class* of possible events.

The scientist persistently generalizes from the seen to the unseen. When he draws a conclusion from an experiment his statement concerns more than the specific objects or events that were part of the experiment. He observes that 43 specific chicks, fed a particular drug, grow faster on the average than 43 other specific chicks not fed the drug; he reports this as a fact, but his conclusion is the inference that *all* chicks would grow faster under certain conditions. (As we will see shortly, what he says is, "The difference between the means is statistically significant"; and this statement distinguishes between the fact of a faster average growth for his particular chicks—this is a fact, there is no argument about it—and the inference about the growth of all chicks in such conditions. When a difference is found to be "significant," it implies a generalized conclusion.) When I measure the rate of learning of college students in a particular set of circumstances, my concern is not primarily with those particular students but the way in which people in general—or mammals or vertebrates in general—learn.

This inference from the particular to the general is of course not peculiar to science; it is a fundamental feature of human thought, and so too is the other (the descriptive) function of statistics. In this book, consequently, statistical thinking is of interest in two ways: to help the student understand how research is made more precise and controlled; and also as a feature of human thought that has intrinsic interest psychologically, something from which we can learn about the thought process.

If, for example, the student has come to the conclusion that men are taller than women, not restricting his statement to the specific men and women that he has seen personally, he has made a statistical inference. If he has ever taken an average, he has made a statistical description. If he has even, without any adding up of quantities and dividing by the number of cases, concluded that the average day in July is warmer than the average day in June, or has estimated how high the temperature may go in August, he has made a statistical summary from his own past experience (which is necessarily limited), and has gone on to generalize, with an implied prediction about what is going to happen next year and the year after.

STATISTICAL CONCLUSIONS WITHOUT COMPUTATION

If the present chapter is not an example of statistics without tears, it may be that at least fewer tears will be shed than usually. A good deal of analysis of data can be done by simply arranging them in an orderly way (especially in graphic form). The object here is to show the student how to think statistically, and perhaps he will succeed better this way than if he was given an elaborate set of mechanical computations to carry out, which sometimes act as a substitute for understanding.

First, two conceptions about which it is quite important to be clear: The scientist works with a *sample* from which he draws conclusions about a *population* or *universe.* The sample is a sample set of the items making up the population. It is one's collection of facts or observations, the empirical data available to work with, their number of course being finite and often rather small. The population is not necessarily a population of people or animals—this is another scientific figure of speech—but usually comprises events or properties of objects or events; in an experimental science a population is characteristically hypothetical and indefinitely large. The sample is a set of properties or events that have actually been observed; the population or universe includes all the properties or events in this class (i.e., of the same kind) that could have been observed in the past or that may conceivably be observed in the future. To illustrate:

An astrophysicist investigating shooting stars wants to know what they are composed of. He manages to find, let us say, fifty meteorites and determines their composition. This is his sample. The population in which he is interested, however, will include future meteorites and past ones which were not recovered. He may go on to draw conclusions about the bodies in space that hit other planets, thus going even farther beyond his facts—but going beyond the facts is of the essence, in the scientific method.

A psychologist breeds rats selectively for maze learning ability, mating males that do well with females that do well, and males that do badly with females that do badly. After several generations of such selection he finds that the descendants of the good learners always do better than descendants of the poor learners. He has tested perhaps 20 rats of the sixth generation in each strain, bright and dull. He has therefore a sample of 20 animals from each of two infinitely large populations: namely, rats with heredities determined in certain ways. Apart from his two samples, these populations do not exist in actuality, for no one else has bred animals in this way. But this does not prevent him from concluding that future samples will show the same difference that he has found. This means that he is talking about learning ability in two indefinitely large, hypothetical populations of *all rats that will be, or might be, obtained by the breeding operations that he has carried out.* No one really cares, scientifically, about the maze learning of a particular rat, apart from its implications for larger questions. The question here concerns the relation of heredity to the learning ability, or intelligence, of rats in general and of mammals, including man, in general. Drawing such conclusions about hypothetical populations, making such generalizations, is certainly subject to error; but we must generalize, and there are statistical methods for evaluating the inevitable error.

The first step in all this is to describe the sample. Consider, for example, the error scores that were made by 31 rats in a simple maze problem: 27 9 13 32 23 16 18 21 15 24 23 19 19 4 29 22 33 7 30 17 26 17 10 22 17 16 36 27 22 12 26. Each number gives the total errors for an individual rat. The properties of the sample become easier to see merely by rearranging in order: 4 7 9 10 12 13 15 16 16 17 17 17 18 19 19 21 22 22 22 23 23 24 26 26 27 27 29 30 32 33 36. The highest and lowest values, or the range of values, are evident at a glance, and the *median* value, 21, can be found by counting to the mid-point in the series from either end (when there is an even number of scores the median is halfway between the two middle scores). The distribution of values becomes clearer from the next step, which is to group the scores by larger steps as shown in Table 3, or to represent the same grouping as in Figure 54. With this change some detail is lost—one no longer sees what the lower limit of error is, for example; it could be anything from 0 to 4, whereas in the raw data it was 4. But we now see clearly the bunching of scores near the middle; we see that the distribution of scores is approximately symmetrical, and we can estimate the *mean* directly. The mean is the "average" of elementary arithmetic, the sum of the quantities divided by their number. (Technically, there are several averages, of which the arithmetic mean is one.) By inspection, the mean is found a little above the dividing line between 15–19 and 20–24—that is, above 19.5. (By actual computation from the raw scores it is 20.4.)

TABLE 3. FREQUENCY DISTRIBUTION OF ERROR SCORES BY 31 RATS IN A MAZE TEST

Interval	Frequency
0–4	1
5–9	2
10–14	3
15–19	9
20–24	7
25–29	5
30–34	3
35–39	1

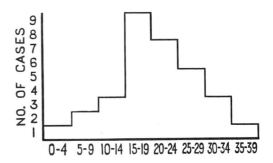

Figure 54. Histogram showing the errors made by 31 rats in a maze test (Table 3). One rat made errors in the 0–4 range, two rats made errors in the 5–9 range, and so on.

Two values here are of primary interest: the *central tendency* and the degree of *dispersion* or *variability.* The central tendency is the average, the single representation value which, if you must report a single value, best stands for the whole set of values concerned. The meaning of "best" here differs according to circumstances, but for most psychological experiments the mean or (less often) the median is used. As soon as we have this central value, however, the next step is to ask how much the single cases differ from it. How variable are the values in the sample? Here also there are several ways in which the answer may be given, but we will consider only two: the *range* and the *standard deviation,* or SD.

"Range" is easily determined simply by inspection of the highest and lowest values. Often it gives a sufficient description of the degree of variability. In an experiment comparing the intelligence of dogs and rats, for example, the score for rats ranged from 5 to 20, for dogs

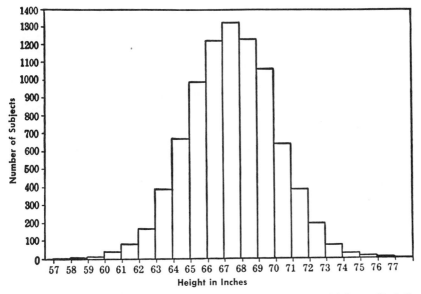

Figure 55. Histogram for heights of 8585 men. (From K. J. Holzinger, Statistical Methods for Students in Education, *Ginn.)*

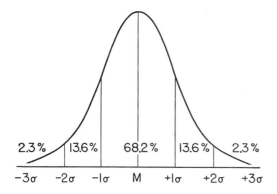

Figure 56. Normal probability curve, showing the frequencies with which certain deviations from the mean occur. Sigma (σ) stands for SD, or standard deviation; 68.2% of all cases fall within 1 SD of the mean, 95.4% within 2 SD (68.2 plus 13.6 plus 13.6), and so forth.

from 24 to 27, in a test in which 27 was a perfect score. For the purposes of the experiment in question no further analysis was needed: the superiority of the dog was evident.

However, range is apt to be unsatisfactory as an index of the amount of variability, because it is determined by the two most extreme cases only and does not tell us much about the less extreme ones. In the experiment referred to, for example, one exceptionally stupid dog might have made a score of 12: then the range for dogs would be 12 to 27, and this fact would not tell one that almost all dogs make scores over 20. A more stable index—less susceptible to being deflected by one individual subject—is provided by the standard deviation. To find the SD one must do some computing (it is the square root of the average of the squares of deviations from the mean), but this is not necessary in order to understand how the value is used.

It is generally used in conjunction with what mathematicians call the *normal probability curve.* Distributions which are approximately symmetrical and bell-shaped, as in Figure 55, and which as the number of cases increases come closer and closer to the smooth curve of Figure 56, are frequently found with biological measures such as men's heights or weights. The smooth curve applies only to an infinitely large population—an idealized conception. A finite number of cases, even as large a number as that presented in Figure 55, can only approximate it; and when we have a small number, as in Figure 54, the irregularities loom large. But Figure 54 is about as close to the smooth curve as we could expect for a sample of this size, and we can assume that it is a sample from an infinitely large population to which the normal probability curve, the idealized distribution of Figure 56, applies.

In that case, the standard deviation has certain quantitative properties shown in the figure. About two-thirds (68 per cent) of all values will fall within 1 SD of the mean value; one-sixth fall more than 1 SD below, and one-sixth more than 1 SD above the mean. About 2.3 per cent fall more than 2 SD above (or below) the mean, and 0.1 per cent more than 3 SD's above.

For example: consider adult IQ's on a particular test with a mean of 100 (which is what the mean IQ is supposed to be: p. 155) and an SD of 15 (approximately what is given by existing tests). If these values hold for the general population, and if IQ's are normally distributed, we know without being given any further information that about a sixth of the population have IQ's above 115, or that a man with an IQ of 135 is in approximately the top 2 per cent of the population. If it is said that all students who do well in college have IQ's above 115 (as it has been; the accuracy of the statement does not matter for our present purposes), it is implied that no more than one-sixth of the population could do well in college, as things stand at present. It is usually considered that IQ 70 is the dividing line between those who can assume control of their own lives and those who cannot (between "normal" and "retarded"). Since intelligence tests are subject to error, a test score should not be the sole basis of judging such a question in the individual case; but statistically, for the general population, it is implied by this definition that about 2.3 per cent of the population are retarded.

Now let us look more closely at the inference from sample to population. Suppose that we want to know how tall the average male college student is. Having searched out and measured 20 of these rare creatures, we find their mean height to be 69.8 inches. Is this the value we are looking for? We know that men differ in height, so we cannot just measure one, or two or three. We need a large group; is 20 large enough? We track down 20 more and measure them, and this time we get a mean of 70.3 inches. Three more groups of 20 give means of 70.1, 67.7 and 71.6. *The means of samples are variable too.* We pool the five groups and get a mean for the 100 men: 69.9. But another group of 100 would give us still another mean. The larger the samples, the less variable their means will be, but the variability will not disappear. We cannot get a final, precise answer, and we must try another approach.

We first get as large a sample as is practical. The mean of this sample is the best *estimate* of the mean of the universe from which the sample is drawn. In the example just discussed, our best estimate of the mean of height of all college men is 69.9 inches. Next we determine the variability of values in the sample, and from it estimate the variability in the universe.

Now we can look at our estimates critically, and ask how far off they are likely to be. We can ask, for example: could the true value be as low as 69.5 inches? We have a sample of 100 heights with a mean value of 69.9; is it probable that such a sample could be drawn at random from a population with a mean of 69.5? Mathematically, it is possible to determine exactly how often this would happen. It turns out to be, let us say, once in 25 times. The probability that the true value is as low as 69.5 therefore is only one in 25, or 4 per cent; it can be concluded with reasonable certainty that the true value is higher than this. Could the true value be 69.6, if it is not 69.5? The probability of this degree of error in our estimate can also be determined. We cannot ever say what the true value *is;* but we can determine the probability that it differs from the estimate by a specified amount, or that it lies within a specified range. With these fictitious data we might be able to say, for example, that there is a 50 per cent probability that the true value lies between 69.7 and 70.1; a 90 per cent probability that it lies between 69.6 and 70.2; and so on.

Now for scientific purposes it is customary to emphasize two levels of probability in asking such questions: the 5 per cent and 1 per cent levels. In the example just used, we may say that the mean obtained differs *significantly* from 69.5 *at the 5 per cent level.* In other words: the difference can be given some weight, since a chance difference as great as this would be found less than 5 per cent of the time. (The student must remember, however, that the chance difference at this level of significance does occur—once in 20 experimental determinations.) For a higher degree of confidence the 1 per cent level is adopted, with a 1-in-100 chance of being wrong. When one encounters the statement that a difference is "significant" it signifies, by common convention, that the probability is at least 19 to 1 against this being due to the operations of chance in obtaining our sample; "highly significant" may be considered to mean that the probability is 99 to 1 against. Alternatively, one may say that a difference is "significant at the 5 per cent level," or at the 1 per cent level.

Summarizing: we can never say what, precisely, is the true value of the mean of the universe from which a sample is drawn. But we can, with the proper computations, determine the probability that it differs from our *estimate* by more than any given amount. Also, we can state limits within which it must lie, with a probability of 20 to 1 or 100 to 1—or if we wish, 1000 to 1.

No one can do more. Improved methods of measurement and larger samples cut down the size of probable error but do not abolish it. They decrease the uncertainty range within which the true value lies, but do not decrease it to zero.

RESTATING MATTERS, WITH SOME FURTHER (IMPROBABLE) EXAMPLES

Statistics asks the student to think in a new way about the meaning of averages and related matters. He is used to thinking that we know—or could determine—the *exact* value for the height of the average man, or the income of the average family. Is this not the sort of thing the census does for us? If it is impractical to do it for all men, considering some of the out-of-way places in the world, why should it be impossible to obtain a precise value for the mean height of all adult male Americans, or Indonesians, or Greeks? But as we will see in a moment, precision in this sense is chimerical. The scientific use of statistics really does ask for a new way of thinking, which though inherently simple is at first hard to achieve. It is unlikely that the preceding pages have fully conveyed this point of view, so the purpose of the present section is to restate it with some bizarre examples that may help to make it intelligible.

Let us see why it is chimerical to ask for an exact figure for the mean height of American male adults. First, there is the fact that *every* measurement has its probable error. Next, any biological population is not static but changing. A number of American males die daily, and a number reach the twenty-first birthday that marks adult status. If we are really to have a precise figure for the whole population and not a sample (however large), we must fix on some date and hour—say 12 noon, July 1, in the year following the decision to undertake the project—and with the aid of 10 or 12 million assistants we get everyone measured within a few minutes of the hour, including all those on their sickbeds, aloft in airplanes, at sea or abroad.

Now, assuming that we could succeed in this improbable undertaking, we must recognize that the mean we obtain will be out of date by July 2; in fact, well before the necessary computations could be completed. The net result of all this labor would therefore be, at best, a precise value for the population at a particular time in the past, not the present. To apply it to the present at once involves an element of estimation. We cannot treat census figures for this or any other aspects of the average man as precise factual values, independent of inference; they are estimates—from very large samples, it is true, and with correspondingly small deviations from the "true" value—but still estimates that are subject to error. For most purposes we will thus be better off if we recognize this fact in the first place, and frankly use a sampling-and-inference method.

Now another improbable example, which may help us in understanding the logic of this method. Let us suppose that an explorer who has penetrated to some fastness in the mountains of Mexico, where no one has been before as far as he knows, discovers and traps a single specimen of an elephant 10 inches high at the shoulder. He has seen no others, nor heard of any. What information has he about the species, the population from which his sample of one has been drawn? His best estimate of the mean height of the species is 10 inches; but having only one in his sample he has no basis for estimating variability and thus no basis for saying how far off his guess about the average height might be.

Even with a single specimen, however, he is bound to have formed some idea of the size of other members of the species, and there are some conclusions that can be drawn quite logically. He can rule out the hypothesis, for example, that the mean of the population is 40 inches, the standard deviation 12. This situation is shown roughly by the larger curve, diagram *A,* Figure 57. He can also rule out the hypothesis that the mean is 15, SD 2 (smaller curve, diagram *A*). Both hypotheses imply that the first animal he happened to encounter is one of the very smallest—$2^1/_2$ SD's away from the mean. The probability that this would happen is well below the 5 per cent level. Similarly, he can rule out the hypothesis that the mean height is

6 inches, standard deviation 1.5 (diagram *B*, Fig. 57). Many hypotheses cannot be ruled out, but some can be.

His most probable hypothesis is represented by one of the curves of diagram *C:* some distribution centered about a mean of 10 inches. The different curves in diagram *C* are meant to show that, with a single specimen, nothing is known about variability and so the SD may be large (considerable spread in the curve) or small (little spread). As *D* shows, these curves may be shifted somewhat to left or right and still represent tenable hypotheses, as long as the given sample value, 10 inches, remains in the central part of the curve.

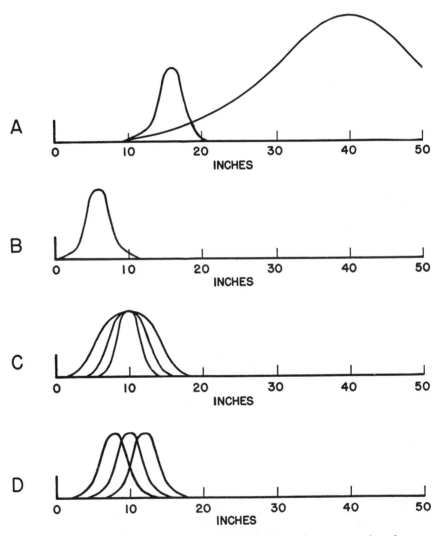

Figure 57. *Possible hypotheses about the heights of a new species of pygmy elephants, given a sample of one, 10 in. high. Diagram A: two hypotheses, (1) that the mean for the species is 40 in., SD 12 in. (larger curve, to the right); and (2) that the mean is 15 in., SD 2 in. (smaller curve). B: mean, 6, SD 1.5, and so forth; see text.*

When 4 more animals are captured, giving values of 9.6, 9.7, 9.8, 10.0, and 10.1 inches, an estimate of variability can be made — it is small — and now the distance becomes smaller by which the curve can be shifted to left or right and still represent a tenable hypothesis. The point for the student to get from this example is that we can quite freely form hypotheses about the population, after seeing a sample from it, but must then proceed to test them rigorously. The elaborate machinery of statistics, the formulas and computations omitted in this book, make it possible to state precisely what the probability would be of getting a known sample from any given hypothetical population. If the probability is low we disregard that hypothesis (but cannot rule it out absolutely and finally, for the very improbable sometimes happens).

However, this process cannot pick out, from among those hypothetical populations which might reasonably have produced our sample, *the* one correct hypothesis. The larger the sample, the more we can narrow the zone within which probable answers lie, but we are always left with an uncertainty range, even if small. This is represented in principle by diagram *D,* Figure 57.

To be epigrammatic, science works not with absolute truth but with a probable error. Its hope is to reduce error to a minimum, only. The scientist *thinks* in terms of truth when he sets up a hypothesis for testing, for what he says in effect is: Let us suppose that the true mean has such-and-such a value; if so, what would be found in a sample? But the result, the only conclusion that can be justified, is that the "true" value has a thus-and-so probability of lying within such and such a range of possible values.

COMPARING TWO VALUES

Now a different but related case: the comparison of values and the determination of significant differences between samples.

Take first a familiar case, the comparison of the heights of men and women. Suppose that we have two samples, 100 in each, of the heights of college men and women. The two means are 69.9 and 65.4 inches. Are men taller than women? That is, if we had the mean of all men's heights would it differ from the mean of all women's?

We attack the question by saying, Assume that the heights of men and women are *not* different. This is the *null hypothesis.* It amounts to assuming that the two samples of heights come from the same population. Now we can ask, What is the probability that we would draw from the same population two samples like these, with means that differ as much? We know that any two samples from the same population will give different means, just by chance; is that what has happened in this case? But the answer here might well be that two such different samples could come from the same population less than one in a thousand times; it is thus very unlikely that the null hypothesis is true. We therefore reject it. This in turn means that we conclude that men and women differ in height. The usual way of reporting such a result is to say that "the difference between the means is significant" (or in this case, of course, very highly significant).

This method of analysis might be applied in an experiment as follows. We want to know whether the frontal part of the brain is more important for maze learning than the occipital part. We remove equal amounts of brain tissue, on the average, from two groups of rats. Those with frontal damage make, let us say, a mean of 42.1 errors; those with occipital damage, 55.7 errors. Our two samples are certainly different, but is the difference significant? We apply the null hypothesis, assume that there is no difference in the means of *all* rats with such frontal lesions and *all* with such occipital lesions, and see how often two such samples would be drawn from a single population. The variability in our two groups is great, indicating a wide "spread" in the curve representing the parent population (Fig. 57), and this implies that the uncertainty range is rather great. As a result, computation shows that our two samples might be obtained from a single population about 20 times in 100. The difference is far from the 5 per cent level of significance, so we cannot reject the null hypothesis. We have not yet established the proposition that occipital damage is worse than frontal damage in its effect on maze running.

The student should keep in mind, however, that the odds still favor the proposition; by increasing the size of the samples, and thus decreasing the uncertainty range—the amount by which the means may vary—a further experiment might find a significant difference after all.

In the preceding examples we have dealt with measurements and normally distributed values. One is not limited to measurements, and normal distributions, in statistical thinking. Suppose we are interested in the relation of wildness to heredity in rats. We bring up 20 rats from an albino laboratory strain and 20 from a wild gray strain, all separated from the mother at weaning and brought up singly in identical cages. Heroically, the experimenter reaches into each cage when the occupant has reached 70 days of age, and picks up the animal once. He counts the bites received: 1 bite from the albinos, 13 from the grays. There are methods of computation (e.g., chi-square, which need not be described here) that make it possible to determine that this result is highly improbable on the assumption that biting rats are equally likely to occur with either heredity. The result is therefore highly significant. We reject the null hypothesis (that there is no difference in the frequency of biters in the two universes, all hypothetical albinos and all hypothetical grays, brought up in this particular way). Rejecting the null hypothesis is equivalent to concluding that there is a relation between heredity and wildness. Here we treat biting as an index of wildness, but the procedure does not measure wildness in the individual animal, and we have no idea whether it is normally distributed.

THE CONTROL GROUP

The experiment just considered brings us to the use of the control group. In the physical sciences it may often be possible to hold constant all but one of the factors that might affect the outcome of an experiment; this one, the *independent variable,* is changed systematically, and the experimenter observes the effects in the *dependent variable.* In a study of the pressure of the atmosphere, for example, the independent variable may be height above sea level; the dependent variable is the height of a column of mercury in a barometric tube. Other influences that might affect the outcome are eliminated or kept constant: temperature, contaminating substances in the mercury, movement of the surrounding air, and so forth. In the biological sciences one can only approach this ideal procedure; and only too often fundamental questions have gone unanswered because it was not possible to get anywhere near it. In psychological research there are two great difficulties which frequently demand the use of control groups as a substitute for the ideal procedure.

One is that taking a psychological test usually changes the subject; a later test does not give the same result because of *practice effect*—the subject as we say "remembers" the first test. The second difficulty is that we are dealing with extraordinarily complex material; after we have used up our first sample of the material (the first subject or group of subjects) we cannot get a second that is identical with the first, because animals and men differ in many ways which we cannot identify before beginning an experiment.

Suppose, for example, that we want to find out whether removing the frontal lobes of a monkey's brain affects his ability to learn a visual discrimination. In an ideal procedure we would measure his learning ability, remove the frontal lobes, and measure his learning ability again. But in reality the second measurement is disturbed by memory of the first. We must measure learning ability by the number of trials, or the number of errors made, in achieving the discrimination. In the second measurement there will almost certainly be a practice effect, and we do not know how great it will be. Next best, in a slightly less ideal world, we would obtain two monkeys identical in all respects; we would remove the frontal lobes from one, have both learn the task under identical conditions, and see how much faster the normal monkey learned, compared to the one operated on. But in practice we cannot find two identical subjects, animal or human. (Identical twins are identical with respect to heredity, but it is impossible that everything that has happened since birth which might affect them psychologically is exactly the same. Also, of course, there are not many of them.) Thus we are driven to the comparison of two groups, an *experimental group* and a *control group,* large enough to make individual differences average out. If the original learning capacity of two subjects is not identical, the average for two groups is likely to differ much less, and the probable degree of difference can be dealt with statistically.

The ideal cases referred to, however, should be kept in mind, for they tell us what we are trying to achieve by the use of the control group. In the frontal-lobe question referred to, what we would like to do is measure the learning ability of the same monkey with and without his frontal lobes, with the second measurement not being affected by the first. This is impractical. So is the hope of finding two identical monkeys; but it is not impractical to find two groups which, if they are large enough, will be much more similar, as groups, than two individual monkeys. Our choice of a control group, then, is a matter of choosing animals which are as much like the animals in the experimental group as possible, in every way that affects visual learning.

The experiment may then proceed in one of two ways. First, we can operate on one group, and test both. We compare the mean scores of the operates and of the normal control subjects, and see whether they differ significantly. Statistics at this point enables us to evaluate the probability that the difference we have found is due simply to accidental differences in our two groups, treating them as two samples in the way already described. The second procedure would be to test both groups, operate on one, test both groups again, and see whether the increases in score by the normals (due to practice effect) are significantly greater than the increases by the operates (though the experiment might come out with a still clearer result, the normals all showing increases and the operates all showing losses).

The principle is clear: make your control group like the experimental group in every way that would affect the outcome of the experiment, except for the one variable in which you are interested. The pitfalls and gins besetting the path of the investigator on this point mainly consist of not recognizing a variable that affects the results. If one is picking rats out of a colony cage, and puts the first 10 into the experimental group, the second 10 into the control group, one overlooks the possibility that the most easily caught animals, or the ones that come to the front of the cage and allow themselves to be picked up, are tamer than the others; and this difference is likely to affect any experimental result. The easiest solution is to put no. 1 into the first group, no. 2 into the second, no. 3 into the first, and so on. (There are also more sophisticated ways of doing this by the use of random numbers assigned to the animals, but we need not go into this.)

Again, in clinical investigations one does not have the choice of one's "experimental" group, and one perforce must try to find a similar control group. This is usually difficult. The clinical group (corresponding to the experimental group of the laboratory) generally includes people of all sorts of occupations, rural as well as urban, educated and uneducated, old and young. It is difficult indeed to persuade a group of similar persons, who are not ill and have no reason to take tests, to give up the time to act as subjects—especially since they are apt to view any psychological test with suspicion. But if one wants to know whether removal of the human frontal lobe affects intelligence, and if the clinical group with frontal lobe operation has a mean age of 40 and a mean of 8 years' schooling, for example, one must make one's comparisons with a group that is similar in these respects, as intelligence test scores vary with amount of schooling and with advancing age.

CORRELATIONS

Correlation is the degree of relation between two variables. A *coefficient of correlation* is a quantitative statement thereof. It is even more time-consuming to compute than the quantitative values we have been dealing with so far, but—once more—the student's aim here should be to understand it, instead of memorizing a formula and methods of computation.

Correlation coefficients range from plus 1 to minus 1; plus 1 represents a perfect relation between the two variables, high values accompanying high values, intermediate values accompanying intermediate values, and so on. Minus 1 *also* represents a perfect relation, though it is reversed: the highest score on X goes with the lowest one on Y, next highest on X with the next lowest on Y, and so on. The relation is perfect in this sense. Once you knew what a man got on test X you would also know what he got, or will get, on Y. Finally, a correlation of zero means no relation at all; here a high score on the first test might go with a high, a medium, or a low score on the second.

To see better what is meant, consider Figure 58. Tests A and B (first of the three diagrams) have a zero correlation. Knowing what a man has made on test A tells us nothing about what he will make on test B. Now consider tests P and Q (second diagram). These two are perfectly and positively related (perhaps we may note that such perfection simply does not occur in psychology). If we know a child's

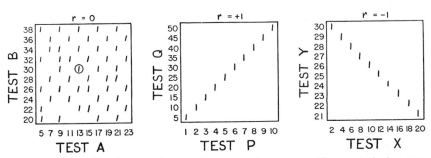

Figure 58. *Correlations of zero, plus one and minus one. The symbol* r *is a particular index of correlation (the Pearson product-moment coefficient). Each mark represents a single subject's scores on the two tests being correlated. In the first diagram, for example, the encircled mark is for a subject who made 12 on the first test (test A) and 31 on the second (B).*

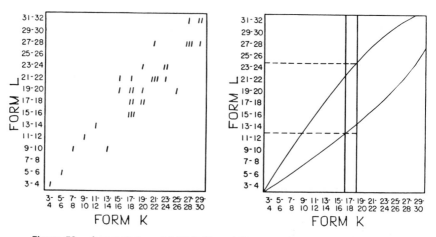

Figure 59. *A correlation of 0.93 (left) and the accuracy with which prediction of a second score (on form L of the test) can be made from a first (on form K of the same test). Even with as high a correlation as this, the accuracy is not great; on the right is shown the roughly drawn "envelope" enclosing the entries. The vertical lines enclose the entries which represent scores of 17 or 18 on form K; the width of the envelope at this point determines how much variability may be expected in the scores on form L —roughly, from 13 to 24.*

score on *P* we do not have to give *Q*; the two tests correlate 1.00, so the second score can be determined as soon as the first is known. Similarly with tests *X* and *Y*, though now the relation is negative; if a subject makes a poor score on *X* we can predict, without further testing, that he will make a good score on *Y*.

These, however, are only the extreme cases. One thing the student needs to know is the degree of relation, roughly, that is represented by such correlation coefficients as 0.30, 0.50, 0.70, and 0.90. In general, one may say that the relation is not nearly as close as one of these figures makes it sound. The first, 0.30, represents a barely discernible relation. A correlation of 0.70 is not 70 per cent correspondence, or agreement 7 times out of 10, but 49 per cent; a correlation of 0.90 represents 81 per cent correspondence.* In psychology, because we must often deal with coefficients below 0.60, it is common to speak of one above this value as representing "a high correlation." But this is misleading, suggesting as it does a close relation between the two variables; it would be better to reserve the term for coefficients above 0.90.

All this has more meaning for the student if expressed graphically. Figure 59 shows a plot of two sets of scores, on parallel forms of the same test, in which the correlation is 0.93. It is reasonable to speak of this as a high correlation, but let us see how close the correspondence really is. The vertical lines in the second diagram of Fig-

---

*In a manner of speaking. These values are obtained by squaring the coefficient of correlation (0.70 × 0.70 = 0.49, 0.90 × 0.90 = 0.81), and what they represent more exactly is the proportion of the *variance* (SD^2) in one test that is predictable from or determined by variance in the other.

ure 59, on each side of the 17–18 value on the base line, contain the entries for all subjects who made 17 or 18 on the first form of the test. On the second test, these subjects made scores ranging from the 15–16 bracket to the 21–22 bracket. (From the raw data it could be seen that one man who made 18 on the first test made 15 on the second; another who made 18 on the first made 22 instead, on the second.) Evidently no very close prediction of the second score is possible, despite the correlation of 0.93.

Figure 60 shows a somewhat lower correlation, 0.72. A comparison of Figures 59 and 60 shows clearly that the thickness of the diagonal band made by the entries on such a correlation plot is the essential factor in predicting the second score from the first. With a high correlation we have a thin band; when the vertical lines are drawn, as in Figure 59, only a short segment from the diagonal band is enclosed, which means that the amount of variation in the second test is small—and prediction is good. When the correlation is lower, the band is broader and prediction is poor. In the perfect case, the correlation in the second diagram of Figure 58, the band would have no width whatever (all the points plotted fall on a single straight line), and prediction is perfect.

This graphical analysis is of course rough, and there are much more exact ways of dealing with the predictions that can be made, and their degree of error. But it is still true here, as elsewhere, that a good deal can be learned about complex data by simple inspection, and there is no other way that is as good for conveying the fundamental meaning of a correlation coefficient, high or low.

With a correlation, it is clear that we are always dealing with a causal connection. The connection may be very indirect, however, and a correlation, in and of itself, does not tell us what causes what. If *A* and *B* are correlated, *A* may cause *B*, *B* may cause *A*, both may be caused by an outside factor *C*, or there may be a mixture of these relations. It is known, for example, that intelligence-test scores are correlated with years of schooling—but we cannot leap to the conclusion that one's IQ is determined by one's education. The relation may be just the opposite—those who have not the intelligence to do well

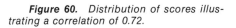

Figure 60. *Distribution of scores illustrating a correlation of 0.72.*

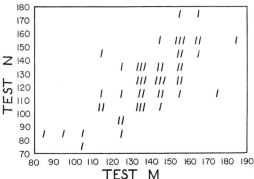

in school tend to leave earlier than others, which means that intelligence affects amount of schooling. A more important factor may be that intelligent parents tend (1) to have intelligent children, and (2) to encourage their children to keep on at school. In this case, the parent is the outside factor, *C,* that determines the level both of *A* (intelligence) and of *B* (schooling); *A* and *B* could thus be correlated without one's causing the other.

Intelligence in the growing child (mental age, not IQ: see Chapter 9) is known, for example, to be correlated with length of the big toe. This old joke might well be remembered by the student; the statement is quite true, for as a child grows his capacity for solving problems increases at the same time that his bones are growing in length, and the two therefore show a significant correlation. This may help the student to see that, though a correlation shows a causal relation *somewhere,* it does not necessarily mean that one of the two things correlated causes the other.

SUMMARY

Statistics is a fundamental feature of the scientific method; it is concerned with evaluating the errors which must occur in any measurement, or in generalizing from known data (a sample) to the larger class of values or events to which the data belong (a population or universe). The elaborate mathematical methods of statistics increase the exactness with which the estimate of error is made, but they are not the essence of the matter; graphical methods, and simple inspection, are often sufficient for a particular problem in which results are relatively clear-cut. (Some scientists say they make no use of statistics; what they really mean is that inspection is sufficient for their purposes, without formal computations.)

The first step of analysis is a description of the available data, the sample. Two values are of primary importance: a measure of central tendency, and a measure of dispersion. Central tendency is a single representative value, an average; there are several kinds of averages, of which the most important is the (arithmetic) mean. Dispersion is the extent to which individual cases deviate from the average; one index of it is the range, but a more useful one is the standard deviation, or SD. This is particularly so when we are dealing with the "normal probability distribution," the symmetrical bell-shaped curve frequently found with biological data.

Given the mean and the SD, we can then ask how probable it is that our sample has come from any given hypothetical population. If the probability is low, we reject the conclusion that the sample has come from that population. For scientific purposes, it is customary to work with two levels of "significance" (i.e., of probability) in drawing such conclusions: the 5 per cent level (when it is reasonably sure that the sample has not come from that population) and the 1 per cent level (still surer).

To determine whether an experimental treatment of some sort has had an effect on a group of subjects, we use essentially the same method. We have an experimental group and a control group, the latter treated in exactly the same way as the experimental group except for the one treatment in whose effects we are interested. What we ask is whether the two samples, the data from the two groups, could have come from the same population. That is, we make the null hypothesis: we assume that the treatment did *not* have an effect. (The difference between our two groups may have occurred by chance, since any two samples from the same population are likely to differ.) Statistics allows us to determine just how probable such a result would be – how often we would get, from the same population, two samples as different as these two. If the probability is below 5 per cent, we reject the null hypothesis: that is, we conclude that the treatment did have an effect. The chance of being wrong in this conclusion, of course, is 1 in 20; if we wish to be more certain to avoid a wrong conclusion, we may use the 1 per cent level instead.

Correlation is the degree of relation between two variables; a coefficient of correlation is a quantitative measure of the relation, ranging from plus 1 to minus 1. Graphical analysis is very useful here as well, especially since calculating the coefficient may be very laborious.

When two variables are correlated, there is a causal relation, but from the correlation alone one cannot determine what causes what: *A* may cause *B*, *B* may cause *A*, or they may share a common cause, *C*.

NOTES AND REFERENCES

Obviously this chapter does not deal with all aspects of statistical thought, and offers no help to one who wants to make active use of statistics himself. The intention here is only to enable the student to comprehend the meaning of certain commonly made statistical statements. A number of books are available in this field and the student should consult his instructor when he wants to go further, for these texts vary in the extent to which they involve the reader in details and thus vary in difficulty. However, an authoritative and effective treatment will be found in either of the following books:

Ferguson, G. A.: *Statistical Analysis in Psychology and Education.* McGraw-Hill, 1971.
Hays, W. L.: *Statistics for Psychologists.* Holt, Rinehart and Winston, 1963.

For the beginner, a valuable preparation for tackling statistical texts is the following programed-learning text:
McCollough, C., and Van Atta, L.: *Introduction to Descriptive Statistics and Correlation,* McGraw-Hill, 1964.

9

intelligence

Among the great names of psychology—such names as Freud, Pavlov, Thorndike, Watson—are two that are great because their owners learned how to measure something that could not be measured before. Hermann Ebbinghaus invented nonsense syllables and then could measure memory, by counting the number of syllables a subject could remember at some time after having memorized a list of them. Alfred Binet, with whom we are now concerned, invented a set of simple questions and problems to put to children and, by counting the number of satisfactory performances and comparing them with those of other children, could measure a child's intelligence. The problems were simple indeed, related to common everyday experience, and it was a stroke of genius to realize how revealing they could be of a child's mental development. Binet made the great discovery, and all later work is really a development of his original idea. Test items (the individual questions or problems) have been extended and improved, tests suitable for older persons and for measuring different aspects or kinds of intelligence* have been developed, but it was Binet who showed in principle how all this could be done.

The kind of material that is used for the measurement of intelligence might include asking a child what a match is used for; what time of day it is when the sun is in the west; what the meaning of the proverb "Once bitten, twice shy" is; or what holds airplanes up, or in what respect an airplane is like a balloon. The subject may be asked to complete an analogy like "Boy is to girl as man is to ___," or the more difficult "Raindrop is to air as bubble is to ___." One can ask who Einstein was, or Hitler. One can put a pattern before the subject and have him copy it with blocks, and here of course the problem can range from very easy to very hard, so that a whole series of the same

---

*E.g., verbal vs. nonverbal intelligence, where there are sex differences; the girls do better with verbal tests, the boys with mechanical, spatial and quantitative ones. Males, who are inclined to think that verbal skill is due simply to talking too much, may be reminded that language is man's distinguishing mark as a species. The lower animals also do better with nonverbal tasks.

kind of tasks can be used. Some of the "problems" that have been suggested would be suitable only for very young children, some only for older ones, but a list of such items, running from easy to hard, could be prepared and used to find out, for any one person, what level of difficulty he could deal with. A total score could be determined by giving him one point for each item on which he succeeded, and this score could be used to compare the subject with others.

Having made up such a list — the first intelligence test — Binet determined the average score made by three-year-old children, four-year-olds, five-year-olds, and so on. Now when he tested a child of six years who made a score that was average for children of five, he knew that the child was retarded in his intellectual development and he could say that the child had a *mental age* of 5; or if the score was half way between the averages for seven years and eight years, the child was ahead of his age group with a mental age of 7.5.

The next development was to define an *intelligence quotient** or *IQ. MA* is mental age, *CA* chronological age. The IQ is then defined as follows:

$$IQ = \frac{MA}{CA} \times 100.$$

Thus an eight-year-old with a mental age of 6 has an IQ of 75; if instead he has a mental age of 10, his IQ is 125. The IQ therefore is an index of the *rate of intellectual development.* An IQ of 100 means an average rate of development, 95 a slightly slow rate, 90 a slower one, and so on.

For adults, the situation is somewhat different. The intelligence that is measured by such tests does not continue to rise much after the age of 15 or thereabouts (no exact figure can be given, since the cessation of development is not abrupt). But we know that those with low IQ's during childhood continue to make low scores at maturity, and high IQ's lead to high scores at maturity. What we can do therefore is to work out IQ's for adults that correspond to their probable IQ's in childhood. The mean IQ for the whole population is considered to be 100, and the standard deviation of IQ's is 15 (p. 141). So we take the mean score of the adult population on some test and say that those who make that score have an IQ of 100 — by definition. A score that is made or exceeded by only 15.9 per cent of the population is 1 SD above the mean (Fig. 56) and equals an IQ of 115; one made or exceeded by only 2.3 per cent, 2 SD's above the mean, equals an IQ of 130; and so on, with in-between scores treated accordingly. A child's IQ makes a direct comparison of his rate of development with that of others; an IQ at maturity compares his ultimate attainment with that of others, and refers only by inference to the rate of development.

*This important step was made by Wilhelm Stern.

RELIABILITY AND VALIDITY

There are two questions one must ask about any mental test: How accurate or dependable or reliable is the measurement it makes; and, Is it measuring what it is supposed to measure? The first is technically the question of *reliability,* the second the question of *validity.* Ideally, to answer the second question one must have a perfect test, or practically perfect, to compare the new test with; we have no perfect tests, so we must approach the matter indirectly.

Reliability is fairly straightforward. It is defined quantitatively as the correlation between the scores on a test made by the same subjects on two different occasions — preferably using different forms of the test. With repetition of the same form the subject is likely to remember and repeat the answers he gave to questions on the first time of testing. Figure 59 (p. 150) is an example in which the correlation between the two forms of a pictorial test of intelligence in adults was 0.93. Here we say that the *reliability of the test* is 0.93.

Validity is more difficult. On the face of it, a child's ability to name common objects or to say what is missing in a picture of a horse with three legs may not have much to do with his powers of thought. When Binet published the first intelligence test, how were people to know that it did in fact measure intelligence? Many people today have their doubts about the validity of such tests; what evidence can one cite in reply? As far as reliability is concerned, values for the well-established tests run over 0.90, which allows one to say how large the error of measurement is likely to be — accuracy is not perfect, but it is, on the whole, very good.* But no quantitative value can be given for validity, except by comparing one test with another, which means nothing when one asks whether *any* existing test is valid.

We have no simple answer we can give, especially where the intelligence of older subjects is concerned. Existing tests are mostly tests of *academic and clerical aptitude:* that is, they measure intelligence only as it is related to school and college, and to desk-work occupations. They do not measure intelligence as it is needed for chess, for understanding and getting on with people, for interior decorating or for being an inventor. Even in academic matters they may predict who will do well in advanced examinations but tell us nothing about who will be leaders in research; in officers' training school they may tell us who will be well trained but nothing about which cadets will become leaders of men.

A particular problem concerns the evaluation of adult intelligence. The widely used tests are all developments of material

---

*Fortunately, the error of measurement is least with low IQ's. Variability of measurement is fairly large with higher IQ's, and the subject who gets an IQ of 125 on one test might get 118, perhaps, or 130, on a second test; but at this level no one's future is likely to be determined by the precise value of his IQ. But a low IQ may determine whether the subject is to be classed as feeble-minded, or whether he would benefit from being put in a special class for the retarded, and here the error is small. An IQ of 56, for example, is likely to remain within one or two points of that value on retesting, and is unlikely to vary as much as five points.

Figure 61. *Two items from a pictorial test of intelligence for adults. The task is to point to the part of each picture that is "funny" or "out of place." (Note, not what is impossible—rather the opposite.) Left, Is it loaded? Right, interior decoration. Left, easy; right, moderate difficulty.*

Figure 62. *Two further test items as in Figure 61. Left, costume for church-going? (especially since this was prepared about 1940). Right, the little guy shows his muscle (if any). Left, moderate difficulty; right, hard.*

designed originally for school children: to test adults, they use the same kind of questions but make them harder—and more bookish. For a good evaluation (unless one is simply trying to predict academic performance) something closer to adult interests is needed. One example is provided by the accompanying pictures (Figs. 61 and 62) which were designed as part of a nonverbal test (the subject has only to point to "what is funny or out of place").

For their primary purpose—the prediction of school performance—the existing tests are good though far from perfect. The real validation comes from the experience of several generations of testers. But these "intelligence tests" are not tests of general intelligence—at least not after the age of six, seven or eight—for there are important aspects of human intelligence that they do not touch at all.

SELECTION OF TEST MATERIAL

The student understands intelligence testing much better when he knows how one selects the problems that make up a test. The process is highly empirical rather than theoretical. One chooses items that work and discards others, no matter how attractive the latter may seem. The meaning of this statement will be clearer if we first consider a problem that touches the student closely: the problem of devising an examination to measure comprehension of a college course.

Traditionally, the essay examination was used for this purpose. It is a relatively direct measure and has a fair degree of validity. It is however known to be not very reliable; when two examiners mark the same set of papers the correlation between the two sets of marks in a large class is not apt to be above 0.60, and as we have seen this is not a high correlation. The correlation would be still lower between two different examinations on the same subject matter.

Reliability can be increased by the use of objective examinations; but unless validity is also kept in mind, we may get results that are even farther from our goal of measuring *comprehension.* For example, the objective questions may simply test memory for the exact words of the textbook; a student who has worked hard to understand it, and has intelligently worked out its implications, would make a poor mark; another who has simply memorized, with little attempt at rational understanding, might make a good one. Devising objective examinations that do not sacrifice validity in this way is not easy, even after one has been in the business for some time. For the inexperienced examiner it can be very laborious. The experienced examiner has a stock of questions from past years to use as a guide, or even to use again together with new ones; and he is more likely to hit on a satisfactory wording for a question at first try. What we are concerned with here, however, is not the discomforts that examiners must undergo, but the principles of mental measurement, which will be illustrated best if we see how one might go about developing an objective examination from the ground up.

In practice, one might proceed as follows: First one would devise the best questions one could, in rather large numbers, since some of them will turn out to be unsatisfactory. Next, one needs some way of sorting out the class, roughly, into good, fair and poor students. If the class has had to prepare a term paper or do laboratory work, from which an independent evaluation of the students is available, nothing more is necessary, and the final paper may consist of the objective questions only. If not, the paper may include some essay questions. From the term paper or essay questions one then finds a group with good comprehension of the course work, and a group with poor comprehension. Finally, one looks at each objective question to see whether the more capable group did better with it than the less capable, and discards all questions for which this is not true—a procedure known as "item analysis."

In this method, one cannot be sure that the "high" group contains all the best students, and only the best; nor that the "low" group is made up only of the poorest. Essay questions, or term papers, have not sufficient reliability to determine this. But the essay questions are reliable enough to discriminate between groups, and allow one to pick out two groups that differ greatly in level of ability. On the average, the group of high scorers on the essay section of the paper will be much better students than the low scorers.

For each objective question (or "item"), one determines the number of correct answers by each group. If, for example, 47 out of 50 in the high group answer a question correctly, and 14 out of 50 in the low group, the question is evidently valid. But on another question, one may find 35 correct in the high group, 34 in the low group; this one clearly does not discriminate sufficiently, and should be excluded from the examination because it increases the amount of chance error. Worse still, one may find a question which gives: high group 22, low group 28. In fact, whenever an item analysis of this kind is done with an objective test one finds such questions, which are clearly invalid and are better left out of the final reckoning. Having thrown these out, one then proceeds to rescore the shortened examination for all students. This gives the final mark.

It does not matter how logically justifiable a question may be; if in fact it confuses the better student or misleads him into looking for subtleties that are not there, but fails to confuse the student who perhaps does not know enough to be misled, the question is a poor one.

Exactly the same principle applies in constructing an intelligence test. Its whole success will depend on asking what problems *are* solved by the more intelligent, and rigorously refusing to use problems that an intelligent person *should* be able to solve, in the opinion of the test constructer. One might, for example, try to devise a measure of intelligence by saying, "Intelligence is the capacity to solve problems, so we will get a set of puzzles to use as a test." Or one might say, "Intelligence is the capacity to adapt to the environment, so we will test our subjects by putting them into strange situations"; or, "It is the capacity to learn, so we will measure their ability to memorize lists of nonsense syllables." But these theoretical approaches do not work. Binet tried a different one, which did. In effect he asked simply, What do bright subjects do that dull ones do not? and when he found questions that distinguished the bright from the dull, he used them, whether they looked like tests of intelligence or not.

Here of course the problem of validity enters, as troublesome as ever. Until we have a test of intelligence how do we know which subjects are bright, which dull? Binet met this difficulty by assuming that older children have more intelligence than younger ones—on the average. Some five-year-olds are better problem-solvers than some six-year-olds, but as a group the younger children are inferior. Binet then kept the test items on which performance improved with age in growing children and discarded the others.

This method cannot be used with adults, and the great American psychologist E. L. Thorndike proposed another approach. He first defined intelligence as that quality in which a group of geniuses, such as Newton, Einstein, Leonardo da Vinci, Shakespeare and Rabelais, differs most from the occupants of a home for the mentally deficient (the best definition, by the way, that anyone has come up with so far). This defines two groups for use in choosing test items, in the way described above for making a class examination. The procedure is not practical as it stands, since most of our genius group are dead; but one might modify it in practice as follows. In any society there are persons who are known, from long experience in the community, to be skillful, quick learners, and ingenious about everyday problems; and there are other persons who are known to be the opposite. These judgments are none too reliable in the individual case, but one cannot doubt that two large groups chosen by such evaluations would differ very much, as groups, in their average intellectual capacity. We could then validate our test items.

As a practical matter, the procedure would hardly be exactly that described above, but it is in principle the procedure by which one can select valid test items. *The real validation for intelligence tests as a whole is the fact that they have been found to make sound predictions.* The child who shows a high IQ turns out, in general, to do well in his schooling and in later life. The child with a low IQ, in general, does not. (This does *not* mean that he has a poor brain: see the next two sections.) It has already been said that an IQ determination is not infallible, even in the hands of a competent tester; to this it must be added that an inexperienced tester, and particularly one using group tests (paper and pencil tests that can be done by a whole class at once), may obtain results that are way off the mark. In this case, a low IQ particularly should not be trusted, since the subject may not have understood what he was supposed to do. A trained, experienced tester using an individual test proceeds with the test only after he is sure that the subject knows what he is to do and has adjusted to the test situation. Then the IQ, though it still has no magical accuracy, can be given weight as a predictor of the subject's future level of intellectual performance.

THE HEREDITY-ENVIRONMENT QUESTION

The classical view in psychology was that intelligence is determined essentially by heredity. This view seemed to be supported by such experiments as the following:

Learning ability was tested in a large number of laboratory rats. The brightest males and females, those with the fewest errors, were then bred with each other, and the dullest likewise. The second generation was tested and the brightest males and females of the bright group were bred with each other, and the dullest males and females of the dull group. This was continued till by the seventh generation it was found that there was little or no overlap in the scores of the bright and dull groups; practically all of the bright strain made better scores in maze learning than any of the dull strain (R. C. Tryon).

This experiment appears to show that intelligence is dependent on heredity alone. However, there are other experiments that contradict the conclusion. We can take litters of rats and divide them in two groups. Bring up one group in a restricted environment, each animal alone in a small cage which he cannot see out of, containing no objects and presenting no opportunity for problem solving. Bring up the other group in a "free environment," a large cage containing the whole group, and laid out as a sort of amusement park for rats with a variety of barriers to give experience with varied paths from point to point (B. Hymovitch; Forgays and Forgays). Or rear dogs as described in Chapter 7 (p. 123), some in restricted cages, some as pets in normal homes (another form of free environment). Then compare the restricted rats or dogs at maturity with those reared in the wider environment. When such experiments have been done, the animals reared in restriction show marked deficiencies in maze learning and the solution of simple problems. These experiments show that intelligence is determined by environment, not by heredity.

But do they? Look again at the two kinds of experiments in the light of Chapter 7. In the breeding experiment all the animals were reared in identical small cages; this keeps environmental differences from affecting the results. In the study of restricted vs. free environment, heredity is prevented from having any systematic effect by splitting litters. In effect, the two groups (as groups) have the same heredity, just as in the other experiment the two groups had the same environment. What the experiments show, therefore, is that both heredity and environment determine adult intelligence. If one source of variability in adult performance is held constant, all the variability (the difference between individuals or groups) comes from the other source, as one might expect.

With this point in mind, we can examine the result of a related investigation of human intelligence. Identical twins are twins that originate from a single fertilized ovum and thus, according to genetics, have the same hereditary characteristics. If they are brought up in different environments, we should be able to see what kind of effect variations of environment have upon intelligence. Psychologists have therefore been very interested in identical twin orphans adopted by different families. It has been found that their IQ's are very similar, and this fact has sometimes been used as argument that man's adult intelligence is determined by heredity and not by environment.

But when we look at the evidence, we find that most of these pairs of children have been brought up in very similar environments. When a pair of twins is orphaned, one of two things happens. They may be adopted by the neighbors, which implies similar environments—the same community, plus the fact that all the families in one neighborhood are apt to have about the same economic and social status. Or the twins may be taken charge of by a social agency, to oversee adoption, and this again means that they will get into environments that have much in common, social workers having strong ideas about who is fit to bring up children. In this kind of "experiment" differential effects of environment are minimized, and it is hardly surprising to find similar IQ's in identical twins with similar environments. The fact that identical twins have IQ's which are more alike than those of fraternal twins shows that heredity is important, just as the rat breeding experiment did; but it does not show that heredity is the only variable.

Sometimes it is recognized that heredity and environment both affect intelligence, but the writer then goes on to say *how* important each is. The student may find it said, for example, that 80 per cent of intelligence is determined by heredity, 20 per cent by environment. This statement is, on the face of it, nonsense. It means that a man would have 80 per cent of the problem-solving ability he would otherwise have had, if he were never given the opportunity to learn a language, to learn how people behave, and so forth. Conversely, it means that any animal would develop 20 per cent of a man's capacity for thought if reared in a good environment, no matter what its heredity, be it that of a mouse or a cow. What we must say is that both these variables are of 100 per cent importance; their relation is not additive, but multiplicative. That is, asking how much heredity contributes to man's intelligence is like asking how much the width of a field contributes to its area, and how much its length contributes. Neither can contribute anything by itself.

Though we cannot experiment with the effect of environment on the intelligence of the growing child, there are cases in which its importance has been unequivocally demonstrated. Goldfarb, as we saw earlier (p. 11), showed that an orphanage environment may be sufficiently unstimulating to account for a deficiency of 23 points in the IQ, comparing orphanage children with foster-home children. Also, children who grew up about 1920 on canal boats in England, re-moved from many of the normal experiences of other children, showed a sharp decline in intelligence. Their mean IQ was 90 at the age of six, 77 at age seven and a half, 60 at age twelve. An IQ below 70 is ordinarily considered to mean mental deficiency, whereas 90 is within the range of normal ability. Again, a very similar picture (mean IQ for seven-year-olds, 84; for fifteen-year-olds, 60) was found for children growing up in isolated mountain communities in the United States. The higher IQ's for the younger children show that the low IQ's at later ages do not mean deficient heredities – if they did, all the scores would be low. Instead, it appears that the social and cultural environment is sufficiently stimulating for a normal development of intelligence in the first four or five years of life, but progressively inadequate from then on.

INTELLIGENCE A AND INTELLIGENCE B

It is implied by these facts that the child at birth has a certain capacity or potential for intellectual development, but a stimulating environment is needed if the potential is to be realized. The extent to which intelligence can be developed may be low, in which case no environment can produce a high IQ; then heredity sets a limit on the development. But the child may have inherited a better brain, capable of developing a high IQ, and yet in a poor environment his IQ remains low – just as with a child that inherited a poorer brain.

Now it happens that in much of the literature, the term *intelligence* is used to refer both to (*A*) the original potential and (*B*) the ultimate level of development. This has produced confusion since, as we saw in the preceding paragraph, *A* might be high and *B* low. They are not the same thing. "Intelligence" at best is not a very precise term, but things will be less confused if we recognize two quite different meanings, as follows.

The term *intelligence A* refers to an innate potential for the development of intellectual capacities and *intelligence B* to the level of that development at a later time, when the subject's intellectual functioning can be observed. Intelligence *A* cannot be measured, for intellectual functioning is not observed in the newborn; the IQ, therefore, is a measure of intelligence *B* only. The student should note that *A* and *B* are not wholly separate; on the contrary, intelligence *A* enters into and is a necessary factor in intelligence *B*. What these two terms distinguish is not two different things but two different ways in which the more general term, intelligence, is used.

Another point: The *constancy of the IQ* is an important conception, but must be interpreted with caution. In general, the IQ is stable, changing only very slowly (here it is important for the student to remember the difference between IQ and MA). The IQ is very "constant" in the adult, showing little change between age 15 and age 25 or 30, then declining slowly with further age. In the child, however, constancy of the IQ depends on an adequate environment, as the canal boat children referred to in the preceding section show clearly. Their IQ's were not constant at all but fell steadily, their environment providing inadequate intellectual stimulation for the older child.

It appears that the effects of the environment during childhood tend to be permanent, for good or ill, and that the IQ tends to change less and less as the child grows older, stabilizing about the age of 15. A subject may have a good intelligence A and be reared in a stimulating environment, producing a good intelligence B; thereafter he will always have that level of intelligence (unless he becomes a victim of disease, malnutrition or injury that affects brain function). But the same subject, if he is reared in an inadequate environment, will have a low intelligence B: and manipulation of his environment after the age of 15 will not significantly raise it.

From these considerations it is clear that the level of intelligence B, which we can measure, does not necessarily reflect the level of intelligence A, and hence that we cannot really measure A. B reflects A if we assume an adequate environment for the full development of A's potential. If the environment is good and B is low, A must have been low also; but a low IQ obtained by a subject reared in an inadequate (or doubtfully adequate) environment leaves a question as to whether the result is due to a low intelligence A or not.

THE RACE QUESTION

This approach allows us to understand the issues involved in the question of the intelligence of different races, and specifically the intelligence of the Negro as compared with the Caucasian — a question that is currently of the greatest social importance, and as confused as it is important. The confusion arises from that term "intelligence," and the failure to distinguish its two meanings, A and B.

In general, it is true that the Negro in the United States and in Africa has on the average a lower IQ than the Caucasians in the same countries, but it is also true that the average Negro has not had an equally favorable environment for the development of intelligence in childhood. It is further true that many Negroes are far more intelligent at maturity than many Caucasians. The lower mean IQ therefore offers no justification for the conclusion that the Negro's native potential is lower, and no justification for not trying to find means of providing more stimulating conditions of growth for the Negro child. A low intelligence B does not necessarily mean a low intelligence A. On the existing evidence, the mean native potential of the Negro may be higher or lower than (or the same as) the Caucasian's. There is no scientific basis for belief in any essential relation between intelligence A and skin color, whether black, brown, yellow or white.

That last statement is the important one. There is always the possibility of an accidental and transient relation that would not affect the conclusion above. It is conceivable that centuries of slavery and peonage have resulted in a genetic selection temporarily favoring a lower average intelligence A in the Negro, just as it is conceivable that centuries of a different kind of oppression, and of having to live by his wits, have led to selection favoring a higher intelligence A in the European Jew. But even if this should be so, the mean for a whole group would shift extremely slowly, and the resulting difference between means, if there is one at all, would be trivial in comparison with the wide range of individual differences within a group. *Conceivably,* something of the sort has happened; but if so, the existence of some highly intelligent Negroes as well as stupid ones, and the existence of some stupid Jews as well as intelligent ones, shows that level of ability has no essential connection with group membership in either case, and a change in the relation of the group to the larger social environment could reverse these deviant trends. Knowing that a man is a Negro or a Jew (or a Malay or an Englishman or an American Indian) does not tell you how good a brain he has inherited.

It is a well-established principle in psychology that no valid comparison of native ability (i.e., intelligence A) can be based on a comparison of IQ's obtained by persons brought up in different cultures. The principle was established during the First World War, when mass testing was first used to screen recruits for the U.S. Army. Negroes in general were found to have lower IQ's than the white population in general; but it was easily shown that the Negroes had, as a group, less exposure to the intelligence-test materials by which the IQ's were determined. It was also shown that Negroes living in the North had a higher mean IQ than the rural white population in the South: a clear indication, if not proof, of the importance of environment in determining the level of the IQ.

As soon as it is realized that any intelligence test assumes an adequate knowledge of or exposure to the test materials, it becomes obvious that the IQ provides no basis for comparing intelligence A in persons from different cultures. We cannot compare the native abilities of Swede and Italian, or of American and Russian. Even apart from the language problem, even assuming that one's test has been adequately translated, different patterns of living and thinking and talking would still exist and the same score of, say, 20 items correct in a test of 50 items, would have a different value in the two social environments.

This conclusion must hold also for different social strata in the same culture. If we cannot legitimately compare Negro and Caucasian in the United States because they have not had the same exposure to the test material, neither can we compare Caucasian and Caucasian when one has grown up in a well-to-do home and the other in the slums of a big city. Such comparisons within one culture can effectively be made with respect to intelligence B at the age of 15 years or later, because the intelligence test does have this kind of validity. If the IQ is low because of a poor environment, intelligence B will be low also—the poor environment will have had its effect on the subject's general ability in the culture. But once again the low IQ in a subject coming from a poor environment does not permit the conclusion that intelligence *A* is low and that the subject would still have been unintelligent if he had grown up in a better environment.

THE COURSE OF DEVELOPMENT: PIAGET

The development of thought, in man, must be as complex a matter as thought itself and we are far from understanding it yet. But much has been learned and, of that, much is due to the work of the great Swiss psychologist Jean Piaget. Beginning as Binet did with observation of his own children in their natural environment (the household), Piaget has traced out the way in which the infant's apparently uncomplicated reactivity, at a more or less reflex level, develops into adult intelligence — via some surprising steps.

Actually, some of the results surprise us more than they should. If we as adults saw ourselves and our society objectively and in perspective (as some being with greater intelligence or from another universe might see us) the thinking of the child might seem more akin to that of the adult than it does at present. Piaget has shown, for example, that there are magical and animistic stages in the child's thought; intelligent people in civilized society have outgrown such things: or so we claim. But have we? Magic is the action of symbols — ideas expressed in words, gesture or ritual — upon things at a distance and in the future: we disavow some of its cruder forms, but a superstitious belief in lucky and unlucky actions affects the behavior of most of us, at least to some mild degree. Again, animism is the idea that an object, inert by itself, is active because inhabited by some nonphysical agent. We have seen that an animistic theory of behavior is intellectually respectable and an important feature of society (p. 3). Also, one's thinking is tinged with animism whenever one attributes any sort of consciousness or intention or personality to a physical thing such as sailing vessel, car, light plane or computer; and it may be very hard indeed not to think at times of an angry sea, of a threatening sky, or of hurricanes as malignant entities to whom names such as Carol or Dolly (feminine, naturally) are suitable. The child's thinking therefore is less different from ours than at first it seems.

This does not invalidate Piaget's delineation of distinct stages in development. Qualitatively different patterns of thought at different ages must still contain threads of continuity. From one point of view, it may be suggested that the child's magic and animism is simply spread over a wider segment of his environment than the adult's; but at the same time it is true that a predominance of such ideas must give thought a qualitatively distinct character.

At an early stage in its development the child's understanding is at a level of simple association. Things that are connected in thought are connected in the environment. Thus a kind of magical thinking occurs, as for example when the child concludes, because sleepiness occurs in the evening, that his sleepiness brings on the night (magical, because his feelings determine events outside him). Or he has seen a difference between the color of things that sink and the color of ones that float, and thinks of the color as determining the buoyancy. For one child, live things are ones that move; therefore clouds are alive but trees are not. For another, live things are warm things; the sun is warm, so it is alive, *because* it is warm.

Great caution is needed in all this. We must be careful in dealing with the child not to put words into his mouth, or ideas into his head, when trying to find out how the world appears to him; but with care it is possible to find out that, for the child referred to, the sun would belong with non-living things if it was cold instead of warm.

As thought develops further with experience, the idea of usefulness or apparent purpose enters. Why do boats float? because they are needed to carry people. Clouds move because rain is needed somewhere else. Still later the child begins to think of *how* such things happen, of the means involved, and introduces an agent of some kind (one might say a supernatural agent, except that the thinking has not reached a stage at which natural and supernatural are differentiated; such conceptions have not yet developed). The clouds must be moved by *someone*. (Primitive as this may be, it is at a more rational level than the preceding.) The someone may be God, but if so God is thought of as one would think of a very powerful human being; it is important to remember that for the very young child his parents and other adults have indefinitely great powers—an almost unlimited capacity for making things happen. Rivers and lakes have been made (Paul Bunyan!) so boats can travel on them. Things in general exist because they have a use, are needed, as in Molière's old joke about noses shaped as they are so that spectacles can rest on them.

These points have been discussed by M. Laurendeau and A. Pinard who have also provided us with extensive quantitative information about causal thinking in the child, taking as example a peculiarly psychological phenomenon that has long fascinated mankind: the dream. They have defined four stages of development, as follows: *Stage 0.* The child does not know what a dream is or does not understand the questions. *Stage 1,* the dream is "real" and exists apart from the dreamer. It is in the bedroom and others can see it; or, if they cannot, it is because the dream disappears when the lights are turned on, or because the dream is under the bedclothes, and so on. *Stage 2,* intermediate: the dream is in the child's eyes or in his head, and if one could look inside his head one could see the dream, which is like a little show. *Stage 3,* real understanding: the child may say that the dream is in the eyes or in the head, but it is from one's memory, in one's thoughts or imagination. Now the child may have a harder time finding words to say what he wants to, since understanding may have outstripped vocabulary.

The rate of development is shown in Table 4.

TABLE 4. DEVELOPMENT OF UNDERSTANDING OF DREAMS
PERCENTAGE OF CHILDREN CLASSIFIED AT EACH STAGE, BY AGES
(DATA OF LAURENDEAU AND PINARD)

Stage	Age 4	Age 6	Age 8	Age 10
0	55	10	0	0
1	20	10	0	0
2	24	38	18	2
3	0	41	82	98

Table 4 will have more meaning if it is illustrated by giving some protocols of the questions asked and the answers.

Age four: When your mother is in your bedroom, can she see your dream too? *Yes.* And if I were in your room, could I see it too? *Sure!* Why do you say that I could see your dream? *Because I think it is still there.*

Age four and a half: Is the dream in your room really, or do we just say that? *Really there.* When you dream, are your eyes closed or open? *Closed.* Then where is your dream? *In my room.* How can you see it with eyes closed? *I don't know.* And a five-year-old, asked the same questions, replies that the dream is under the bedclothes (Stage 1).

Age six: When you dream are your eyes closed or open? *Closed.* Then where is your dream? *In front of me.* There is something in front of you when you dream? *Yes.* When your mother is in the room, can she see your dream? *No.* And I...? *No.* Why do you say I could not see your dream? *Because it is inside me, but in front of me. I don't understand, I'm mixed up!* (Stage 2.)

Age eight: When you dream, where is the dream? *In my eyes. Not near my eyes, in my eyes.*

Age nine: When you dream, where is the dream? *In my head.* In you or in your room? *In me.* (Stage 3.)

This provides but the barest example of the work done on the development of intelligence by Piaget and others who have followed his lead. A separate problem is to determine the conditions which maximize the development: a tremendously important social problem but one which, unfortunately, we know too little about.

Technological development and automation are steadily increasing the levels of education and intelligence required to hold a job, and decreasing the demand for unskilled labor. Unless we are willing to accept a high rate of chronic unemployment in a country like the United States, and an increasing economic gap between "have" and "have-not" countries (a gap that is already far too great), the level of functioning of large numbers of people must be raised. How to do it? More and better schools are only part of the answer, for educability depends on the IQ—on intelligence *B*—and this in turn depends largely on the intellectual stimulation the child has received in the home and in his wider social environment outside the school. It also depends, of course, on his heredity, but even if something can be done to decrease the number of children born with poor intelligence *A,* it remains essential that existing children realize their full potential intelligence *B*. It appears certain that large segments of the present population in every country are far from having done so. That is, the average intelligence *B* of the unskilled and semiskilled classes is not as high as their genetic constitutions would allow.

The difficulty in raising it, for the next generation (remember that the IQ appears to be fixed by about age 15, for all practical purposes), is that the intellectual climate for the growing child is mostly determined by the level of intelligence *B* of the adults of the generation to which the child is exposed. *By the time the child reaches kindergarten or first grade the effects of a deficient intellectual environment are already in evidence.* Various attempts to counteract the deficiency have been made, for example, using television (*Sesame Street*) or putting the child in a special nursery school for a summer. Valuable as these have been, they are limited. Many children have no access to TV, and all our theoretical information says that no program beginning at three or four years of age can make up fully for the preceding lack of an intellectually sufficient environment. An hour or two a day may be all that is needed, but it must begin early and continue. It has been asserted that such attempts at "compensatory education" have failed. To this it must be replied that a real try to correct the deficiency completely has never been made. The striking results that *have* been achieved show how much more could be done.

SUMMARY

This chapter is concerned first with the measurement of intelligence, and second with the conditions and course of its development. Binet solved the essential problem of measurement when he abandoned a priori definitions of intelligence and asked instead what differences of response could be found between a more intelligent child and a less intelligent one. No question was included in his test because intelligent children *should* know the answer; only ones to which they *did* know the answers. Test items are *valid* if they separate bright from dull, the bright doing well and the dull doing poorly with them. A test is *reliable* to the extent that it gives the same result on repeated testing, preferably with different forms of the test so that the subject does not simply remember his earlier answers and repeat them.

The heredity-environment problem reappears in virulent form as related to we turn to the topic of intelligence, and the student should keep Chapter 7 in mind as he works through this one. The adult's level of performance is fixed by hereditary potential *and* by environmental conditions that determine to what extent that potential will be realized. Thus heredity may be thought of as setting limits to intellectual development. Animal experiments have demonstrated the importance of both heredity and environment, and naturalistic observation of identical twins, and of children reared in isolated communities, show that these conclusions apply to man as well.

Guide to Study

In reviewing, the student should make sure that he can give definitions for IQ, MA and CA; for reliability and validity; and for intelligence in sense *A* and in sense *B*. He should know the meaning of the term, "constancy of the IQ," and what limitations this concept has for the growing child. He should understand clearly why a low IQ does not necessarily mean possession of a poor brain, and why or in what sense IQ's of persons from different cultural backgrounds cannot be compared.

This chapter gives only a sketchy introduction to Piaget's important studies of the way in which human intelligence develops, but the student should understand the meaning of animistic and magical thought, and what kind of evidence shows its existence in the young child.

NOTES AND REFERENCES

Forgays, D. G., and Forgays, J.: The nature of the effect of free-environmental experience in the rat. *Journal of Comparative and Physiological Psychology,* 1952, 45, 322–328.
Ginsburg, H., and Opper, S.: *Piaget's Theory of Intellectual Development: an Introduction.* Prentice-Hall, 1969.
Goldfarb, W.: Effects of early institutional care on adolescent personality. *Journal of Experimental Education,* 1943, 12, 106–129.
Hunt, J. McV.: *Intelligence and Experience.* Ronald, 1961. An important review and synthesis, especially of the human data.
Hymovitch, B.: The effects of experiential variations on problem-solving in the rat. *Journal of Comparative and Physiological Psychology,* 1952, 45, 313–321.
Laurendeau, M., and Pinard, A.: *Causal Thinking in the Child.* International Universities Press, 1963.
Neff, W. S.: Socioeconomic status and intelligence: a critical survey. *Psychological Bulletin,* 1938, 35, 727–757. Included is a summary of the study of intelligence in the canal-boat children.
Piaget, J.: *The Psychology of Intelligence.* Harcourt, Brace, 1950. Piaget is a difficult writer, and the student would be well advised to start with Phillips (below), or Ginsburg and Opper (above.)
Phillips, J. L.: *The Origins of Intellect: Piaget's Theory.* Freeman, 1969.
Thompson, W. R., and Heron, W.: The effects of restricting early experience on the problem-solving capacity of dogs. *Canadian Journal of Psychology,* 1954, 8, 17–31.
Tryon, R. C.: Genetic differences in maze-learning in rats. *Yearbook, National Society for the Study of Education, 1940.* The classical demonstration of genetic differences in learning ability and intelligence.

10

motivational mechanisms

The function of behavior in evolution is simply to keep an animal alive and well long enough to mate and in other ways to get the next generation established, the process then repeating itself and leading to still another generation.

Obviously, Darwin's "natural selection" must operate to shape behavior accordingly. Strong food seeking and mating tendencies, for example, must be present in every generation, for if they are weak or absent the species will cease to exist. A species may arise with a large brain, capable of speech, and given to abstract problem-solving and artistic creations, but it can continue to exist only if, along with these great intellectual endowments, it has also a biologically primitive tendency to mate. (Incongruous or not, man's sexual motivation must be overwhelming in strength, at least some of the time, and in an animal with such small litters, survival of the species requires that this should be true of all or nearly all its members.) Similarly, hunger and pain motivations make for survival of the species, pain by diminishing the probability of repeated damage to the body and so of early death, hunger by ensuring that the animal will expend enough effort to obtain the substances necessary to maintain life. Also, to "get the next generation established" requires some parental assistance to the offspring of many species; thus in all mammals and most birds (with rare exceptions such as the cuckoo), natural selection has produced a strongly marked maternal or parental motivation.

Motivation may be defined as a tendency of the whole animal* to produce organized activity, normally varying from the low level of deep sleep to a high level in the waking, alert, excited animal, and varying also in the kind of behavior that results or the kind of stimula-

---

*Component parts of the organism are more or less active all the time, being made up of living cells that must be active or die, but "motivation" does not refer to these activities. It is a variable which accounts for *fluctuations* in the level or form of the behavior of the whole animal. The heart rate and breathing rate are affected by certain changes of motivation, for example, but we do not consider that there is a special motivation necessary 24 hours a day to maintain pulse and breathing. See p. 186 for the difference between "motivated" and "unmotivated" breathing and temperature maintenance.

171

tion to which the organism is responsive. Thus we may speak of a subject as being strongly (or weakly) motivated, meaning that he has a strong tendency to be active (or is lethargic); or we may speak of his having special motivations such as hunger motivation, sex motivation, and so on. These special motivations are intermittent, they vary in strength, and more than one motivation may be present at the same time, the stronger then being dominant. The four biologically primitive tendencies referred to in the preceding paragraph are commonly referred to as the *hunger, pain, sex,* and *maternal* motivations, and to these we can add a fifth, the *exploratory* motivation, which if it is not as strictly necessary for survival, is just as widespread, and must favor species survival by installing the species over a wider territory and making it less vulnerable to local catastrophe.

It should be noted that this terminology is convenient, but not precise: "hunger" used in this way must include a need of oxygen and of water as well as of solid foods; "pain" must include various discomforts such as those produced by low or high temperatures, and so on; "maternal" and "sex" motivations in man may not be wholly distinct but perhaps have elements in common, and "maternal" must in many species refer to the father as well as the mother.

However, all this is still far from being the whole story. As the brain has increased in size in the evolution of mammals, certain motivational characteristics have appeared which are of the greatest significance. The sleep-waking difference assumes more importance, covering a much wider variation in readiness for response than it does in lower animals, and makes it necessary to consider the level of general *arousal* in the behavior of the mammal. Also, the *emotions* are motivational states which seem to be peculiar to the larger-brained animal, and these too must be taken account of.

In this chapter and the next we will be concerned with the whole problem of motivation. The present chapter deals with its neural basis and the more primitive motivations. The following chapter will deal primarily with the "higher" motivations; not all of them admirable, by any means, but characteristic of the higher animal.

NONSPECIFIC AFFERENTS AND AROUSAL

There are two main ways in which a sensory excitation affects cortical activity. In Chapter 3 the specialized sensory pathways were described: the direct routes from eye, ear and skin to the corresponding cortical sensory areas. They are specialized not only to keep each sense distinct from others; they also keep messages within the same sense distinct, so that excitation from the toe, for example, travels by a special sub-pathway and is not mixed up with excitations from the thumbs or the lips. But there is also a second way in which excitations reach the cortex.

The second kind of pathway is *nonspecific.* It does not keep sensory excitations distinct according to their place of origin but pools them and delivers the result to all parts of the cortex. The *specific afferents,* the ones described in Chapter 3, convey information, guide behavior, determine specific responses. The nonspecific afferents instead have the function of "toning up" the cortex, providing a general facilitation to aid cortical transmission (cf. footnote p. 73) and so make it possible for the messages from the specific pathways to reach the motor system and have their guiding influence on behavior. The nonspecific pathways produce *arousal:* alertness, responsiveness, wakefulness, vigilance.

Each main afferent path branches as it approaches the thalamus, as shown by the diagram of Figure 63 (only two sensory inputs are represented, for simplicity). The main branches go to their own specialized thalamic nuclei* (represented by the hatched circles) which in turn project—send fibers—to the corresponding sensory areas of the cortex. The other branches go to the *arousal system* (or "non-

---

*A nucleus is a cluster of cell-bodies. The sensory nuclei of the thalamus are the final relay points of the specific afferent pathways, receiving axons from below and in turn sending their own axons to the proper cortical sensory area.

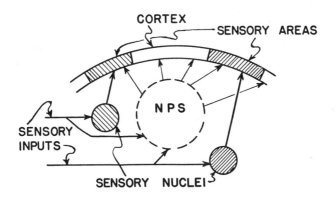

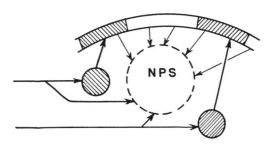

Figure 63. *Diagram of the "nonspecific projection system" (NPS) or arousal system. Two specific sensory paths are shown, the hatched circles representing two thalamic sensory nuclei, each connected with its own special cortical area. Each sensory input also sends branches into the NPS, which mixes up excitations from these different sources and transmits them indiscriminately to the cortex (upper diagram). The cortex also sends excitations to the NPS (below), so cortical processes can contribute to the level of arousal.*

specific projection system'': *NPS* in Figure 63). Though some cells in the system may be fired only by branching fibers from the visual afferent path, others only by auditory or olfactory ones, the level of activity in the whole system is the result of a pooling of the excitatory effects of sensory stimulation—from all sources. The general excitation is in turn transmitted to the cortex, producing a general level of behavioral excitability; that is, arousal. A low level of activity in the arousal system makes the animal unresponsive, higher levels produce normal alertness or emotional behavior.

The arousal system is not a neat circular structure—as the student might think from looking at Figure 63—but a series of well-organized separate nuclei in the midbrain (lying parallel to the aqueduct: Figs. 10 and 11), plus some in the thalamus. Their physiological role is to activate the cortex, and physiologists generally refer to these structures as the *ascending reticular activating system* or *ARAS*. From a behavioral point of view, however, ''arousal'' is more relevant as well as a handier term, and it is customary to distinguish between cortical *activation* (low-voltage fast waves in the EEG) and behavioral *arousal* (the animal is awake).

For our present purposes the arousal system can be treated as one system, with a single mode of action. The student should know, however, that it has at least two patterns of activity, probably more. All produce arousal, but the arousal shows differences. There is strong arousal in both laughter and fear, for example, but recovery from disturbance in one case is quick, in the other slow. Another simplification made here is to talk about the effect of arousal on ''cortical transmission.'' It was observed earlier (p. 69) that the transmission is really through a series of closed loops or systems of closed loops many of which join cortex and subcortical structures. The cortex does not function at all as a separate organ: it is an anatomical unit but not a functional one.

The branching of the path from a sense organ, one branch going to the cortex and one to the arousal system, means that a sensory stimulation has two quite different functions. The first can be called a *cue function:* a guiding or steering or informational effect. The second is the *arousal function:* it determines the level of excitement or excitability or wakefulness of the animal, without determining what the animal's behavior will be. The sensory messages that go straight to the cortex guide behavior. They excite specific pathways which tend to produce specific responses, or modify connections between cell-assemblies so that other messages will produce specific responses (*set*, p. 86, or *knowledge,* p. 32). That is, the messages that reach the cortex do this if the arousal system is active, not otherwise.

For higher functions the arousal system is crucial. Without its support cortical processes cease, as far as behavior is concerned. Sensory excitations may still reach the sensory projection areas, but they stop there. The need of summation for synaptic transmission has already been discussed, as well as the way in which parallel transmission provides for summation, thus guaranteeing that excitations will reach the sensory cortex (p. 71). But the loop circuits or cell-assemblies which appear to be the main basis of cortical transmission do not function unless the arousal system is providing a sort of general summation to all cortical synapses. It was suggested (p. 73) that assembly *A* may transmit to or excite assembly *B* only if assembly *C* is also active and supporting *A*'s action; but this of course cannot happen unless the assemblies themselves are active, and they are not active unless they receive support from the arousal system. Though unconditioned reflexes still function, all conditioned reflexes and mediating processes cease when activity in the arousal system ceases. *All the mammal's learned behavior, that is, and all thought processes or consciousness, depend on the arousal system deep in the brain stem.**

The level of activity of the system varies normally from a low level in deep dreamless sleep to a high level in the waking, emotionally excited subject. The primary source of excitation of the system is the sensory input represented in the upper diagram of Figure 63; monotonous (i.e., unvaried) stimulation from the environment allows the level of excitation to fall, and thus facilitates sleep. However, this is not the sole avenue by which excitation is transmitted to the arousal system; the lower diagram in Figure 63 shows a "down-flow" from the cortex, which also contributes to arousal. What this means is that the main source of arousal is sensory stimulation, but that another source lies in the thought process. There can be exciting thoughts as well as exciting sensations. The subject put in a monotonous environment does not necessarily go to sleep.

For some reason, not very clearly understood, a repeated sensory event not followed by other events tends rapidly to lose its capacity to produce arousal (though there are sensations, such as pain, of which this is not true). The result is known as *habituation* or "negative adaptation." Familiar scenes and familiar events are not exciting. One can "learn" to sleep even in a quite noisy environment if the noises are the usual ones, but the learning appears to be the habituation referred to. A strange environment, on the other hand, is exciting, and this appears to make it both frightening and attractive, as we will see in discussing exploratory motivation.

AROUSAL AND THE EEG

Behavior is the most important index of the level of arousal, but it does not always provide us with full information. When the lecturer in the classroom sees a student slumped back in his seat with eyes closed, he cannot tell immediately whether the student is asleep, or daydreaming, or thinking hard about the lecture. Another source of information about arousal level could be obtained by *electroen-*

---

*As Wilder Penfield first observed in 1938, giving the name *centrencephalic system* to the structures involved and proposing that consciousness is more closely related to the brain stem than the cortex is. It was in 1949 that G. Moruzzi and H. W. Magoun discovered the vital part in this that is played by the midbrain reticular formation ("reticular" only means that the region looks like a network after being stained for microscopic study).

cephalography: an instance of technical jargon to make anyone shudder, even electroencephalographers, who consequently are accustomed to speak of the *EEG* instead. Though it is hardly practical to use it to detect sleep in the classroom, the EEG is an index of arousal that has a good deal to tell us about what is going on in the brain.

When the same electronic amplifying methods that are used to pick up disturbances in the atmosphere, otherwise undetectable, and turn them into music or speech on the radio—when these methods are applied to the scalp of the living human subject, it is found that the brain, too, is broadcasting, though not always in an equally entertaining way. Instead of turning the broadcast into sounds, we make it operate a pen on a moving sheet of paper and thus produce a lasting record of the brain's activity. Such records of "brain waves" are shown in Figure 64.

The figure shows how the EEG changes with different states of arousal. Small fast waves mean that the arousal system is active, large slow waves that it is inactive. The *alpha rhythm* (so named because it was the first one to be recognized and studied, by Hans Berger about 1928) represents an intermediate level of arousal; it

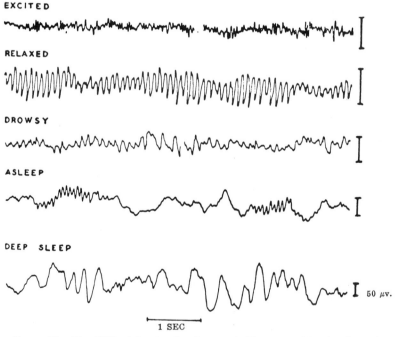

Figure 64. *The EEG at five levels of arousal. The second tracing from the top ("relaxed") is the alpha rhythm. In the fourth one ("asleep") the two places where a burst of short, faster waves occurs on top of a slow wave are "sleep spindles." The vertical line at the right of each tracing permits comparison of voltages (e.g., the bottom tracing would have much higher waves if on the same scale as the top tracing). (From H. H. Jasper, in W. Penfield and T. C. Erickson,* Epilepsy and Cerebral Localization, *Charles C Thomas.)*

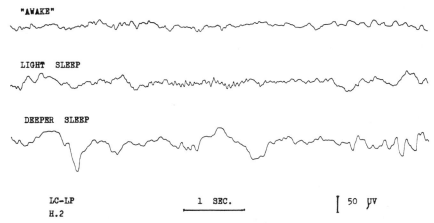

Figure 65. *EEG records from a human infant 90 hours old, for comparison with the adult records of Figure 64. The waking record of the infant has slow waves, though of much lower amplitude than in the two sleep records, and a marked lack of both alpha and beta frequencies. (Courtesy of A. K. Bartoshuk, Hunter Laboratory, Brown University.)*

consists of moderately large regular potentials, at about 10 cycles per second, and appears when the subject is instructed to close his eyes and relax. If he opens his eyes and attends to his surroundings, or if with eyes closed he is given a problem to solve, the *beta rhythm* appears: small fast waves characteristic of the actively thinking subject. At times in sleep, on the other hand, and when brain function is impaired by disease or anesthesia, there are large irregular slow waves called the *delta rhythm,* about 2 to 5 cycles per second.

Things are not really as clear-cut as this may suggest. The alpha rhythm is the only really distinctive pattern of the EEG, and some subjects do not show it while in others it is much less regular than the one shown in the second record in Figure 64. The beta rhythm is really a range of irregular frequencies, from 12 cycles per second up. In sleep, there is, as we will see, an activation pattern at times ("REM sleep") and when slow waves appear it is usually in combination with faster ones. Also, sleep-deprived subjects may produce slow waves at the same time that they are — more or less — awake and responsive to the environment. Finally, the newborn infant shows slow waves as well as faster ones during periods of behavioral wakefulness (Fig. 65), which suggests that the infant's consciousness (and that of the sleep-deprived adult) falls far short of what we know as consciousness in the normal waking adult.

Some writers, especially on psychoanalysis, have been puzzled at the lack of memory for the events of infancy. They seem to think that the infant is conscious in the same way as an adult, with the same kind of memory. It is even suggested that the fetus is conscious in the uterine environment, and later can be nostalgic for this idyllic state of existence. Such ideas, surely, are nonsense. We do not need to suppose that there is some special repression that explains the "forgetting" of uterine and early postnatal awarenesses; it is far more likely that no such awarenesses, in any adult sense, ever existed. It is likely, in other words, that the newborn infant is not fully conscious, and only gradually becomes so in the first five to ten months of life.

The EEG has something important to tell us concerning the way in which the arousal system affects cortical activity. The electrode from which the record is obtained is at some distance from the surface of the cortex, separated from it by scalp and skull, which means that the potentials it records must be averages from a rather large number of cortical neurons. A large potential (a high wave) therefore means that most of the neurons near the electrode are active at the same time, and inactive at the same time; that is, they act synchronously. Otherwise the negative potentials produced by cells that have just been active (p. 60) would cancel out the positive potentials produced by inactive cells, and a flat EEG record would result. Figure 64 therefore shows that a low level of arousal means synchronized or simultaneous activity of neighboring neurons in the cortex; a higher state of arousal, in the actively thinking or perceiving subject, means that neighboring neurons tend to fire independently of each other. This fits in with the idea that cortical activity in consciousness is the firing of neurons arranged in loops, as in Figure 33 (p. 70) and Figure 34. To function effectively, the neurons must fire one after another, not simultaneously. If the cell-assemblies are intertwined, as they must be, the neurons would all be in the same cortical region and so, if the assemblies *A, B, C* and *D* are active in succession, the individual neurons in this region must not all be active at the same time. The EEG tells us that the neural activity of consciousness is a diffuse firing, a coordination of cells at some distance from each other rather than a local synchrony.

THE AUTONOMIC NERVOUS SYSTEM

A basic role in motivation and emotion is played by the *autonomic nervous system.* This is a primitive, though still complex, set of motor pathways to *smooth muscle* and glands. *Striate* or skeletal muscle is what moves the limbs, the chest (in breathing), the jaws, tongue and eyeballs; it has a striped appearance under the microscope, hence the term striate. Smooth muscle lines the walls of the arteries and regulates the blood pressure of different parts of the body; it controls the size of the pupil of the eye, movements of stomach and gut, and erection of hair. (In man it produces goose pimples, each of which is caused by the contraction of a small muscle which would make one hair "stand on end" if men were as hairy as their ancestors.)

The autonomic nervous system is made up of two subsystems, the *sympathetic* and the *parasympathetic.* The parasympathetic system has two parts, one at each end of the neural tube (Fig. 66). Thus the autonomic nervous system has a total of three segments: the sympathetic, in the middle regions of the spinal cord; the upper section of the parasympathetic, emerging from the brain stem; and the lower section of the parasympathetic, emerging from the tail end of

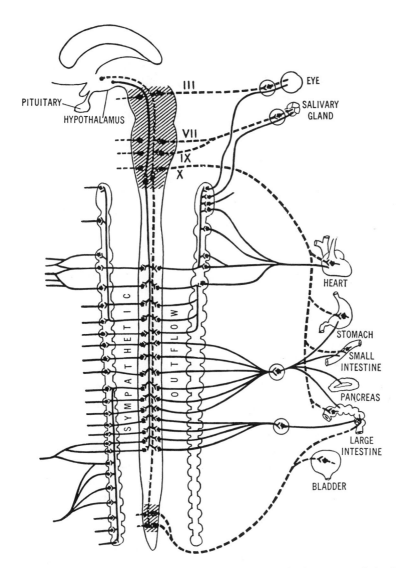

Figure 66. *The autonomic nervous system. The sympathetic segment is in the middle region, its connections shown in solid lines; the parasympathetic has two divisions, the cranial (above) and the sacral (below). Its connections are shown in broken lines. (From E. Gardner,* Fundamentals of Neurology. Saunders.*)*

the spinal cord. As Figure 66 shows, most organs are controlled by both sympathetic and parasympathetic systems. These are motor systems only; the afferent neurons from smooth muscle are not called autonomic but are simply thought of as sensory fibers, mixed in with those from other bodily structures, which serve to control non-autonomic responses as well as autonomic ones.

Sympathetic and parasympathetic systems are in general opposed to each other. What one excites the other inhibits. Sympathetic fibers, for example, increase the heart rate and slow down the digestive processes of the stomach; parasympathetic fibers slow the heart and promote digestion. The sympathetic is regarded as designed for action in emergency situations, mobilizing the resources of the body for maximal expenditure—a spendthrift, while the parasympathetic is the skinflint that builds them up and conserves them. This is an oversimplification—the sympathetic, for example, has a role in the normal activity of the body—but useful to keep in mind, with reservations. Also, sympathetic and parasympathetic are not completely opposed in their actions, and do collaborate to some degree. But the student may think of the parasympathetic as dominant in quiet periods, and of the sympathetic nervous system as preparing the animal for "fight or flight": increasing the heart rate and the flow of blood to the muscles for violent emergency action, causing the sweating that controls the resultant heat production, and making the hair stand erect in the picture of the emotionally disturbed animal.

The sympathetic, then, is directly concerned in that picture of emotional disturbance. But the student should also remember that this is only part of the total picture; emotional behavior involves the striped musculature also. The autonomic nervous system is a primitive motor system, much of whose action is diffuse rather than specific and not well controlled by cortical mechanisms. The sympathetic, especially, tends to go into action as a whole. The result, in "emotional situations" in which there is a high level of neural activity, is that ideational or mediating-process activity may be able to control skeletal muscles completely and at the same time have little or no control of smooth muscle and gland. The man who is angry or frightened may not attack anyone or run away, but his heartbeat increases, his blood pressure rises, and there is sweating and pallor or flushing, because these things are not under voluntary control.

Now most studies of emotion are made in the laboratory with student subjects taking a course in psychology. They want to pass the course, and consequently restrain themselves from striking the experimenter when he makes them angry. If they become afraid they do not show it, at least not by running away. But though ideational processes can inhibit the action of arms or legs, they cannot inhibit autonomic activity in the same way. Thus the effect of emotional situations seems autonomic only, and psychologists have talked mostly as if emotion and autonomic activity were the same thing. But this is a misleading conclusion. The normal—uninhibited—expression of

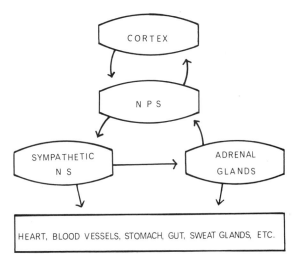

Figure 67. *Diagram of the relations between the arousal or nonspecific projection system (NPS) and certain other structures. NPS and cortex form a closed (or feedback) circuit; so do NPS, sympathetic nervous system and adrenal glands. The last two also excite visceral structures; the diagram does not show the feedback, via sensory pathways, from the viscera to both NPS and cortex, nor the close connection of NPS to the limbic system.*

anger is attack, and attacking is done with skeletal muscles. It is the same with fear and running away. *Skeletal muscle is as closely related to emotion as smooth muscle is.* The autonomic nervous system more or less reflects the level of excitement in the CNS, but this includes activity that is not primarily emotional (as in a sudden dash for the bus), and when emotional disturbance does occur it excites skeletal muscle as readily as that of the viscera. Trembling of the limbs, disturbance of breathing, and incoordination of the fingers—all produced by skeletal muscle—are signs of emotion just as much as sweating and increased heart rate.

An important link in the action of the sympathetic nervous system is the adrenal gland, situated close to the kidney, whose inner portion secretes a hormone, *adrenalin,* into the blood stream. Adrenalin acts directly on smooth muscle, and on the glands of external secretion, in about the same way that sympathetic fibers do. Also, it excites the arousal system directly; and since the arousal system excites the sympathetic nervous system (which excites the adrenals), this makes a closed circuit (Fig. 67). We have already seen that the arousal system and the cortex form a closed circuit, each exciting the other, so we see now that the arousal system is the focal point where two such feedback systems meet, as Figure 67 shows. The arousal-sympathetic-adrenal circuit in particular must be part of the reason why a generalized excitation, or strong emotional disturbance, takes so long to die down, instead of stopping at once when the exciting cause is removed.

In this respect the autonomic nervous system has a special relation to emotion, as part of a more extensive system whose activity is not readily damped once it has been excited, and which is readily aroused by strong or unusual stimulation (i.e., events such as pain to which the arousal system does not habituate, and the strange event to which it has not yet habituated).

THE LIMBIC SYSTEM

A vital factor in motivation is provided by the *limbic system:* a loosely organized set of structures, some cortical, some subcortical, that are closely connected with the arousal system. There is not complete agreement on what is limbic and what not, but in the main the system includes the cortex near the base of the brain, and where it borders on the corpus callosum (where it dips deep into the midline fissure separating the two hemispheres); the hippocampus; the *amygdala* (a small group of nuclei in the temporal lobe not far from the hippocampus); and parts of the thalamus and hypothalamus.

The functions of the limbic system are still being worked out, but it is clear that the system is at the heart of motivation and emotion. It is not large, but it almost seems that the rest of the brain has been developed to serve it. A large cortex makes an animal better able to reach its goals, but the limbic system has much to say about what the goals will be. The arousal system is necessary if a large brain is to function effectively but it likewise does not determine what goals are sought; and arousal is an essential part of the animal's emotional reaction, determining its strength, but it is the limbic system apparently that determines whether the emotion will be fear or anger or sexual excitement, love or hate.

The hypothalamic centers controlling hunger and satiation (p. 187) are part of the system. There is also a hypothalamic region from which the hunting and attack behavior of cats is controlled: a cat that is usually friendly with a rat in the same cage will stalk and kill it while this region is stimulated, but promptly stops when the stimulation stops (J. P. Flynn). (An electrode is inserted into the brain and cemented to the skull under anesthesia, leaving the upper end protruding through the scalp. This causes no discomfort when the animal has recovered from the operation, and now the part of the hypothalamus reached by the electrode can be stimulated while the animal is moving around, as in Figure 68.) Other regions of the hypothalamus are involved in the control of sexual and maternal behavior.

Fear and pleasure, emotional avoidance and emotional seeking, are at the heart of motivation, and it appears that the limbic system provides for these emotions directly. J. M. R. Delgado, W. W. Roberts and N. E. Miller have shown that stimulation of a lateral anterior part of the hypothalamus produces true fear in the rat—not a mere withdrawal, but an emotional state that has the same properties as the state produced by electric shock to the feet, for example. On the other hand, there are points in the hypothalamus and elsewhere that produce something like pleasure.

The procedure is illustrated in Figure 68, the stimulation being carried out by J. Olds (right) and P. M. Milner, the original discoverers of the effect. The rat is free to move about in the apparatus. If shock is delivered whenever he goes to one corner, the rat remains there. If in-

Figure 68. *Rat with implanted electrodes, connected with a light flexible wire so he can move about freely. If the experimenters give a brain stimulation in this corner of the maze, the rat will persist in coming back to it, just as if he were hungry and found food there.*

stead he is put in a Skinner box (Fig. 5, p. 27) and the lever is connected with a switch so that each press—or every second or fifth or tenth press—produces a brief stimulation, very high rates of pressing may result: sometimes as high as 2000 or more per hour.

R. W. Doty has remarked that damage to the cortex or to sensory and motor structures may diminish intelligence, impair perception or paralyze, but leave one otherwise the same *kind* of person; but damage to the limbic system changes personality and may strike at the very heart of human nature. Removal of the amygdala will turn a wild animal into a tame one, and small lesions in the ventromedial nuclei of the hypothalamus can have the opposite effect, making a gentle cat permanently vicious. And attacks of spontaneous hyperactivity in a diseased amygdala (like a tiny localized epileptic process) can turn an otherwise peaceful human being into a ferocious attacker (V. H. Mark, F. R. Ervin). The problem of depression, or of a schizophrenic loss of motivation, may well turn out to be a problem of limbic-system functioning.

SLEEP AND THE CIRCADIAN RHYTHM

One of the most striking characteristics of mammals and birds is the need of sleep. Sleeping is instinctive behavior, if any behavior is; it is species-predictable and necessary to survival (G. Moruzzi). It is evidently a form of rest for the nervous system, a process with restorative action, yet it has peculiarities that make it something more than merely a suspension of activity while recovering from fatigue. A fatigued muscle can be rested at once, and the amount of rest that is needed depends on the amount of work done. But if sleep is rest for the nervous system, it has to occur on a more or less fixed schedule, and the amount of sleep does not vary greatly with the amount of mental work. Hard thinking does not make one sleepy; it is more likely to make one turn to a different form of mental work, such as some kind of game or reading, until the appointed time for sleep arrives. In fact, what makes one sleepy is not mental activity but a lack of it, in what we call boredom.

Also, the brain does not become inactive in sleep; as the EEG shows, cortical neurons are very active during sleep, but in a different pattern. The large potentials of sleep (Fig. 64) are not chiefly due to all-or-none firing of cell-body and axon, although there is a good deal of such firing during sleep. The potentials are mainly the product of the activity of dendrites that is not all-or-none (p. 58) and in some way that we do not understand this must have something to do with the recuperation of cortical neurons.

Sleep involves a lowered activity in the arousal system (with some fluctuation), but again this is not all that is involved. We can think of the arousal system as a "waking center," since its activity causes wakefulness; and there is also something like a "sleep center" in the brain stem, paralleling the arousal system in the midbrain and continuing forward into the posterior hypothalamus.

The two systems alternate in a 24-hour sleep-waking cycle, known as a *circadian rhythm.* "Circadian," from the Latin *circa diem,* means "about a day," but may be used also to refer loosely to other built-in rhythms such as the crab's tidal rhythm (below), or annual hibernation by bears. The control mechanism that does the timing is not known, but it is internal—does not depend on external events—and is commonly referred to as a *biological clock.*

F. Brown, whose work first brought the phenomenon to our attention, has shown that certain crabs that forage on the seashore at low tide have both a 24-hour cycle and a 12-hour 25-minute cycle (the period of the tides). A protective color change in the crab is normally coordinated both with the day-night cycle and with the tidal cycle. The change continues thus coordinated even when the crab is kept in the darkroom away from the seashore, and keeps quite good time. The clock can be reset, however, by exposing the crab to a different lighting schedule: turning on the lights in the darkroom from 6 p.m. to 6 a.m. for several days reverses the crab's timing—and the new timing will continue if the crab is again left in darkness.

Man's 24-hour clock works in much the same way. In mammals, at any rate, the clock is not exact but loses or gains a little. Travellers in the Arctic night continue to need their sleep at approximately the usual times. Air travellers who suddenly move from their own time zones to ones that are four or five hours different find that their internal clocks may take several days to reset, and there is some disorganization and discomfort while this is going on.

Man's clock might run fast or slow by as much as half an hour a day, possibly, in extreme cases. This helps to account for some common complaints. If the clock is fast, the owner will become very sleepy early in the evening and be unable to sleep in the early morning. Actual exposure to the day-night alternation will tend to reset his clock each day (otherwise he would go to bed earlier and earlier and get up earlier and earlier) but he must remain in a chronic state of maladjustment. A slow clock, on the other hand, means that the subject gets to sleep half-an-hour later each night but is waked up at the usual time. The result is an increasing sleep deprivation during the week, till the weekend makes it possible to make up the sleep debt — only to start the process over again on Monday (L. J. West).

Being deprived of sleep may have extreme effects. The need eventually becomes overwhelming, and it is reported that soldiers have actually fallen asleep on their feet while marching. When a subject is kept awake in the laboratory, hallucinations and mild delusory ideas appear, usually about the third day. R. B. Malmo and W. Surwillo have described three subjects who were kept awake, with repeated periods of active psychological testing, for 60 hours. One subject had dream-like hallucinations in which sounds turned into people, arranged in rows and squares. A second subject had no hallucinations, but lost the tactual perception of the knobs he was required to handle in the tests, and had to look at them to see what their shapes were. The third found that some of his visual imagery became hallucinatory (changed so as to seem as if he was actually looking at real objects). He also had momentary delusions (i.e., he actually believed) that the experimenters were controlling his hallucinations.

Dreaming is accompanied by rapid eye movements (REM), and by an activation record in the EEG (small fast waves) as if the subject was awake and thinking. If a human subject is awakened when he makes such eye movements, he reports dream content, but not if awakened at other times. It seems also that dreaming is an important part of the recuperative process of sleep. Experimental subjects were wakened on some nights whenever they started to dream (as shown by their eye movements); as a control procedure they were wakened on other nights when they were not dreaming, for an equal degree of sleep deprivation. When dreaming was prevented on successive nights the subject became irritable and disturbed, but not merely because his sleep was interrupted, for the same disturbance did not occur following the nights when he was awakened between dreams. Loss of some special state of sleep that goes with dreams was what caused the trouble. When normal sleep was permitted following several nights of dream deprivation, the proportion of dreaming time went up from a normal 20 per cent to 30 per cent — the subject, so to speak, had to catch up on his dreaming.

One other aspect of sleep must be mentioned, concerning individual differences. Eight hours is commonly considered the normal sleeping time, but some persons need only six hours or even less, others ten hours or even more. The differences seem to be familial and thus genetic in origin (though no study of this question has been made), and very deep-seated. The six-hour sleeper cannot believe that the ten-hour man really needs all that time in bed, and the ten-hour man is apt to suspect that the other really spends his day cat-napping; how else could he pretend to get along with only six hours of sleep? W. B. Webb and J. Friel found no evidence of personality differences between a group of long sleepers and a group of short sleepers, and they suggest that the long sleepers are simply less efficient at sleeping and so must put in more time at it.

HOMEOSTATIC MECHANISMS

When we turn to the primitive tendencies to action that are represented in hunger and so on, an important conception to be clear about is *homeostasis*, which is defined as a process that maintains a constant internal environment. Inside the skin of a healthy, uninjured normal human being the temperature stays the same within a degree or so, and the circulating fluids maintain a remarkably constant chemical composition. A slight deviation from normal sets off activity in a homeostatic mechanism, tending to restore the normal condition.

For example, breathing is part of the homeostatic mechanism that tends to maintain a constant level of oxygen and carbon dioxide in the blood stream. If the CO_2 level falls, or if the O_2 level rises, breathing slows down and reverses the trend. A rise of CO_2 and a fall of O_2 cause faster breathing. Certain receptors in the brain stem (for CO_2) and in the carotid artery and aorta (for O_2) act like the home thermostat that turns on the furnace when the temperature falls and cuts it off when the temperature rises. The body, of course, has its temperature-regulating mechanism also. When body temperature rises above the normal limits, sweating and panting occur: these dissipate heat. When it falls, shivering occurs: this is heat-producing.

The oxygen–carbon-dioxide mechanisms, and those regulating temperature, function reflexively. As long as a reflexive mechanism is adequate, so that the rest of the nervous system is not called into play, we do not consider the homeostatic process to be motivational (i.e., it does not produce arousal, nor affect the course of other behavior). But when the reflex process is inadequate, motivation is affected at once. If breathing, for example, is interfered with there is a prompt and vigorous reaction from higher neural centers that dominates all other activity.* Ordinarily, the need of oxygen remains at a reflexive

---

*That is, when choking occurs; not if there is merely too low a level of oxygen in the air that is breathed. Pilots have to be specially trained to put on their oxygen masks at the proper altitude. This lack of an automatic protective reaction is like the lack of a pain reaction to strong ultraviolet light: the warning signals come too late, after the damage (sunburn) is done.

level and does not involve motivation. Temperature needs, however, differ. Because the temperatures to which man is exposed daily go well beyond the capacity of the sweating-shivering mechanism, maintenance of body temperature within normal limits involves the general course of behavior, rather than being reflexive only. The motivation that is involved in the search for warmth or coolness is the activity of a homeostatic process.

Hunger and thirst are also homeostatic mechanisms, since they act to produce behavior whose direct effect, in turn, is to maintain the normal concentration of certain substances in the blood stream. The motivation to avoid pain is not as clear a case; it does not directly concern the constancy of the internal environment, but it does act in the long run to do so by preventing injury to the defensive barrier of the skin, for example, or preventing the loss of blood. But sexual motivation is clearly not homeostatic. Copulation does not act to raise sex hormones in the blood stream to a normal level, or lower them from a higher level.

Behavior can be considered homeostatic only if its effect is to regulate the internal environment, correcting deviations from some zero point or norm, and sex behavior as far as we know does not do so. Motivation may therefore be biologically primitive, and very powerful, without being homeostatic.

Hunger

The primary control of eating is hypothalamic. There is a "hunger center" and a "satiation center." (As we saw in Chapter 3, the nervous system is constructed in two symmetrical halves, so these "centers" are dual, each consisting of two nuclei, one on each side of the midline.) When both ventromedial nuclei of the rat's hypothalamus are destroyed, the rat settles down to eat almost continuously if the food is easily available. That is, he can no longer stop eating and becomes as a result enormously obese. If instead a more lateral region of the hypothalamus is destroyed on both sides the rat stops eating, at least for some time, and unless fed by hand will die.

This is the rat's food thermostat, so to speak. The lateral region starts eating, so it is the hunger center. The ventromedial region stops it, so it is the satiation or I've-had-enough center. The two apparently function reflexively in the control of eating. But there is also an important role for learning.

Short-term learning is involved to a different degree in different hungers. Experimentally, we take a laboratory rat that has always had food available, and remove the food from his cage for 24 hours. The food is then put back, and eating time is recorded. We find that in the first 60 seconds the experimental animal eats no more than the control animal which has had food present continuously; in one experiment with 10 rats, the range of times spent eating was from 0 to 55 seconds. In the next five minutes, however, the rate of eating increased. As the experiment was continued, making food available for a 30-minute period daily, the eating behavior in the first 60 seconds of each day changed, and by the tenth day or so every animal ate voraciously at the first presentation of food. (The same experiment with water deprivation gives a different result: a definite thirst appears quickly. Either learning is not involved in the same way, or it is more rapid.)

A sudden acute lack of food does not produce a strong motivation in the subject that has not experienced it before. A rat does not run well in the maze for a food reward until he has been put on a 24-hour feeding schedule for some time; only with repeated experience of hunger, followed by eating, will the rat work energetically for food. In human subjects, similarly, an acute need of food in a previously well-fed subject is far from being as strong a source of motivation as chronic starvation; in the latter case the need may dominate behavior completely.

The homeostasis of hunger is selective for a number of substances — carbohydrate, protein, fats, vitamins and salts — as well as for water. The animal whose food lacks calcium salts, for example, will prefer to drink a weak solution of calcium salt rather than plain tap water. If the diet lacks fat, or thiamine, a food choice is made that tends to correct the lack. But learning is again involved in some of these choices, and learning has effects that are not always desirable. Both rat and man tend to avoid novel foods even though they would correct a deficiency. A most interesting discovery is that when a rat eats a novel food and then becomes sick — even hours later and even if the food was not the cause — any food that tastes the same will be avoided afterward. This obviously protects the rat that nibbles at poisoned food and avoids it later, but it keeps the rat from the same food when it is not poisoned. In man, also, this may account for the otherwise unexplained food aversions that are so common: a child eats onions, develops a fever that night, and then has a permanent dislike of onions. The mechanism apparently involves the amygdala. (For a review of the experiments on acquired aversion, see G. E. Hargrave and R. C. Bolles.)

Artificial Hunger: Addiction

The various addictions of this society, to caffeine, nicotine or alcohol as well as to less frequently used drugs such as morphine or cocaine, are commonly referred to as "habits." They are not merely bad habits, however, like eating with one's knife, or mispronouncing some word. "Habit" implies learning, and this is certainly involved in addiction as it is in hunger; but like hunger, the addiction has the further effect of maintaining the level of a specific substance in the blood stream. In short, an addiction is a homeostatic process, even though the presence of the drug in the blood stream was not originally necessary, or biologically desirable. Once the addiction is well established the drug becomes necessary to stable neural functioning, and lack of it can be very strongly motivating.

There are two stages in the establishment of morphine addiction and presumably of others also: an intermediate stage of physiological dependence, and addiction proper. When young chimpanzees were given injections of morphine daily by S. D. S. Spragg, physiological dependence developed in five or six weeks. Now when the animal was not given his injection he showed the typical signs of physiological disturbance with restlessness, yawning, scratching and so forth; these are called withdrawal symptoms. The chimpanzee was clearly "unhappy" but at this intermediate stage had not yet learned that it was the injection that made him comfortable again. If it was omitted, he did nothing about it.

The experiment required one to three months of further injections before addiction proper occurred. Then the animal would try hard to get the injection, dragging the experimenter to where the drug and hypodermic needle were kept, taking out the needle from its case and handing it to the experimenter, and so on (Fig. 69). At this stage, the chimpanzee would do anything in his power to get the injection, and now the need of the drug had become powerfully motivating.

In human beings who know that they are taking a drug, and know that it is the drug that produces the feeling of well-being, the intermediate stage and true addiction may coincide. Essentially, however, the two stages represent different kinds of processes, the first being some physiological modification of bodily tissues, so that they now require the presence of the drug for "normal" (i.e., reasonably stable) functioning. Without it, there is irritability, restlessness, and disturbance of work habits and social behavior. The second is a learning process.

There is a good deal of evidence to indicate that there are considerable constitutional differences, from one person to another, which determine susceptibility to addiction. It is often thought that al-

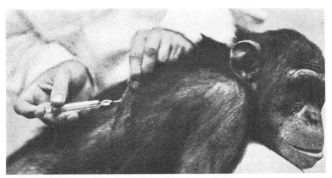

Figure 69. Frank voluntarily taking an injection of morphine. (Courtesy of Yerkes Laboratories of Primate Biology.)

coholism, for example, is simply an attempt to escape from personal troubles, or is due to some form of neurosis. This may be partly true, but there are some neurotics who fail to solve their problems in this way, and despite using alcohol do not become alcoholics. Others with little emotional excuse become addicted at once. It seems clear that emotional difficulties are often the decisive factor that turns the susceptible person into an alcoholic; but it also seems that physiological susceptibility is not the same for all persons. For some, *alcohol is a deadly poison* because of its capacity for rapidly making, in these persons, a homeostatic modification which is in effect irreversible and which thereafter is likely to dominate behavior, with personally and socially disastrous consequences. This is not true for others, and *if* the student is going to drink it is of the greatest practical importance to find out in which class he belongs before he gets finally caught. It is at least a danger sign if alcohol immediately gives great pleasure.

We do not know at present whether marijuana is addictive or, if addictive, whether it is more so than coffee (though coffee can sink a hook deeply in some people). But it should be realized that marijuana, like alcohol, may affect two people very differently. If it has not harmed some people this does not mean it is harmless for others. It might be kept in mind that for some ten years cocaine was thought to be a nonaddictive substitute for morphine. Some caution is still advisable in the use of marijuana.

PAIN

Pain in normal persons appears to comprise two distinguishable processes: one a sensory event, the other a central reaction with a strong motivational component.

The most striking feature of pain as a sensory process is its tendency to take control of the animal's whole behavior. Unless light or sound becomes very intense it can be disregarded for fairly long periods (i.e., the animal may not respond at all to visual, or auditory, cues); but even a weak pain stimulus tends to be dominant over all others in determining the direction of behavior. How this comes about we do not know.

Pain is sometimes spoken of as if it was simply a sensation like other sensations, but it is more than that. There is a sensation to start with, but as R. Melzack and P. Wall have shown the cortex may suppress the incoming sensory message way down at the level of the spinal cord—or, on the contrary, may act to greatly increase the strength of the reaction to the sensation. When the skin is burned or some other injury happens to the body, there is a fast message to the cortex and also a slow message that travels by separate paths in the spinal cord. When the cortex is deeply involved in some activity—that is, when the subject is strongly motivated—it may act on the fast message and send impulses back to the spinal cord to inhibit further transmission. This explains how one can take the skin off a knuckle in the workshop and not be aware of it if an interesting job is demanding close attention at the time, or how sometimes a football player may even break a leg and not know it till he tries to stand up.

There is no specialized cortical area for pain. The sensory information when it does reach the cortex arrives at the somesthetic area along with other body sensations. The *reaction* to the information, when one does react, is due to the involvement of other structures including the arousal system and the limbic system.

At this level, therefore, pain may be more a motivational state, a generalized emotional reaction, than a sensation. Patients suffering from intractable pain are sometimes subjected to "lobotomy," a deep cut made in the frontal lobe at a level anterior to the motor pathways. These patients give us a very curious report after the operation: they say that the pain is the same as before the operation — but it no longer bothers them as it did. They are still able to identify the sensory event — that is, to recognize a pain stimulus — as well as before, but the pain has lost much of its dominating control of behavior.

Animal experiments suggest that some of the motivational aspects of pain are a product of normal experience during growth (Factor IV). The chimpanzee reared with cardboard tubes over hands and feet preventing normal somesthetic experience, and presumably with little or no experience of pain (p. 125), reacted very differently from normal animals to a pin prick. Dogs reared in extreme isolation from the normal environment (p. 123), and with no experience of pain except what they may have inflicted on themselves, showed a most extraordinary unresponsiveness to noxious stimulation. They made little observable response to pin prick, or to having their tails stepped on. They would investigate a lighted paper match by putting a nose into the flame (thus extinguishing it); when another was lighted, it was investigated in the same way. A normal-control dog, if he had not encountered flame before, might put his nose into it once, but would not do so again. For the experimental animals, it was evident, pain stimuli had not acquired the same dominance as for the normal.

We cannot be certain yet concerning the meaning of such data, but it appears that some of the problems concerning pain would be much less puzzling if this interpretation is sound: namely, that "pain," as the term is ordinarily used, refers both to a discriminable sensory event, which in itself does not have strongly motivating properties, and to a motivational state to which the sensory event gives rise on the basis of past experience with pain. In short, it is suggested that "pain" in normal subjects is to a large extent an acquired motivation.

SEXUAL MOTIVATION

In birds and lower mammals, the most important single factor in sexual motivation is humoral: estrogens in the female, androgen in the male, both controlled to a considerable extent by the pituitary gland. As we will see, however, sexual motivation is not completely dependent on this mechanism, especially in the male and in higher species.

In some mammalian species the male is sexually responsive at only one time of year (the rutting season), but in others, including the primates, the male will respond at any time. The female on the other hand always shows cyclical motivation, ranging from a yearly cycle (in sheep, for example) to one of four days (in rats). This is directly related to the cycle of changes in the ovary. In lower species the period of estrus, or heat, is clearly distinct; copulatory behavior cannot be elicited except when the blood-estrogen level is high. In the chimpanzee, however, a few females show sexual responsiveness at all times during the ovarian cycle, though it is very weak at the stage at which other females are unresponsive. Motivation in the human female is still less controlled by the ovarian cycle but though there are great individual differences, the fluctuations of sexual responsiveness still show some relation to the cycle.

The nervous system of the normal animal, male or female, contains the patterns of organization for both male and female behavior. The presence of androgen in the blood stream of the male sensitizes the neural structures involved in the male behavior pattern, but also sensitizes those of the female pattern. The male pattern is dominant and is always displayed when a receptive female is available, but sexual arousal in the normal male makes it more probable, not less, that the female pattern can be elicited from the same animal if he is mounted by another excited male. Conversely in the female: one reliable sign of estrus is often the occurrence of mounting by the female. These facts are evidently of significance for the problem of homosexuality in man. It seems probable that constitutionally, by his nature, man is hetero- and homosexually motivatable, with heterosexuality dominant; and that the establishment of one of these modes of behavior as exclusive depends upon a learning process—that is, it is a function of the culture in which the subject lives, and of the accidents of his experience.

The relation of sexuality to cortical function and learning is of considerable interest. In the male rat, copulatory behavior is correlated with learning ability. It is also dependent on the cortex, and is impaired by cortical destruction in the same way as maze-learning scores. In the female of lower species, however, this relation does not hold. The behavior is much more at the reflexive level, and rather large cortical destructions do not lower the frequency of effective mating (F. A. Beach. See also p. 130). Also, there is little evidence that the female's copulatory behavior is affected by past experience. But at the anthropoid level, this changes. The experienced female chimpanzee copulates much more promptly than the inexperienced, though the difference is not nearly as great as with males. In the chimpanzee, and still more in the human species, ideational factors ("attitudes") determined by earlier learning are capable of greatly modifying sexual responsiveness in both male and female; stimuli that have no directly sexual significance can heighten responsiveness or suppress it. In lower mammals copulation is a compulsive, stimulus-bound form of behavior, especially in the female but essentially in the male also. Strong as the sexual motivation of anthropoid or man may be, the behavior at this phyletic level has come under the control of mediating processes and is far removed from the reflexive characteristics to be seen in dog or cat.

EXPLORATORY BEHAVIOR, AROUSAL AND AMBIVALENCE

Exploratory motivation as we have seen is biologically primitive; it occurs far down in the evolutionary scale and must have survival value. In man and other higher animals this investigative tendency has broadened to include all that comes under the head of *curiosity*, much more than a matter merely of exploring new regions of space. Here, however, we are concerned only with exploratory motivation in an animal such as the laboratory rat, in order to examine its relation to arousal and the ambivalence that is characteristic of this and other motivations.

Ambivalence is a mixture of opposing motivations. In exploratory behavior it is a simultaneous tendency to move toward, and to avoid, a new territory. Placed in familiar surroundings, but with access provided to an unfamiliar region, the animal orients toward the latter. If he is in his home cage with the door open, in a part of the room he is not used to, he moves toward the exciting outer world, but acts as though he was moving to a point of balance between the exploratory tendency, on the one hand, and fear of the strange on the other. Any sudden noise, even slight, produces a prompt retreat, followed again by an advance. The rat's hair is apt to be erect, showing activity of the sympathetic nervous system. Each advance tends to reduce unfamiliarity, so the "point of balance" becomes farther and farther from home base and eventually the whole new territory will be explored.

What we know about the arousal system gives some glimmering of what is going on here, even if final explanations are still in the future. Familiar perceptions lose their power to cause arousal (habituation: p. 175), so arousal is low in the home cage. Looking at strange objects and moving closer, so they are seen more clearly, increases arousal. As long as this increase stays at some moderate level it tends to support whatever cortical activity is going on, by providing additional summation at cortical synapses (p. 173). But this cortical activity is what is causing the animal to move toward the strange outside world, so looking and moving toward the strange tend to make the animal continue doing so, as long as the resulting arousal is not too high. But high levels of arousal tend to produce disorganization in behavior, and constitute emotional disturbance, so a point will be reached at which the strange, which at first attracted, becomes disturbing instead.

An increase from low to moderate arousal must tend to have an organizing effect on behavior, by improving cortical transmission and cell-assembly activity. If a high level of arousal facilitates cortical transmission still more, however, it may begin to make possible conflicting cortical processes. The divergent-conduction regions of the cortex will no longer have their important screening function, which allows only sensory-motor transmissions that are supported by facilitation from the cell-assemblies already active (p. 73). A very high level of bombardment from the arousal system of the brain stem provides other facilitation and may make cortical support unnecessary. The result is that other messages get through; new cortical processes are excited, and these may inhibit the already existing processes, or their motor outflow may excite behavior that conflicts with existing behavior. For example, a limb may receive efferent impulses to its extensor and flexor muscles simultaneously, causing either muscular rigidity or tremor (which is a rapid alternation of extension and flexion). Thus there may be either a cortical conflict (by inhibition) or overt motor conflict (trembling, paralysis of movement, etc.). If in this state of affairs the animal looks back at the home cage, or if his random movements take him back toward it, arousal is decreased; the cortical process that caused the backward movement thus has a chance to continue, since conflicting processes are diminished, so the animal will tend in the first place not to continue moving forward to the point at which arousal is too high, or if he does will tend to move back so that arousal can drop to a moderate level.

This is too simple an account of what goes on, of course, particularly because it leaves out of account the earlier learning the animal has done in arousal-producing situations. But it does suggest how we may be able in principle to understand ambivalence in the emotion-producing situation.

SUMMARY

This chapter is concerned with the neural basis of the primitive motivations of hunger, pain and sexual behavior, and of a peculiar ambivalence found in an animal's exploratory behavior. It is also concerned with the neural mechanism of emotion as it relates to the arousal system, the autonomic nervous system and the limbic system. Arousal determines the level of cortical function in the range from deep sleep to full alertness, and this level is recorded in the various wave patterns of the EEG. The autonomic nervous system has two divisions, the sympathetic and the parasympathetic; the latter acts like a miser, storing up energy, whereas the sympathetic exists as a spendthrift, designed to mobilize the energy for rapid expenditure in emergencies. The limbic system is a fundamental determinant of personality, and of such things as tameness or friendliness and wildness or ferocity.

Other topics dealt with in the chapter are sleep and dreams; circadian rhythms; the homeostasis of hunger and of the acquired hunger known as addiction; pain; and sexual motivation.

Guide to Study

Here as elsewhere, the student would do well to devise his own questions — as if he were preparing an examination for another student — but he should make sure at least that he can answer the following ones himself: What are the two routes by which a sensory excitation may affect cortical activity, and what is the meaning of the terms cue function and arousal function? How does the brain stem regulate consciousness, and why does thought depend on arousal? What does the size of an EEG wave tell us about what is going on in someone else's head? Draw a sketch to show the three segments of the autonomic nervous system; explain why this ANS has sometimes been thought to be the whole story of emotion, and sketch the dual closed circuit (involving the adrenal gland) which partly accounts for the persistence of an emotional disturbance. What function has the hypothalamus in hunger? Where is the amygdala and what does it do? What is the evidence for the existence of pleasure centers?

The student should be sure that he knows the meaning of the term "biological clock," and its relation to sleep; the evidence concerning the value of dream time; the meaning of homeostasis, and which primitive motivations are homeostatic and which are not; what parallel there is between hunger and addiction; and what reason there is to think that "pain" refers to two different things. He should know what the comparative evidence tells us about the relation of sexual motivation to learning ability in the male, the differences between male and female in this respect, and the tendency of each sex to respond like the other in certain circumstances. Finally, what has exploratory behavior to tell us about the nature of ambivalence?

NOTES AND REFERENCES

SPECIAL TOPICS

Arousal System

Lindsley, D. B.: Emotion. In S. S. Stevens (Ed.): *Handbook of Experimental Psychology*, Wiley, 1951. The first application of the discovery of the arousal system to behavioral problems.
Moruzzi, G., and Magoun, H. W.: Brain stem reticular formation and activation of the EEG. *EEG and Clinical Neurophysiology*, 1949, 1, 455–473. Truly an epoch-making paper.
Penfield, W.: The cerebral cortex in man: 1. The cerebral cortex and consciousness. *Archives of Neurology and Psychiatry*, 1938, 40, 417–442.

Limbic System and Motivation

Delgado, J. M. R., Roberts, W. W., and Miller, N. E.: Learning motivated by electrical stimulation of the brain. *American Journal of Physiology*, 1954, 179, 587–593. Describing aversive effects.
Doty, R. W.: Limbic system. In A. M. Freedman and H. I. Kaplan (Eds.): *Comprehensive Textbook of Psychiatry*, Williams & Wilkins, 1967.
Olds, J., and Milner, P.: Positive reinforcement produced by electrical stimulation of septal area and other regions of rat brain. *Journal of Comparative and Physiological Psychology*, 1954, 47, 419–427.
Wasman, M., and Flynn, J. P.: Directed attack elicited from hypothalamus. *Archives of Neurology*, 1962, 6, 220–227.

Biological Clocks and Sleep

Aschoff, J.: Circadian rhythms in man. *Science*, 1965, 148, 1427–1432.
Brown, F. A., Fingerman, M., Sandeen, M. I., and Webb, H. M.: Persistent diurnal and tidal rhythms of color change in the fiddler crab, *Uca pugnax*. *Journal of Experimental Zoology*, 1953, 123, 29–60.

Kleitman, N.: Patterns of dreaming. In J. L. McGaugh, N. M. Weinberger, and R. E. Whalen (Eds.): *Psychobiology,* Freeman, 1967. (Originally in *Scientific American,* November, 1960.)

Malmo, R. B., and Surwillo, W.: Sleep deprivation: changes in performance and physiological indicants of activation. *Psychological Monographs,* 1960, 74, 1–24 (whole number 502).

Moruzzi, G.: Sleep and instinctive behavior. *Archives Italiennes de Biologie,* 1969, 107, 175–216.

Siegel, P. V., Gerathewohl, S. J., and Mohler, S. R.: Time-zone effects. *Science,* 1969, 164, 1249–1255.

Webb, W. B., and Friel, J.: Sleep stage and personality characteristics of "natural" long and short sleepers. *Science,* 1971, 171, 587–588.

West, L. J.: Psychopathology produced by sleep deprivation. *Research Publications, Association for Research in Nervous and Mental Disease,* 1967, 45, 535–558. Chronic deprivation in normal life is dealt with as well as acute deprivation. Note, in the Discussion (p. 556) Lubin's report of the man who thought he was being followed by a telephone pole.

OTHER REFERENCES

Beach, F. A.: The neural basis of innate behavior: III. Comparison of learning ability and instinctive behavior in the rat. *Journal of Comparative Psychology,* 1939, 28, 225–262.

Hargrave, G. E., and Bolles, R. C.: Rat's aversion to flavors following induced illness. *Psychonomic Science,* 1971, 23, 91–92.

Mark, V. H., and Ervin, F. R.: *Violence and the Brain.* Harper and Row, 1970.

Melzack, R.: The perception of pain. In J. L. McGaugh, N. M. Weinberger, and R. E. Whalen (Eds.): *Psychobiology,* Freeman, 1967.

Melzack, R., and Wall, P.: Pain mechanisms: a new theory. *Science,* 1965, 150, 971–979.

emotion and motivation: the social context

We saw, in the introduction to Chapter 10, that evolution must build into an animal certain prime directives: especially, to eat, to mate and to avoid injury. Hunger, sex and pain motivations are essential if a species is to exist. But evolution also endowed the mammal with a large brain and a cortex, and this has certain other consequences that one might not anticipate if one was designing a mammal for the first time.

A large brain has direct evolutionary value, making its owner more adaptable by making him more capable of learning and of solving problems, but it appears to have some indirect motivational effects also. There are motivations, that is, that seem dependent on intelligence and are characteristic of the higher mammal, less strong in the lower mammal and wholly absent in most other animals. These characteristics are most marked in man, and they are closely related to the structure of human society. The whole of this large area is the concern of the present chapter. There is no topic in psychology that is more important, and none in which comparative data are more significant. Although enthusiastically ignored by most social psychologists, the behavior of dog, porpoise and chimpanzee has much to tell us about the nature of man and his society.

EMOTIONS, MOTIVATION AND AROUSAL

Emotion is not a term that can be defined precisely, though we know what it means in a common-sense way. It refers to such states as joy, love, pride, and fun, which the subject likes (that is, he does not act so as to terminate them when they occur, and at other times acts so as to make them recur); it refers to anger, jealousy and fear, states which the subject tends to terminate by attacking the source of anger or jealousy, or by running away from the source of fear; and it refers to grief, shame and depression, disliked states whose causes are not terminable by the subject's behavior. Emotion is both organizing (making behavior more effective) and disorganizing; it is both energizing and debilitating. In other words, "emotion" is a term that refers to some very different conditions, apparently little related.

However, they do have something in common. They are all special states of motivation, and closely related to arousal. Anger for example is a temporary heightening of arousal accompanied by a tendency to attack. Fear is a temporary heightening of arousal accompanied by a tendency to withdraw or flee. When fear is chronic, because the threat cannot be escaped, or when there is no external threat and the fear is due to some disorder within the nervous system itself, it is called anxiety. Thus for some purposes we can discuss emotion as an entity, as a single kind of process, but for others we will be better able to deal with the specific named emotions such as anger or fear.

Let us begin by considering the inverted-U curve of arousal in Figure 70. This shows the relation of *cue function* to *arousal function* (p. 174). What the curve says is that the capacity of sensory stimulation to guide behavior is poor when arousal is very low or very high. We saw, in the discussion of exploratory behavior and ambivalence, that cortical function is at its best only in the middle range of arousal; with low arousal cortical transmission is poor and with high arousal it is too good, permitting the occurrence of irrelevant and conflicting cortical activities (p. 194). With very low arousal, the sensory message does not get through; with very high arousal too many messages get through and prevent the animal from responding selectively to any one set of stimuli. In other words, the animal is unresponsive when arousal is low and too responsive, to too many things at the same time, when arousal is high.

Now we can see the relation between emotion and motivation. Emotion in the general sense is closely related to arousal (D. B. Lindsley); as arousal increases so does emotion. But if motivation is a tendency to produce organized, effective behavior (p. 171), the curve of Figure 70 shows that motivation rises at first with arousal but then begins to fall off at some higher level and may practically disappear at the highest levels.

Though we ordinarily think of emotional excitement as a cause of vigorous, effective response—that is, we think of it as motivating—there is well-authenticated evidence showing not only that it can impair behavior but also that it can reduce the effectiveness of response to near zero. Apparently it does this by abolishing the thought or intention of acting: a loss of motivation. The term "paralysis of terror" is somewhat misleading, but this is what we are talking about. (The term is misleading because there may be no paralysis in the literal sense, the subject usually being capable of movement, and also because, in extreme cases, the subject's thought may be so impaired that he really does not have what we would ordinarily consider

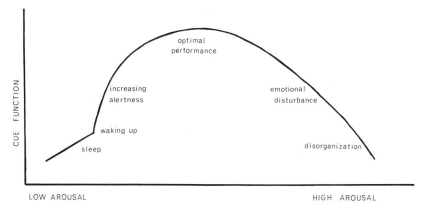

Figure 70. Relation of the effectiveness with which stimuli guide behavior (cue function) to the level of arousal, varying from deep sleep to disorganizing states of emotion, with maximal behavioral efficiency at an intermediate level of arousal. The shape of this curve must be different for different habits: See Figure 71.

to be fear or terror. These terms refer to a state of mind which includes *ideas* of being injured, of feeling pain and so on. But there is something that approximates paralysis, either of thought or of bodily movement.)

J. S. Tyhurst has described the behavior of people caught by a fire in a vacation steamship or apartment house, or by a flash flood. About 15 per cent show really organized and effective behavior; about 70 per cent show varying degrees of disorganization, but are still able to function with some effectiveness; but another 15 per cent (the proportion varied from 10 to 25 per cent in different disasters that were studied) show completely ineffective behavior: screaming or crying, confusion, inability to move or to get out of bed, or aimless or unsuitable movements. One man, told that the ship was on fire and that he had to get on deck at once, was last seen ineffectually searching for a cuff link. S. L. A. Marshall has reported very similar figures for the stress of battle: repeated studies in various armies have shown that only about 15 to 25 per cent of infantrymen in the presence of the enemy can be relied on to fire their rifles, with or without careful aiming, and some are incapable of doing so even when prodded by an officer. Again, the newspapers every now and then report the case of a pedestrian caught in traffic who could escape but makes no move and is killed, or a driver whose car stalls on a railroad track before an oncoming train and who sits motionless, apparently unable to stir, and is killed in the subsequent collision.

Such behavior shows that emotion-producing situations can severely impair the processes that control organized behavior, even when the cues are present that should guide the appropriate response. Motivation, that is, can be impaired by too high a level of arousal.

There are other phenomena with the same implication. Stage fright is something most of us have suffered from, and "buck fever" is well known (suddenly being given one's great opportunity, and being unable to act appropriately). There is a common opinion that the prize fighter's skill may be impaired by anger, and that a physician or surgeon should not try to deal with a serious illness in one to whom he is emotionally attached, the implication being that *his* skill is similarly impaired by worry.

All such examples show that arousal can have a disorganizing effect on behavior. But we must not forget, of course, that lower levels of arousal are organizing, and it is essential to remember that different habits will have different degrees of resistance to disorganization. Logically, a simpler and longer-established habit should be less likely to be disrupted than a complex mode of response that depends on a delicate interaction of mediating processes: if anger produces a trembling of the fingers it would disturb a watchmaker's skilled behavior but not his ability to swat a fly. Similarly—at a cortical level—worry about his wife's future could impair a physician's skill in diagnosing her illness when cancer is in question, but not when his diagnosis is hay fever. In effect, what this says is that the inverted-U curve has different shapes for different habits, as in Figure 71. Also, we may note that the same degree of arousal may be disorganizing at one point in a series of actions but organizing at a later point. Stage fright, for the experienced actor, is disturbing *before* the performance, but there seems to be general agreement that if there is no stage fright at any time in the proceedings, the performance itself is less likely to be effective.

This discussion can be summarized as follows: Emotion in its general sense is directly correlated with arousal. Emotion, or arousal, is motivating up to the point at which conflicting activities in the cor-

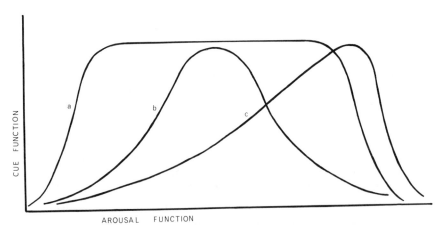

Figure 71. *Possible differences in the curve relating arousal to cue function or effectiveness of response, in three habits. In a, a simple, long-practiced habit such as giving one's name when asked, maximal efficiency is reached with low arousal and maintained over a wide range; in b, a complex skill, the maximum appears only with a medium degree of arousal; and in c, a performance such as running a race which is relatively uncomplicated but demands full mobilization of effort, the maximum appears with higher arousal.*

tex begin to interfere with one another, preventing the dominance of one activity that would produce *one* set of organized responses to the situation. How high arousal can be and still be motivating varies with the kind of behavior. It presumably varies also from one person to another.

Emotion is "directly correlated with" arousal but cannot be simply identified with it, because the limbic system evidently has a crucial (but not yet fully understood) contribution to make, and because thought processes are an important feature of any emotion. *Fear* can be defined as arousal accompanied by mediating processes which constitute the idea of being injured, and which tend to produce avoidance and flight. *Anger* can be defined as arousal accompanied by mediating processes which constitute the idea of hurting the person or animal at whom the anger is directed, and which tend to produce the corresponding behavior. *Disgust* or *horror* is arousal with no accompanying ideas of being injured, but simply of avoiding the sight, sound, touch, taste or smell of the thing that disgusts. *Joy* or *love* is arousal accompanied by mediating processes which make for a deeper immersion in, or continued contact with, the activity or thing that gives joy or is loved. The arousal of joy is presumably not the same as the arousal of strong fear; presumably the pleasure centers (p. 182) are active in one and not in the other, though mild fear may be pleasant, as we will see below, but the clearest distinction between the different emotions is found in the ideas that go with them, and the actions that these ideas (mediating processes) give rise to. No definition of emotion can omit reference to the cortical activity that gives any emotion its identity.

EMOTION AND INTELLECTUAL LEVEL

Next we come to an important proposition: that an animal's susceptibility to emotional disturbance is directly related to the level of its intelligence. Man is the most rational animal, but also the most emotional; his near neighbors in evolution, the great apes, show their kinship with him more clearly in their emotional characteristics than in their capacity for learning and solving problems; and it is the older rather than the younger animal that is more subject to emotional disturbance from a variety of causes and shows the greater severity and duration of disturbance. Thus there is a species correlation between emotionality, in this sense, and level of intelligence, and also a correlation with the growth of the animal, as its intellectual functions become more complex.

The correlation is so close that one can hardly avoid the notion that there is a direct causal relation. The facts suggest that emotional disturbance is like a temporary breakdown in a piece of mechanical or electrical equipment; the more complex the equipment, the greater number of things by which its operation may be disturbed, the greater the aberration from normal function may be, and the longer it may take to get it back in working order.

Has this analogy any value? It is consistent with the idea that mediating processes (more complex in the higher animal) are a factor in emotion, and it implies that having mediating processes increases the strength and duration of arousal. It does seem that this is so. One important cause of emotional disturbance is some discrepancy between perception and expectancy: why this should cause a sharp rise in arousal is not entirely clear, but it is known that cortical events have a down-flow action on the arousal system (p. 175), so something of the sort could conceivably take place. We may note also that the complex perceptions of the more developed brain would allow the more intelligent subject to detect discrepancy when another subject would not, and that a capacity for thought allows the subject to dream up imaginary injuries and insults.

Let us look at the evidence for the statement that emotion is characteristic of the more intelligent subject.

Anger and its close relative *jealousy** are not conceptions that one needs for classifying the behavior of the laboratory rat. The rat bites to escape capture, or in the course of fighting for food, or to protect the young, but rarely for other reasons. Anger as we know it in higher animals involves a sort of social perception that is beyond the rat's ken. The dog is definitely capable of jealousy and occasionally, in some dogs, there are signs of sulking. In the chimpanzee, however, we have the full picture of human anger in its three main forms: anger, sulking and the temper tantrum. The peculiar feature of sulking is refusing to accept what one tried to get in the first place. The peculiar feature of the temper tantrum** is the inclusion of apparent attempts at self-injury, the child holding his breath, pulling his hair, banging himself against the wall — and watching meanwhile to see what effect this is having on the adult who is denying him what he wants. There is a purposive element that is also clear in the year-old chimpanzee infant who takes surreptitious looks at his mother in between his attacks of choking to death or pounding his head on the floor.

The main cause of anger is the perception of someone else's doing something one does not like. It is common to say that the cause is *frustration,* frustration meaning that one is prevented from getting something one wants. This is unsatisfactory; the sight of food out of reach does not produce anger in the hungry chimpanzee. But he does get angry if one offers the food, then pulls it away — that is, if he is given an expectancy of getting it, and then perceives the caretaker

---

*It seems that jealousy differs from anger only in the circumstances in which it appears — in other words, jealousy is anger arising from a particular social situation.

**"Temper tantrum" refers only to a distinctive pattern of behavior in the half-grown primate infant, as characteristic of the young chimpanzee as of the human child and as easily recognized. The term is also used in common language to refer to other outbursts, in child or adult, that are quite different. They might be called "frustrated rage," since they do not have the purposiveness characteristic of the true temper tantrum.

as deliberately refusing it. Also, anger may occur when there is no frustration at all, in the sense defined. Rain water from the roof that wetted Bokar's back did not make him angry, though he did not like it; but he was enraged when Dick spit water at him from the next cage, even if he was not hit. Pan took food from Mona, whom he dominated, in the same cage; her noisy frustrated rage then angered him so that he gave her a beating. The only frustration *he* suffered was of his desire for peace and quiet after he had got what he wanted.*

The close relation of chimpanzee and man, with respect to the forms and causes of anger, is clear; the only difference between the two species is the greater variety of things that cause anger in man, with his greater social perceptiveness and consequently greater capacity for being slighted or insulted, and with language to increase still further the range of possible provocations.

THE CAUSES OF FEAR

With fear we find the same increasing variety of causes as we go from lower to higher mammals, and the same increase in duration and apparent severity of disturbance. Pain, sudden loud noise and sudden loss of support cause fear in any mammal. For the rat, we need add only strange surroundings to have a complete list of the causes of fear as far as we know them. With the dog, the list becomes longer: strange persons, certain strange objects or situations (such as a balloon being blown up before the dog), a large statue of an animal, the dog's owner in different clothing, or a hat being moved across the floor by a thread that the dog does not see (R. Melzack). Not all dogs are equally affected — H. Mahut has shown, for example, that working dogs, bred for intelligence, are more susceptible to fear than bulldogs and terriers, bred for pugnacity. Monkeys and apes are affected by a still greater variety of stimulating situations than dogs, and the degree and duration of disturbance is greater.

Causes of fear in the captive chimpanzee make up an almost endless list: a carrot of an unusual shape, a biscuit with a worm in it, a rope of a particular size, color and texture (but not other ropes), a doll or a toy animal, a particular piece of apparatus or part of it, and so on. What one animal fears another may not, but as a species chimpanzees are much more susceptible than dogs to fears that do not arise from pain or threat of pain.

Figure 72 is a picture of two objects that are capable of producing a remarkable reaction in chimpanzees. The "death mask," left, in particular produced screaming, panic-stricken flight in a fifth of the adult animals who were simply shown the object, carried in the experimenter's hand as he walked up to the cage. The response of

*See the preceding footnote. The chimpanzees referred to were inmates of the Yerkes Laboratories of Primate Biology.

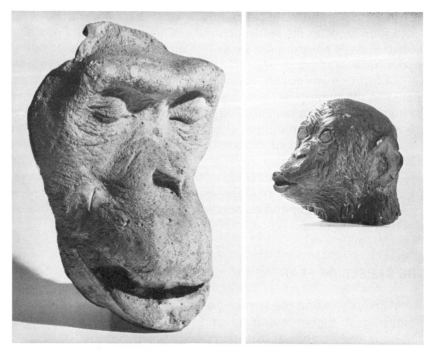

Figure 72. Objects that caused fear in adult chimpanzees: left, a plaster of paris cast from a death mask of an adult; right, a clay model of an infant's head, nearly life size.

the remaining adults varied in strength, but most were very frightened and no animal failed to show erection of hair and avoidance of the test object. The same reaction was produced by a clay model of an adult chimpanzee head about half life-size (this was more frightening than the modeled infant head shown in Fig. 72); an actual chimpanzee's head that had been preserved in formalin; a life-like model of a human head, sawn from a display dummy; and various related objects, such as a detached human hand (from the same dummy). With repeated testing there was some habituation (p. 175), but no animal got to the point of coming near any of these objects. A doll, representing a human infant, was placed in the cages of five adult chimpanzees, one after another, but despite the chimpanzee's well known curiosity and destructiveness with things he can take to pieces, the doll remained intact and untouched.

These were the results with adults. The behavior of younger animals was quite different. One- and two-year-olds (corresponding roughly to human two- and three-year-olds) paid no attention at all to the test objects; as the experimenter approached carrying one of the objects the infants came toward him and apparently not noticing the object at all, tried to get the experimenter to pick them up. All their attention was focused on his face. Half-grown animals of five and six years (corresponding ages in man: eight to ten) were fascinated by the objects; as the experimenter neared an enclosure containing half a dozen of these youngsters they approached as close as they could (quite unlike the adults), forming a tight cluster clinging to the cage wire and poking their fingers through to prod the model head being shown them. The same things that terrified the adults—or horrified them—were exciting but not frightening to the half grown, and not even noticed by the infants.

There is a clear parallel in the different reactions of human children and adults to distorted and damaged human bodies. To the limited intelligence of the chimpanzee a model of a head may be in the same class as an actual head severed from the body for man. (In both cases there is a perceived identity with part of a living person, and at the same time a clear discrepancy.) It is not children but their elders who are most upset by scenes of violence and broken bodies on TV; a color movie of a major operation can produce nausea and fainting in adults, but not in children; we tolerate the extraordinary brutality of many of the classic fairy stories as adults, presumably, only because we were introduced to them at the more bloodthirsty age of five or six years.

An experiment by H. E. and M. C. Jones provides direct evidence of the increase of emotional susceptibility with age. They recorded the reactions of children and adolescents to a snake, which was rather torpid and which was shown to be quite harmless. The subjects were city dwellers and had not had contact with snakes before. There was little fear in the youngest (about five years old), increased interest with only slight signs of caution in those of intermediate ages, and strong avoidance by most of the older subjects. "Fear" is not the right word to apply to the older subjects' reaction; "horror" is better since they did not expect to be injured (they knew the snake could not hurt them), but in general it can be said that the reaction of most adults to a snake that they know is not capable of injuring them is hardly less vigorous than to a dangerous one. (It should be emphasized that the "fear" of snakes is not learned. Why it should be so strong is not understood, but it is a product of psychological maturation (p. 129) rather than learning. The year-old chimpanzee is not disturbed by contact with a snake, but the adult who sees one for the first time is disturbed, very much so, his reaction being about as strong as a man's.)

EMOTION AND THE SOCIAL STRUCTURE

It was proposed in the preceding section that emotionality increases as mental age increases in the growing child. Now at first sight this seems false. It is true that temper tantrums and unreasoning fears increase in frequency and strength between the ages of one and four years, but in the study of a large number of children by A. T. Jersild and F. B. Holmes this trend reversed itself about the age of five, and though we know that some things such as the fear of snakes continue to increase in strength, are these things not exceptions to a more general tendency to become *less* excitable at maturity?

To ourselves as adults we seem civilized, urbane, not given to senseless fears and outbursts of rage like the young child or the explosive chimpanzee. The reason, however, may not be that we are less susceptible, but instead that we are sheltered by what we call a civilized environment, within which we are not much exposed to the causes of emotional disturbance. It offers actual physical protection from wild animals or freezing to death and, mostly, makes it possible to avoid starving to death, but it also offers psychological protection from emotional disturbance by reducing the causes to near zero. In a "civilized environment" one never has to be in strange places in darkness (thus many adults never discover that they are subject to fear in such circumstances). The adults in it have learned elaborate rules of courtesy, good manners, and how to behave in public, so their behavior is predictable and usually will not cause one embarrassment, shame, anger or disgust. All this is achieved by prolonged training in childhood and later enforced by legal penalties (e.g., for slander, indecent exposure, dumping garbage in the street) or by social ostracism. In this environment, in short, one can count most of the time on not being suddenly exposed to the causes of strong emotion without warning and without adequate opportunity to avoid them. All this of course implies also that we as adults have been trained to suppress strong emotion when it does occur, as far as we can. Emotional outbursts are thus rare in the civilized adult on his own ground, but there is no reason to conclude from this that he is less susceptible to attacks of emotion than his five-year-old son, who must live in an environment tailored to adult needs rather than those of a five-year-old.

The social problems of race and religious prejudice should show us what we are like as a species, if nothing else does. It is common to assume that social prejudice is wholly learned, and that if one never let the child hear bad things about other groups he would grow up to be without prejudice. We know, however, that more is involved. Such learning does occur and it is important to prevent it whenever possible, but prejudice can spring up where there has been no occasion for learning, and the learning, when prejudice is taught, occurs with extraordinary ease. An essential component in prejudice is the emotional reaction of human beings to the strange, to what is the same and yet different, to the thing that can cause a conflict of ideas.

At first it seems unreasonable to suppose that emotions as strong as those involved in social prejudice could be set off by such small things as a difference of skin color or the knowledge that the other person does not share some religious belief. Here the comparative evidence has great weight. The chimpanzee's outright panic at the sight of a model of a chimpanzee head shows how strong the effect of a perceptual discrepancy, as such, can be. Also, if a human being is excited and hostile on seeing a stranger, we might think that this is because he has been taught that strangers are dangerous, but the chimpanzee born in captivity and never before exposed to a stranger, chimpanzee or human, shows the same thing. Clearly the hostility is not something that needs to be learned.

Clearly, strong emotional reactions may be induced by apparently trivial things, in man as in chimpanzee: consider that healthy young men, known to be capable of withstanding very serious injury without crying out, are also known to be capable of fainting at the *idea* of hypodermic injection, before a needle has even touched them. Or, among trivial differences with large consequences, consider the social use of two words that mean precisely the same thing, one a Latin anatomical term, one coming from Anglo-Saxon and classed as obscene.* All that "obscene" can mean in this case is that one word is taboo and the other is not. Society is shot through with taboos, and failure to observe them involves considerable risk. These are taboos in the most primitive sense.** The whole structure of society contains a large irrational or emotional factor; failure to recognize it means failure to understand the social behavior of the human animal.

The attempt to explain race and religious prejudice as products of learning arises from the assumption that man, being a rational animal, makes his important decisions on the basis of reason. Once we see this is not so, and that the possession of intelligence may in fact, through imagination, *increase* the causes of emotional disturbance, we can see better the nature of our problem in dealing with prejudice, and how dangerous is the assumption that prejudice will disappear if the child is not taught bad things about others.

Left to itself, the child's emotional reaction to the other, to the one who differs, is likely to result in hostility. *But it need not do so.* Learning, which can have bad effects and increase hostility, can instead guide the emotional reaction in the direction of warmth and friendliness. Man's motivational characteristics are not all undesirable. The same comparative approach which shows us that unreasoning hostility can arise spontaneously, allows us also to see another and more favorable side of man's nature. To this we will turn in a moment.

To sum up the argument of this section: the comparative evidence indicates that the capacity for emotion increases with intelligence. It is the higher animal of whom fear of innocuous objects, or unfounded hostility, is characteristic. Also, it is the older rather than the younger chimpanzee that is more fearful and hostile. At first it may seem that these conclusions cannot be extended to man: adult civilized man is less emotional than the fearful wild animal, and less emotional than the young child? But looking at the environment in which the traits are manifested, we see that something has

---

*The publisher advises that the student be allowed to think of his own examples. These are the words that in English are generally spelt with four letters but in Latin take five or more, showing the superiority of English to Latin.

**Consider some of the sexual taboos, for example. A prison sentence for statutory rape or indecent exposure does not require evidence that the behavior has done anyone any harm, physically or mentally — all that must be shown is that the taboo has been broken. Or consider the taboos attaching to the dead body: there are severe legal penalties for "offering indignity" to a corpse, as for example stuffing one into the trunk of your car when taking it to be buried.

been left out of account. The structure of "civilization" is such as to cushion the adult's sensitivities, to protect him from the causes of fear, anger and disgust. The extent and strength of social prejudice (in which reason is used only to reinforce one's unreasoning emotional responses) show how deeply rooted these sensitivities are. Thus the lack of emotional outbursts in the civilized adult is evidence, not of a lack of susceptibility, but of the effectiveness of the social cocoon in which we live. It does not refute the proposition that emotional susceptibility rises with intellectual capacity.

This susceptibility often has undesirable results, but this, fortunately, is not always so, as we will now see. Man and ape can feel fear *for others,* and man, at least, can be angered by injury or injustice to others.

ALTRUISM IN THE HIGHER ANIMAL

Among the distinctive features of behavior in the human species is the frequency of *altruism,* defined as intrinsically motivated purposive behavior whose function is to help another person or animal. In this definition, "intrinsically motivated" means that the behavior does not depend on primary or secondary reinforcement: that the helper receives no benefit except the knowledge that he has helped; and "purposive" implies that the behavior is under the control of mediating processes, thus excluding the reflexive cooperation of the social insects (ant, bee, termite).

Common experience tells us how frequent such behavior is. Giving money to a beggar, working in societies for the prevention of cruelty, helping a stranger start his car, contributing to disaster funds, helping with the dishes, lending a set of notes to another student or giving him a match—trivial or not, there are endless ways in which human beings do things for others with no expectation of a return. Often, of course, such things are also done with hope of later benefits, but this does not change the fact that truly unselfish acts, great and small, are frequent. Some of them are great indeed, considering the number of persons who die annually in the attempt to rescue someone from drowning or from a burning building.

The facts are clear. What do they mean? There is a long tradition of interpreting *all* of man's motivation as selfish; generosity is not in the child's nature but imposed by rewards and punishments and maintained at maturity by social pressure. It is assumed that the adult is generous—when he is generous—only because of habit or because he is rewarded by social approval and punished for selfishness by disapproval. It is difficult to refute this proposition directly, because of the multifarious learning of the growing child in society. But there is a disproof in animal behavior.

H. W. Nissen and M. P. Crawford have shown that begging, for example, is a very powerful stimulus for the chimpanzee. Two animals are in adjoining cages and one is given food; if the two are friends, the second may get as much as half the food as a gift. If they are not friends, the importunate begging of the second animal may still be irresistible, but annoying, and the rich animal may end up by throwing the food violently at the beggar. There is no suggestion in this latter case that the "rich" animal gets any pleasure from giving to the poor. There is some deeper compulsion, and it is quite clear from the history of the animals, reared in the laboratory, that the gift is not made because the giver was trained as an infant to be kind to beggars.

Chimpanzees and gorillas living free in the wild have been observed giving help to half-grown youngsters in trouble, sometimes when it meant that the helper himself had to venture into the dangerous neighborhood of the human observer. A similar kind of behavior has been observed experimentally.

Two adult female chimpanzees, Lia and Mimi, are caged together. A disguised human observer approaches, playing the part of the "bold man," one who is unafraid of chimpanzees. Thanks to the cage wire between him and them, and a stout pair of gloves, he can pretend to answer attacks in a most intimidating manner. Both Lia and Mimi, seeing a stranger approach without the caution usually shown by strangers, attack; Lia is frightened by the vigor of the stranger's responses and runs away, but Mimi is not. Mimi stays close to the wire trying to catch hold of him; then Lia, though clearly afraid, returns and repeatedly tries to pull the reckless Mimi out of the danger zone. This scene is repeated on subsequent testing.

The porpoise, or dolphin, a sea-going mammal, must be classed as a higher animal on the ground of its behavior as well as its large brain, a fifth larger than man's with a highly developed cortex. There is well-attested evidence of adults helping other adults in trouble. J. B. Siebenaler and D. K. Caldwell report two cases in which a stunned animal was supported at the surface till he could swim again (for porpoises of course must breathe). Other females besides the mother have been seen helping the newborn porpoise to the surface to breathe for the first time. Finally, W. N. Kellogg reports two separate instances in which a porpoise helped a human swimmer to reach safety.

In short, the evidence from infrahuman mammals indicates that altruism is a product of evolution and not something that must be beaten into the growing human child because of the needs of society. Here, apparently, we have another motivational consequence of the development of complex mediating processes. It is clear in the chimpanzee and porpoise, at least on occasion, but it is most evident in man and obviously an important element in the structure of human society.

PLAY, BOREDOM AND THE SEARCH FOR EXCITEMENT

Living things must be active, and this is as true of brain as of muscle. Ordinarily both are kept exercised as a result of environmental stimulation and in the satisfaction of biological needs. There are times however when an animal has no threat to escape, no need of food and no young to care for, no sexual motivation and no need of sleep. One need remains: to be active, physically and mentally.

The play of birds and the lower mammals seems largely muscular, though there is evidently a neural component also. The animal does not merely tense and relax his muscles alternately, but indulges in activities that require elaborate neural control, generally ones that depend on past learning. In monkey, ape and man, however, a kind of play occurs that is almost entirely mental, with a minimum of muscular activity.

H. F. Harlow has shown that monkeys will work for hours at solving simple mechanical puzzles, with no reward other than finding a solution (Fig. 73). The chimpanzee will work for a food reward, but he works much better if the task interests him, and then he may work even if he does not want the food. One female solved a series of problems, getting a slice of banana for each solution, but not eating it; instead, she piled the slices in a neat row on top of the apparatus. Then she repeated the whole series of problems, putting one slice of banana back into the food dish after each trial, apparently for the experimenter.

Such behavior is *play*, when play is defined as work done for the

Figure 73. A monkey solving a problem for its own sake. All the experimenter has to do is to "set" the simple mechanical puzzles (which would offer a six-year-old child no problem at all), and the monkey will work at them. (Courtesy of H. F. Harlow.)

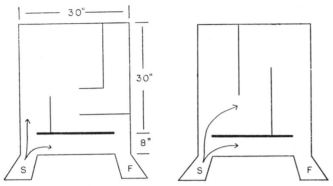

Figure 74. *Two "problems" in a variable-pattern maze, the rat having always the option of going directly from the start (S) to the food (F) instead of going through the problem area. The arrows indicate the two routes from which the animal could choose. (From Hebb, D. O., and Mahut, H., J. Psychol. Norm. & Pathol., 1955.)*

sake of doing it. Obviously it is not primarily physical play, but must exercise the brain more than the muscles. Even the laboratory rat shows something of the same kind. Figure 74 shows the plan of an apparatus allowing the rat the choice of a direct route to food, versus an indirect route through a simple maze. Figure 75 shows that about 40 per cent of the time the rats preferred to take the longer path, provided that the "problems" (so simple that they hardly deserve that name) were changed on each run. Figure 75 also shows that an unchanging problem did not have the same attraction. Here only 12 per cent of the runs were through the maze area, the difference showing up even in the first block of five trials. The effect of varying the problems shows that the rat was not merely seeking physical exercise, since the unchanged problem provided as much muscular activity on the average as the changing ones.

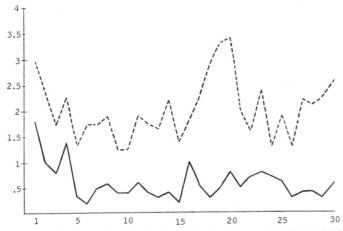

Figure 75. *Mean number of choices of the longer route in each block of 5 runs by 11 rats, in maze problems of the kind shown in the preceding figure. A mean of 3 thus represents 60 per cent choice of the longer route.*

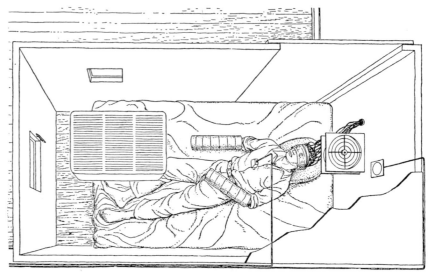

Figure 76. *The subject in the isolation experiment seen from above, with the ceiling cut away. Cuffs were worn to prevent somesthetic perception by the hands; the plastic shield over the eyes admitted light but prevented pattern vision. The subject had a foam-rubber U-shaped cushion covering his ears; here it has been removed so that EEG tracings can be taken. An air-conditioner is shown where it would be on the ceiling, upper left, and the microphone by which the subject could report his experiences is seen just above his chest. (From "The Pathology of Boredom" by W. Heron. Copyright © 1957 by Scientific American, Inc. All rights reserved.)*

It is evident therefore that "mental play," involving the brain as much as the muscles, is a characteristic of the mammal and one that becomes more prominent in the higher mammals. Much of man's mental play—in bridge, chess, and so on—is competitive, and we tend to think of it as motivated by the secondary reinforcement of the "prestige" or social approval that comes from being better than someone else. But there is also noncompetitive play such as knitting or singing or birdwatching, and the lower-animal data just discussed show that the need of mental exercise exists in its own right. *Boredom* is a state in which the subject seeks a higher level of excitement, usually in some form of play, and the avoidance of boredom is a most important factor in human behavior.

The extent to which we are dependent on our normally varied environment and the mental activity it gives rise to is seen in perceptual-isolation* experiments (W. H. Bexton, W. Heron, and T. H. Scott). College students were paid $20 a day to do nothing, lying on a comfortable bed with eyes covered by translucent plastic (permitting light to enter, but preventing pattern vision), hands enclosed in tubes (so that the hands could not be used for somesthetic perception, though they could be moved to prevent joint pains), and ears covered with earphones from which there was a constant buzzing except when the subject was being given a test (Fig. 76). These conditions were

---

*Sometimes referred to as "sensory deprivation."

relaxed only to allow the subject to eat or go to the toilet. Few could stand the monotony for more than two or three days, the upper limit being six. The subjects became willing to listen to childish or meaningless talk that otherwise they would have avoided contemptuously — anything to break the monotony. Eventually the need became overwhelming to see, to hear, to be in normal contact with the environment, to be *active*. Nothing like the same pressure develops when a subject is equally immobilized (with a broken leg, say) but has books, radio and friends to keep him occupied mentally. The need thus is more for mental than for physical activity.

The experiment showed that man can be bored, which we knew, but it showed, too, that boredom is too mild a word for some of the effects. The need for the normal stimulation of a varied environment is fundamental. Without it mental function and personality deteriorate. The subjects in isolation complained of being unable to think coherently, they became less able to solve simple problems, and they began to have hallucinations. Some of them saw such things as rows of little yellow men wearing black caps, squirrels marching with sacks over their shoulders, or prehistoric animals in the jungle. These scenes were described as like animated cartoons. More fundamentally disturbing were somesthetic hallucinations, when the subject perceived two bodies somesthetically or felt as if his head was detached from his body; closely related to this was "a feeling of bodily strangeness," for which the subject could give no more adequate description, and the report of several subjects that they felt that their minds were detached from their physical bodies. The subjects' very identity had begun to disintegrate. We saw in Chapters 7 and 9 that the development of personality and intelligence depends on exposure to an adequately stimulating environment during infancy; the isolation experiments show that adult man continues to be dependent on it in the same way, for the maintenance of normality.

MAN'S AMBIVALENT NATURE

Man is a mammal and a product of evolution, and fundamental to his motivation is the satisfaction of basic biological needs; when these are not met — particularly if the lack is chronic — the attempt to satisfy them generally becomes a dominant motive. (Even here, however, the mediating processes of a large cerebrum have a powerful influence; the starving man may share his food, the man in danger may invite even greater risk to help another, and sexual need is characteristically subordinated to the rules and customs of society.)

But when the individual's biological needs are satisfied we see a very different picture. The ambivalence of the exploratory tendency that is evident in the lower mammal (p. 193) now extends itself over a much wider field, but apparently still with the same function of reaching a balance between low and high arousal, between boredom and emotional disturbance. We all know that man dislikes work, but if he has none he invents it—though then he calls it play. By definition, fear entails avoidance, and so do horror and disgust; yet man seeks situations that produce fear, in the guise of "thrill" or "adventure," he is fascinated by newspaper accounts of the mangled human bodies in Monday's report of the weekend highway toll, and he is notoriously charmed by risqué joke and bawdy song. Presumably these ambivalent attitudes are to be understood in the same way as the rat's exploratory tendency: as the manifestation of a tendency to increase arousal up to the point at which conflicting cortical processes interfere with a closer approach or greater exposure to the source of excitation.

One must see how extensively these tendencies penetrate into, and determine, the structure of society. It was suggested above that "civilization" is a protective cocoon, an ordering of the physical environment and of man's own social behavior of such sort as to insulate the adult member of society from most of the emotional provocations that he would otherwise be subject to. This is still its primary function. But the result in an economically successful society, such as that of Rome (because of its tributary provinces) or of the United States today, is that life may become dull and the need to find excitement pressing—at least for part of the time and for a majority of citizens. In this light we can recognize a source of motivation that underlies mountain climbing, skiing, and auto racing: activities all of which depend largely on thrill for their attraction, which means to say that they are ones in which some degree of fear is deliberately courted. We can recognize the *raison d'être* of golf, which might be an old ladies' game if it were not for its furious frustration and constant threat of frustration. It is a notoriously anger-provoking game, as bridge is also. But only relatively few people get a chance to climb mountains or play golf, and above-average intelligence is needed to be really frustrated by bridge. These occupations offer escape for only a minority of the population. Rome made the great discovery that the populace needs circuses as well as bread; our circuses are the organized sports. The brutalities of Canadian hockey and American football are a pallid substitute for tossing Christians to the lions, perhaps, but they serve the same function. When we add soap opera, TV, movies, comics and paperback thrillers, it can be seen that we do fairly well in this respect, and the important thing for our present purposes is to realize that such things are not luxuries but necessities, at least at the present stage of development of social institutions.

SUMMARY

The development of a large cortex in mammals presumably increased their capacity to learn and to solve problems but it also increased their susceptibility to emotional disturbance and their capacity for altruistic behavior. Emotional susceptibility is correlated with intelligence in the growing animal also, so it is the older rather than the younger subject that is most easily disturbed.

Man's emotional sensitivities have led him to organize social patterns that reduce the frequency of emotional stimulation, allowing him to think of himself as unexcitable. But apparently trivial things can cause strong reactions, and the persistence of racial, religious and national prejudice—because all people do not look alike, think alike, and talk alike—and the violence that goes with it, show how far man is from being the unemotional and peace-loving creature he thinks he is.

Two other motivational characteristics are major factors in our social structure. One is the capacity for altruism, which is fundamental to man's nature but for some reason has always been disregarded or denied by social scientists. The other is a need for excitement when the social cocoon becomes too effective and thus causes boredom. Man avoids strong fear but seeks mild fear; and so with frustration (in mental or physical work) and disgust (avoiding outright obscenity, but enjoying off-color jokes). The stability of society appears to require harmless sources of mild excitement. If they are not provided, worse ones may be found.

Guide to Study

For review, the student might consider first the differences of motivation and emotion in their relation to arousal, make sure he understands the meaning of the inverted-U curve, and the reason why the exact shape of this curve may be different for a simple habit and a complex one. The text says that emotion continues to rise with arousal whereas motivation first rises, then falls, but the text also says that in extreme arousal emotion may disappear (in the "paralysis of terror," p. 198). How should the curve be drawn to show this relation of emotion to arousal?

What parallel is there in the chimpanzee's fear of a model head and man's disturbance at the sight of a badly mutilated human face? What other human sensitivities might be analogous? Could you justify in psychological terms the idea that reading an adventure story is a mild form of fear-seeking, by relating this to a "down-flow" from cortex to arousal system? Fear and anger are known to be related; is it possible that arousal is the same in both, and that they differ only in the ideas that go with each (expectancy of being hurt in one case, of hurting in the other)?

What evidence indicates that prejudice need not be learned, though it is dependent on learning (Chapter 7, p. 129)? How much weight would you give to the chimpanzee evidence indicating that altruism is inherent in man's nature?

But the best device for reviewing this chapter might be to see how you would have organized the material yourself.

REFERENCES

Lindsley, D. B.: Emotion. In S. S. Stevens (Ed.): *Handbook of Experimental Psychology*, Wiley, 1951.
Hebb, D. O., and Thompson, W. R.: The social significance of animal studies. In G. Lindzey and E. Aronson (Eds.): *Handbook of Social Psychology*, Addison-Wesley, 1968, Vol. 2.

SPECIAL TOPICS

Altruism

Kellogg, W. N.: *Porpoises and Sonar*. University of Chicago Press, 1961. See pp. 13–15.
Nissen, H. W., and Crawford, M. P.: A preliminary study of food-sharing in young chimpanzees. *Journal of Comparative Psychology*, 1936, 22, 383–419.
Siebenaler, J. B., and Caldwell, D. K.: Cooperation among adult dolphins. *Journal of Mammology*, 1956, 37, 126–128.

Fear and Anger

Hebb, D. O.: The forms and conditions of chimpanzee anger. *Bulletin of the Canadian Psychological Association*, 1945, 5, 32–35.
Jersild, A. T., and Holmes, F. B.: *Children's Fears*, 1935.
Jones, H. E., and Jones, M. C.: A study of fear. *Childhood Education*, 1928, 5, 136–143.
Mahut, H.: Breed differences in the dog's emotional behavior. *Canadian Journal of Psychology*, 1958, 12, 35–44.
Marshall, S. L. A.: *Men Against Fire*, Morrow, 1947.
Melzack, R.: Irrational fears in the dog. *Canadian Journal of Psychology*, 1952, 6, 141–147.
Tyhurst, J. S.: Individual reactions to community disaster. *American Journal of Psychiatry*, 1951, 107, 764–769.

Need of Work

Bexton, W. H., Heron, W., and Scott, T. H.: Effects of decreased variation in the sensory environment. *Canadian Journal of Psychology*, 1954, 8, 70–76.
Harlow, H. F.: Mice, monkeys, men and motives. *Psychological Review*, 1953, 60, 23–32.
Hebb, D. O., and Mahut, H.: Motivation et recherche du changement perceptif chez le rat et chez l'homme. *Journal de Psychologie Normale et Pathologique*, 1955, 52, 209–221. The report of rats seeking a more interesting route to food (Figure 74).
Heron, W.: The pathology of boredom. In J. L. McGaugh, N. M. Weinberger, and R. E. Whalen (Eds.): *Psychobiology*, Freeman, 1967. (Originally in *Scientific American*, January, 1957.)

sensation and perception

12

Though their activities are closely related, sensation and perception are different in kind. The sensory information that determines response may do so in quite different ways. It may be transmitted directly to muscle and gland, or it may be transmitted instead to the higher centers of the cortex and only have its effect by making changes in the activity that is going on at that cortical level. In the first case the behavior is sense-dominated and does not depend on perception. In the second, perception occurs, and the sensory information if it affects behavior does so only in conjunction with the concurrent cortical processes. Very often it has no immediate effect on behavior, but produces latent learning that may or may not have an effect at some later time.

Writers on perception have often spoken as though sensation was a simple perception, or perception merely the pattern of sensory input to the cortex. But we saw in Chapter 4 that transmission up to the sensory cortex must be of a different kind from transmission from that point onward, as the excitation leaves the sensory area and becomes incorporated into the ongoing cortical activity. Physiologically there are two kinds of process, and if we think of perception as the incorporation of sensory information into the thought process, then the first kind of transmission is sensation, the second kind perception. As we will see, the psychological evidence also indicates that sensation and perception must be different in kind.

Accordingly, *sensation* is defined in this text as the activity of receptors and the resulting activity of afferent paths up to the corresponding sensory cortical area in mammals, or other highest point of afferent conduction in animals without a cortex. *Perception* is the activity of mediating processes to which sensation gives rise directly (and here we make the assumption that a mediating process is a cell-assembly activity). Where there are no mediating processes—where there is no thought, where behavior is reflexive—there is no basis for speaking of perception.

There is no reason for example to think that the flea or the mosquito first perceives a human being, then attacks. Most birds and fish may also lack perception, since no one has provided evidence of mediating processes in control of their behavior (the lack may not apply to birds like the crow and some of the larger parrots, which are highly intelligent—for birds). Also, perception is not a factor in human reflexive behavior. As light fails the pupil of the eye widens and the student happily engrossed in some work on psychology may not even realize that the change in light level has occurred; sweating in a warm room may be accompanied by a perception of the warmth but if so the perception is apt to come *after* one notices that one is sweating.

Sensation is in effect a one-stage process; a sensory surface is stimulated and the sensation results. Perception is characteristically sequential: started by a sensation, there is a preliminary motor reaction with feedback that adds further information, and perhaps a rather long series of such exploratory reactions, building up to *one* perception. Visual perception in general depends on complex eye movements, tactual perception on movement of some part of the body (a hand, paw, snout, or beak is characteristically brought into play). Auditory perception of strange sounds usually involves head movement (and ear movement in lower mammals); also, it often deals with series of stimuli, extended in time, a fact that is especially evident in the perception of a melody or of speech. Taste, or gustatory perception, utilizes movements of lips and tongue, smell utilizes changes of breathing (i.e., sniffing), unless the substance to be identified is very familiar. In short, perceiving involves a sequence of events. Most past discussions of the problem have dealt with the apparently instantaneous identification of events in the environment—usually optical events—but this is a very misleading emphasis. With very familiar objects or events no overt activity may be needed, and identification is apparently immediate. A single glance, one contact with the hand, is enough; no further investigatory movement is made. But even here, perception may consist of a temporal series of mediating processes instead of a single unitary event.

In summary, perception is a mediating-process activity which normally occurs with some preliminary responses, such as eye movement or touching. Obviously the feedback from them contributes essentially to the end product. With highly familiar things perception may seem to occur instantaneously, but in some of these cases there may still be a serial order of events within the mediating processes even though it takes only milliseconds to reach completion. Perception is a preparation for response, just as *knowledge* is; in fact, knowledge is perception whose effects last for some period of time (p. 32). The response that is made depends on circumstances, and very often the "adequate response" is to do nothing. You see a leaf fall from a tree, hear the dormitory phone ring, feel the pack of cigarettes in your handbag as you reach for your lipstick and—if you do not collect leaves, are not on answering duty, or do not need a smoke—the perception leads to no further action. But it is a real event and in each of the above cases there is an indefinitely large number of possible responses the perception might prepare you for. There is no one response called for by a perception, so we cannot think of it as an incomplete action. It is a setting of the central switchboard. While it lasts, it is knowledge.

SENSORY STIMULATION

We have already seen, in Chapters 3 and 4, by what paths sensory information reaches the cortex, how parallel conduction guarantees transmission as far as the sensory projection areas (p. 71), and how information from different sources is kept sorted out and delivered to different cortical areas; not only separating, for example, vision from somesthesis, but also keeping one part of the visual field or one part of the skin surface separate from another (p. 47). Now, to understand sensation better, we need to take the story a bit further. First, the sense organs themselves.

Vision

The eye is both an optical instrument and part of the brain. Figure 77 shows the lens system in front (the cornea, which acts as a lens, and then the lens proper), the iris which contracts or opens up to

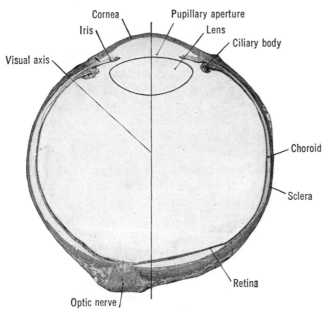

Figure 77. *Horizontal section of a human eye. The ligaments that support the lens and control its curvature have been omitted, and the retina has partly separated from the back of the eyeball. (From E. Gardner,* Fundamentals of Neurology, *Saunders.)*

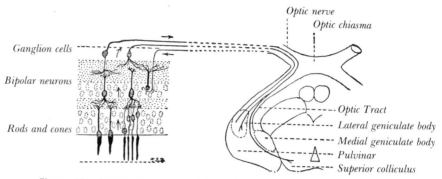

Figure 78. *Schematic representation of the retina and its afferent connections, from rod and cone to the brain. Cross section of retina at left, light entering from above. (From S. W. Ranson and S. L. Clark,* Anatomy of the Nervous System, *Saunders.)*

control the amount of light that enters, and the "ciliary body" or ciliary muscle which (though its connection with the lens is not shown) controls the degree of curvature of the elastic lens and thus adjusts it to produce a good focus on the back of the eye, the retina. The retina is a thin sheet through which light passes easily, which is a good thing, since the light-sensitive cells are at the back, pointing away from the *pupil* (the aperture in the iris through which light enters). The light-sensitive cells are *rods* and *cones*: the rods are more sensitive to low light intensities but not sensitive to differences of wave length (i.e., they are "color-blind"); the cones respond selectively to different wave lengths (permitting color vision). Both are neurons, connecting with an intermediate set of "bipolar cells" which in turn connect with the "ganglion cells" which send their axons over the surface of the retina to gather at one point as the *optic nerve* that connects with the rest of the brain. (See both Figs. 77 and 78. Figure 78 shows why the retina is part of the brain. The only cells corresponding to sensory nerves are the rods and cones, which connect with bipolar cells in the same way that afferent neurons from the skin connect with spinal cord cells; thus the "optic nerve" is really a *tract* in the CNS, though it looks like a nerve.)

The *fovea* is a small depression in the center of the retina where cones are packed in very tightly. It is the point of clearest (or central) vision, the point on the retina where the image of what one is looking at is focused. However, foveal vision is clearest only in normal lighting; the rods are the basis of "twilight vision" (being most sensitive at low intensities) and they are not found in the fovea. Thus at night one finds that one can see best by looking a little to one side of what one wants to see.

The *blind-spot* results from the absence of rods or cones at the point where the fibers from the ganglion cells gather to form the optic nerve, on the nasal side of each retina. If the student will close his right eye, look at some object across the room such as a doorknob, and then move his gaze slowly to the right but at the same level, the knob will disappear when his gaze is about 15° away from it, then reappear as he looks still farther to the right.

Figure 78, for clarity, has omitted the neurons ("association cells") which connect *across* the retina, from bipolar cell to bipolar cell, and which may in some cases produce summation but in others inhibition. There is certainly inhibition from each small retinal area to neighboring areas, but some of this may be caused by *efferent* fibers in the optic nerve—feedback from higher centers directly to retinal cells—one such fiber being diagramed in Figure 78. It is supposed that the inhibition helps "sharpen" the perception of an edge or a thin line.

There is another important effect of inhibition. It was mentioned earlier (p. 120) that there are neurons in the visual cortex that are excited only in looking at a line or contour of a particular slope. This was shown by D. H. Hubel and T. N. Wiesel, and they explain it as follows: A cortical neuron receives excitation from a number of retinal cells, which may be arranged in a row, more or less straight; if a line of light falls along this row the cortical neuron is fired, but if the line falls across the row it excites more of the surrounding inhibitory cells than the central excitatory ones, and the cortical neuron does not fire (Fig. 79). There will be cortical neurons with different connections, of course, that will fire instead. There are plenty of retinal cells to permit such a specialization of connections, as the human eye has about a million cones and 37 million rods.

What Hubel and Wiesel describe is a sensory mechanism, as we

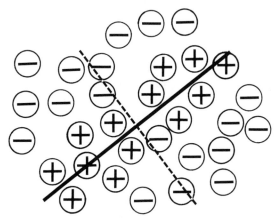

Figure 79. *Representation of the receptive field of a cortical visual cell. Circles enclosing a plus sign represent retinal "on" points: stimuli here make the cortical cell fire. Circles enclosing a minus sign represent "off" points: stimulating one of these points tends to make the cortical cell stop firing. Consequently, a line of light slanting from upper right to lower left, as shown, will make the cell fire strongly since it excites the "on" points in the receptive field; a line at right angles (broken line) excites mainly "off" points, and makes the cell stop firing (however, it will make other cells fire—ones with different receptive fields). (After "The Visual Cortex of the Brain" by D. H. Hubel. Copyright © 1963 by Scientific American Inc. All rights reserved.)*

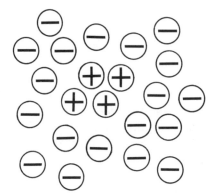

Figure 80. Possible arrangement of "on" and "off" points in the frog retina (see Fig. 79) to account for the frog's tendency to snap at small objects in his visual field.

use the term sensory here. No mediating processes are involved. Somewhat similar mechanisms would account for a certain selectivity in frogs without having to suppose that they are perceiving and conscious. The frog will attack — flick out a tongue at — any small moving objects, avoiding larger ones (J. Y. Lettvin, *et al.*). In this way he catches flies for a living. The behavior is instinctive and it has seemed mysterious, but the mystery vanishes if the frog retina contains receptive areas made up of small groups of *on* cells, surrounded by *off* cells as in Figure 80. (In the same way the tendency of the newly hatched chick to peck at rounded rather than angular objects may be accounted for by receptive fields that are roughly circular.)

The retina is connected directly with motor centers in the brain stem and can thus control a directed reflex response in the frog (or chick). In man also there is a direct motor connection (with the "superior colliculus") as well as with the visual cortex. Thus the baby's eyes shortly after birth tend to follow a bright light reflexively. R. L. Fantz has shown that baby will scan visual objects and will spend more time with some than with others. This "preference" may suggest that the newborn is perceiving, aware of the visual environment, but the behavior can be explained on a reflex basis. The method as used by P. Salapatek and W. Kessen is shown in Figure 81, where the baby lying on his back sees a triangle above him.

Hearing

The ear is less open to observation than the eye, its sensory mechanism being buried deep in the petrous ("rocky") bone, and it took correspondingly longer to work out the principles of its operation. The outer ear we know; essentially a funnel to direct sound waves on to the eardrum. The *middle ear* is a cavity filled with air, and connected with the mouth by the eustachian tube which permits air pressure inside to stay the same as that outside (Fig. 82). Swallowing

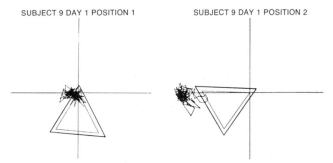

SUBJECT 9 DAY 1 POSITION 1   SUBJECT 9 DAY 1 POSITION 2

Figure 81. *Recording eye movements in the newborn baby exposed to a large solid black triangle in the "ceiling" above: 9 inches from the baby's eyes. The triangle was 8 inches on the side, and was presented in two orientations, as shown in the two records of eye movements below (for the same baby). (From P. Salapatek and W. Kessen, J. Exp. Child Psych., 1966.)*

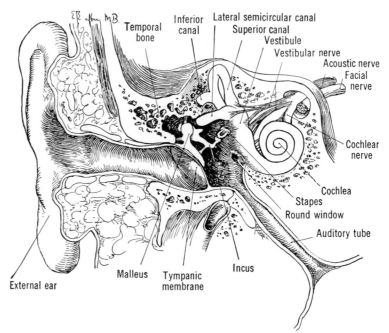

Figure 82. *Structures of the ear. "Tympanic membrane" equals eardrum. The middle ear is the cavity containing the three ossicles, malleus being attached to the eardrum and transmitting (with magnification) its movements via incus and stapes to the "oval window" (not shown) and the fluid of the inner ear. "Auditory tube" equals eustachian tube. "Superior canal" is one of the three semicircular canals. (From E. Gardner,* Fundamentals of Neurology, *Saunders.)*

opens the tube, which is why swallowing relieves ear discomfort when air pressure changes in an airplane. Three small bones, or "ossicles," transmit sound vibrations from the eardrum to the "oval window," the entry to the *inner ear.* Here things become more complicated.

The inner ear actually has two functions, hearing and the sense of balance or of head movement. It is filled with a fluid throughout its two parts, the *cochlea* (for hearing) and the *vestibule* (for balance). The cochlea is a coiled-up tube (hence the name, which is Latin for snail shell) which can be seen coiled in Figure 82 and schematized, uncoiled, in Figure 83. The vestibular system on each side contains three semicircular canals, lying in three planes at right angles to one another, so that any movement of the head should make the fluid move in at least one of the canals. One canal is shown in Figure 83, schematically, and the relation of the three to the head is shown in Figure 84.

The three tiny bones (ossicles) of the middle ear ("hammer, anvil and stirrup," or "malleus, incus and stapes") transmit vibrations from the eardrum to the fluid of the cochlea, where it produces movement of the *basilar membrane* on which the receptors for hearing are found. Low frequencies of vibration produce deformations (move-

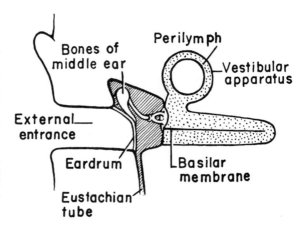

Figure 83. *Schematic representation of the human ear, showing the bones that connect the eardrum with the inner ear, the basilar membrane that carries the auditory receptors, and the cavity of bone filled with fluid (perilymph) which is continuous with the fluid of the semicircular canals, one of these being shown schematically. The eustachian tube connects with the mouth, permitting air pressure in the middle ear to be equalized with external air pressure. The basilar membrane and the tube-like hollow of bone in which it lies are not straight as shown in the figure, but coiled like a snailshell. (After G. v. Békésy, in S. S. Stevens [Ed.] Handbook of Experimental Psychology, Wiley.)*

ments) of the upper end of the basilar membrane, high frequencies deformations of the lower end (G. v. Békésy). Thus a primary cue to pitch is found in the locus of stimulation on the basilar membrane, which means that different fibers in the auditory nerve are active in the response to tones of different pitches.

In each of the six semicircular canals—three on each side—there is a small protuberance, or "cupula," which is believed to move when the fluid in the canal moves. Disturbing the cupula excites nerve endings contained in it, providing one of the two cues of *proprioception* or *kinesthesis:* the sensation of movement. (The other kind of cue comes from nerve endings in the muscles, tendons and joints which are stimulated when a muscle contracts and produces a change in the position of one bone with respect to another.) The semicircular canals are stimulated by any movement of the head, but their activity comes particularly to one's attention in the dizziness produced by rapid rotation or rapid irregular movements. The canals are connected directly with the eye muscles; if the student will take the trouble to roll down a steep grassy bank, or have himself rotated rapidly

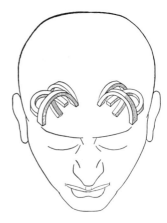

Figure 84. *The relation of the semicircular canals to each other and to the head. (From E. Gardner, Fundamentals of Neurology, Saunders.)*

on a piano stool by another student long enough to produce dizziness, he will see the world rotating around him after he has stopped: this is due to the fact that his semicircular canals continue to stimulate the eye muscles so his eyes continue to move without his being aware of it, and thus the world instead seems to be rotating. These eye movements are easily seen by another person. Seasickness, airsickness, and carsickness are due also to overstimulation of the canals.

Skin Senses

The skin is a sense organ, even if we do not usually think of it as such. It contains free nerve endings and also some specialized organs, but these need not be described since no one has any very good idea of what they do. The skin has four main sensory functions, *touch, warmth, cold,* and *pain.* The adequate stimulus for touch is not merely contact with the skin, but enough pressure to bend it (if only to a slight degree) or bend a hair. The hairs provide the most sensitive mechanism, each hair having a nerve ending coiled around its base and being stiff enough so that it acts as a lever. Warmth and cold will be discussed shortly. The pain referred to above is the sensory component of the total process; there is also a component that is emotional rather than sensory (p. 191).

SENSORY CODING

We have seen that the nervous system can keep different sensory messages distinct from each other by keeping them on separate lines to the cortex. There is also another mechanism which allows two different messages to use the same channel if they are *coded* differently (see below).

How the messages can be kept distinct is an old question. Stimulation of the optic nerve always produces visual perception. Sensation from the left foot never gets mixed up with sensation from the right hand. These facts are known as the *law of specific energies.* It does not matter how the optic nerve is stimulated; applying pressure or passing an electric current through it still makes the subject "see" light, so the optic nerve is "specific" for visual perception, once it is activated. And, clearly, the specificity is because the nerve leads to the visual cortex. Stimulation of this region is enough, by itself, to produce the effect. A blow on the head that stimulates it mechanically makes one "see stars"; the surgeon, operating on the brain of a conscious patient, applies electrical stimulation to the occipital cortex and the patient reports seeing a light—though his eyes may be closed and there is in fact no activation of the sense organ. So-called visual *awareness* thus consists of the activity of certain paths beginning in the visual cortex, auditory awareness is an activity beginning in the auditory cortex, and so on. The difference between these processes, their distinctiveness, is evidently related to the fact that each sense organ connects with a different region in the brain. Basically, the routes involved in tactual perception are separate from those of auditory or visual perception. A difference between two perceptions means the possibility of making distinctive responses; this is easy to understand if the sensory excitations reach different parts of the brain, and thus have clearly separate paths from receptor to effector.

The same separation of routes, of course, occurs within a single sensory system. We have already seen that each part of the retina is connected with its own part of the visual cortex: the existence of these different pathways within the visual system helps to account for the subject's ability to make different responses to stimuli in different parts of the visual field. A person *knows* what direction a light is coming from, whether he responds to it or not. This means that if further stimulation of various kinds occurs he can point to it or direct his gaze toward it or tell you where the light is. Similarly, there are separate paths within the somesthetic system for different parts of the body. The subject knows when he is touched on the hand; if the stimulus is strong enough to produce a response, it is the hand that is likely to move. But specificity in sensation goes further than is accounted for by a complete separation of routes.

Two sensory messages may use the same incoming lines, at least in part, and still be completely sorted out at higher levels in the CNS. This is achieved by a kind of *coding,* which consists of the frequency pattern of the impulses (one message, for example, may consist of regularly spaced impulses, another of intermittent bursts) plus the combination of afferent fibers.

As a first simple example of what this means we may consider the transformation of strength of stimulation (intensity) into (1) frequency of firing, and (2) the number of afferent neurons firing. In Figure 85, a weak stimulus may fire cells A only, at a low rate. A strong stimulus produces a higher rate of firing in A, and also brings in B. The second-order neurons X and Y may thus be exposed to a low or a high rate of bombardment. Neurons differ not only in limen (the number of impulses at the synapse that are necessary to fire them) but also with respect to their frequency of firing. If pathway X therefore has a low limen, or is most readily fired at a low frequency, it is possible that a weak stimulus would activate pathway X and not Y. A strong stimulus might excite Y more than X, when both X and Y are exposed to a strong bombardment; and if, as suggested in the figure, activity in Y inhibits activity in X, the result would be that with a strong stimulus only Y would be active, while with a weak stimulus only X would be active. Thus two "messages" use the same incoming lines, in part, but are sorted out in the CNS.

The details of how this occurs are not established experimentally. They are suggested here to show how the same afferent neurons, A, might contribute to two different sensory events, and to show what is meant by the term "coding." The sorting out into spatially discrete paths might not occur at this level, but in the cortex.

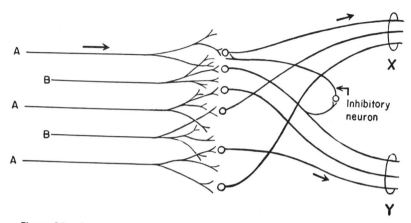

Figure 85. *A possible mechanism of sensory coding. A and B are afferent neurons, A having a lower limen than B. A weak stimulus fires A only; a strong one fires A at a higher rate and also fires B. At the next synaptic level, internuncial neurons X may have a lower limen than Y, or respond more readily to a lower frequency of firing. With low-level activity in A alone, X will fire and Y will tend to be inactive. When the level of bombardment goes up, however, Y begins to fire and inhibits X (for clarity, only one inhibitory neuron is diagramed). Note that this is quite speculative; also, this sorting out into spatially discrete paths need not occur only at the first synaptic junction, but may occur farther on in the system as well.*

What we do know is that discriminable sensory events do not always have entirely separate incoming paths; and we do know that, if they are discriminated, they eventually get on to separate paths in the CNS.

This last point, concerning the ultimate spatial separation, is a straightforward inference from behavioral evidence. If we have two sensory events *A* and *B* which can be discriminated by the subject, we can train him to raise his left forepaw or left hand in response to event *A,* and his right forepaw to event *B*. The excitation from *A* may use some of the same incoming paths as *B*, yet ultimately it is conducted *only* to the motor neurons that lead to the left forepaw. Even before this training, therefore, we may say that though the excitations from *A* and from *B* utilize the same lines for part of their course, they ultimately get on separate lines, or are capable of getting on separate lines, at some point in the CNS. They may of course be brought back to the same lines, since we can train the subject to make the same response to different stimuli; but the principle is clear that perceptual discriminability means a spatial separation in the CNS at some point.

A more interesting example of the problem of specific energies and coding occurs in taste (C. Pfaffman). A weak acid on the tongue (which tastes sour) produces firing in three sets of afferent neurons, *A, B* and *C*. Salt solution fires set *A* plus set *B;* quinine, which is bitter, fires set *A* plus set *C* . Despite having a common activity in the *A* neurons, these three afferent processes produce effects at higher levels that are quite distinct from each other. (Sour, salt and bitter, together with sweet—for which less physiological information is available—constitute the four primary taste qualities.)

Activity on line *A*, therefore, may contribute to any one of three different awarenesses (considered as neural activities in the cerebrum), depending on the total pattern of activity: *A-B-C* activates one central process, *A-B* another, *A-C* a third.

Another example is found in the perception of temperature. Steady warmth and steady cold have a considerable overlap in their use of afferent connections; but warmth produces a slow, irregular firing, cold a faster and more regular firing (R. Granit). Ultimately these messages get completely sorted out, at some point in the CNS. They must, since they determine quite different responses.

It is not difficult to see how the sorting out might be achieved, although the synaptic mechanisms are not known specifically. In taste, *A* and *B* fibers may produce summation and fire cells that *A* and *C* do not (these cells in turn inhibiting any others that happen to be excited by *A* alone). As for warm and cold and differences of temporal pattern, we have seen that some cells may have a low limen for impulses at one frequency, other cells a low limen for another frequency, and this may be a factor in sorting out the "warm" message from the "cold" message.

To sum up: the specificity of sensory input is primarily in the existence of separate routes from different parts of the sensory surfaces. Secondarily, this is extended by the patterning and timing of impulses. Two different inputs may use, at least in part, the same afferent lines. But if so, they must be sorted out at some higher level. If the organism can respond differentially to two sensory events, either by giving them different names (i.e., making distinctive verbal responses) or by acting in one case to maintain the stimulation and in the other to discontinue it, then at some point in the nervous system there is a spatial separation of the two processes.

SPACE PERCEPTION

A fundamental feature of perception must be to inform the perceiver about spatial relations, and in particular about the direction and distance of the objects he perceives. The classical problem of space perception concerns *visual depth:* how far away is the object that is seen? It seems easy to understand how one can perceive the direction of an object, from the direction in which the eyes must be turned in order to see it clearly. But the retina functions as a two-dimensional surface (even though it is a curved surface) like a photographic plate at the back of a camera: why does the world not look flat, like a photograph? Why is visual depth so immediate and inescapable? There is also auditory space perception—it is possible in the proper circumstances to *hear* where something is and how far away, even if it makes no noise itself—and this too has been a puzzle.

Visual Space

The primary cues to visual depth are summarized as *accommodation, convergence* and *retinal disparity.* Of these, accommodation is the least effective: it is the degree of curvature of the crystalline lens that is necessary to produce a good focus on the retina. The lens is elastic, and its curvature is reflexively controlled by the ciliary muscle. The amount of tension in the muscle that is necessary to focus the image, and the resulting proprioceptive sensation (sensory feedback), is one cue to depth. Such effectiveness as this cue has is for near distances, up to about six feet from the eye.

A much more effective cue (but also mainly for near distances) is the convergence of the two eyes which is necessary if the image of an object is to be projected on the fovea in both eyes. For far objects the axes of the eyeballs are parallel; for near objects the axes cross, and the position of the eyes in their sockets becomes a cue to the distance of the object looked at. This is chiefly effective for distances up to perhaps 20 feet.

Retinal disparity, or *parallax,* refers to the difference in the retinal images that are formed when an object is seen from different angles. Binocular disparity occurs when an object is observed with both eyes open, because the eyes, separated in space, necessarily see the object from different angles. The student can demonstrate this for himself by holding a pencil so that it points directly at his nose, at a distance of a foot or a foot and a half. By closing first one eye, then the other, he will find that the two eyes have distinctly different views of the pencil, one seeing the point and the right side, the other the point and the left side. *Movement disparity* is more obvious, either with one eye or two; one gets very different views of a three-dimensional object or scene as one moves the head from side to side, or up and down.

Both forms of disparity have a strong effect in the perception of the third dimension. The effect of binocular disparity is demonstrated best in the *stereoscope,* a device that allows one to see two slightly different photographs simultaneously, as if they were one. One photograph is seen by the right eye; the other, made from a viewpoint slightly to the left, is seen by the left eye. The eyes then deliver to the same parts of the visual area in the brain slightly different patterns of excitation. Instead of two conflicting two-dimensional scenes, a single scene is perceived in depth. The brain, in some manner not at all understood, integrates the discordant patterns and adds a dimension in so doing.

There are a number of other cues to depth (Fig. 86): the smaller retinal angle of familiar objects farther away; the overlap of near objects over farther ones, partly hiding them; the loss of fine detail in farther objects, and their change of color (increasing blueness) when distances become great.

But all these are cues that apply to a single object (or two

Figure 86. Other cues to the perception of visual depth (distance from the eye) can be found here.

overlapping objects) without regard to the surrounding environment; and our discussion up to this point might suggest that in judging the distance of an object all one takes into account is the appearance of that object. In fact, except when one is dealing with objects flying or floating in the air, all one's judgments concern objects that are connected with (supported by) extended surfaces such as the ground, walls of buildings, ceilings, and so on; and these background surfaces have a most important influence on depth perception. As they extend away from us, they show gradients of *visual texture,* the units into which the surface is divided (Fig. 87, left) and the irregularities within the units (not shown in the figures). These gradients provide cues to the direction of slope of the surface, with respect to the line of vision, and thus provide cues to the size and distance of objects close to or touching the surfaces (J. J. Gibson: Fig. 88).

Auditory Space

To a surprising degree, there is such a thing as the auditory perception of space. The design of the auditory system, apparently, is such as to permit discrimination of frequency and intensity, but nothing else. In a sense this is true; but just as the visual system uses binocular disparity and other cues to produce depth discrimination, though it seems at first not suited for such a function, so the auditory

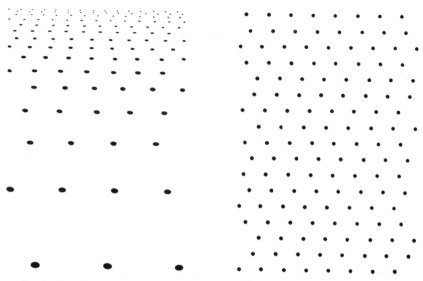

Figure 87. *On the left, gradients of visual texture — of size and spacing — give the perception of a receding surface; on the right, the absence of gradients suggests a "frontal" (non-receding) surface. (From J. J. Gibson,* The Perception of the Visual World, *Houghton Mifflin.)*

system uses the cues of frequency and intensity to produce discriminations of direction and distance that in some cases are surprisingly accurate. Sound travels at a limited speed (about 1100 feet per second, compared with 186,000 miles per second for light), so the time of transmission from a sound source becomes a factor in discrimination: one slight advantage for the ear over the eye. Another is that *sound shadows* (blocking of the sound waves by an interposed object) are selective; long waves are not blocked while short waves are, whereas with light the blocking is practically complete. Suppose therefore that a complex sound, made up of high (short wave) tones and low (long wave) tones, comes from the subject's left side. His left ear gets both high and low tones, but his right ear is in the sound shadow cast by the head, so the right ear gets the low tones, but little of the high ones. This binaural discrepancy is a cue to which side the sound source is on. With high-pitched sounds, also, the sound shadow cast by the outer ear makes possible a discrimination of front from back.

The most important cues to direction, the ones that tend to dominate, are the relative times of arrival at the two ears, and the relative intensity. Ordinarily these two cues work together, but it is found experimentally that either is effective alone, other cues being held constant, though the time factor is the more important of the two. If a sound reaches both ears simultaneously and with the same intensity, the source must be equally distant from them: that is, it must lie in the median plane, directly in front, above, or behind the head. If it reaches the right ear first, it must be on the right side; but with a low pitched sound (when the shadow of the outer ear is not effective) this gives no cue as to whether the sound source is higher or lower, front or back. This is in fact what is found with a momentary sound, when echoes (reflections from the ground, walls, or other surfaces) are excluded. But with a continuing sound, or one that is repeated, the subject tilts his head, and at once can discriminate up from down; or turns his head to one side, and discriminates front from back. (Here is an example of the importance of response for auditory perception, not unlike the importance of eye movement for visual perceptions.)

The discrimination of the times of arrival of a sound at the two ears is astonishingly fine. The time differences involved are of the order of one or two tenths of a millisecond. The same capacity affects the perception of auditory depth. A sound made near one ear produces a binaural difference, in time of arrival, of something under a millisecond; farther away, the difference is slightly less, yet this difference permits reliable judgments of distance. Echoes also become very important. The subject can judge the distance of a reflecting sur-

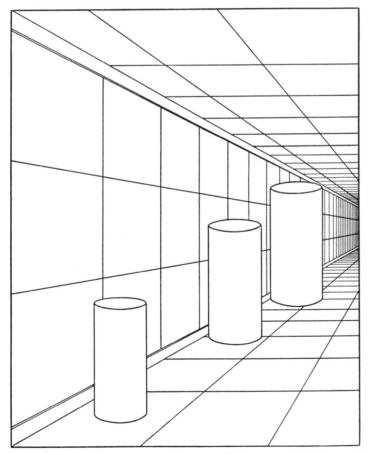

Figure 88. *Perception of size and distance of objects as related to receding surfaces. The three cylinders are drawn the same size. (From J. J. Gibson,* The Perception of the Visual World, *Houghton, Mifflin.)*

face on the basis of the time difference between hearing a noise that he makes himself and its echo: about two milliseconds for each foot of distance. Many animals and birds have developed similar auditory skill. The bat is the best known example. When flying it emits very high-pitched sounds, and is guided by the echoes: so much so that it can fly among a number of obstacles without hitting any of them, even when its eyes are completely covered. If the ears are covered, the ability disappears.

It is the same cue that tells us when we are about to bump into something in the dark. This is sometimes a very puzzling experience; one is suddenly aware of some large object in front of one, without knowing how. It used to be thought that the trick was done by something called "facial vision," some kind of sensitivity of the skin of the face to radiations from nearby objects. Actually, the object is detected by means of the echoes of the sound of one's footsteps or of one's breathing. It is easy to show that one is dealing with auditory space perception in this case, because the ability disappears when the ears are plugged. This ability, of course, becomes very important in blindness. When the blind man taps his cane hard on the sidewalk he is not feeling for obstacles; he is setting up echoes from nearby objects, and the echoes tell him where he is with respect to those objects.

One does not of course perceive the echoes as separate events, estimate their time of arrival, and on the basis of the time differences in milliseconds work out the direction and distance of an obstacle, any more than we see visual depth as a result of conscious calculations about retinal disparities. There is instead an automatic transformation of the sensory stimulation into the perception of an object, as a preparation for further response. How it occurs has not been worked out.

DISTINGUISHING PERCEPTION FROM SENSATION

The clearest evidence that perception is something more than a complex sensation—that we must consider it to be a different kind of event—is the fact that the same sensory stimulation can give rise to completely distinct perceptions, and different stimulations can give rise to the same perception. All our knowledge of the sensory process says that the same stimulation produces the same activity in the sensory cortex time after time, but the evidence is quite clear that it need not produce the same perception.

The classical demonstration of variability in perception with the same stimulation may be observed by looking at Figure 89 or at Figure 6 (p. 30). These are *ambiguous figures*, a conception that we owe to the Danish psychologist E. Rubin. Figure 89 may be seen either as a bird bath or vase, or as two faces. If the student will keep his eyes fixed on the black dot between the two noses (or in the center of the

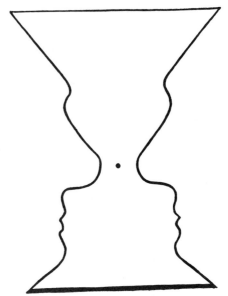

Figure 89. *Ambiguous or reversible figure. (After Rubin.)*

bird bath), he will find that the reversal, the change from one perception to the other, does not require eye movement; though the movement definitely permits a clearer perception and affects the rate of
reversal. The significance of this observation is that two very different
perceptions can occur with the same sensory input.

   Nothing in the sensory process itself accounts for this "flip-flop"
action. Slow, steady changes might be intelligible, but not the discon-
tinuous alternation of two distinctly different perceptions. But alternation becomes quite intelligible with the mechanism diagrammed in
Figure 90, which assumes that the two perceptions consist of different sets of assembly actions, each of which prevents activity in the
other.

   Figure 89 also illustrates the *figure-ground phenomenon.* The *figure* is
the region in the total configuration that is perceived at the moment, the rest
being ground (the alternation that occurs with Figure 89 can thus be described as an alternating figure-ground relation). The student will find, when
the vase is being perceived, that the space in the center of the figure appears
closer and, in a vague way, more solid. When perception shifts to the two
faces the central space recedes, and the two lateral spaces appear closer.

   The figure-ground relation is fundamental in the perception of objects
and regions of space. The unity of simple, clearly demarcated figures is
present in first vision, as far as can be determined from the behavior of the
congenitally blind who are given sight at maturity. With such objects, then,
the figure-ground relation is independent of experience, but it also seems
that with other figures it is much more a function of experience, and that the
kind of variability in the figure-ground relation that is demonstrated in Figure
89 increases as a result of perceptual learning.

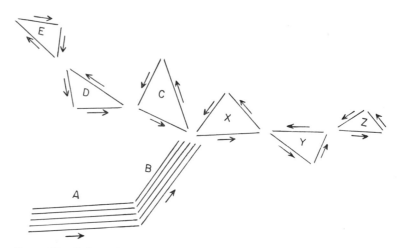

Figure 90. *Schematic representation of an explanation of the reversal of the ambiguous figure. A, B, afferent conduction (in parallel); C, X, alternating assembly actions. It is assumed that C inhibits X and vice versa. C-D-E constitutes one perception; X-Y-Z another (these assemblies must lie intertangled in the same regions of the brain, not spatially separated as above).*

Variability is a general property of perception, not found only with such special stimulus patterns as Figure 89. The ambiguous figure is significant only because it provides an especially clear case. If the student will fix his eyes on some point of his environment, he will find himself perceiving sometimes this detail, sometimes that; sometimes the larger scene instead of details, and so on. If he looks even at as simple a diagram as Figure 91 *A*, he will still find that his perception is sometimes of the crookedness of a line, sometimes the gap at the lower right; sometimes the whole triangle as such, or perhaps as a badly formed "4." With the dots of Figure 91 *B*, he will see sometimes one group, sometimes three; sometimes individual dots, sometimes the areas between them; and so on. The sensory input sets limits on what may be perceived — there is no chance that the perception of Figure 91 *B* will be identical with that of Figure 91 *A* — but within these limits variability is pronounced. The constancy of perception with a given sensory stimulation consists of a frequent recurrence of the process which is "the" perception, rather than the maintenance of a single process.

Brightness and *size constancy* are two important examples of the case in which the stimulus varies while the perception remains the same. Brightness constancy refers to the obvious fact that a white object looks white whether it is in the light or in shadow. Now this is, in fact, rather surprising. "White" means that an object reflects much light, "black," that it reflects little light. A lump of coal lying in the sunlight reflects much more light than a piece of white paper in a deep shadow, yet the coal still looks black and the paper white. What is actually involved here is a phenomenon of *contrast:* though the coal reflects the light, it reflects much less than surrounding objects.

When one arranges experimentally to focus intense light on a shiny piece of coal, and *only* on it (e.g., by fastening it with sealing wax to the end of a piece of wire, and suspending it in the middle of a room with no other surface near it to be equally illuminated), the coal becomes a brilliant silver in appearance. A piece of white paper in a dark shadow, seen through a reduction screen (which does not permit one to see the surroundings), becomes a dark gray. In ordinary circumstances, where contrast effects are not prevented, white paper moved in and out of a shadow does not appear to change its color but is perceived as white under both conditions: two different conditions of stimulation, but the same perception with respect to the color of the paper.

Size constancy is equally familiar, and equally surprising when one stops to consider what is happening. Visual size is basically dependent on retinal angle of projection; but it is also basically related to the perception of visual *depth* (i.e., distance from the eye), as shown by the fact that one's hand does not seem to be larger when it is 9 inches from the eye than when it is 18 inches from the eye. (If there is any difference it is slight.) Yet a hand at the 9-inch distance has a retinal projection approximately twice as great as at the 18-inch distance. A picture on the wall does not expand and contract as one moves closer or farther away; the face of a friend across the table does not appear three or four times as large as that of another friend at the far end of the room. This is size constancy. The constancy is not absolute, and at great distances apparent size is sharply decreased. Also, for some reason, the constancy is much less marked with objects seen in the vertical dimension, up or down. A related phenomenon is the moon illusion, which makes the moon on the horizon seem larger than the same moon at the zenith.

Another case in which the same perception results from different stimulations is found in the *phi-phenomenon,* the perception of motion where no motion exists, as in moving pictures and illuminated signs. Nowadays the phenomenon is commonplace, but it involves a

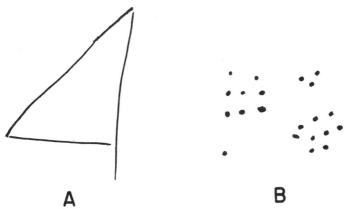

A   **B**

Figure 91. To illustrate variability in the perception of simple configurations.

A   B

Figure 92. *A demonstration of the phi-phenomenon. A light* A *goes on, then off; a fraction of a second later* B *goes on and off. With proper timing, the subject sees, instead of two lights, a single one that moves from one locus to the other.*

really remarkable transformation between what happens on the sensory surface and what happens in perception.

In Figure 92 two light sources are represented. *A* is lighted for 200 milliseconds; 60 msec. after it has been extinguished, *B* is lighted for 200 msec. Instead of two lights, one after the other, the observer sees a single light that *moves all the way* from *A* to *B*. This is the phi-phenomenon. If the interval is too short, two lights are seen simultaneously; if it is too long, two lights are seen one after the other, without movement. The timing that produces the effect varies with the intensity of the lights and the angular distance between them. A number of suggestions have been offered to account for the phenomenon in physiological terms, but as yet there is no satisfactory explanation in detail. It cannot be accounted for by eye movement from *A* to *B* because, with two pairs of lights, apparent movement can be perceived simultaneously in opposite directions.

Now let us ask how all this is to be dealt with in objective terms. The subjective approach has continued to dominate the discussion of perception long after it has been abandoned elsewhere. Whether it is right or wrong, it has great logical difficulties (how does the mind "look inward?") which are as serious in the study of perception as in that of learning or emotion; and it has wholly failed to deal with the motor effects of perception. In modern psychology we are committed to a different approach, which must be applied in perception as much as elsewhere.

What does it mean when a subject reports that he sees a light move, under the experimental conditions of Figure 92? It means, simply, that these conditions of stimulation produce, at some level in the brain, the same process that is produced by a light that does move from *A* to *B*. There is no reason to conclude that there is any movement of an excitation in the visual cortex from one point to another; instead, it seems certain there is not. The probability is that events in the sensory cortex follow the course of retinal excitation faithfully, and there is of course no excitation moving across the retina. We *can* conclude that the same assembly activities are aroused either when the retina is stimulated by a light moving from *A* to *B*, or when the two corresponding points are stimulated with the proper timing. *Sensation* in the two cases differs, *perception* is the same. Both are theoretical constructs, events inferred from our knowledge of anatomy and physiology and from the responses made by the subject.

What does it mean when, with Figure 91 *B*, a number of dots appear as a unified group, a single entity? We can interpret this as signifying that the processes aroused in some part of the brain are the same as would be aroused by a single object occupying the same space. The unity of such perceptions is not a mysterious thing. It implies that any response made to the group, or any tendency to respond, is being determined by all members of the group in the same way and at the same time.

ORGANIZATION IN PERCEPTION

Now we turn to some further experimental evidence of the complexity of perception, showing that it has an internal structure. Perception was defined as composed of mediating processes, and we will look first at an experiment by D. E. Broadbent which demonstrates holding in auditory perception. Holding is a mediating activity, and the experiment also shows how holding makes it possible to restructure a sensory input.

Human subjects wore earphones, through which were delivered two series of three spoken digits simultaneously, one series to the right ear, one to the left. The digits were separated by intervals of half a second. The right ear might receive 3-7-5, for example, at the same time that the left ear received 8-2-9. The 3 and the 8 would be heard at precisely the same time, and so with 7 and 2, and 5 and 9. The subjects could correctly report all the digits they heard on 62 per cent of the trials, which itself is an interesting result; but much more interesting for the theory of perception is the fact that in 157 out of 160 trials the subjects of their own accord (i.e., without being instructed to do so) reported the whole series for one ear, in the proper order, before reporting the series for the other ear. In this sort of experiment subjects report that they hear the digits as two separate sets, one in each ear: they do not hear one set of six digits which then must be sorted out in thought, but *perceive* them sorted out. The perception is not a loose aggregation of sensory events but tightly structured.

A quite different line of experiment throws light on the organization of visual perception. About 1952 D. W. Ditchburn and L. A. Riggs discovered independently that stabilizing the image of a line on the retina leads to its rapid disappearance. In normal vision there is always some tremor of the eye muscles. Consequently the retinal image of something looked at, even when one tries to look steadily with no movement of the eyes, is never quite still. There is always some slight variation in the rods and cones that are excited. However, there are several ways of preventing this. One is to use a very small object as target, and mount it on a short stalk fastened to a contact lens worn by the subject. Another tiny lens is attached so that the target can be seen and focused on without effort even though it is very close to the eye (Fig. 93). Now when the eyeball moves, the target—the object looked at—moves with it, and the image is stabi-

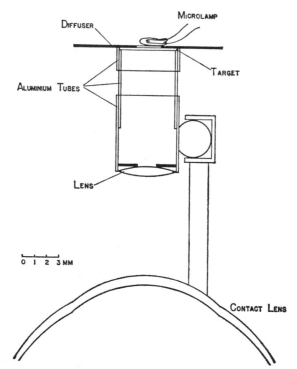

Figure 93. *The apparatus used to produce stabilized images on the retina, with contact lens mounted on the cornea of the eye. (From R. M. Pritchard, W. Heron, and D. O. Hebb,* Canad. J. Psychol., *1960.)*

lized on the retina. In these circumstances, a straight line will disappear in perhaps 10 to 20 seconds. With more complex figures, part or all may disappear (R. M. Pritchard, W. Heron). This is illustrated in Figure 94.

The same kind of disappearances are obtained with luminous figures in a dark room (J. P. McKinney) or figures drawn with black lines in a *ganzfeld*—an evenly lighted field extending to the periphery in all directions so that the black lines are the only visual objects. The main difference is that disappearances may not occur as quickly as with the stabilized image. The student can easily observe the effect for himself by drawing an outline figure such as a triangle on a sheet of cardboard with luminous paint, and then in a dark room looking steadily at one point in the figure. (Disappearances do not occur if one moves one's eyes from point to point in the diagram.) The disappearances are all-or-none, a whole line or whole figure disappearing at once, though there is some fading first. It seems, from our present knowledge, that the disappearances can be explained as the sudden cessation of the activity in cell-assemblies that constitutes perception.

The evidence clearly supports the theory of cell-assemblies, which proposed originally that the perception of a triangle, for example, is a com-

Figure 94. *Partial disappearance of stabilized images. A and B are targets; to the right of each are patterns that may be perceived at different times as one or more parts disappear, or reappear after the whole target has gone.*

posite, and that the perception of one side or one angle is the activity of a separate cell-assembly. The assembly functions as a system, its reverberatory activity allowing the neurons in the system to support each other's firing. Some neurons may fatigue and drop out while the reverberation continues, but a point will be reached at which one too many has dropped out, and then the reverberation will cease suddenly. The line first fades, then suddenly disappears completely.

However, the support from this experiment is limited. If the theory is as it seems on the right track it is not yet satisfactory. When a different kind of figure is seen with stabilization, such as the solid square of Figure 95, the disappearance is not all-or-none but gradual, as Figure 95 shows. Cell-assembly theory says that perception is a complex of *unitary* processes; as it stands at present it cannot account for the graded disappearance represented in Figure 95. There are other related difficulties from the same set of experiments. The difficulties may perhaps be handled by assuming that an assembly consists of a number of sub-assemblies, temporarily functioning as a single system. A sub-assembly might perhaps be as small as one of Lorente de Nó's closed loops (Fig. 33). However, this has not been worked out in detail, and the evidence of Figure 95 at present stands as evidence opposing the theory. It is worth drawing this to the student's attention as an example of the fact that a theory may be useful, introducing new order into existing data and guiding new research, *and still not be true* or worthy of unquestioning acceptance.

One thing at least the stabilized-image experiment shows: visual perception of a complex object such as square or triangle may seem to the perceiver to be a completely simple unitary event, and be actu-

Figure 95. *Fading observed with a solid (i.e., not an outline) square. Unlike those observed with outline figures, the disappearances are not all-or-none. (From D. O. Hebb, Amer. Psychologist, 1963.)*

ally a complex that under the right conditions can be broken down into constituent parts. Next we will see that certain evidence from the memory image enables us to carry this analysis a step or two further.

MEMORY IMAGES

There are several varieties of images: the after-image referred to on page 2; memory image and the closely related eidetic image; hypnagogic image; and hallucination. The *after-image* is an effect that follows immediately on intense or prolonged stimulation. A *memory image* is the reinstatement of a perception, as a form of recall; an *eidetic image* is an exceptionally vivid memory image that occurs immediately after the perception (but is not an after-image). *Hypnagogic imagery,* usually occurring before going to sleep (hence the name hypnagogic), is a prolonged reinstatement of some unusual activity that occurred during the day: like a moving after-image except that it may occur hours after the unusual experience has ceased. *Hallucination* is any strongly convincing imagery of central origin, due to spontaneous firing of cortical and subcortical neurons.

The after-image is distinct from the others in being under sensory control. When you stare at a bright surface as you were invited to do earlier (p. 2), you fatigue the rods and cones of the retina in a pattern that corresponds to the shape of the bright object; now when you look away at a plain surface, the fatigued cells can only fire at a slow rate, as if they were not being stimulated very strongly, whereas the surrounding cells of the retina

Figure 96. *For a demonstration of the negative after-image. Stare at one point in the picture while counting slowly to 40. A good point to look at is the inner corner of the person's right eye (on your left as you look at the picture). Then look at a sheet of white paper. The negative after-image will appear. (It may not at first; if so, stare for 40 seconds at the same point again, not moving your eyes, then try it. Blink your eyes once or twice.)*

fire at a normal rate. The result: a *negative after-image,* a dark object being seen instead of a bright one. If instead it is a dark object you stare at, as in Figure 96, the rods and cones in central vision are being rested while you look at the dark surface, and so when you look away at a lighter surface the same cells are ready to fire strongly. The after-image therefore is of a light-colored object on a dark ground. *Positive after-images* are produced by a sudden brief flash of light, very intense if the eyes are adjusted to daylight, less so if they are dark-adapted. The positive after-image is easy to observe if you happen to wake up at night in darkness. Go to the light-switch and flick it on and off as quickly as you can. For some seconds afterward you will see the scene exactly as you saw it during the brief moment when the light was on.

The visual memory image has something important to tell us about perception. In visual perception eye movements occur constantly, but have they any importance apart from enabling us to see the details better in what is perceived? It seems in fact that they enter into and make part of the perception itself. An image of a sports car or a plane or a bicycle is a reinstatement of a perception, with some loss of detail—the perception is happening again, in its main outline. Now if the reader will close his eyes and recall the appearance of one of these objects—the sports car, let us say—he will find that it is not possible to have a complete image of the car all at once. Instead he must see now this part, now that, and he will find that he moves his eyes as, in the image, the point "looked at" changes from the door to the bumper to the steering wheel. It is not possible to have a clear visual image of a complex object without eye movement, or imagining eye movement (which you may be able to do with some practice; but it is easier just to make the actual movements). In the image, in other words, we have a reinstatement of what happened in perception, *including* the eye movement. It appears that the perception is a complex, with its various parts being linked together by motor processes. We may think of it as a series of cell-assembly activities. One assembly fires, which excites a motor activity, which excites another assembly, and so on. The memory image includes those motor links.

The motor component helps us to understand the eidetic image. R. N. Haber and R. B. Haber have shown convincingly that the eidetic image does occur, in a small proportion of school-children mainly. There has been some skepticism, perhaps because the eidetic image acts in some respects like an after-image (positive), but not in other respects. It is vivid, it occurs only in the period immediately after the stimulation, and it is transient: all of which sounds like an after-image; but it does not move as the eyes move, and the child is capable of "looking at" any part of it to see it more clearly, which of course is impossible with an after-image.

The child is shown a picture, such as the one in Figure 97, for 15 to 30 seconds. Then the picture is taken away, leaving behind it a gray surface of about the same size. The child talks as if he can still see the picture on the gray surface, and when he wants to describe what was at the top he looks at the corresponding point and then describes

Figure 97. Picture used in an early study of eidetic imagery by G. W. Allport. Some of the "eidetikers" (children with eidetic imagery) could even spell the long German word on the front of the building, in addition to reporting much other detail, after looking at the picture for 35 seconds only.

it—very accurately, in detail, and in greater detail than the rest of us could. This sounds like mysticism, as if the picture had left something behind it that the child could see. Hence the skepticism.

But if motor movements do make up part of a perception and of a memory image, all this becomes intelligible. If the child's image consists of a number of part-images, and if one of these is excited not directly by another but by the intervening motor link, then when the child wants to "see" a particular feature of the picture again the eye movement he makes toward the corresponding part of the gray surface is a stimulant, helping to re-excite the part-perception that followed such eye movements earlier, when he looked at the real picture. This means that the eidetic image is an exceptionally detailed and vivid memory image, and need not be considered mysterious—no more mysterious, at least, than other memory images.

The memory image for printed words is also of interest, as a reinstatement of perception. Some people with good memories seem to have a sort of photographic record of what they read. In exceptional cases the subject says he can close his eyes and still see the page he has just read. These people tend to explain their memories for verbal material by saying that they just call up an image of a page and read it off. Many people report having memory images of single words that help them with spelling or, in memorizing verse, report having images of whole lines and even of short stanzas.

If the student or one of his friends is such a person, he can make an interesting test. The image in these cases seems just like something out in front of one, that one can look at as one could look at an actual page. With a real word to look at, one could read the letters off backward nearly as fast as forward. So, think of a long word such as Louisiana and form a clear image of it, or have your friend do so. When this has been done, look at your image of the word and try to spell it backward, or get your subject to. You, or he, will be surprised by the result. Again, the person with a "photographic memory" of a familiar poem cannot repeat the last word of each line, going from bottom to top, without first thinking of most of the rest of each stanza. He seems to have a clear picture in his mind, to look at—but he can only look at it in a certain order: the same order in which he saw the actual words on the page, as he read from left to right and top to bottom.

Such an image differs from the image of a car, discussed above, in which the parts can be seen in any order. The difference arises from the difference in the way in which perception happened: printed words are perceived, ordinarily, in a certain order; a car's parts are perceived in any order, and the order differs from one time to another. The image, then, is really a reinstatement of perception, including the motor components. A perception of the whole is unitary, but a complex whole has a structure and in addition to perceiving the whole one may also perceive its parts.

SUMMARY

The chapter makes a distinction between sensation and perception, sensation being the input process, perception the mediating activities to which sensation gives rise. Perception, that is, is the beginning of a thought process and cannot occur where there is no thought. The chapter includes a brief description of the structure of both eye and ear—about enough to tell the student he has an eye and an ear—and for details of what is known about the very complex processes of vision and audition the student should consult a text such as Milner's or that of Ruch and Fulton (p. 76). Other sensory topics include Hubel and Wiesel's receptive fields in vision, coding in sensations of taste, warmth and cold, and the sensory basis of visual and auditory space perception. Emphasis is put on the difference between sensation and perception from a behavioral point of view. Emphasis is also put on the sequential and motor aspects of perception, as shown both in visual and auditory experimentation (stabilized images, binaural digit reception) and in certain aspects of the memory image (including the eidetic image).

Guide to Study

Here is a list of terms that should be known and understood: after-image, ambiguous figure, accommodation, basilar membrane, blind spot, constancy, convergence, cochlea, disparity (including movement disparity), eidetic image, fovea, gradient of visual texture, outer and inner and middle ear, parallax, phi-phenomenon, receptive field of a neuron, rod and cone, semicircular canal. The student should be able to list four skin senses, so-called, and the four elementary tastes. He should be able to say what is surprising about the relation between warmth and cold, physiologically, and how in general terms different fibers interact to determine different tastes. He should be able to list the cues to visual depth, explain facial vision, describe a sound shadow. The text says that perceptions of auditory distance are possible, but does not elaborate: how would this work with echoes of your own footsteps when approaching a wall? and, assuming that high-pitched sounds do not travel as far as low-pitched ones, how would it work in telling how far away another person is from the sound of his voice?

Why are a baby's eye movements not necessarily an evidence of perception? How might the ambiguous figure be explained? What is peculiar about the visual imagery of printed material? How is movement a factor in visual imagery of nonverbal material?

NOTES AND REFERENCES

Good modern accounts of perception are given by Gibson, Hochberg, and Neisser, and for anatomical and physiological background, Milner is recommended:
Gibson, E. J.: *Principles of Perceptual Learning and Development,* Appleton-Century-Crofts, 1969.
Hochberg, J. E.: *Perception,* Prentice-Hall, 1964.
Neisser, U.: *Cognitive Psychology,* Appleton-Century-Crofts, 1967.
Milner, P. M.: *Physiological Psychology,* Holt, Rinehart and Winston, 1970.

SPECIAL TOPICS

Vision
Fantz, R. L.: The origin of form perception. In J. L. McGaugh, N. M. Weinberger, and R. E. Whalen (Eds.): *Psychobiology,* Freeman, 1967. (Originally in *Scientific American,* May, 1961.)
Hubel, D. H.: The visual cortex of the brain. *Psychobiology (vide supra).*
Hubel, D. H., and Wiesel, T. N.: Receptive fields, binocular interaction and functional architecture in the cat's visual cortex. *Journal of Physiology,* 1962, 160, 106–154.
Lettvin, J. Y., Maturana, H. R., McCulloch, W. S., and Pitts, W. H.: What the frog's eye tells the frog's brain. *Proceedings of the Institute of Radio Engineers,* 1959, 47, 1940–1951.
McKinney, J. P.: Disappearance of luminous designs. *Science,* 1963, 140, 403–404.
Pritchard, R. M., Heron, W., and Hebb, D. O.: Visual perception approached by the method of stabilized images. *Canadian Journal of Psychology,* 1960, 14, 67–77.
Salapatek, P., and Kessen, W.: Visual scanning of triangles by the human newborn. *Journal of Experimental Child Psychology,* 1966, 3, 155–167.

Hearing
Békésy, G. v.: The ear. In McGaugh et al. (eds.): *Psychobiology,* Freeman, 1967. (Originally in *Scientific American,* August, 1957.) It was von Békésy who solved the problem of pitch perception.
Broadbent, D. E.: The role of auditory localization in attention and memory span. *Journal of Experimental Psychology,* 1954, 47, 191–196.
Licklider, J. C. R.: Basic correlates of the auditory stimulus. In S. S. Stevens (Ed.): *Handbook of Experimental Psychology,* Wiley, 1951.
Supa, M., Cotzin, M., and Dallenbach, K. M.: "Facial vision": The perception of obstacles by the blind. *American Journal of Psychology,* 1944, 57, 133–183.

Other Senses

Granit, R.: *Receptors and Sensory Perception,* Yale University Press, 1955. See page 44 onward, and (for warm vs. cold) p. 54 especially.
Pfaffman, C.: Taste and smell. In S. S. Stevens (Ed.): *Handbook of Experimental Psychology,* Wiley, 1951.

Imagery

Allport, G. W.: Eidetic imagery. *British Journal of Psychology,* 1924, 15, 99–120.
Binet, A.: *L'etude experimentale de l'intelligence,* 1903.
Haber, R. N., and Haber, R. B.: Eidetic imagery: I. Frequency. *Perceptual and Motor Skills,* 1964, 19, 131–138.
Hebb, D. O.: Concerning imagery. *Psychological Review,* 1968, 75, 466–477.
Kling, J. W., and Riggs, L. A.: *Woodworth and Schlosberg's Experimental Psychology.* Holt, Rinehart and Winston, 1971.

13

thought and language

This chapter is concerned with man's thought: with consciousness, purpose, insight and creativity, and also with the thought processes that make language possible. The discussion does not deal with man only, because the perspective of comparative study is as useful here as anywhere in psychology, and a look at communication in birds, for example, or the solution of problems by chimpanzees, helps us to see how remarkable man's capacities are. But we are turning now to the central problem of psychology, the human mind, and though in the present state of theory one cannot pretend to do much explaining, one must define the problem as best one can. When we know more, we will understand the problem better, even if then we still do not have adequate answers.

CONSCIOUS AND UNCONSCIOUS

We can start by trying to clear up an important point. In this book, *conscious* describes a person or a higher animal who is in a normal waking state and responsive to his environment. *Consciousness* is the state of being awake and responsive, or the state of the brain's activity at such a time. This is the way the terms are used in objective psychology.

In psychoanalytic theory however, and in popular language, "conscious" has a quite different meaning. There are conscious ideas and unconscious ideas. Here the term does not describe a state of the whole mind, but a part of the mind—the part one knows about. The student should see the great difference in meaning. It is one thing to say that I am conscious of the world about me. It is another thing to say that an idea is conscious, meaning that I am conscious of it, and implying that I can introspect and be aware of some of my mental activities and not others.

The idea that man has an unconscious mind, or a separate part of his mind which acts independently of the conscious part and whose actions are not known to him whereas those of the conscious part are known, goes back to the philosopher Herbart, about 1825. This may be a conception that is useful in a subjective psychology, one that assumes the possibility of introspection and direct awareness by the subject of his own mental processes. For modern objective psychology, which has good reason to conclude that introspection does not exist—that mind is not able to observe itself directly—there is no *conscious* in this sense (i.e., no part of the mind that we are conscious of or observe directly) and hence no need to speak of an unconscious.

In psychoanalytic theory the unconscious is capable of perceiving complex social situations and being jealous or hostile, and making the subject act accordingly without his knowing why. Such powers imply that the unconscious has separate mechanisms of thought parallel to those of the conscious mind. In effect, the unconscious is discussed as if it was a separate mind that competes for the control of behavior (and often wins).

All this is reasonable, even necessary, if the mind knows itself directly, if we are conscious of consciousness. If we assume that we know our ordinary thoughts directly, and then find that we also have unpleasant or indecent thoughts that we do not know, are not aware of, we may conclude that these thoughts lie in a different part of the mind: the unconscious. That is, we conclude that there is an unconscious because we have immoral or mean or vicious ideas and tendencies that we do not know we have.

But if we go as far as this, we must go further. It is not only our disreputable thoughts that we do not know directly. There is plenty of evidence from scientists, poets and musicians that new ideas have on occasion come to them suddenly, already worked out. They are new, they are creative, so the working-out must have been done by the unconscious. In mathematical discovery, it is the beautiful, harmonious, elegant idea that is likely to be powerful. From this J. Hadamard, the eminent French mathematician, basing his argument on the analysis of a very great mathematician, H. Poincaré, has concluded that the unconscious is the real creator in such discovery and that it has great powers of esthetic judgment. All this is based on the fact that the mental processes in question are not known to, cannot be described by, the person in whose mind they occur.

When we add to this, however, that the most ordinary mental acts are in the same class, are not observable by introspection, and by the same logic must also take place in the unconscious mind, the whole thing begins to be absurd. For example, the mechanism that enables a subject to say "ten" when he is shown a 9 and a 1 if he has one set, but "eight" if he has another set (p. 86), was shown by Oswald Külpe and his students to be unobservable by introspection, about 1910. That is, ordinary arithmetical calculation must be done by "the unconscious." *All* mental mechanisms are in this class, a fact that may help the student to see why objective psychology (a) considers that all mental processes are "unconscious" in the sense that they are not reportable or known directly by the subject but must be studied theoretically, and (b) consequently denies that we need to talk about a separate unconscious mind.

BEHAVIORAL SIGNS OF CONSCIOUSNESS

In other respects also the term consciousness must be used with care. For some persons it refers to something not part of the physical world, implying dualism (p. 4). The term could be avoided in scientific discussion, except that we would at once have to invent another one with the same meaning to designate the normal state of the waking adult of a higher species, as contrasted with one under anesthesia or in concussion or in deep sleep, and to make a distinction between the level of neural function in higher and lower species. "Conscious" and "consciousness" are useful terms, if used cautiously. The behavioral difference between consciousness and unconsciousness is not simple, as we can see by taking some examples which also clarify our whole discussion.

Our first pair of examples show that responsiveness, by itself, is not enough to show that consciousness is present. In comparing a conscious and an unconscious animal, one might think that the only difference is that one responds to stimulation and the other does not. But this is not accurate. Reflex responses can be obtained from a man in coma, when he is considered to be unconscious. Also, the reflexes of breathing and heart action continue in unconsciousness, or else death follows at once; some reflexes disappear, and others are altered, but the point is that the unconscious organism is not wholly unresponsive or inactive.

Secondly, vigorous reflex activity can be elicited from the tail end of a "spinal" dog (i.e., one in which the spinal cord has been severed at the level of the neck) which is likewise not considered to be conscious. Some persons see consciousness in any living thing, plant or animal, but such views need not concern us. Scientifically there is no justification for ascribing consciousness to sensitive plants (such as Venus's flytrap, which makes a reflex-like response to trap the insect that alights on it) or bacteria, or houseflies or earthworms or jellyfish. These conclusions apply to any animal whose behavior is entirely reflexive, including the ants, bees and termites, the social insects whose behavior is very remarkable but has not been shown to be more than a reflexive (or sense-dominated) adaptation to the environment.

On the other hand, it is not possible to avoid the inference of consciousness in such higher animals as the chimpanzee or rhesus monkey—or in the dog or cat, though we do not consider these latter to be quite as high in the scale of psychological complexity. None of these animals has language, so a verbal report is not a necessary sign of consciousness. (This point is also clear when one identifies consciousness in a stranger, seen for the first time, without hearing him speak a word—a common occurrence.) *The higher animals then share some feature of man's nonverbal behavior which leads us to classify them as having consciousness,* and this feature is not shared by the ants and bees.

The distinction we are discussing is evidently related to the distinction between sense-dominated behavior and behavior in which thought—or complex mediating activity—takes part. We have seen that there is probably no hard and fast distinction between these two classes of behavior. Accordingly, we can make a distinction between conscious higher animals and unconscious lower ones without supposing that these are two quite separate classes. There is a continuum of higher and lower species; at one end consciousness is clearly in evidence, at the other not. There is no need to try to dichotomize, to determine at just what point consciousness appears in this hierarchy. Let us agree that the presence of consciousness is not demonstrated by reflex responsiveness alone, a conclusion which implies that mediating processes are required as a minimum; we can then go on to see what other complications are involved without treating this as an all-or-nothing question.

Similarly, consciousness in man can be impaired in various ways, and there is no good purpose to be served by trying to say just what the impairment must be before we decide that the subject is not conscious. Is the sleeper who is dreaming, but unresponsive to the world about him, conscious or not? Is a man conscious after a blow on the head, if he can talk intelligently about himself but does not know where he is or how he got there, and later cannot even recall being helped to the hospital? (E. G. Boring). In either case, some of the processes normally present in the conscious subject are present, others are absent or impaired, but these are in-between cases, and we do not need to classify them in one or the other category.

However, it is worth while paying some attention to them, because they tell us something about normal consciousness. Evidently it is not a single function but a group of functions, rather loosely associated, so that one can be decreased or abolished while another is not greatly affected. Normally, one feature of consciousness is immediate memory (memory for the immediate past), so that the subject remembers what he was thinking about and can reproduce much of it on request. He remembers what he has said and done, and does not unnecessarily repeat an action that is already complete, or bore his listeners by telling the same joke twice at the same sitting. Normally, he perceives most of what goes on around him, unlike the sleeper, though he may not give any overt sign of having done so; but if he is deep in a book or a TV program he may actually be *less* responsive to other stimuli than one who is dozing.

Evidently the state of consciousness is something that varies greatly from one time to another, even in normal subjects. This variability, in degree of responsiveness and in what the organism is responsive to, is in fact one of the marks from which we infer consciousness or the capacity for consciousness. If at times the higher animal is unresponsive to his environment (even when his eyes are open, and the EEG shows a waking pattern)* at other times he prowls restlessly about or seeks ways of manipulating, and being excited by, the world about him. Further, when he is responsive, the aspects of the environment to which he responds differ greatly from time to time. That is, his interests are variable.

At times, of course, interest is determined by biologically primitive needs: at one time the animal is motivated sexually, at another time by hunger; and this degree of variability is just as characteristic of the lower as of the higher animal. But when such needs are fully met, other complex motivations appear in the higher animal. Given activity in the arousal system, the thought process appears to be intrinsically motivated, and the complexity of behavior that emerges when no primitive need is present is an excellent index of level in the psychological hierarchy.

Finally, another index of consciousness, or of behavioral level, is an intermittent appearance of purposive and insightful behavior, to which we will return.

Summary up to this Point. "Consciousness" is equivalent to "complex thought processes," and hence is not present in animals whose behavior is at a reflexive, sense-dominated level. (On the other hand, verbal behavior is not a necessary requirement.) It is very variable, qualitatively, in the behavior it determines: it may diminish or increase responsiveness, and may produce periods of sustained purposive behavior or periods of almost complete immobility. With this goes a great variability of motivations. An important feature of normal consciousness is immediate memory, making it possible to coordinate past experience and action with future action. Immediate memory and purpose (which involves anticipation of the future) together mean an extension of temporal integration in behavior for longer blocks of time. (So-called instinct, in lower animals without mediating processes, may also produce long-term temporal integrations, but here the behavior remains under sensory dominance and there is no evidence that the animal acts purposively, or anticipates the end effects of the instinctive act.)

INSIGHT AND PURPOSE

A definition of insight will be more intelligible if we look first at some examples from a classical series of experiments. A chimpanzee is shown food—a banana—suspended above his head out of reach. In sight, but at the other side of the experimental room, is a box upon

---

*A common domestic situation provides an example: "Why can't you answer when I speak to you?" "Well, I was thinking."

which he could stand. He jumps repeatedly for the food without success, gives this up, and paces restlessly back and forth. Suddenly he stops in front of the box, then rolls it over under the food, climbs up and seizes the food. At this point insight is said to have occurred (W. Köhler).

In a later test the box is left outside the room, where the chimpanzee sees it as he is being led to work. It is not visible from the experimental room, but the door is left open. At first the animal stays close to the point above which the fruit is suspended, jumping for it and trying one way after another of reaching it directly. All at once he stops these efforts, stands motionless for a moment, then gallops out into the corridor and returns dragging the box, with which he secures the prize.

This sudden thinking of the answer or "seeing the light" is of course well known in human problem-solving. The student should not get the impression that insight occurs only in this way, after a delay period — it must be present also when the subject sees the answer at once — but the sudden solution has a special interest because the sharp break in behavior identifies for us the moment at which a reorganization of thought processes occurs.

Like consciousness, insight is not all-or-nothing; it can be defined, essentially, as the *functioning of mediating processes in the solution of problems,* and from this point of view it is clear that some mode or degree of insignt is present in all problem-solving by the higher animal. The dog shows his superiority to other animals, such as the hen, in his perception of situations that require taking an indirect route to food (*umweg* behavior, Fig. 98). The chimpanzee shows his superiority to the dog in using objects as stepping stones, as described above; it is of great interest that there is no reliable report of a dog's ever pushing a chair or a box into a position from which he could climb up to food. This is physically possible for the dog; his failure to do so shows that the chimpanzee's superiority with "tools" is due to intellectual capacity and not solely because he has hands — though these are also an important factor in such behavior.

The insightful act is an excellent example of something that is not learned, but still depends on learning (p. 129). It is not learned, since it can be adequately performed on its first occurrence; it is not

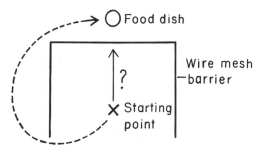

Figure 98. The umweg *(round-about) problem. The animal starts at the point shown, with food in sight through the wire mesh. The insightful solution is to turn away from the food, as shown by the broken line.*

perfected through practice in the first place, but appears all at once in recognizable form (further practice, however, may still improve it). On the other hand, the situation must not be completely strange; the animal must have had prior experience with the component parts of the situation, or with other situations that have some similarity to it.

The chimpanzee, for example, is capable of using a stick to pull in objects that are out of reach; but he does not do so if he has never had experience in manipulating sticks. Six young chimpanzees were tested with food out of reach, and a stick lying in plain view. Only one animal used the stick to get the food; this was a female who had been frequently observed playing with sticks in the past. All six animals were then given sticks as playthings for a three-day period, and at the end of this time were tested again. Never in the intervening three days had one of them been observed using a stick to pull anything to him — instead, the stick was used to poke at other chimpanzees, or at the experimenter outside the cage — but on being retested three used the stick at once to rake in the food, and the other three did so after one false start. This was a new act, and thus insightful; but it also depended on the prior occurrence of other experience (H. G. Birch).

Similarly, dogs reared in isolation, without the normal opportunity for learning to deal with barriers, were markedly inferior to normal dogs in a situation like that of Figure 98, as well as other "insight situations," and we have seen that experience occurring in infancy affects problem-solving in the adult rat as well (p. 161). All our evidence thus points to the conclusion that a new insight consists of a *recombination of preexistent mediating processes,* not the sudden appearance of a wholly new process.

Such recombinations must be frequent in man's everyday living, and in a theoretical framework we must consider them to be original and creative. The terms "original" and "creative" as applied to human thought are commonly reserved for great intellectual and artistic achievements, but from the point of view of behavioral mechanisms one sees that originality is a question of degree, and that in principle the housewife who thinks of a new way of serving potatoes is as truly creative as the novelist who shows us a new view of human nature. The child who imagines her doll talking to her is being creative — and so is the drunk who has hallucinations.

We speak of insight chiefly in the context of overcoming some obstacle or disposing of a difficulty, but we can recognize that the same kind of process is also involved in suddenly realizing, for example, that a friend is annoyed. Even in one's dreams, when one creates improbable situations, or in daydreams when one imagines how entertaining it would be if the lecturer in a large class fell off the platform, one is recombining ideas to produce what is, to a greater or lesser extent, a new idea. Such products of thought may be bizarre or impractical, but they share a common creativity with insight.

Purpose goes hand in hand with insight in problem-solving. Behavior is classed as purposive when it shows modifiability with circumstances in such a way as to tend to produce a constant end effect; it is behavior that is free of sensory dominance, controlled jointly by the present sensory input and by an expectancy of producing the effect which is its goal. When the situation changes, the behavior changes accordingly.

For example: the chimpanzee that has solved the problem of using a box to climb on to get food is given the same problem, but no box is within reach. He goes over to the experimenter, standing nearby, and tugs at his clothing to bring him near the suspended fruit; then he climbs the experimenter and gets the reward. This is clearly a purposive action. When a dog in the *umweg* problem turns away from food, he is showing a capacity for purposive behavior in his avoidance of the barrier; in each of a number of variants of the situation the dog immediately modifies his behavior to suit the circumstances and find the shortest route to food.

In principle, a number of examples of a given kind of behavior have to be observed before we can conclude that purpose is involved, since it is only in this way that we can demonstrate that the behavior adjusts itself to circumstance. In practice, however, one may know enough about the species—or about a particular animal—to be able to identify purpose in a single trial. Knowing that chimpanzees as a species are capable of complex insightful and purposive behavior, and that a particular chimpanzee has previously used a box to climb on, one need have no doubt about the purposiveness of the whole pattern of behavior when this animal pulls the observer over to the right place and uses *him* as a stepping stone.

In the purposive behavior of man we encounter longer unified chains of action than in any lower animal: "unified" since it is clear that the earlier links in the chain are not done for their own sake but because they make the later links possible. When a chimpanzee goes to get a stick, returns and rakes in food, getting a stick does not in itself meet the need for food, but it makes the later part of the whole action possible. In man such temporally integrated patterns are much longer. The fisherman in need of food may spend a day or more weaving his net before he even goes near the river. Man builds a shelter before he needs it, as winter approaches, and such anticipatory and purposive behavior may involve periods not only of days or weeks but even years.

We customarily think of man's intellectual superiority as shown in (a) his capacity for language and related symbolisms, and (b) his capacity for solving a difficult problem as presented to him here and now. But to these, it seems, we should add also (c) a long-range anticipation of future difficulties (including some that may never arise, and some that would not arise without his help).

COMMUNICATION AND LANGUAGE

The term *communication* is used here in a broad sense, comprising three levels of behavior: (1) a reflexive or nonpurposive level, exemplified by the social insects and by the emotionally-tinged danger cries of mammals as well; (2) a purposive level, clearly evident in some subhuman mammals, which nevertheless falls short of language; and (3) language itself, which appears to be exclusively human. However, these are broad categories, and it would be unwise to think of them as sharply distinct from each other. It is not inconceivable that insects have purposive behavior. The chimpanzee, or the porpoise, or the elephant, may border on the possession of language, and in one case a chimpanzee, after extensive training, has met the criteria proposed below (Gardner and Gardner).

1. Reflexive Communication.   The social insects live in highly organized colonies, in which the behavior of one animal must be coordinated with that of others if they are to survive. The coordination is so good that one can hardly help thinking of it as intelligent and purposive, but as far as is known this is not so; the individual worker ant responds compulsively to stimuli from other ants, and by her behavior in turn stimulates them to respond, in such a way as to promote the life of the colony, without thought processes or any anticipation of the long-term effects of the behavior. In one wasp species the larvae in need of food extend their heads from their cells, which stimulates the workers to provide them with food. In various species of ants, odor determines whether a worker is admissible into the colony; if an actual member is given a strange odor she is attacked and killed by other workers, but if a stranger is given the colony odor she is unmolested. In some species the nest entrance is guarded by a soldier who blocks it with her large head; when a worker approaches, to enter or leave, she strokes the head or abdomen of the guard, who then moves backward and permits her to pass. The ant is capable of learning, so this behavior may be of the order of a conditioned rather than an unconditioned reflex, but in either case it is sensorily controlled.

In much higher species, where purposive communication occurs, there still may be many examples of an almost equally reflexive and unintelligent, or nonpurposive, level of communication—particularly in the context of fear or hostility. We will return to these examples in the discussion of purposive communication, because they provide a contrast that makes purposiveness, when it does occur, more recognizable. Before doing so, however, we may look briefly at an extremely interesting example of communication in bees.

The worker bee who has encountered a food source at a distance from the hive is able to give other bees the direction and distance to the food by means of the "dance" which she performs on a vertical comb in the hive, upon her return. She climbs the comb with a peculiar waggling movement, making a number of rotations in doing so. The angle of climb corresponds to the angle between the direction of the sun and that of the food source. The number of turns corresponds to the distance (a smaller number when food is farther away). Other workers watch her closely, and thereafter fly more or less directly to the food (K. v. Frisch).

Such behavior has been called "the language of the bees." We have, however, no reason whatever for regarding this as more than a figure of speech. Though its *effect* is the same as if the bee possessed a sign language, it has not been shown that any purposive element is present in it.

2. Purposive Communication Short of Language. Now let us consider some purposive forms of communication in higher animals, together with some nonpurposive ones for comparison.

The essential distinction is whether the "sender" acts in such a way as to affect the "receiver's" behavior, and modifies the communication according to its effect on him (or lack of effect). In purposive communication the sender remains sensitive to the receiver's responses. A dog that wants to be let out may go to the door, turning his head at first and looking at his owner. If at this point the owner gets up and starts toward the door the dog simply waits, but if not, after a moment or two the dog barks—the bark being more restrained than when the dog hears a stranger outside. If nothing happens then, the barks become more vigorous. The behavior is effectively adapted toward achieving a change in another with a minimum of effort, and stops as soon as this objective is attained. A caged chimpanzee begging for food beyond his reach similarly adapts the means to the end, using begging gestures with the hands as well as vocalization. The purposive aspect of the behavior is further confirmed by the use of other means of getting the food, such as a stick, if they are available. The individual begging act is one of a repertoire of acts, any one of which may be employed depending on circumstances.

Contrast this with the alarm call of the wild monkey that detects a human observer. This is communication, for it alerts the rest of the band so that they all flee. But there is no reason to consider it purposive, because the screaming continues after the others have received the "message," and are well out of danger. The whole behavior fits into a picture of generalized emotional disturbance; it may have a purposive element also, but this has not been shown. The same considerations apply to the growl or bark of a dog at a strange dog, or an intruder. The dog, like the monkey, is known to be capable of purposive behavior and conceivably some of these acts also combine the purposive with the emotional—that is, the dog may growl with the intention of scaring off another dog—but again this has not been shown to be so.

3. Language. In man we have behavior that parallels both of the preceding classes (a cry of pain or a look of disgust may be quite reflexive, and some purposive gestures and sounds may be at no higher level of complexity than a chimpanzee's begging); but we also have a kind of behavior that, with one apparent exception, is not known to occur in any other species. This is *language.* It includes sign language as well as spoken and written words so the chief problem does not concern the ability to make the sounds of human speech, since lower animals in general are not capable of sign language either.

What puts language on a higher level than the purposive communication of dog or chimpanzee is the *varied combination* of the same signs (words, pictures, gestures) for different purposes. The parrots and other talking birds can reproduce speech sounds very effectively—but without the slightest indication of transposing words, learned as part of one phrase or sentence, into a new order, or making new combinations of them. The phrase is "parroted," repeated as a whole without regard to circumstances and with little change from the form in which it was learned. The human child, on the other hand, uses his separate words singly or in new combinations to influence others' behavior, as well as using the words in the arrangement in which they were originally heard. We do not have to analyze long sentences to see the difference between human speech and the parrot's; the two-year-old's use of four words to form the propositions "I thirsty," "I not thirsty," "Mommy thirsty" and so on, is enough to make the point.

The criteria of language, then, are (a) that it is usually purposive communication (though a nonpurposive use is common also, as in talking to oneself), and (b) that two or more items of the behavior are combined in one way for one purpose, and recombined for other purposes. This applies to sign language as well as speech. In ordinary circumstances the chimpanzee, which makes free use of gesture to invite contact, to threaten or to beg, never seems to combine two gestures as a man does when he points to an object and then points to the place where it should be put.

Until recently these minimal criteria were sufficient to distinguish man's language from any known purposive communication by other animals. (They are minimal criteria and do not pretend to offer an adequate description of language.) Now however an important change has been made. One young female chimpanzee, Washoe, has been taught sign language (a modified form of American Sign Language). By intensive training, R. A. Gardner and B. Gardner have developed communication in Washoe to a point that clearly meets the criteria proposed above. She combines and recombines, with considerable freedom, the separate gestures she has learned. Evidently this does not make Washoe the equal of the human two-year-old, since her achievement is the result only of special training and since it remains to be seen to what extent the underlying mediating processes are the same as the child's. The experiment, however, has clarified the problem of language, and is of value also in throwing into relief the remarkable capacity of the human baby in acquiring a more complex language with little or no training—simply by exposure to the language.

A fundamental difference between man and chimpanzee seems to lie in man's capacity for having several sets of mediating processes at once, relatively independent of each other (parallel trains of thought: p. 91). The three levels of communication that have been defined may be seen as representing three stages of intellectual development. In the first there are no mediating processes at all, and the animal remains sensorily tied to his environment. In the second, mediating processes occur but (to state the general idea crudely) only one or two at a time; there is a certain detachment of thought processes from the immediate sensory environment, but not a great one, so purposive behavior and planning remain rather limited. In the third, the human, stage, there is a greater fluidity of mediating processes and a greater independence from the immediate sensory environment.

LANGUAGE LEARNING

But language is not determined simply by the higher level of human intelligence. There is also a special readiness to react to speech sounds, in the baby, and a special learning capacity that may well be called instinctive. So little special experience is needed, so slight is the role of incentive or reinforcement in the acquisition of language, that it has seemed to Noam Chomsky that any learning that is needed is only superficial: that the essential mechanisms of language must be determined by the inherited structure of the brain. He has suggested that they pre-exist, and all that is needed is exposure to a language-filled environment in order to activate these language mechanisms. Vocabulary of course must be learned, and the superficial style of speech, since these vary from one country or one part of a country to another. But as Chomsky has shown convincingly, the real problem in understanding language is not vocabulary or pronunciation but the underlying mechanisms which he has called the "deep structure" of language. This is the problem of grammar, and the kind of comprehension that permits the child to make new sentences without effort even when they include words that he has heard for the first time.

The student who has understood what has been said here about instinctive behavior, in Chapter 7, will recognize that these views are perhaps more extreme than they need be. Chomsky has effectively reoriented the problem and shown us its real dimensions in demonstrating the difficulties to be met in a learning-theory explanation of language, but it is not necessary to go to another extreme and rule out learning. It seems certain that he is right in refusing to accept a straightforward learning explanation, especially learning that depends on reinforcement; man does not speak because he is intelligent and learns to speak just as he learns other skills. It seems certain that the baby is born with a special sensitivity to the sounds and patterns of sound in human speech, and with special equipment in the left temporal lobe for the understanding, organization and production of speech. But this equipment, to become functional, may still require the effects of experience. In other words, learning still has its part to play even if that part is to develop a very special innate aptitude.

A great difficulty here is that we do not know what that special equipment of the left temporal lobe is or how it differs from the rest of the cerebrum. The only way at present by which to discover the dimensions of the innately available "special equipment" is by seeing what kind of learning does go on: what is necessary and what is not. K. S. Lashley, like Chomsky but basing his argument on other considerations, has shown that language cannot be the product of learning according to the S-R formula. Language is a cognitive process, and involves more than the association of stimulus with response. However, the latent learning discussed in earlier chapters opens up other possibilities.

For example, it is known that the baby develops a kind of "competence" with language some months before he begins to talk. The baby has a certain comprehension, but what this is or how it takes place has been left unexplained. In stimulus-response analysis it remains a mystery. But we have seen the possibility in Chapter 4 (p. 66) that the first learning is a perceptual (and conceptual) development in brain function: latent learning that lays the basis for the very different learning that is characteristic of older children and adults. The baby's competence then may consist of that latent learning.

From this theoretical point of view, moreover, learning to say "doggie" at sight of a dog is S-S rather than S-R learning, though there is also some S-R learning as the child associates the sound of his own vocalizations with the motor process of vocalizing. Learning the name doggie depends on an association between two perceptions, which is S-S learning. One perception is the visual perception of the dog; the other is the auditory perception of the name spoken by the mother. This association must be preceded by other latent learning, the development of the two perceptions: the visual one from the sight of dogs and related objects such as toy animals, the auditory one from hearing the word doggie repeatedly and from hearing other words containing the same sounds. At this stage, before he produces the word doggie himself, the baby perceives it when it is spoken, recognizes it, and has a visual association for it. The word is in his competence. Before it is spoken, S-R associations must have been established between the component sounds and the corresponding motor processes. Hearing a sound he has practiced himself, he now tends to make the sound again.

That is, the child *imitates* what he hears (not necessarily at once, since a child is a cognitive animal capable of latent learning whose behavioral effect need not be seen at once). But notice what this means. The child at this stage is not learning to talk by imitation. He imitates only what he has already learned to perceive. Learning precedes imitation rather than the other way round.

One more example of the contribution of cognitive theory to the problem of understanding language: one of the great problems concerns active and passive voice, and how the child becomes able to change from one to the other. No grammatical rule can be formulated that will cover all the cases. But language does not exist in a vacuum, subject only to its own internal rules. Taking into account some aspects of perception and of nonverbal thought makes the active-passive relation easier to understand.

It was emphasized in Chapter 12 that a perception is a sequence, not a single static process, and the same object or event may be perceived in different sequences of part-perceptions. Now suppose I am a six-year-old who observes a playground battle between Annie and Billy. Suppose also that I am attending to Annie when this happens. My perception then runs as follows: I perceive Annie, I see her attacking, I see the contact with Billy and Billy's disturbance. When asked by the teacher, my report is: "Annie hit Billy." But suppose instead that I had been attending to Billy when war broke out. My perception would then run as follows: I perceive Billy, I see a blow and Billy's upset, I see the source, Annie. *Now* my verbal description of the event would be, "Billy was hit by Annie." The same event can be seen in two ways, one of which naturally gives rise to the active voice, the other to the passive voice.

And this shows how sentences may be transformed from active to passive and vice versa. Given the sentence, Annie hit Billy, to put in the passive voice, all one need do is reconstruct the scene in imagery (which also is sequential in structure), attending first to Billy, and make a verbal report in the form that readily results: Billy was hit by Annie.

The examples in this discussion have been made as simple as possible, and it is perhaps wise to remind the student that nothing about human behavior is as simple as these may suggest. The discussion is meant first to show how the problem of language may relate to other aspects of behavior, theoretically, and secondly to draw attention to a possible line of cognitive theory for dealing with language, avoiding the extremes both of nativism and empiricism. No simple theory of learning can account for the phenomena of language; there is evidently a major hereditary determinant of the course of development; but we have no good idea of what this is or how it has its effect, and the only way to find out is to explore the various possibilities offered by theories of learning. When we find out what is not learned, we have found out what is innate.

PROBLEM-SOLVING IN MAN: LABORATORY STUDIES

We know human problem-solving in two contexts: first, as it is studied in the psychological laboratory; and secondly, as it occurs in the daily life of students, scientists and citizens. Unfortunately the two are not always closely related, and there are some characteristics of

real-life solutions that cannot be observed in the controlled experiment—or at any rate, have not been observed so far. To learn something about these aspects we will turn in the following sections to a
consideration of scientific thought, after looking in the present section at problem-solving as it is studied in the laboratory.

The chief limitation of laboratory study is that it must deal, in
general, with short-term solutions, ones that can be reached in a reasonable period of time; consequently the problems presented must
be rather clearly defined for the subject. In real life the barrier to intellectual achievement often lies in the choice of problem, or which of
its aspects to attack first, and in selecting the relevant information;
and success or failure depends often on whether the thinker keeps on
coming back to his problem and worrying about it for months or
years. When the undergraduate enters the laboratory to act as subject, one has only an hour or so of his time. One must define the
problem instead of waiting for him to find it, and put before him the
necessary data and materials. As to motivation, the student usually
finds it advisable to please his instructor, and so keeps on working
whether the problem interests him or not. But despite its limitations,
laboratory study of human problem-solving has told us much about
the process, especially in the light of the various records of scientific
thinking and of experimental studies with infrahuman animals.

Animal studies have already shown us that thinking need not
depend on language (since animals do not have language but do
have fairly complex mediating processes). Human studies allow us to
go further; not only do important steps of thought occur without language, they cannot be put into language after they have occurred.
This may be true with quite simple problems (adding 8 and 2) as well
as in the complex thought of the mathematician (Hadamard, p. 249).
When the flash of insight occurs in scientific thought it can be
without warning, and without any recollection of the steps of inference immediately preceding. Suddenly the answer is there, and that
is all. There are evidently links in the chain of thought that are quite
"unconscious" —and not unimportant ones either.

This is also illustrated by a relatively difficult problem in the psychological laboratory, but one in which the solution, when it is found,
is simple. The subject is given the task of tying together two strings
which hang down from the ceiling, just too far apart for him to be able
to take hold of one and then reach the other. The solution is to take a
pair of pliers—left lying about by the experimenter but in the eyes of
most subjects having no bearing on the problem—tie them to the end
of one of the strings, and start it swinging like a pendulum; then it
becomes possible to take hold of the other string and catch the pliers
when they swing close, detach the pliers, and tie the knot. When the
subjects failed to see this possibility the experimenter "accidentally"
brushed against one of the strings and set it swinging, whereupon a
number of the subjects solved the problem promptly, but without any
realization that they had been steered to the solution. For them the

idea had arisen spontaneously, and they were quite unaware of a decisive factor in their thinking (N. R. F. Maier).

Set in thinking is both advantageous and disadvantageous. A set to solve in one way blinds one to other solutions; but one's habitual solution may work efficiently, and it would be very inefficient indeed not to have ready-made procedures to apply to common problems. Life would hardly be possible if every time one wanted to wash one's face, for example, one had to return to first principles, examine one's ideas for possible misleading assumptions, and make sure again that the use of soap and water is a good way of removing dirt. In most of the problems of everyday life the accustomed solution is still the efficient one. But it is not always so; and the difficulty is to know when to stop and take a fresh look at a problem, to discard one's present solution and seek a better one.

Also, it is not always easy to identify one's tacit assumptions, or to change them even when one knows what they are and that it is time to make a reassessment. It can be very difficult to do so in science when the assumption is a long-used, and useful, theoretical conception. Laboratory studies have shown that the more confirmations an assumption has had the less likely it is to be abandoned, even though it is no longer working. In some of these experimental situations, human subjects can be incredibly blind to alternative methods and approaches when a set has been established to deal with problems in one particular way which has worked with other, apparently similar, problems in the past.

If this is true with the small artificial problems used for experimental purposes, it is much truer with the complex problems of science. Here a further obstacle may be encountered. The theoretical idea which must be given up, or changed, may affect wider matters. It was hard for the physical scientist about 1900 to deal with the problem of radioactivity, because the solution required changed assumptions, concerning the atom, which involved the whole structure of physical and chemical theory. Even when the trouble-making assumption is identified and the problem is solved, it may be difficult for someone else to accept the solution. If it affects his view of the cosmos and man's place in it, then he may fight to the bitter end to suppress Galileo's ideas about planetary motion, or Darwin's theory of man's origins, or Freud's view of human nature.

DISCOVERY, INVENTION AND LOGIC

Refusing to accept a cogent argument because one does not like it is illogical but not necessarily stupid. We tend to identify "good" thinking and intelligence with the use of logic, but some doubt about this conclusion should arise when we find intelligent people acting in an illogical way. In laboratory experiments, for example, it is not uncommon to see a subject who is baffled by the problem given him come back repeatedly to try something that has failed before—even when he remembers that it has failed. This is puzzling in an intelligent subject—as long as we are thinking of problem-solving as solely a logical process. But is it? It may be recalled that the airplane was invented despite mathematical proof that a heavier-than-air machine could not fly, and as we will see shortly, there are records of other highly successful problem-solving by the great scientists, that also departed at times from the use of logic.

The same scientists are eminently capable of using logic when they choose to (e.g., in demolishing an opponent's argument). Here, it seems, we should distinguish between two modes of thought: (1) *discovery* or invention, the attaining of new ideas, and (2) *verification,* the process of testing, clarifying and systematizing them. When an apparent absence of logical thought is observed in a competent problem-solver, it is mostly in mode (1), not (2). With this distinction, the aimless or futile moves of the baffled problem-solver become more intelligible. When the thinker is completely stuck, having tried everything he can think of, logic is of little use. What can he resort to? One possibility is to leave the problem entirely, hoping that his thought will be running in different channels when he comes back to it (this in fact is a recommended procedure, which often works); or he may continue to react almost at random to the different elements of the situation, manipulating it this way and that hoping that sensory feedback from one of his moves will "give him an idea." In such a process—which also results frequently in success—logic plays no recognizable role.

What is happening here? We assume that a new perception or new idea is a recombination of mediating processes; and that the mediating processes which occur at any moment are a joint product of the sensory input and of the immediately preceding central processes (p. 90 and Fig. 42). The thinker does not know in advance what combination of ideas he is looking for but must act more or less blindly, to increase the probability that other combinations will occur besides those that have already done so, and hope that the effective one will be among them. Dropping the problem for a time, trying to forget it by doing other things, can help by permitting changes in the mediating-process activity with which the problem is approached on the next attempt; turning the problem around, looking at it from every possible aspect, juggling its component parts—even though these moves include repetitions of previously unsuccessful ones—can increase the probability that some sensory event will occur just at the moment when a central process is occurring which, with that particular sensory input, adds up to the idea that is needed for solution of the problem.

It is not implied that blind manipulation is the only source of new ideas; what we are concerned with here is what happens after the possibilities of logically consistent analysis have been exhausted. Then it becomes, essentially, a matter of waiting for the lightning to strike. There is repeated testimony from the great mathematicians and scientists that they have arrived at solutions after deeply immersing themselves in the problem, thoroughly familiarizing themselves with the relevant ideas and phenomena, trying this attack and that without success—and then, often with little warning, the line of solution became evident. A new idea, a new insight, is the adventitious occurrence of a certain combination of mediating processes. It can be prepared for in advance, but it cannot be commanded at a particular moment; having made available the component parts of the idea (as far as he can guess what they may be) the thinker must then, so to speak, open his mind—avoid a too narrow concentration on a particular line of thought—and wait. The element of chance is inescapable, which means that the waiting may be for a long time.

The role of chance (which of course works only for the prepared mind) becomes very evident in another aspect of scientific discovery. It is notorious that many great achievements of experimental science have been made as a matter of accident: accident, except that it must happen to one who can see its possibilities. An early example is the discovery of the magnetic effects of electric current, because a compass happened to be lying near a wire through which Oersted passed a current. Another is the discovery of natural radiation (from uranium salts) because Becquerel kept unexposed photographic film where (as we now know) he should not have. A more modern example is the discovery of penicillin, because Fleming had failed to keep his culture dishes clean. These are examples of great discoveries which required great men for their making, but less earthshaking ones made in the same way are a common occurrence in the laboratory—in fact, they are a main pillar of ordinary, everyday research. There are few scientists who have not had the experience of setting out to solve problem *A* and ending up instead with the answer to *B*, a problem that was not even thought of when the research began. This is *serendipity*, the art of finding one thing while looking for another.*

Examples of psychological serendipity from the present text: Melzack and Thompson were looking only for a loss of learning ability when they observed the insensitivity to pain and the personality peculiarities in their isolation-reared Scotties (p. 123), Bexton, Heron and Scott were interested in motivation and intelligence-test performance when they discovered hallucinatory activity in the isolated college student (p. 212); Olds and Milner were investigating the relation of the arousal system to learning when they found the pleasure areas (p. 182); and McKinney was investigating the ability of athletes to judge verticality in a dark room when he discovered the same kind of disappearance that occurs with stabilized images (p. 240). Perhaps it may be added that Boring was only looking for a bookshop when he was knocked

---

*The term serendipity has come into common use in discussions of the scientific method but often, it seems, half jokingly. Joke or no joke, the name is needed to refer to a main factor in fundamental research. Actually the word is well established in the English language, dating from Horace Walpole's *The Three Princes of Serendip*, 1754. The princes "were always making discoveries, by accidents and sagacity [this describes the scientific case precisely], of things they were not in quest of" (*Shorter Oxford English Dictionary*).

down by an automobile and was able to make his subsequent observations on post-traumatic amnesia (p. 251).

Another point that emerges from the scientific record is that some of the most brilliant successes do not involve any intellectually difficult ideas. Once the discovery is made, the new idea formulated, the whole affair looks obvious. Any high-school student can understand it, and we wonder how generations of brilliant men could have failed to do so. It is sometimes said that a problem well stated is half solved, and this is often (but not always) so. The true difficulty in such cases is to select the relevant facts and ideas, disregarding the rest. When this is done, the solution may be child's play. To us, who know what the relevant information is, the "problem" is absurdly simple; but when we put it this way we mistake the nature of the real problem, which was to select the relevant facts, to create the effective new ideas, and to get rid of the mistaken ideas of the past which were blinding the thinker.

The great scientist is not always one who thinks more complex thoughts. He is great frequently because his thought somehow has *avoided* complexities in which others are bogged down, because he sees the relevant issues and—often enough with no logical justification except that in the end it works—has pushed apparently contradictory data to one side, leaving them to be explained later.

Two cases will illustrate these points. The student of physics today has no difficulty understanding how the mercury barometer works, and why it is that water cannot be lifted with a suction pump for more than 34 feet or so. He knows that air has weight, and can see that it must press down on the surface of a well like a gigantic plunger. If we put a pipe into the well, and use a pump to remove the pressure from the surface of the water *inside* the pipe, the water in the pipe will rise—pushed up by the pressure outside—until the weight of water balances the weight of air outside, after which it will rise no higher. Galileo failed to find this answer, from which we may reasonably conclude not that Galileo was stupid, but that his pupil Torricelli, who did find the answer, performed an intellectual feat of the first order by abandoning a principle that others were working with ("Nature abhors a vacuum") and asking whether the facts could be accounted for by the weight of the air. Once it was placed in this context, the question could be clearly and finally answered by the experiments with mercury columns (which are more easily handled in a laboratory than 34-foot columns of water) that gave us the barometer.

The second case concerns the phlogiston and oxygen theories of combustion. It is common to poke fun at the phlogiston theory because even when it was being used it did not comprehend certain facts which make no difficulty for the oxygen theory. Actually the phlogiston theory was powerful. It explained much that was unexplained before and introduced new order into the field. We know now that the oxygen theory produces a greater order, but at the time when Priestley and Lavoisier were arguing the matter (Priestley, though he himself had discovered oxygen, supporting the phlogiston theory) there were *also* facts that denied the oxygen theory completely. Logically, one might say, both theories should have been abandoned; in fact, each scientist was confident that the contradictory evidence against his side would be explained with further work. Lavoisier was right,* Priestley was wrong; but here the point to note is that both men, highly capable and critical thinkers, selected the data by which to theorize and refused to accept contrary evidence.

From another point of view, of course, neither man was in the slightest degree illogical. Each was thinking in terms of a total picture of the future, when more would be known. No scientist would for a moment consider a theory really satisfactory, or "true," if he thought that the evidence would always be opposed to it, but it is a persistent characteristic of scientific thought that it deals with what is going to happen, or might happen, as well as with those things that have happened already. We have already seen, in Chapter 8, that a test of significance (p. 136) may depend logically on asking whether two sets of data (two samples) have been drawn from a population that does not yet exist, or whether one must conclude that they have been drawn from two separate populations, also nonexistent. Scientific thought largely deals with an imagined world where logic and order and predictability prevail (or in nuclear physics, an ordered lack of predictability), and this fact must be taken into account when evaluating an apparent lack of logic by a Lavoisier or a Priestley.

Where formal analysis and logically formulated inference really come into their own is in the testing and communication of ideas. The thought process produces ideas, as we have seen, more or less unpredictably and at random. Many of these have a short life, not being "attractive" or "interesting" — that is, the new combination of mediating processes does not have the capacity to persist and set off further series of mediating processes. Other combinations interact more strongly with the ideas resulting from the period of preparation, and thus persist, because the new combination of mediating processes excites other mediating processes, which in turn re-excite the new combination — which means that the thinker continues to "think about" the new idea. This is the point at which the powerful tools of logically consistent analysis make their contribution to thought. In short, they are the means of discovering error, and of winnowing the multifarious ideas produced in thought.

As to formal logical analyses, the use of syllogism and systematic induction, it seems likely that these are never used except in trying to

---

*The difficulty for the oxygen theory disappeared when chemists developed methods for distinguishing between gases such as nitrogen and carbon dioxide, neither of which supports combustion, or hydrogen and carbon monoxide, both of which are inflammable. But Lavoisier died (on the guillotine) before these advances were made, and thus never knew how the obstacle would be overcome.

pin down error in an opponent's argument or to convince skeptics of the clarity of one's own reasoning. In other words, their primary function is communication. It seems quite clear that the propositions "All men are mortal," and "Socrates is a man," from the classic example of a syllogism, do not occur in thought as two separate processes. A neurologist finding a case of hemianopia (p. 46) would never say to himself, (1) This is hemianopia, (2) What causes it? (3) All hemianopias are caused by injury to the visual pathways, (4) This man must have an injury in his visual pathways. But he might very well say so if he had to convince a skeptic.

Similarly, scientific generalizations or laws are not arrived at by a slow process of accumulating cases and gradually formulating the idea, with increasing confidence as the number of cases increases. Instead, the conclusion is likely to be formulated on the basis of one or two cases, and the remaining cases are gathered *in the light of that idea,* as a means of testing it or of convincing others of its value. Both man and animal have a way of generalizing from one specific type of experience to others; the generalization may then be supported by further experience, or alternatively it may be extinguished. An example is the dog that generalizes from one sound to others in Pavlov's experimental procedure but is fed following that one sound only and stops responding to other sounds. We may regard this as a simple experimental analogue of the procedure of the scientist who leaps to a tentative conclusion concerning a new phenomenon ("I wonder whether it could be caused by. . . ?") but finds the idea not confirmed in further observations. All this implies that the generalizations of science do not arise by induction, as that term would be used in logic, but on the other hand they must be ones that survive the *test* of an essentially inductive method.

SUMMARY

The preceding chapters have touched repeatedly on thinking, as an aspect of motivation or perception or some other topic, but here we are concerned with it for its own sake, and primarily in man. However, the comparative method is still useful, giving us perspective. Scientific thought is important not because it is really different from that of a businessman or a housewife but because we have such a good record of its course of development.

Consciousness is a complex and variable activity of mediating processes, its manifestations in behavior ranging from immobility (as in attentive listening) to extreme activity (as in a tennis match); from aimless wandering about ("just looking for something to do") to long-term temporal organization ("Don't bother me, I have an exam next week"). Insight and purpose are important characteristics of consciousness. Insight may occur at the moment of seeing a problem situation, when the solution follows immediately; but we learn more about it, as a reorganization of mediating processes, when there is first a failure to solve and then a sudden change of behavior leading to the solution. At that moment we know that insight occurred. Purpose is closely related to insight. It involves an expectancy of achieving some end effect, and an expectancy also of the effect of each preliminary step toward this goal. Behavior thus varies not only with the present situation but also according to what the behaver expects the situation to be at a later stage in the proceedings.

Language is a human monopoly. One chimpanzee by intensive training has acquired a form of sign language but the human baby develops the skill without apparent effort. There is little certainty about how the development occurs.

The study of man's problem-solving in the laboratory is restricted by practical considerations, but it has told us much and has special value when taken in conjunction with the naturalistic study of the behavior of scientists. Set is an essential component in solving problems, but may also blind the thinker to alternative possibilities: success with the laboratory problem or in research is often a matter of finding the right set.

Guide to Study

The student should be sure that he understands the two different meanings of the term "conscious," as it is used behavioristically and in psychoanalysis, and should go back to Chapter 1 and review the discussion of the objective vs. the subjective theory and treatment of mind. He should be able to give his own examples of the different behavioral manifestations of consciousness and thinking, and thus be able to show why there is no simple criterion of the presence of consciousness. He should be able to give examples from his own experience of the occurrence of insight, in himself and also in friends. A good idea is to experiment on friends with puzzles or anagrams, to see the behavior that tells us at what moment a recombination of mediating processes has taken place. The more surprising the solution, the more effective the behavior is likely to be as a demonstration.

The student should know what "the language of the bees" is and why it is not a language (or what kind of evidence would be needed to show that it is), and should be able to say why the fundamental difference between a chimpanzee's begging for food and a child's asking for a cookie is not merely that the child can pronounce English (or French, or Swedish) words.

The student will be able, from his own experience, to find examples in which solution of a problem was hindered by not looking at it in the right way. He should see how this can happen in science, and again should be able to find other examples besides those in the text. He should be sure that he understands the reason for saying that the procedures of induction are likely to follow a scientific idea rather than lead up to it, and he should in general see the difference between logical thought and creativity.

NOTES AND REFERENCES

First, a group of references that have general value for the study of human thought:

Conant, J. B.: *On Understanding Science,* Mentor, 1951.

Ghiselin, B.: *The creative process,* Mentor, 1952. Testimony from scientist and nonscientist about the way in which their creative ideas were achieved.

Hadamard, J.: *The Psychology of Invention in the Mathematical Field,* Dover, 1954. Most readable, not a technical presentation; fascinating material.

Leeper, R.: Cognitive processes. In S. S. Stevens (Ed.): *Handbook of Experimental Psychology,* Wiley, 1951.

Ray, W. S.: *The Experimental Psychology of Original Thinking,* Macmillan, 1967. Part I is a review of the literature; Part II is a collection of papers, including the famous report of Henri Poincaré of how he made his mathematical discoveries.

Woodworth, R. S., and Schlosberg, H.: *Experimental Psychology.* Holt, 1954. Chapter 26 is an admirable account of thought and problem-solving.

SPECIAL TOPICS

Language

Chomsky, N.: The formal nature of language. *Appendix A* in E. H. Lenneberg: *Biological Foundations of Language (vide infra).*

Gardner, R. A., and Gardner, B. T.: Teaching sign language to a chimpanzee. *Science,* 1969, 165, 664–672.

Hebb, D. O., Lambert, W. E., and Tucker, G. R.: Language, thought and experience. *Modern Language Journal,* 1971, 55, 212–222. The argument against a one-sided emphasis on heredity.

Lashley, K. S.: The problem of serial order in behavior. In L. A. Jeffress (Ed.): *Cerebral Mechanisms in Behavior,* Wiley, 1951.

Lenneberg, E. H.: *Biological Foundations of Language,* Wiley, 1967. A valuable book, though it may seem to over-emphasize innate factors. It also contains an appendix by Chomsky (*vide supra*), whose views if they are somewhat extreme are important and have led us to see the true dimensions of the problem of language.

"Language of the Bees"

Frisch, K. v.: *Bees: Their Vision, Chemical Senses, and Language,* Cornell University Press, 1950. The report was subjected to experimental criticism by:

Wenner, A. M., Wells, P. H., and Johnson, D. L.: Honey bee recruitment to food sources: olfaction or language? *Science,* 1969, 164, 84–86. This criticism was itself criticized experimentally by:

Gould, J. L., Henery, M., and MacLeod, M. C.: Communication of direction by the honey bee. *Science,* 1970, 169, 544–553. At present, then, Gould *et al.* hold the field: Bees do communicate.

OTHER REFERENCES

Birch, H. G.: The relation of previous experience to insightful problem-solving. *Journal of Comparative Psychology,* 1945, 38, 367–383.

Boring, E. G.: *Psychologist at Large,* Basic Books, 1961. This autobiographical account includes, on p. 39, the incident in which he was knocked down and had post-traumatic amnesia.

Köhler, W.: *The Mentality of Apes,* 1927.

Maier, N. R. F.: Reasoning in humans: I. On direction; II. The solution of a problem and its appearance in consciousness. *Journal of Comparative Psychology,* 1930, 10, 115–143; 1931, 12, 181–194.

psychology and the scientific method

This chapter is a kind of summing up, a look at objective psychology in perspective. It provides some historical background to help the student understand certain aspects of modern psychology. It considers the advantages and the limitations that may result from the use of neurological ideas in the attempt to understand mind and behavior. It also considers what the limitations are that result from treating psychology as an objective science. How are we to know what goes on in the minds of others, and how indeed are we to understand ourselves if there is no introspection, no immediate self-knowledge?

Psychology made its first stumbling moves toward experiment and the scientific method about 1860, after a long history of philosophical speculation. From the first the new approach was quantitative, in the hands of G. T. Fechner, a German physicist who is credited with being the first experimental psychologist. He set out to measure sensations and did so, after a fashion. He could of course measure the intensity of a physical stimulus, and he wanted to relate this to the strength of sensation, considered as a mental event. What he concluded was that the strength of sensation equals a constant times the logarithm of the intensity of the stimulus. This is the *Weber-Fechner law* (Weber, a physiologist, had preceded Fechner in this field). The law in this form has turned out to be not really satisfactory, but Fechner's results were such as to convince others that mental measurement was possible. Systematic work also was undertaken on the measurement of *reaction time* — the time needed to respond to a simple stimulus, such as putting on the brake when you see a light turn red — and people now began to think of psychology in a new way, as an experimental science.

This early work left little of value behind it, except as a beginning. Fechner's real contribution lay in persuading others that experiment and measurement were possible. In particular, it was his work that inspired Ebbinghaus with the idea of measuring memory, and with Ebbinghaus we come to the real beginning of modern psychology.

Following Ebbinghaus, the next major step was made by Thorndike with the cat experiments described in Chapter 2. This is the point at which Darwin's influence began to be felt for the first time in psychology, the point at which psychology took its place among the biological sciences. Darwin himself saw that there is an evolution of behavior along with the evolution of bodily structures, and attempted its study in 1872 in *The Expression of the Emotions in Man and Animals.* The book, however, had little effect on psychologists, who were still preoccupied with a very different set of ideas. G. B. Romanes, a friend of Darwin's, tried to make an evolutionary study of intelligence using second-hand evidence, but the attempt was not successful. Lloyd Morgan—very critical of Romanes' methods—undertook experiments on animal learning. None of this got much attention in the psychological world. Capable as they were, Romanes and Morgan did not depart far from traditional lines of thought: Morgan, for example, assumed that learning requires consciousness (p. 22). Thorndike was a radical and asked radical questions. He got the wide attention that Romanes and Morgan had not got.

Thorndike's questions may not seem stupid or radical now, but they did in 1900. They earned him a certain amount of scientific abuse, and they stirred up others to find new experimental evidence to show that his answers were wrong. Do animals think, or do they merely learn mechanically? Does learning consist only of S-R connections? Why are some responses learned and others not? What is the function of reward? These were questions that became central in psychological thought (especially in the '30s and '40s, in the "continuity-noncontinuity" and "latent learning" controversies).

If Thorndike looked radical, it was only to other psychologists; John B. Watson looked radical to a still wider audience, whom he outraged by asserting that mind and consciousness and thought do not really exist. In 1913 Watson founded a movement called Behaviorism, saying that psychology is the study of behavior, not of mind. Pavlov had completely excluded consciousness from consideration in his animal work but he insisted that what he was doing was physiology, not psychology, and in this earlier work did not concern himself with human behavior at all. Watson attacked man directly. A mind is a collection of habits, nothing more. Images are verbal responses. Consciousness is a myth. It is known that in some of this Watson was intentionally overstating his case, but some of it he meant. His views were ridiculed widely, but they were more solid and better thought out than those of some of his critics. He was later shown to be right in rejecting introspection as a method of study (see the references to Humphrey and Boring, p. 18). His idea that thinking is a series of muscular reactions was too extreme, but it had value. This is the idea that thinking consists mostly of subvocal speech—talking inaudibly to oneself—or in the case of a deaf-mute, movements of the fingers. Each movement of the vocal organs produces proprioceptive feedback, which is the stimulus for the next movement, and so on: the

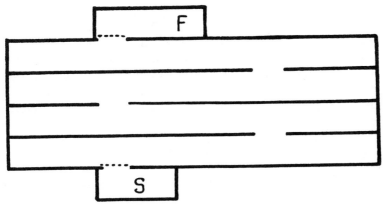

Figure 99. *Maze used by K. S. Lashley in his study of the effects of brain injury on learning by the rat. S, starting box; F, food. The broken lines represent the doors that were used to prevent the rat from re-entering the starting box, and from leaving the goal-box to re-explore the maze.*

motor theory of thought. There is little doubt now that sensory feedback plays an important part in thinking, and in general Watson's views were not so silly that they could be easily disposed of. He was cleaning house, getting rid of ideas that had been uncritically taken for granted. Some of those ideas were brought back later but only when supported by solid evidence.

This was a period when the study of animal learning was at a peak. Here the white rat had the central position, and a maze-path was what he had to learn. Some work was done with primates, but mostly it was the white rat learning to traverse a maze such as the one whose floor plan appears in Figure 99. Some studies of visual learning were being made, using discrimination apparatus like the Yerkes box shown in Figure 100, and this increased when K. S. Lashley dis-

Figure 100. *Yerkes discrimination box. A trial begins when the sliding door of the starting compartment is raised by the experimenter. On each trail one of the two swinging doors is unlocked, one locked. In front of each door is an electric grid (horizontal lines) by which the animal can be "punished" for the choice of the wrong door in addition to being rewarded by food for choosing the correct one. (From K. S. Lashley,* Comparative Psychology Monographs, *1935.)*

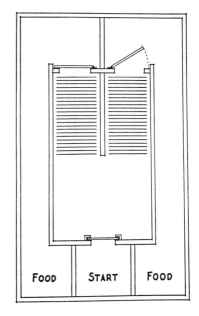

covered that the rat has pattern vision. It is almost incredible that until 1930 it was thought to be an established scientific fact that the dog – and still more the rat – may discriminate between objects of different sizes, and between different brightnesses, but does not perceive visual patterns. The reason? In apparatus like that of Figure 100, the patterns to be discriminated were put above the door where the animal paid no attention to them and so did not learn. We now know that learning is prompt when the patterns are put *on* the doors, where the animal must push against them, but the discovery was actually made in a different apparatus, like that of Figure 101: where the rat must jump against the pattern he chooses and so pays attention to it. All mammals have pattern vision, and so have birds, as may be readily shown in the Skinner box (Fig. 102). (In the figure the pigeon is shown discriminating between brightnesses, but a discrimination between simple patterns is easy to establish.)

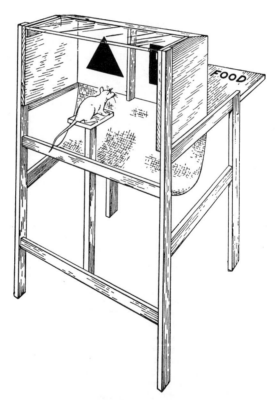

Figure 101. *Lashley's "jumping stand" for studying perception in rats (having to jump makes the rat pay better attention to the stimulus object). There are two windows, each closed with a piece of light cardboard bearing the positive or negative diagram (on the left a triangle; on the right, partly hidden, a square). When the rat jumps to the positive diagram the card falls away and he reaches the food platform. The negative card is locked in place; if the rat jumps to it he falls into the net below. (After Lashley, from N. L. Munn,* Handbook of Psychological Research, *Houghton Mifflin.)*

Figure 102. Pigeon in a Skinner box, discriminating a brighter from a darker spot of light. At left a choice is being made (the darker spot is obscured by the bird's beak); at right, the bird receives food following a correct choice. (Photographs by Roy DeCarava, from D. S. Blough, Sci. Amer., July, 1961.)

THE ROLE OF NEUROLOGICAL IDEAS

In all this period of the development of psychology as an experimental science, certain theoretical ideas about the nervous system played a significant part. Theory, like rum, is a good servant and a bad master—this book has emphasized at one and the same time the importance of theory and the importance of not believing it—and the proposition applies as much to neurological theory as to other kinds. Let us now see what value this particular intoxicant has had, and what its limitations are.

The S-R formula is the cornerstone of modern psychology. In itself it is clearly a fundamental explanatory principle; it comprises all the behavior of animals low on the evolutionary scale and some of the most vital behavior of higher animals (i.e., reflexive behavior), including man. Now the S-R formula is based on a purely physiological conception of the operation of neural paths leading from sense organ muscle or gland, and of stimulus evoking response immediately by this means. As we will see in a moment it is possible to forget physiology, and talk as if psychology had nothing to do with the nervous system, but the origin of this particular conception is clear.

The benefits that psychology has got from the S-R conception are also clear. All of Pavlov's work, still of fundamental significance for psychology, was cast in this mold. Thorndike's attempt to explain problem-solving in S-R terms showed us how to attack the theoretical problems of learning. Thorndike and Watson between them achieved the first comprehensive theory of behavior, all by consistent use of the S-R formula.*

The theory omitted thought, intelligence, insight, expectancy — any mental activity that we would now think about in terms of mediating processes — and so we must regard it as inadequate. But the theory was still a great achievement. It did explain much that had not been explained before and, just as important, it led to new and important experimental problems. Thorndike's clear statement that an animal's problem-solving is all trial and error and learning to repeat successful responses (because they are rewarded), formulated an equally clear experimental problem for L. T. Hobhouse: Can we find cases of problem-solving in which the successful response is not learned but comes suddenly? The result was the first insight experiments (by Hobhouse), later followed up by Köhler (p. 253).

Watson's clear statement that all problem-solving, including man's, can be analyzed in S-R terms had a similar value. He proposed, as we saw above, that thinking is merely talking to oneself — not really something going on internally but a stimulus-response series — stimulus, subvocal response, feedback stimulus, subvocal response, and so on. No holding, no activity in the brain except S-R transmission, would occur. These views led Hunter to devise the delayed-response procedure showing that holding does in fact occur, and later led to the demonstration of expectancy by Tinklepaugh in Tolman's laboratory (p. 87; probably a case of serendipity).

More examples might be given to show how extensively the theory of behavior is based on the S-R formula, either to strengthen it or to attack it. C. L. Hull and K. W. Spence devoted their careers to developing the explanatory powers of this conception, and N. E. Miller and B. F. Skinner have used it in their important discoveries of new behavioral phenomena; E. C. Tolman and K. S. Lashley devoted their careers to showing its limitations and in doing so made other important discoveries. Psychology in this century has revolved around three issues: the problem of thought or higher processes, the problem of reinforcement, and the problem of heredity and instinct. The first two arose directly from Thorndike's work with the S-R formula, and even the last was affected by it, the S-R psychologist attempting to reduce everything to learning and thus, in an earlier day, denying that there *was* any problem of instinct (p. 16).

In short, the S-R formula has played an essential part in twentieth-century psychology. Obviously it is a physiological conception, but it is possible to forget this fact because its behavioral ramifications are so extensive and the formula could be used by someone who had never heard of the nervous system. The formula defines a class of behavior in which observable response follows observable stimulus at once. Applying it then reveals the existence of another

---

*Their theories differed in one important respect. Thorndike's was "reinforcement theory," treating the law of effect as essential for learning; Watson's, like Pavlov's, was "contiguity theory," with no reinforcement principle.

class of behavior in which there is a delay between *S* and *R,* so we can go on to postulate the existence of mediating processes to bridge this gap in time—all without stopping to ask what neural mechanisms carry out these functions. It may be thought that psychology in this way can detach itself from neurological ideas, and that knowledge of the nervous system is not useful to a psychologist.

But such knowledge has been useful and stimulating in the past and is likely to continue to be so. Psychological theory goes well beyond what is known about the nervous system and for most psychologists it is unnecessary even to have seen a brain, let alone put an electrode into one, but it is essential that *some* psychologists should "neurologize" (i.e., work directly with the nervous system) and thus be able to keep the rest of us in touch with results that are relevant to the concerns of psychology in general.

Limitations of Neurology

There is also another reason for having at least a nodding acquaintance with neurological ideas, besides their possible stimulating value. The idea that was useful at one stage in the development of theory may become constricting later, and its deleterious effects may only be recognized if one knows where it came from.

The S-R formula again provides a clear example. Despite its value it has had a limiting effect when its neurological origin was forgotten by psychologists who thought that neurological ideas were unimportant and who thus did not find out that later developments in neurological knowledge had considerably modified the significance of the stimulus-response idea. When Thorndike and Watson and Pavlov were establishing S-R theory, the nervous system was thought to be a set of paths running from receptor to effector, some longer and less direct (i.e., through the cortex, in learning), but all one-way streets; no back connections, no feedback within the system, no loop circuits in which an excitation could maintain itself without sensory stimulation. The self-re-exciting paths of Figures 32 and 33 had been described by the great Spanish anatomist S. Ramón y Cajal but physiology had paid no attention to them. For physiologists as much as for psychologists, all neural transmissions had to be straight through, from sense organ to muscle or gland. The alternative, that some other activity might go on inside the brain, seemed to be denied by hard facts. For the hard-shell behaviorist especially, to speak of consciousness or any thinking except Watson's motor thinking was to talk dualism: and dualism was totally unscientific.

Thus theoretical development was at an impasse until R. Lorente de Nó again demonstrated Ramón y Cajal's closed circuits and this time got the attention of physiologists and psychologists, about 1940. Neurological theory has been a stimulant, providing us with basic conceptions for analyzing behavior besides provoking people like

Köhler and Hunter and Lashley into devising new experiments to test the theory, but it has also been limiting: more limiting to those who *believed* S-R theory, less so to others.

All theory needs to be held skeptically, and this applies all the more to neurological theory because it can be so useful. The time to be especially skeptical is when theory says something cannot be so. Our knowledge of neural function is far from complete, and theories based on it must be deficient: incomplete, certainly, and quite possibly containing gross errors. The student should understand and be able to use the theoretical ideas that have been developed in the preceding chapters, but — once more — he should maintain his capacity for disbelief.

FURTHER LIMITS ON NEUROLOGIZING: PSYCHOLOGICAL CONSTRUCTS

What has been said is this: Until neurological theory is much more adequate, the psychologist has to take it with a grain of salt. But we must go further. It seems that some aspects of behavior can never be dealt with in neurological terms alone. We turn next to the necessary limitations of neurologizing, and the use of *psychological constructs:* conceptions for dealing with behavior that do not derive from anatomy or physiology though they may be compatible with physiological knowledge.

The essential point is that the simplest behavior of the whole animal involves a fantastic number of firings in individual neurons and muscle cells, as the animal moves, for example, out of the starting box in a maze, or as the student reads a line of this text. There is no possible way of keeping track of more than a few of these cells, and little prospect that it will become possible to do so in the future. To describe mental activity in such terms would be like describing a storm by listing every raindrop and every tiny movement of air.

We must have units on a larger scale for the description. To deal with the storm, the meteorologist speaks of showers or inches of rainfall (instead of counting raindrops), a moving weather system (extending over hundreds of miles) and so forth. For our problem, we can use neurological constructs such as a volley of impulses, the level of firing in the arousal system, or the occurrence of widespread summation in the cortex. But the intricacies of brain function are such that this still does not take us far enough, and we reach a point at which the use of psychological conceptions, on a still larger scale of complexity, becomes inevitable.

To discuss what goes on inside a rat's head as he runs the maze, for example, we use such terms as "hunger," "expectancy of food," "stimulus trace" and "the stimuli of the choice point." Such constructs have little direct reference to neural function. They were invented and subsequently refined in the context of studying behavior, and their use does not depend on first knowing how the brain functions. Instead, we can learn about how the brain functions *from the behavior,* beginning with these psychological constructs. Perception, for example, can be discussed from this point of view. The behavior of the child who calls a sea urchin a ball, when he sees it for the first time, tells us that sight of the sea urchin must excite some of the same activity in the brain that sight of a ball does. We don't know what the activity is, as yet, but this kind of information is an important guide in our study of the neural processes of perception. In the meantime, we use the psychological construct, "perception of similarity." When eventually we learn in detail what the neural processes are, we may still find that they are as complex and variable as the raindrops in the meteorologist's weather system, and that just as the meteorologist needs his large-scale construct of a weather system for convenience in thought as well as in communication, so we as psychologists will continue to need such constructs as perception and the perception of similarity.

The situation is that we have, broadly speaking, two ways of knowing about the functioning of the brain and of mind as the highest level of brain function. One is physiological and anatomical, one is behavioral. The physiological tends to be more *molecular,* or fine-grained, dealing with units rather than the whole, concerned more with the trees than with the wood; the behavioral tends to be more *molar,* large scale, looking at the wood rather than the single tree or small clump of trees. Both kinds of information about brain function are essential. One adds to or may correct the other. Logically, the physiological and anatomical data have priority in the analysis of brain function, but conclusions drawn from these data alone may be wrong and may be corrected by the evidence from behavior.

For example, papers by German psychologists about 1920 gave one picture of how the afferent path must function in vision; neurophysiology gave a different one and thus—it seemed—showed that the psychological theory was wrong. But 20 years later it became evident that here it was on the right track.* Another example is Hunter's work on the delayed response: as we have seen, his results in 1914 said that holding must occur, but the then-current ideas about brain structure said it could not, that all brain activity must be straight-through transmission conforming to the S-R formula. Hunter, however, was right, though at that time neurophysiologists were not accustomed to the idea that psychological evidence should be given much weight and his results did not stimulate them to any reexamination of their ideas. It was in 1938 and 1939 that Lorente de Nó managed to convince fellow scientists that the closed pathway is an

---

*See W. Köhler, Zur Theorie der stroboskopischen Bewegung, *Psychologische Forschung,* 1923, 3, 397–406, and W. H. Marshall and S. A. Talbot, Recent evidence for neural mechanisms in vision . . . *Biological Symposia,* 1942, 7, 117–164. Köhler's idea of the phi-phenomenon has not been confirmed in some respects, but in others his treatment of the sensory process has a striking similarity to that of Marshall and Talbot—which itself has not been confirmed in detail but which in its main lines is now standard.

important feature of the nervous system, and in 1940 that E. R. Hilgard and D. G. Marquis drew the attention of the psychological world to this physiological development—which Hunter had, in effect, anticipated by purely behavioral research.

The theory of cell-assemblies is based on this work, and on an attempt to coordinate the physiological-anatomical evidence with the behavioral. The behavioral evidence says that holding can last for seconds, perhaps minutes, whereas the single loops that Lorente described might reverberate for much shorter periods (perhaps a tenth of a second). If a number of loops worked together, however, it might be that the reverberation would last longer. How would they work together? If a learning process is involved, making synaptic connections between the individual loops and combining them into larger systems, the question arose whether evidence of this learning could be found in infancy. From this kind of question some of the experiments on early experience and "Factor IV" originated. Such experiments add to our knowledge of brain function and of mental development, even if the theory turns out to be inadequate.

It has already been said (p. 85) that "cell-assembly" and "mediating process" refer to the same thing, the first being a hypothesis concerning the way in which the second might function. "Cell-assembly" refers to a bridging conception, relating the mediating process—known from behavior—to brain function. Physiological psychology makes hypotheses about the nature of psychological constructs, on the assumption that the hypotheses may have clarifying value, but it does *not* try to get rid of all psychological constructs.

Psychology cannot become a branch of physiology. We cannot escape the need for large scale units of analysis, nor the need for the special methods of behavioral study on which such analysis is based. Some of the most important aspects of brain function, that is, can only be known and studied by psychological methods.

It seems on occasion to be thought that neurological entities are somehow more substantial, more "real," than psychological entities: that the study of nerve impulses is a more scientific affair than the study of anxiety or motivation. This is entirely mistaken. It may be that the "probable error" of a psychological conception is larger than that of the neural conceptions of anatomy and physiology; our conceptions, that is, may need more revision and sharpening, but they are not less related to reality. The wood is as real as the trees, a shower of rain as much an entity as the drops that compose it. There must be different levels of analysis in natural science, from the microscopic (or submicroscopic) to the large-scale macroscopic. At any given level, "reality" consists of the unanalyzed units whose existence is taken for granted as the basis for analyzing the next higher level of complexity. Otherwise we should have to deny the reality of the raindrops as well as of the shower, for the drop is "only" a group of molecules, and such reasoning would lead us to the ultimate conclusion that the only fit objects for scientific discourse are the subatomic particles of nuclear physics—this page would not exist as an entity, nor would the student who is now reading it.

THE INFERENCE FROM BEHAVIOR

It seems that we have no real choice about the liaison between psychology and neurology. Psychological ideas, even those that seem furthest from any talk about neuron and synapse, are inextricably involved with ideas about sensation and how the brain works. Similarly, we have no choice about the objective method, whether we like it or not. Direct self-observation, of the mind by the mind, does not exist. To suppose otherwise is to deceive oneself. G. Humphrey showed that even E. B. Titchener and the Cornell group, introspectionists *par excellence* in the first decades of this century, described the external event instead of describing the sensations it gave rise to as they thought they were doing. What one knows about one's own mental processes is inference, not observation. The inference it seems has much in common with that made about the mental processes of others.

How is the inference from behavior made? We can begin by seeing how we find out what the world looks like and sounds like to others, animal or man.

What Others Perceive

Ingenious methods have been developed by which to study animal perception. Pavlov showed that the dog's auditory range goes up to 40,000 cps, whereas man's upper limit in practice is about 15,000, and also obtained a remarkable discrimination between tones of 1000 and 1012 cps, presented at different times and not one right after the other for immediate comparison. Not only does the dog have a wider range than man, therefore; his discrimination of fine differences also is very good indeed—as good as one could expect in man.

By using the same methods, one can show that the dog distinguishes between temporal patterns of sound. One can easily condition him to respond to a series such as 500 cps—600 cps—400 cps, and not to respond to 600 cps—500 cps—400 cps, just as man distinguishes between two such simple "tunes." Furthermore, one finds that the dog will also respond to the series 550—660—440, which has the same pattern, but not to these new stimuli in another order: just as man recognizes a familiar tune in a new key. We recognize the tune, the auditory pattern as such, as distinct from the particular notes that make it up.

This is the method of *transfer* and it has been used extensively in the study of the visual world of animals. By means of it for example it has been shown that the laboratory rat has a good perception of horizontal and vertical, but not of triangularity. In the jumping stand (Fig. 101) the rat is first trained to discriminate between the two top diagrams of Figure 103, rewarded with food for choice of the horizontal stripes (top left) and punished for choice of the vertical (very mild punishment: falling 12 inches or so into a net). Then he is tested with the second pair of diagrams, and transfers his response to the single horizontal bar, though it has a different size and shape. The rat shows that he sees the difference, for on the first test trial he hesitates long before responding, though with the training diagrams he was choosing promptly. We can therefore conclude that he perceives both similarity and difference between the test cards and the training cards. The similarity is not merely in the horizontal edges and the vertical edges, but something more generalized, for now he will transfer his response also to the horizontal pair of circles though they do not even contain a horizontal line. As far as we know at present, the rat's perception of the horizontal is very like man's.

In his response to "triangularity," the rat still shows some similar-

Figure 103. *Cards bearing diagrams for studying the perception of horizontality in the apparatus of Figure 101. Top pair, training diagrams; below, two pairs of test diagrams.*

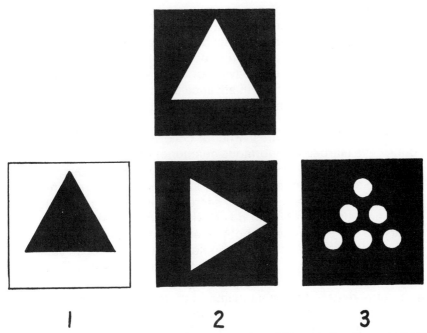

1   **2**   **3**

Figure 104. Diagrams for studying perception of triangularity. Above, training diagram. 1, 2 and 3 are test diagrams. Diagrams 1 and 2 are perceived by chimpanzees as similar to the training diagram; diagram 3 is not, though a two-year-old child perceives it as such.

ity to man, but this is evidently a more complex process and the rat's limitations become clear. If we train a rat to discriminate a triangle from a square, for example, we can make the diagrams bigger or smaller and still get the discrimination; but if we rotate both through 45 degrees the discrimination breaks down—that is, the response does not transfer to a rotated triangle. Or if we train the rat to discriminate an erect triangle from an inverted one, we find that he does not transfer his response to black triangles after training with white, nor does he transfer to triangular masses of small circles (Fig. 104). In other words, his perception of the original triangles was not as generalized as man's, and it seems clear that the rat does not see a triangle as a triangle, as one of a distinctive, unified class of figures, separate from squares, circles, rectangles and so on. The chimpanzee's perception is closer to ours, since he responds selectively to the triangle after it is rotated, and also when brightness relations are reversed; but he still does not transfer to the triangular arrangement of circles, though a two-year-old human child does so.

THE MEANING OF VERBAL REPORT

It may be easier to find out what a human subject perceives than what an animal does: all you need do is ask for a description, a verbal report. But this is true only if you and he have much experience in common. In principle, his verbal report is behavior that functions in the same way as that of a laboratory rat seeking food behind differently marked doors. In both cases we must (a) find out what events the subject is sensitive to or is capable of responding to; (b) see what events are discriminable; and (c) find out what events are discriminable, but similar. The only saving of effort with human subjects is that we need not train them in advance but can make use of the fact that they have already learned to make verbal responses to common objects.

The situation is clearest when a child is learning to talk, since adults have learned an enormous number of separate things that are hard to keep track of. It is only the spontaneous (i.e., untaught) making of the same response to another stimulus that we are concerned with here. I could train a dog to secrete saliva when he is shown a circle, and also train him to do so when shown a triangle; he then makes the same response to both objects; but this is not transfer, and does not mean that circle and triangle look alike to him. In your own experience: you may have a friend to whom you respond with the name Jack, and a contraption for changing tires on a car to which you give — apparently — the same name: but this, fortunately for your friend, does not mean that "Jack" looks like a "jack." It only means that you have learned to make the response independently, in two different situations.

There are many such complications of learning in the adult, which is one of the reasons why special caution is needed in making inferences from human behavior (it is easier to keep track of the past learning of a laboratory animal). However, the situation is simpler with the baby who shows that he sees the similarity of one adult male to another by calling them all "da-da" (until his mother manages to put a stop to it). Or to return to an earlier example, he has learned to call a certain round object a ball; when he sees a sea urchin on the beach for the first time and also says "ball," spontaneously, he shows us that a round ball and a round sea urchin arouse processes in the brain that have something in common. He also shows that the two processes are not completely identical, by picking one up freely and not touching the other or touching it gingerly. His language and manual behavior demonstrate that he perceives both similarity and difference.

All that a verbal description can do is classify the thing described with other familiar things, reminding you of some of your past experience. When I tell you that an object is green, pointed and sharp, and icy cold, what I attempt to do is evoke and combine in you the mental processes produced when you see grass and foliage, when you touch a pin point, and when you touch ice. If I succeed, you may have an "image" or "idea" of something like a pointed sliver of green ice. But this can happen only if you have had some of the same experiences that I have had. If you are color-blind, or if you have lived always in the tropics and have not encountered even artificial ice, I do not communicate. A "strange" object can usually be described, but only because it is made up of familiar parts; its strangeness lies solely in the way in which the elements are combined. If you ever see a unicorn you will be able to recognize it: a horse with a horn in the middle of its forehead. But a genuinely strange experience can only be communicated to those who have also had it, or something close to it: it is not described, it is identified only as "like what you feel when" you are in such-and-such a situation. For example:

Pilots flying aircraft at high altitudes sometimes experience something called the "break-off phenomenon," a name that means little to the rest of us. It is so called because some of the pilots say they felt disconnected from reality—but in some strange way that they cannot really describe, though they have tried (B. Clark and A. Graybiel). What is probably a somewhat similar experience is reported by subjects in the perceptual-isolation experiments (p. 212). We do not know that these experiences are similar, because they cannot be described. The subject says he has "a feeling of bodily strangeness" or "a feeling of otherness" but obviously such words mean little to one who has not actually been in the situation. If one of these students should ever become a pilot and experience the break-off phenomenon he could say something more. If the events *are* the same he could now "describe" that feeling of bodily strangeness to any pilot who knew the break-off phenomenon; *but to no one else.* He could tell him, and the rest of us, that the two events are the same, partly the same, or not the same—and that is all he could tell.

Verbal behavior in man may be enormously complex, and generally is, corresponding to the fact that the mental machinery that controls and produces it is even more complex. Psychology has only got started at the task of working out these complications, and is far from being able to take an ordinary average-length sentence and infer from it the underlying mental processes in any detail. The student should see, however, that verbal behavior is still behavior, and that the principles by which the inference is made are clear, being of the same kind as in the (slightly) simpler case of an animal's performance on a Lashley jumping stand (Fig. 101) or in a Skinner box (Fig. 102).

The Reliability of Report

The inference from behavior is only inference. In some circumstances it may come close to being a sure thing, absolutely reliable, but it is not at all so in others.

The inference from a verbal report is most reliable when it is supported by all the other behavior of the subject, and also when it is in accord with reports from others. If I stick a needle into the subject's finger and he says Ouch! and pulls his hand away, I can infer that he felt pain on the basis of his two responses, verbal and manual; but I *also* know that everyone else in like circumstances, receiving a needle-puncture in cold blood, says he feels pain. I have two kinds of evidence, two bases of inference: the immediate behavior of this subject, and what I know about human beings in general. But what about other cases, in which pain is reported but no injury can be observed? Pain is reported in these circumstances often enough to make us sure that it sometimes happens, but people are also capable of lying.

This can be a serious problem for the doctor. A man claims compensation after an accident because, he says, he has persistent pain, though examination and x-ray can detect no gross injury. There is no really good, clear basis of inference here to allow one always to separate the honest from the malingering. As a result, the insurance company is sometimes victimized — and sometimes the patient.

However, there is one case which for our present purposes is very interesting, and in which we are on a little surer ground. This is the case of pain in what is known as the *phantom limb,* which occurs often enough in predictable conditions to make the inference more secure — though if there was ever a case of a genuinely private event, this is it. The amputation of a leg, for example, does not stop the patient from having "sensations" from it. Since the limb is not there, this is imagery or hallucination. But careful investigation shows that it occurs in almost all (probably all) cases when the loss occurs after the age of six or eight (M. Simmel). The unanimity of report — even from subjects who never heard of such a thing before, who are not just saying what they think they should say but are puzzled instead — this unanimity gives solid basis for accepting the report of the amputee. Further, in a certain proportion of cases (perhaps 10 to 15 per cent), the patient also suffers pain in the phantom. He characteristically complains of cramp, the toes for example being twisted or curled up tightly. Our evidence here is only the verbal report, but we know also that such pain does occur, and particularly when we are dealing with a naïve subject (one who has not heard of having cramps in nonexistent toes), the inference can be made with reasonable security.

The opposite case is the one in which imagery is present but not recognized, not reportable by the subject. It was said in discussing after-images (Fig. 96, p. 242) that it is fairly common for the subject who first looks for the negative after-image not to see it. It was suggested there that the failure may be the result of having learned to pay no attention to after-images. Everything we know about man, about the human eye and nervous system, tells us that the after-image is there; and so we do not trust the subject's report to the contrary but urge him to look again.

Something of the same kind may apply in the case of those who deny having auditory or visual memory images. In the case of visual imagery, Binet in 1903 gave an informal test to those of his friends who said that they did not visualize the scenes when reading a novel. He asked the subject to recall a familiar incident in *The Three Musketeers;* then he started to tell him where the characters stood in the room — at which point the subject discovered, sometimes with great surprise, that he himself had already placed them, visually, in a different arrangement. U. Neisser refers to another test, showing that something very close to visual imagery is occurring where it seems not to. The nonvisualizer is asked how many windows there are in his house, and is able to set up some sort of "internal representation" from which he can count off the windows, just as those with imagery do. All that seems missing in this situation is a separate perception, or cognition, of a *visualness* in the representation,* which must have a visual origin.

TO KNOW YOUR OWN MIND

It has been emphasized that self-knowledge, knowing what is going on in your own mind, has to be achieved by the same sort of inference that allows us to discern—sometimes—what is going on in someone else's mind. The inference may be the same in principle but there are important differences in practice. The inference about your own thoughts and feelings is both harder and easier: Harder, because it is difficult or impossible to see your own behavior as a whole, in perspective; easier, because you have private evidence that is not available to others.

In some respects others have a real advantage in the diagnosis. A close friend may realize before you do that you are worried, or tired, or irritable. The difference in your behavior—restlessness, not paying attention to the conversation or to things that usually interest you, giving sharper answers—may be easily seen by someone who knows you well but not seen by you in the same way. That is, to you it may seem that it is *others* who have changed, become more boring or more irritating than usual: exactly as the deaf man complains that nowadays people mumble instead of speaking clearly. In these and other respects self-knowledge is not superior to others' knowledge.

But not in all respects. Private evidence does exist to aid self-diagnosis. The onset of a headache, when one has learned that headaches make one irritable, may enable one to avoid argument and conceal one's irritability completely. Others may recognize one's hunger when one eats greedily, but one knows about the hunger in advance from stomach sensations or because the cooking food smells particularly good. One's own sleepiness may be detected in sensations from the eyelids, with no betraying sign to others.

So much is obvious. The next step, almost as obvious, concerns imagination, illusion and imagery. Before we go further, however, we must do something about imagery since, as we saw toward the end of the preceding section, there are those who say they have no visual or auditory memory images (after-images they have, like the rest of us).

*See D. O. Hebb, "Concerning imagery," *Psychological Review,* 1968, 75, 466–477, for the possibility that imagery exists at different levels of vividness, more and less sensory, with cell-assemblies of first order, second order and so on.

However, we also saw that they have something that acts in the same way, at least in the case of vision but presumably where hearing is concerned also. This is some kind of "internal representation" that functions like an image and must have originated as images do, in the act of perceiving. We can call this an *internal representation of sensory origin* or *IRSO,* and since this description fits the memory image also we need not talk about imagery at all but can make use of the term IRSO instead.

"Imagination" is a popular term commonly used when an IRSO is mistaken for a real event. I hear a noise as I read, go to the door and find no one in sight, and conclude that I "imagined" the noise. The test, here as in other cases, is whether all the evidence agrees or whether there is a conflict. Here the visual and auditory evidences conflict (I hear something, but nothing can be seen). Again, I measure the cylinders of Figure 88 (p. 233) and find that they are of the same size, which conflicts with the apparent differences as they appear in the figure. The conclusion is that the apparent differences are illusion. It is important to observe that in both these cases (imagination and illusion) one is concluding *from the appearance of the outside world* something about the operations of one's own mind. The conflict of sensory information is crucial. If I hear voices but can find no one in the room when I make a tactual as well as a visual exploration, and if I do not believe in spirits, I must conclude that the voices are hallucinatory IRSOs: something happening in me, not outside. The after-image is recognized as an IRSO because it moves as the eyes move, does not disappear when the eyes are closed, and is not followed by tactual sensation when I reach out to touch what I am (apparently) seeing.

Now we can enlarge the basis on which Peirce knew what he thought (p. 3). He knew when he heard himself speak, but he might also know when he had an IRSO, auditory type, of words that he might have spoken but did not, perhaps because they might hurt someone's feelings. Thought as we have seen is not solely verbal, so visual and tactual IRSOs may be informative too. When X makes a speech and I find my fingertips itching (IRSO) and have further tactual and visual IRSOs of pushing X away from the microphone, I know at once, by inference, what I think of him and his opinions.

And this line of thought explains something else. In the isolation experiments one student reported that his mind seemed to have left his body. A test pilot at high altitude, experiencing a form of the break-off phenomenon, reported that he seemed to be outside his plane, looking in at himself like a puppet at the controls. Such report becomes intelligible if the subject in either case has the hallucination of seeing himself, and if the hallucination is more vivid than the IRSO of ordinary experience and has the full sensory quality that the eidetic image seems to have. The subject then seems to be actually looking at himself. Now to see your body at a distance you—the real you—must have left the body. If you do not believe in a soul that can wander in the void while you are still alive, this must be a disturbing conclusion to come to. A yogi, with a different theory of existence, could properly conclude that the true self had been freed from the husk of the body. He might very well do all in his power to make this happen as often as possible. For the rest of us, an explanation is available that is more in line with our knowledge of the nervous system and of natural science.

SCIENCE AND PSYCHOLOGY

Now a final comment on the nature of modern psychology.

For many philosophers, psychiatrists, neurologists and amateur psychologists, the effect of science and scientific methods on psychology has been calamitous. They feel that in experimental psychology man has lost his humanity, that he is made into a sort of biological machine. To deny man a soul and equate mind with an activity of matter, to make consciousness nothing but nerve impulses running to and fro in the brain, when nerve impulses are nothing but chemical disturbances—for such persons, all this is obviously nonsense. They *know* that mind and consciousness are not like this. What answer should be made to their criticism?

Part of the answer is that psychology is still engaged in laying foundations for the better account of man's mind that will be possible in the future. We are still discovering new complexities of mind and behavior, and if scientific understanding is still inadequate it does not mean necessarily that we are searching for understanding in the wrong direction. It may mean only that we have much farther to go. And on the philosophical point, to equate mind with an activity of matter does not necessarily lower mind but may elevate matter. Instead of reducing the spiritual to the level of dull, inert matter—as we conceive matter to be—it may imply that matter is something different. The modern physicist now tells us that matter consists of pure energy, which reminds one of the poetic outburst of John Tyndall, physical scientist of the 19th century, who suggested that matter is "the living garment of God." Who among the amateur philosophers is so certain about the nature of matter that he can be sure that the movement of ions and the microscopic energy disturbances of the nerve impulse have nothing to do with consciousness?

Modern psychology has not degraded man. It has not denied him free will, and those who suppose that determinism does so have not understood the nature of the problem (p. 91). It has not made man a meaner, more despicable creature: quite the contrary. Earlier psychologists found no rebuttal for the hedonistic theory that man is moved only by the search for pleasure and the avoidance of pain, but a biological and evolutionary psychology can easily show that this is not so. Man by his nature is generous as well as selfish, kind as well as cruel (altruism: p. 208), and how he is brought up may determine which aspect predominates. The mind that was known by introspection (supposedly) was incredibly flat, not even suggesting the complexities of thought shown us by Piaget or those of language shown us by Chomsky. In modern theory man is a far more interesting subject as well as one entitled to more respect.

It is true that some of our assumptions may seem improbable, even incredible, but this is not an effective criticism of a scientific proposition. It may be difficult to accept the idea that your consciousness of the world about you consists entirely of a pattern of nerve impulses in your brain, but the only test of the idea, as a working assumption in a scientific investigation, is whether it does work: whether it helps to organize existing knowledge and leads to the discovery of further knowledge. Science deals in preposterous ideas: preposterous when they are new, that is, and because they constitute a change from existing ideas. Once they are accepted and familiar and have become part of "common sense" we may forget how absurd they seemed when first proposed. No one today talks about the absurdity of saying that energy is a form of matter, and vice versa — not today, when the hydrogen bomb is a practical reality. But it is still in a way an absurd idea. Other scientific ideas have seemed so in the past. The great Galileo laughed at Kepler's suggestion that moon and ocean may have some attraction between them, to account for the tides; Newton found the Royal Society openly skeptical of the preposterous proposition that white light is simply a mixture of the colors of the rainbow; no good defense can be offered for the idea that the sun does not rise or set, that instead the earth is revolving and carrying us through space at speeds up to a thousand miles an hour. There is no defense for these ideas, that is, except that they work, and have led us to new understanding and new knowledge.

If then in psychology the student encounters ideas that clearly contradict common sense, this may be a sign not that the ideas are bad but that psychology is following in the grand traditions of science. We have hardly begun to understand the human mind; if the ideas with which we are working at this stage seem implausible, it can only be expected that they will become more so as the study of behavior progresses. With good fortune psychology may hope eventually to achieve that degree of implausibility — and fertility — that now characterizes the longer established sciences.

SUMMARY

Modern psychological theory has been preoccupied with the problem of learning, a field opened by Ebbinghaus and made of central theoretical importance by Thorndike, Pavlov and Watson. Until about 1930 this theory was very directly influenced by ideas about what the nervous system could or could not do. Since then a number of highly capable psychologists have developed a psychology that on the surface at least is independent of anatomy and physiology. This may be a mistake. Neurological knowledge was evidently a stimulant to psychological thought earlier and may still be so, though it seems clear that psychology cannot be reduced to neurophysiology.

A major problem for the objective study of mind is to know how the "inference from behavior" is to be made, to know what is going on in someone else's mind and, equally, what is going on in one's own mind. The present chapter considers how we can tell what the world looks like to an animal or another person, and discusses the difficulties that arise in the interpretation of a verbal report. It proposes that in learning what goes on in one's own mind one utilizes (a) one's own behavior, just as if one was observing someone else; (b) private evidence of sensations from one's body; and (c) "internal representations of sensory origin" or IRSOs—imagery, or a functional equivalent thereof.

Guide to Study

In the first part of the chapter, you might relate the various topics to what was studied in earlier chapters. Can you see why it is said that the S-R formula is a physiological idea? And how it would be possible to forget this, if no mention of the nervous system is made? Why is Thorndike described as more radical than Lloyd Morgan? What did Hunter have to tell the physiologist of 1915—who, however, did not listen? How would you set out to find out whether a pet dog can recognize his master or mistress visually? What problem has a colorblind person in telling others how the world looks to him? Could you invent a test of your own for seeing whether people who lack visual imagery have some "functional equivalent"—something that serves the same purpose?

Compare the discussion of the mind-body question in the final section of this chapter with the treatment of the same question in Chapter 1 (p. 3). Can you add to the examples of scientific ideas that seemed preposterous when first proposed, or perhaps still do?

NOTES AND REFERENCES

Historical

Boring, E. G.: *A History of Experimental Psychology,* Appleton-Century-Crofts, 1950. Commonly considered the standard work, and beautifully clear in its exposition, this book is thoroughly misleading in its emphasis for the modern period: on Wundt and Titchener in particular, neither of whom left behind him any discernible contribution to psychological knowledge. Boring says that Ebbinghaus left no deep imprint on the psychological world, and refers to Thorndike only as one of the professors at Columbia—and these are the two men who made modern psychology what it is!

Esper, E. A.: *A History of Psychology,* Saunders, 1964. A wholly different approach, concerned with the physiological basis of psychology; stimulating but spotty, and giving no real account of the development from Ebbinghaus and Romanes to Watson, Lashley and Skinner.

Murphy, G.: *Historical Introduction to Modern Psychology,* Harcourt Brace, 1948. More catholic but less detailed than Boring: psychology as seen by a perceptive man in 1928 (date of the first edition).

OTHER REFERENCES

Humphrey, G.: *Thinking,* Methuen, 1951. See pages 122–131 for the evidence that highly trained introspectors (working with Titchener at Cornell) really described objects and not the sensations that objects give rise to.

Lashley, K. S.: The mechanism of vision: I. A method for rapid analysis of pattern-vision in the rat. *Journal of Genetic Psychology,* 1930, 37, 453–460.

Neisser, U.: The processes of vision. In R. C. Atkinson (Ed.): *Contemporary Psychology,* Freeman, 1971. (Originally in *Scientific American,* September, 1968.)

Simmel, M. L.: Phantoms in patients with leprosy and in elderly digital amputees. *American Journal of Psychology,* 1956, 69, 529–545.

glossary

Note: this glossary is, as the term might imply, a set of *glosses* (explanations or comments) on certain words in the text. This is not a dictionary, and for adequate definitions—as far as they are provided at all—the student must consult the text itself. What follows is meant to be a ready and informal guide for the reader in trouble.

a priori assumption   what one takes for granted, does not question, but uses as a basis for questioning other propositions.

absolute refractory period   when the neuron, immediately after firing once, will not fire even with strong stimulation (about 1 msec. in duration).

accommodation   in vision, change in the curvature of the lens to focus on the retina and make a clear image.

addiction   acquired artificial homeostatic need; not a simple habit. (The man who can't quit smoking, or who needs his morning coffee, is addicted to nicotine or caffeine—but "addiction" is now a dirty word and people who should know better say these aren't addictions, just habits. A fine example of using language to conceal distasteful truth from oneself.)

adrenal gland   an **endocrine gland** near the kidney. The inner part (medulla) secretes adrenalin, the outer part (cortex) a complex of hormones, including cortisone.

adrenalin   also known as epinephrine, a hormone secreted by the adrenal gland which acts both on the arousal system and on smooth muscle.

afferent   conducting toward the CNS or toward higher centers in CNS.

all-or-none principle   the mode of action in which a neuron spends all its accumulated energy if it fires at all, the intensity not varying with the strength of stimulation (the frequency, however, does vary).

alpha rhythm   a regular (approximately 10 cps) wave pattern in the EEG, found in most subjects when they are relaxed with eyes closed.

altruism   "other-ism," tendency to act for another's benefit as if the other was oneself—i.e., helping without getting anything in return.

ambiguous figure   visual presentation that is seen alternately as two quite different objects.

ambivalence   simultaneous presence of almost equally strong but

293

opposing motivations: e.g., to fight or to run away, to mate or to fight.

ameba   a one-celled animal, especially *Amoeba proteus,* which moves by flowing in one direction with the rest of the tiny drop of fluid protoplasm following after.

amputee   a bastard word referring to a person who has had an amputation (surgical removal of part of the body).

analogical   changing gradually, not by jumps, contrasted with digital (the difference between a ramp and a set of steps).

androgen   male hormone.

anesthesia   "without sensation," in its literal meaning and in local anesthesia; with general anesthesia, there is loss of consciousness too.

animism   the theory that living things are inhabited by a spirit of some sort.

anxiety   continued fear of a specific event without means of escape; or fear due to some disordered function of the brain, in which case, of course, there is no external threatening object to run away from.

aorta   the great artery from the heart.

aphasia   a general disturbance of language, which may take different forms, with speaking, understanding speech, reading and writing all usually affected to some degree.

aqueduct   a narrow passage connecting the third and fourth ventricles. (A block here is what causes hydrocephalus or "water on the brain," in children.)

arousal   wakefulness, alertness, vigilance, excitation or excitability; at high levels, emotional disturbance.

arousal function   the general excitatory effect of sensory stimulation, as distinct from its function as a guide to response.

arousal system   a network of neurons in the brain stem, of which the reticular formation is the main component; activity of the system is necessary for consciousness and wakefulness.

association cortex   all cortex that is not specialized motor or sensory cortex; the term is a survival from an earlier day, when messages from the different senses were supposed to meet here and become associated.

association of ideas   classical term for what might be called today S–S learning or a connection between mediating processes.

attention   a state or activity of the brain predisposing the subject to respond to some part or aspect of the environment rather than other parts.

auditory area   cortical tissue specialized for hearing, inside and on the lower lip of the sylvian fissure.

autonomic nervous system   a primitive motor system controlling activity of "visceral" structures (including smooth muscle everywhere, not only in the body cavity).

average   see **mean.**

axon   the fiber that constitutes the sending end of the neuron.

basilar membrane structure in the cochlea, in the inner ear, on which are found the receptors for hearing.

behavior technically, the observable activity of muscle and glands of external secretion (but more broadly defined by some writers).

Behaviorism (with capital *B*) originally the S-R psychology of J. B. Watson that excluded mental events from consideration, but now sometimes used (with small *b*) to include all objective psychology.

behavioristic (with small *b*) reference to psychological methods using only public evidence, especially behavior, as distinct from subjective or introspective psychology.

beta rhythm fast irregular small waves in the **EEG,** characteristic of mental activity (loosely, waves of 12 cps and faster).

binocular involving both eyes.

biological clock figurative reference to one of the physiological systems that maintain the 24-hour cycle in behavior (alternation of sleep and waking), the 12-month cycle (hibernation), etc.

blind spot region of no vision in the field of each eye (not coinciding in the two eyes, so there is no blind spot with both open), corresponding to the point in the nasal retina where the optic nerve gathers together and leaves.

brain stem the part of the neural tube that is inside the skull, to which cerebellum and cerebrum are attached; in effect, a prolongation of the spinal cord inside the skull.

break-off phenomenon Clark and Graybiel's description of certain indescribable experiences of solitary pilots at high altitudes.

brightness constancy the tendency of an object to appear of the same degree of lightness or darkness, despite changes of illumination.

buck fever referring to the classical situation in which the novice hunter suddenly sees a deer and makes no move to shoot: paradigm of certain social situations.

CA chronological or actual age, as contrasted with **mental age (MA).**

carotid artery in the throat, the main supply of blood to the brain.

caudal referring to the tail end (the head end is cranial).

caveat emptor Latin for "let the buyer beware" — or in theoretical matters, don't be too trusting.

cell-assembly a hypothetical reverberating system, supposed to be the basis of a mediating process (a mediating process might consist of two or more cell-assemblies, however).

cementing action figurative reference to the idea that reinforcement may act directly to strengthen an S-R connection.

central fissure a cleft in the cortex running from the midline almost down to the **sylvian fissure** and separating the motor (in front) from the somesthetic cortex (behind).

central nervous system   the brain and spinal cord, excluding the autonomic nervous system and peripheral nerves, but including the retina and the optic nerve (this part of the brain got stretched out and nearly detached).

central process   an activity within the CNS as distinct from S–R transmission through the CNS.

central tendency   in statistics, the average; the single value that best represents the set of numbers in question.

cerebellum   a mass of tissue above the fourth ventricle, at the lower end of the brain stem.

cerebral hemispheres   the two halves of the cerebrum, not really hemispherical.

cerebrospinal fluid   bathes brain and spinal cord, and fills the central hollow in the cord and the four **ventricles** of the brain.

cerebrum   the swollen anterior end of the neural tube and the seat of mind (more or less: mental function needs also the lower brain stem, but development of the cerebrum makes the difference between higher and lower animals).

chimerical   unreal, not practical politics, refers to wild-goose undertakings.

circadian   applied to 24-hour biological rhythms and sometimes by extension to other effects of **biological clocks.**

clinical   naturalistic, when referring to a method of research in which phenomena of illness are observed as they occur and are not induced experimentally.

CNS   central nervous system.

cochlea   the snail-like bony structure that contains the basilar membrane and the receptors for hearing.

coding   patterning of nerve impulses that distinguishes two sensory inputs though they travel on the same afferent fibers; the patterning may be in the frequency (e.g., slow and irregular vs. fast and regular) or in the different combinations of afferent fibers that are active.

cognitive learning   includes some effect on mediating processes.

cognitive theory   refers to a line of thought, more or less opposed to **learning theory,** that emphasizes thought processes.

color blindness   partial or complete inability to distinguish hues as such.

commissure   a bundle of fibers connecting corresponding points on the two sides of the CNS.

communication   social behavior varying in complexity from reflex to language.

comparative psychology   the study of behavior which uses a comparison of species as a source of knowledge; not a synonym for "animal psychology," in which only a single species such as the rat may be studied.

conditioned reflex and **conditioned response**   see **CR.**

conditioning method   see **Type-S** and **Type-R conditioning.**

cone light-sensitive cell in the retina, usually fatter than the other such cell, the rod; the cone's specialty is acuity in daylight conditions, and color vision; the rod's, twilight vision.

consciousness refers both to the state of being normally awake and responsive, and to the complex thought processes guiding the behavior of the higher animal when he is awake and responsive.

consolidation in learning, some process necessary for continued retention (i.e., for long-term memory).

constancy of the IQ a supposed fixity found only in the healthy young adult. The IQ declines in old age, and varies greatly in growing children if there are variations of the stimulating environment.

constitutional variables the genetic inheritance of the individual, plus any influence on growth processes, plus any traumatic or toxic influence.

consummatory see **preparatory-consummatory.**

contiguity as a behavioral term, temporal contiguity only: the occurrence of two events simultaneously or close together in time.

contiguity theory the idea that contiguity is sufficient for learning, without **reinforcement.**

control group used in a control procedure.

control procedure obtaining results as they would occur without experimental manipulation, for comparison with experimental results (to see whether the experimental procedure makes any real difference).

convergence in vision, change in the angle between the directions of the two eyes so that both look at the same point.

copulation mating.

cornea the transparent outer surface at the front of the eyeball.

correlation coefficient measure of the degree of relation between two variables; plus 1, perfect correspondence; 0, none; minus 1, perfect inverse relation (top score on one corresponds to bottom score on the other).

cortex the outer layer of the cerebrum or of the adrenal gland (cerebral cortex, adrenal cortex).

cortico-thalamic, cortico-diencephalic describing paths between cortex and thalamus or hypothalamus.

cps cycles per second (in sound, the number of "waves" or pulsations per second: middle C is 256 cps).

CR stands for both conditioned reflex and conditioned response; "reflex" referring to the operation of the S–R connection, "response" to the end result, the motor act.

cranial referring to the cranium or skull, and to the anterior end of the nervous system.

creativity the capacity to produce new ideas (which everyone has, though the term is often used to imply only the production of high-powered ideas by the great artists and thinkers).

CS   conditioned stimulus.

cue function   the guiding or steering role of sensation, as distinct from its effect on **arousal.**

death mask   cast of a face made after death: the object of Figure 72 was a plaster-of-paris cast made from a wax death mask of the chimpanzee Lita.

decortication   removal of all or nearly all the cerebral cortex.

delayed-response procedure   the subject is shown food in one of two containers, but is allowed to choose between them only after a period of delay (e.g., 20 sec.).

delta rhythm   large slow waves, 2 to 5 cps, in the EEG; characteristic of deep sleep and of brain damage.

dendrites   the fibers at the receiving end of the neuron.

dependent variable   see **independent variable.**

depolarization   of a neuron, the movement of positive ions inward, so that there is no longer a difference of potential between the inside and the outside of the neuron.

diencephalon   the front end of the brain stem, consisting mainly of thalamus and hypothalamus (there are also epithalamus and subthalamus, but they don't amount to much).

digital   stepwise, not gradual; contrasted with **analogical** (a digital computer works with digits, and obtains its results simply by counting, an analogical computer does not).

discrimination method   presentation of a positive and a negative stimulus object simultaneously, choice of the positive one being rewarded.

dispersion   variability, the extent to which individual values differ from the mean or other central tendency.

disuse   lack of practice; the cause of forgetting that occurs merely by the passage of time. See **retroactive interference.**

divergent conduction   conduction by two or more neurons from one locus to different loci, as distinct from parallel conduction, where the neurons which start together end together.

dorsal   the side near the animal's back.

dorsal root   the sensory part of a spinal nerve (as the nerve nears the cord it divides into two branches, the dorsal and ventral roots).

dualism   the assumption that there are two kinds of existence or two kinds of being, spiritual and physical, or ideal and material; on this assumption, mind is not part of the brain's activity (which is physical).

early experience   the sensory stimulation of infancy, normally the same, in large part, for all members of a species.

ECS, ECT   electroconvulsive shock, electroconvulsive therapy: electric current passed through the head, producing a momentary convulsion.

EEG electroencephalogram, the record of "brain waves," changing potentials in the cortex measured by electrodes attached to the scalp.

effector muscle cell or an individual cell in glands of external secretion.

efferent conducting away from higher centers in the CNS and toward muscle or gland.

eidetic image exceptionally vivid memory image of short duration, found in a small fraction of children, rarely in adults.

electroencephalogram EEG (q.v.).

embryo see **fetus.**

EMG electromyogram, a record of muscle potentials; like the EEG, but from muscle instead of brain.

emotion special state of arousal accompanied by mediating processes which tend to excite behavior maintaining or modifying the present state of affairs.

empirical related to experience, the practical rather than the ideal, what works rather than what should work (theoretically). Binet's procedure was justified empirically, not theoretically; i.e., it worked but was not theoretically defensible at the time.

endocrine gland one that secretes into the blood or lymph stream as distinct from one (such as kidney or sweat gland) that secretes outwardly ("external secretion").

estrogen one of the female hormones producing sexual responsiveness (heat).

estrus period of sexual responsiveness in the female.

ethology the study of behavior by zoologists—in principle, comparative psychology, but with emphasis on the problems of instinctive behavior and evolution.

eustachian tube connecting middle ear with mouth, permitting air pressure in the middle ear to stay at the same level as in the surrounding atmosphere.

expectancy mediating-process activity occurring in advance of the stimulating situation of which that activity would be the perception: anticipatory imagery or ideation, aroused by association.

experience sensory stimulation.

experimental group the group you do something to (contrasted with **control group**).

experimental neurosis an apparently neurotic disorder produced (especially in the dog) by an insoluble problem.

extensor muscle one that straightens the joint, thus extending the limb; opposed to **flexor.**

extinction producing the disappearance of a habit by removing reinforcement.

facial vision a mistaken early term, used before the phenomenon was understood, for the auditory perception of a nearby surface by means of echoes.

facilitation   stimulation of one neuron by another, which may or may not fire the second neuron.

"Factor IV"   the effect of early experience that is normal for the species.

familial   hereditary, something that "runs in the family."

feedback   in behavior, sensory stimulation resulting from a response; either sensation from the movement itself, or the change of external stimulation as the moving hand touches another surface or as the eye in its new angle of regard sees different objects (e.g.).

fetus   unborn young in the latter part of pregnancy; before that, an embryo.

fibril   a fine branching of axon or dendrite.

figure-ground relation   the figure (constantly changing in ordinary perception) is what one perceives at the moment, the rest of the visual field being ground (i.e., background).

fissure   a cleft in the wrinkled cortex.

flexor muscle   one producing flexion, bending of the joint of a limb, and thus retraction of the limb; opposed to extensor muscle.

form board   a nonverbal intelligence test for children; the subject is required to place a number of blocks of different shapes in corresponding holes in the board.

fovea   central retinal area, the region in which daytime acuity is highest.

fraternal twins   born at the same time but not the product of one fertilized ovum, and thus no more closely related (in terms of genetics) than two children born at different times.

frontal lobes   the two front halves of the cerebrum, anterior to the central fissure.

frustration   failure to reach an expected goal or reward.

ganglion cells   in the retina, the neurons that send their axons to the central structures of the brain, forming the optic nerves.

generalization   spontaneous transfer of response or response tendency, established with one stimulus object, to other objects in the same class.

gin   (p. 148) a trap, not a drink. "O Thou, who didst with pitfall and with gin/Beset the road I was to wander in . . ."

glia   cells supporting, and presumably a nutritive accompaniment of, neurons.

gonads   sex glands: testicles in the male, ovaries in the female.

gray matter   closely packed cell-bodies, as distinct from white matter, which is closely packed connecting fibers.

ground   see **figure-ground relation.**

GSR   galvanic skin response; a change of electrical resistance in the skin, related to sweat-gland activity and an indicator of arousal.

gustatory area   taste area: not discussed in the text, but lying at the foot of the somesthetic area inside the sylvian fissure.

gyrus   the protruding part of a wrinkle in the cortex.

habituation   becoming less and less excited by some stimulation. (If the alarm clock loses its capacity to wake you, or the sound of a plane overhead no longer catches your attention, you have become habituated).

hallucination   exceptionally convincing imagery, such that the subject believes that he is perceiving, or would believe it if he did not have other contradictory information.

hammer, anvil and stirrup   the three bones of the middle ear (tribute to the poetic imagination of the old anatomists).

heat   period of sexual responsiveness in the female of lower species, in which the behavioral difference between being in or out of heat is clear-cut.

hemianesthesia   loss of sensation in all of the right half, or of the left half, of the body.

higher animal   one characterized by more complex behavioral mechanisms; in some contexts, vertebrate as opposed to invertebrate (roughly); in others, mammal as opposed to non-mammal, or again ape, porpoise and man as opposed to other mammals.

higher process   mental process, mediating process, characteristic of the higher animal only; not reflexive.

hippocampus   primitive cortical structure, in man lying near the tip of the temporal pole.

holding   the capacity of the brain to receive an excitation and transmit it to muscle or gland after some appreciable period of time.

homeostasis   maintenance of a constant internal environment, chemically and physically.

homosexuality   preference for sexual activity with one of the same sex; an almost exclusively human trait—with the exception of male porpoises, on two or three occasions, the *preference* has not been observed in lower animals; male-male or female-female sexual behavior occurs, but only in the absence of a receptive animal of the opposite sex.

hormone   substance secreted into the blood stream by an endocrine gland.

hunger   tendency to eat determined by mediating processes (ideas of getting and eating food); not equivalent to a lack of food, since one may need food and not be hungry, or be hungry and not need food.

hypothalamus   the lower half of the diencephalon, the highest level of reflex function (with the possible exception of the cerebellum).

idea   the classical name for what we would call a mediating process today, a single mental activity. As ordinarily used ("the idea of going home," "the idea of having green hair," or "I have an idea that . . .") the term must refer to a complex set of mediating processes.

ideation   a loose designation of the presence of ideas or mediating processes, which commits one to no theory of the nature of mental activity.

identical twins   not necessarily identical, except genetically: differences in their uterine environments may produce significant physical differences even at birth.

imagery   the occurrence of mental activity corresponding to the perception of an object, but when the object is not presented to the sense organ.

imprinting   a lasting social attachment to, or identification with, the species to which the newly hatched bird is exposed.

impulse   nerve impulse, or "propagated disturbance."

independent variable   one that is varied by the experimenter to see what the effect is on another, the dependent variable (i.e., the independent variable is treated as causal). In a study of rat intelligence the experimenter might use animals of different ages, different heredities and different early experiences: these would be independent variables, and maze-learning score might be the dependent variable.

inhibition   technically, an action by one neuron that reduces the probability that another will fire; loosely, any suppression of activity.

inner ear   fluid-filled labyrinth, with two sensory functions, that of the cochlea (hearing) and that of the vestibular apparatus (movement and balance).

insanity   a legal term, roughly equivalent to psychosis, but a patient may be psychotic and not insane (i.e., he can still manage his own affairs though he might be better off if someone else did).

insight   activity of mediating processes leading to solution of a problem, but especially the reorganization of such processes, with sudden success.

instinct   that which controls instinctive behavior (*not* opposed to learning, *not* separate from intelligence). A term not currently in good standing in psychology because of its connotations. (OK if used according to directions.)

instinctive behavior   species-predictable behavior at a more complex level than the reflex.

intelligence A   the innate potential for cognitive development.

intelligence B   the second sense in which the term intelligence is commonly used. It refers loosely to a general or average level of development of ability to perceive, to learn, to solve problems, to think, to adapt.

internuncial connections   paths or fibers in CNS that are neither afferent nor efferent ("lateral" connections between points at about the same level).

intrinsic motivation doing something for its own sake, not in order to get something else (which would be extrinsic motivation, or work for an extrinsic reward).

introspection direct observation of one's own mental processes (figuratively, "looking inward").

inverted-U curve rising to a peak in the middle of the range, then declining—specifically, a reference to a supposed relation of cue to arousal function implying that behavior is most efficient with a moderate degree of arousal.

ion a positively or negatively charged chemical particle.

IQ intelligence quotient, an index of rate of mental development as compared to the average of the population. $IQ = MA/CA \times 100$.

iris the colored tissues surrounding the pupil of the eye.

IRSO "internal representation of sensory origin": a reference in this text to something that functions like an image, but does not seem to be sufficiently sensory to be recognized as imagery.

item in test construction, a single question, problem or task.

kinesthesis sensation of movement, either from receptors in muscle and joint, or from the vestibular apparatus of the inner ear.

knowledge some modification of central processes which affects the response that may be made in any of a number of situations in the future.

labyrinth the fluid-filled canals of the inner ear.

language purposive communication, not necessarily verbal, at a level of complexity known only in man (with the possible exception of one specially-trained young chimpanzee).

latent learning learning without overt response at the time the learning occurs.

law of effect Thorndike's principle of reinforcement: a habit is strengthened if the response is followed by satisfaction, weakened if followed by discomfort.

learning modification of stimulus-response relations, present or potential, resulting from sensory stimulation (including the stimulation of reinforcement). Theoretically, a change in S-R connections or in the connections of mediating processes; also theoretically, fundamentally a synaptic change.

learning theory a special term, not equivalent to "theory of learning," that refers to a line of thought emphasizing the S-R formula, cautious in its approach to thought (whereas cognitive psychologists rush in).

limbic system a set of primitive structures in the brain, believed to be the seat of emotional feeling.

limen the point at which a stimulation becomes capable of causing excitation, as the stimulation becomes stronger or as it varies in frequency, etc. (thus man's upper limen for sound is about 15,000 cps—above this, he does not hear sound, below it he does).

lobotomy   an incision into a lobe (the frontal lobe, in brain operations for mental illness or intractable pain), as distinct from lobectomy, which means the removal of a lobe.

long-circuiting   formation of an S-R path through the cortex.

m   meter(s).

MA   mental age.

macro-molecule   a very large organic molecule.

massed trials   learning or extinction trials presented at short intervals until learning or extinction is complete. See **spaced trials.**

maturation   physical maturation is bodily growth, including neural development; psychological maturation, which is what is actually observed in normal circumstances, includes also the effect of early experience.

mean   the arithmetic mean, an average determined by adding all the values and dividing by the number of values.

median   an average determined by arranging the numbers in order and then taking the middle one.

mediating process   in modern theory, the element of thought, capable of holding an excitation and thus of bridging a gap in time between stimulus and response.

memory   technically, retention of any learning; used popularly to refer only to what the human subject can recall or report.

memory image   imagery for complex material at some time after perceiving it.

mental   referring to **mind.**

mental age   the age of which the subject's level of intellectual function is characteristic. A child with an MA of 7 performs at the level of the average seven-year-old.

midbrain   a short section of the brain stem immediately posterior to the diencephalon, surrounding the aqueduct.

middle ear   air-filled cavity, where three small bones transmit vibrations from eardrum ("tympanum") to the flexible membrane of the oval window, and thence to the fluid of the inner ear.

mind   a loose reference to the processes inside the head that control behavior in its more complex manifestations.

mirabile dictu   Latin, meaning "wonderful to relate."

mnemonic   having to do with memory: a "mnemonic device" is some aid to memory.

molar   as applied to theoretical conceptions, dealing in larger units, less concerned with fine detail (see **molecular**).

molecular   as applied to theoretical conceptions, fine-grained, small scale (contrasted with **molar**).

monism   the assumption, in opposition to **dualism,** that there is only one kind of existence and thus the assumption that mind is a part or aspect of the brain's activity.

monotonous   unvarying (monotony is not a mental state but a state of the external environment).

moon illusion apparent difference between the size of the moon or other objects when seen near the horizon (or horizontally) and when seen near the zenith.

motivation tendency of the whole animal to be active in a selective, organized way ("selective," because not any kind of activity but a particular kind, at any one time, dominates).

motor area a cortical region having relatively direct connections with efferent neurons in the cord; stimulation of the area produces movement in the corresponding part of the body.

msec. millisecond(s): 1/1000 sec.

myelin sheath a fatty white covering of many (but not all) nerve fibers, insulating one from another.

nasal retina the half of the retina nearest the nose.

natural selection Darwin's conception. Nature "selects" the stronger and better-equipped animal to carry on the species, by killing off the weaker one or not giving it an opportunity to mate.

negative adaptation habituation (q.v.).

negative after-image visual after-effect in complementary colors: black after looking at white, green after looking at red, etc.

nerve a bundle of axons or dendrites or both outside the CNS. (Such a bundle inside is a "tract," "lemniscus," "fasciculus," etc.)

nerve impulse the electrochemical disturbance that travels from cell-body to the end of the axon, the means by which the nervous system conducts excitations from one point to another (e.g., from spinal cord to muscle).

neural tube the original embryonic hollow tube which develops into the nervous system; or, in the adult, the spinal cord and brain stem.

neurology study of the nervous system: in one usage, the diagnosis and medical treatment of neural disorder, but also used more broadly to include neuroanatomy and neurophysiology.

neuron the individual nerve cell. Distinguish between neuron and **nerve,** the latter being a bundle of the branches of neurons.

neurosis ill-defined term referring to less extreme forms of personality disorder.

nonsense syllable meaningless short syllables invented by Ebbinghaus for the study of learning and memory: e.g., dom, zik, ral.

nonspecific afferents fibers leading to the cortex via the arousal system, where inputs from different senses are pooled; thus the excitation that reaches the cortex is not specific to any one sense.

nonspecific projection system consists of the ascending reticular activating system plus other nonspecific afferents: NPS or **arousal system** for short.

normal probability curve   a distribution which, it is assumed, many biological values (such as men's heights or women's chest measurements) approximate. Obviously an idealized conception.

noxious stimulation   damaging, or such as normally causes pain.

NPS   nonspecific projection system or, for convenience, **arousal system.**

nucleus   a term with several meanings depending on context; a nucleus is a nub or kernel or central mass: thus a cell has its nucleus, a cell-body may be referred to as a nucleus, and a thalamic or hypothalamic nucleus consists of a cluster of cell-bodies.

null hypothesis   the working assumption, in comparing two groups, that they come from the same population (i.e., their difference does not represent a true difference but results from sampling only): assumption normally made to see whether it can be disproved.

objective psychology   based on public or objective evidence, as contrasted with subjective or introspective psychology; behavioristic.

occipital lobe   the posterior end of the cerebrum.

olfactory area   there is no olfactory area.

optic chiasm   where the optic nerves meet, intertwine, and sort out the fibers that go from each eye to both sides of the brain.

ovum   egg, the cell produced by female mammals as well as by birds: the bird's is much larger since it must carry with it enough nutriment to last through the period of gestation.

pain   refers to two things, a distinctive sensory event and an emotional reaction thereto.

paradigm   a clear representative example (of a mode of thought or of experiment).

parallax   different appearance of an object (or in astronomy, a difference in the pattern of stars) as seen from two points in space.

parallel conduction   where transmitting fibers are laid down side by side, and thus can support each other's action at the synapse with summation, producing reliable transmission to the next level.

paralysis of terror   loose reference to the ineffectual behavior that may accompany strong arousal (including, for example, strong stage fright).

parasympathetic nervous system   the two divisions of the autonomic nervous system found at each end of the neural axis, cranial and caudal, and more or less opposed in their action to that of the **sympathetic** division of the **autonomic nervous system,** which is found in the middle regions of the cord.

parietal lobe   the cerebrum on one side, from the central fissure back nearly to the posterior pole of the brain, and above the sylvian fissure.

partial reinforcement   feeding only on every fifth or tenth trial or on some other scheme by which the animal makes a number of responses for one reward.

perception   activity of mediating processes initiated by sensation.

perceptual isolation   procedure minimizing patterned stimulation and thus perception; sometimes referred to as sensory deprivation, but this would imply eliminating sensory input, which can't be done except for vision.

perceptual learning   modification of perception resulting from prior perceptions.

phantom limb   the somesthetic hallucination of the presence of a limb or some part of the body after it has been amputated.

phi-phenomenon   perception of apparent movement (as in moving pictures).

photomicrograph   photograph from a microscope slide.

pleasure area   one of the regions of the brain whose stimulation is rewarding: the animal will repeat any action that is followed by such stimulation.

polarization   of a cell membrane, the presence of positive ions on one side, negative ions on the other.

population   in statistics the body of numbers or measurements or events—often a hypothetical body, indefinitely large—of which one considers the numbers one has to be a sample.

positive after-image   visual after-effect not in complementary colors (see **negative after-image**).

preparatory-consummatory   Sherrington's conception of two stages in the satisfaction of biological needs, the second being unconditioned reflex (courtship is preparatory, copulation is consummatory; seeking food is preparatory, chewing and swallowing is consummatory).

presynaptic-postsynaptic   when neuron *A* excites neuron *B* (at a synapse, of course), *A* is presynaptic, *B* is postsynaptic.

primary reinforcement   reinforcement by satisfaction of a biological need—in practice, usually the escape from pain, or food or water for a hungry or thirsty animal.

private evidence   sensations and imagery arising in oneself and so not available information for others.

proactive interference   forgetting that is a weakening of learning caused by *prior* learning. See **retroactive interference.**

probable error   deviation from the mean or true value which would occur in 50 per cent of one's measurements.

proprioception   kinesthesis: sensation from active muscles and from joints, supplying information about limb position and movement of parts of the body, and sensations of movement from the vestibular apparatus.

psychoanalysis   refers to both a theory of mental illness and a form of **psychotherapy,** originated by Freud.

psychological construct   a named conception invented for dealing with a particular class of data.

psychological maturation   see **maturation.**

psychosis   ill-defined term referring to the more extreme disorders of personality.

psychotherapy   psychological treatment of mental illness, a form of re-education rather than treatment by drugs, electric shock, etc.

public evidence   data which, for scientific purposes, might be recorded by any competent observer—i.e., objective as distinct from private or subjective or introspective evidence.

pupillary   related to the pupil of the eye; pupillary reflexes, contraction or expansion in response to changes of illumination.

purpose   mediating processes controlling purposive behavior.

purposive behavior   behavior partly under the control of expectancy, the present action being such as to produce a desired goal or suitable to an expected future state of affairs, not determined merely by their present state.

pyramidal tract   a bundle of efferent fibers, mainly those connecting the motor cortex with motor centers in stem and spinal cord.

range   in statistics, the distance from the lowest to the highest value; usually expressed by saying, the range is from (low value) to (high value), or vice versa.

reaction time   technically, the interval between presentation of a stimulus and initiation of the response.

receptor   a sensory cell.

reentrant pathway   a closed circuit in which re-excitation or "reverberation" can occur: e.g., A excites B which excites C which re-excites A and so on.

reflexive   characterized by immediacy and reliability of response to stimulation, as in either unconditioned or conditioned reflex.

reinforcement   any event following a response that increases the probability that the response will be made again when the same situation recurs. (This is the general sense: see also **primary reinforcement.**)

reinforcement theory   the idea that learning does not occur without reinforcement (see **contiguity theory**).

relative refractory period   period following the **absolute refractory period** when the neuron will fire but only with strong stimulation.

reliability   consistency of measurement by a test, expressed quantitatively as the correlation between two measurements.

retina   the light-sensitive structure at the back of the eye, containing rods and cones and connecting fibers.

retinal angle   as a measure of visual size, the angle formed by lines drawn from the center of the lens to each end of the retinal image; in effect, the angle between lines drawn from the eye to the two extremes of the object (a 1-inch line four feet away has about the same retinal angle as a 2-inch line eight feet away).

retinal disparity difference in the images on the retinas, due to the different positions of the two eyes.

retroactive interference forgetting caused by interference between what is learned and subsequent learning, as distinct from **disuse,** and from **proactive interference,** which is an effect of learning that was done earlier.

retrograde amnesia forgetting of the events that happened just before a blow on the head, or the like.

reverberating circuit same as **reentrant pathway.**

rod slender light-sensitive cell in the retina. See **cone.**

salivary reflex mouth watering, which dogs are good at. ("Any dog conditioned well/Slobbers when you ring a bell.")

sample in statistics, one's actual data, regarded as drawn from a population of data.

satiation having enough; with respect to eating, a suppression of hunger.

savings method measure of retention (memory) which compares the number of trials required to relearn with the number in the original learning.

schizophrenia ill-defined but clinically recognizable form of psychosis.

SD standard deviation.

secondary reinforcement stimulation that has accompanied **primary reinforcement** in the past and has acquired some reinforcing value.

semicircular canals part of the vestibular apparatus of the inner ear, involved in the perception of head movements.

sensation activity of receptors and specific afferent pathway.

sensory area a cortical region specialized for one sensory function by receiving fibers from the sense organ; e.g., visual area, auditory area.

sensory dominance full sensory control of behavior, without modulation by mediating processes.

sensory preconditioning refers to Brogden's procedure in which two sensory events are first associated, whereupon one can substitute for the other in a CR.

serendipity discovering what one was not looking for, while looking for something else.

set a state or activity of the brain predisposing to rapid response or to one class of response when others would have been possible (with other sets).

shaping up Skinner's procedure in which the desired pattern of behavior is gradually developed by rewarding any approximation to it, then a closer approximation, and so on.

"significant at the 5 per cent level"   (or 1 per cent, etc.): a result that would be obtained by chance only once in 20 times (or 100 times) and is thus assumed not to be due to chance. (Samples differ, experimental and control groups are samples, and thus expected to differ: the statement says that a mere sampling difference of this size would only occur once in 20 times, so the probability—19 to 1—is that something else made the difference. At the 1 per cent level, the probability is 99 to 1.)

similarity   some degree of perceived identity in objects that are also discriminable.

size constancy   the tendency of objects to appear of the same size, despite changes of distance.

skeletal muscle   striate muscle that moves the parts of the skeleton—limbs, chest wall, hips—in contrast particularly with gut muscle, etc.

Skinner box   apparatus for Type-R conditioning, in which pressure on a lever or a button, etc., is rewarded.

smooth muscle   muscle lacking the striations of limb muscle, etc., and slower acting; found in gut, walls of blood vessels, etc. See **striate muscle.**

somesthesis   body sensation, including touch and temperature from the skin, pain, pressure and kinesthesis.

somesthetic area   cortex posterior to the central fissure specialized for body sensations.

spaced trials   learning or extinction trials with long intervals between them. See **massed trials.**

spatial integration   coordinated activity in different parts of the body at the same time. (Usually combined with **temporal integration**.)

species predictable   characteristic of normal members of a species, and so predictable from knowing with what species you are dealing: e.g., speech in man, nest-building in robins.

specific energy   an old conception: that distinguishable sensory inputs must somehow be distinctive. It is now believed that they are on different input lines, or are **coded** differently on the same line.

speech areas   cortical tissue with a special importance for language; the principal regions are the cortex around the posterior end of the sylvian fissure and the foot of the motor cortex, all on the left side (in the great majority of cases).

split-brain preparation   an animal with a deep vertical incision in the brain, separating most of it into two (left and right) halves.

S-R   stimulus-response.

S-R formula   the conception of response as following stimulation immediately and as predictable from it (i.e., the formula describes reflexive behavior).

stabilized image   a visual image that remains at the same point on the retina, achieved by prevention of the slight movements of the image on the retina which result from the normal tremor of the eye muscles in looking at an object.

standard deviation statistical measure of dispersion, obtained by squaring the individual differences from the mean, adding the results together, dividing by their number, and taking the square root of this result.

stereoscope device showing one picture to one eye, a slightly different one to the other, in such a way that one sees a single picture in three dimensions.

stimulus external energy acting on a sensitive cell (receptor or neuron); in careless language, a stimulus object or event.

stimulus object (or event) something in the environment that gives rise to a stimulus (food is a stimulus object, its chemical action on tongue receptors is a stimulus).

striate muscle under the microscope marked with striations distinguishing from the **smooth muscle** of the gut, etc.

subvocal referring to movements of larynx, etc., corresponding to speech but without sound.

summation the combined effect of two or more stimuli or facilitations, which may be effective when one alone is not.

syllogism a formal mode of deductive thought. The syllogism referred to on p. 268 runs, "All men are mortal, Socrates was a man, therefore Socrates was mortal."

sylvian fissure a great cleft in the side of the brain, slanting slightly upward from front to back.

sympathetic nervous system the central division of the **autonomic nervous system,** active especially in emergency or emotional situations; closely related to **arousal.**

synapse the point at which one neuron makes functional connection with another neuron and the place at which, it is assumed, the fundamental change of learning occurs.

synaptic knob an enlargement of the axon at the point of contact with another neuron. (Also known as *bouton terminal,* or endfoot.)

taboo formalized avoidance, or a combination of detestation or fear with approval or worship, considered in the literature to be characteristic of primitive societies. We have them too, full-blown.

temper tantrum peculiar pattern of behavior commonly seen in ape and human children, involving self-injury, with the apparent purpose of influencing a parent (e.g.). Loosely, any outburst of frustrated rage.

temporal integration coordinated or organized sequence of activities—strictly speaking, a series of actions by the same effectors, but usually involving spatial integration as well, a coordination of different effectors.

temporal lobe the protrusion of the cerebrum below the sylvian fissure.

temporal retina the half of the retina next to the temple, away from the nose.

thalamus   the upper half of the diencephalon, mainly afferent in function.

thiamine   a vitamin, part of the B complex.

threshold   limen (q.v.).

tract   a distinctive bundle of nerve fibers inside the CNS.

transfer   generalization; the making of a response, learned with one stimulus object, to other such objects. "Transfer of training" more broadly refers to the effect of earlier on later learning (positive transfer is learning accelerated by having learned something else earlier).

translucent   permitting the passage of light but not pattern vision.

trauma   injury ("psychic trauma," injury to the soul?).

twilight vision   "scotopic" as contrasted with "photopic" vision; occurring in very low illumination, when human visual acuity is best two or three degrees off center, because there are no rods in the foveal area, only the less sensitive cones.

two-point limen   the distance between two skin stimulations that is necessary for them to be perceived as two, not one.

tympanum   the eardrum.

Type-R conditioning   no specific CS or UCS is used (as in Type-S), but the response to be conditioned is rewarded when it happens to appear.

Type-S conditioning   a neutral stimulation, the CS, repeatedly followed by the UCS (e.g., food), results in the capacity of the CS to elicit responses.

UCR   stands for both unconditioned reflex and unconditioned response (cf.**CR**). The abbreviation UR is also used by some writers.

UCS   unconditioned stimulus, one able to elicit the response without need of a prior learning process to establish the connection. Some writers use the abbreviation US.

umweg problem   one in which the subject must turn away from the goal he can see, in order to reach it (umweg, German for "indirect").

unconscious   in a subjective psychology, the unconscious is part of the mind of which one is not directly aware.

validity   the extent to which a test measures what it is thought to measure; ideally, the correlation between the test in question and a perfect test.

variable   something that varies. Height, skin color, friendliness to strangers, learning capacity, heredity, adequacy of early environment, neuroticism—each of these is a variable. (See **independent variable.**)

ventral   the side near the animal's belly; ventral root, see **dorsal root.**

ventricle one of four cavities in the brain filled with fluid, important anatomical landmarks.

vertebrates animals with a spinal column, excluding thus the octopus, the ant, and the spider.

vestibular apparatus sense organ excited differentially by head movements; part of the inner ear, and including the three semicircular canals.

vigilance readiness to respond to stimulation: arousal, wakefulness, alertness.

visual area cortex specialized for vision, in man at the occipital pole of the brain.

visual depth distance from the eye.

visual field the part of the environment seen at any moment, extending horizontally for more than 180°, for the normal human subject with both eyes open.

visual texture organized detail in the visual field, the fine detail diminishing with distance and larger objects becoming smaller.

volition the will, an old-fashioned conception that we might still use. "Free will," absence of sense dominance.

voluntary behavior behavior not under complete sensory control but determined by the interaction of sensory and central processes.

white matter CNS tissue mainly composed of fibers, not cell-bodies.

author index

315

subject index

319

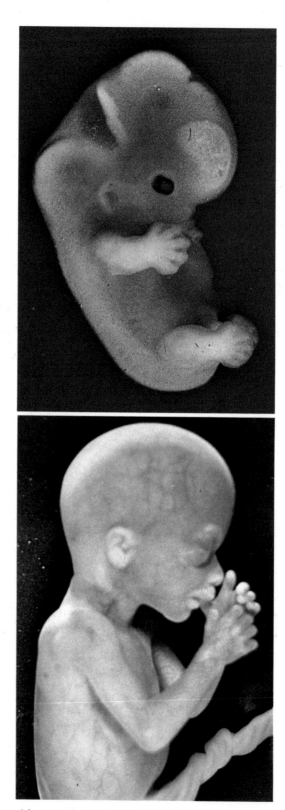

(Top) Normal fetus at 40 days. Note brain vesicles, eye, ear structure, and formation of fingers and toes. The deep cleft in the brain is the isthmus between the midbrain and hindbrain. *(Bottom)* Normal fetus at five months, apparently sucking its thumb. (Courtesy of Drs. R. Rugh and L. D. Shettles, authors of From Conception to Birth: The Drama of Life's Beginnings, New York, Harper and Row, 1971.)